Manufacturing Miracles

Published in association with the
Center for U.S.–Mexican Studies,
University of California, San Diego.

Manufacturing Miracles

PATHS OF INDUSTRIALIZATION IN LATIN AMERICA AND EAST ASIA

Edited by
Gary Gereffi
and
Donald L. Wyman

PRINCETON UNIVERSITY PRESS

PRINCETON, NEW JERSEY

Copyright © 1990 by Princeton University Press
Published by Princeton University Press, 41 William Street,
Princeton, New Jersey 08540
In the United Kingdom: Princeton University Press, Chichester, West Sussex

Library of Congress Cataloging-in-Publication Data

Manufacturing miracles : paths of industralization in Latin America
and East Asia / edited by Gary Gereffi and Donald L. Wyman.
p. cm.
ISBN 0-691-07788-6 (alk. paper)—ISBN 0-691-02297-6
(pbk. : alk. paper)
1. Industry and state—Latin America. 2. Latin America—
Industries. 3. Latin America—Economic policy. 4. Industry and
state—East Asia. 5. East Asia—Industries. 6. East Asia—Economic
policy. I. Gereffi, Gary, 1948–   . II. Wyman, Donald L.
HD3616.L32M36   1991   338.095—dc20   90-35237

This book has been composed in Linotron Sabon

Princeton University Press books are printed on acid-free paper
and meet the guidelines for permanence and durability of the
Committee on Production Guidelines for Book Longevity of the
Council on Library Resources

Printed in the United States of America

10   9   8   7   6   5   4   3

In memory of Donald Wyman

Contents

PART THREE: *Development Strategies: Do They Make a Difference?*

PART FOUR: *Emerging Agendas for Comparative Development Research*

Figures and Tables

Preface

THE PACE, scope, trajectories, and policies of industrial development have shown great variability in the Third World. No two regions capture this diversity better than Latin America and East Asia. Argentina, Brazil, and Mexico have a long history of sustained inward-oriented industrialization dating back to the 1930s, while East Asia's "Four Tigers"—South Korea, Taiwan, Hong Kong, and Singapore—have been acclaimed since the 1960s for the remarkable success of their outward-oriented industrialization based on manufactured exports. While these two paths of industrialization are sometimes portrayed as mutually exclusive, a closer look reveals a complex and fascinating picture of commonalities, divergence, and convergence between the two regions.

The highly industrialized countries in Latin America and East Asia have been the focus of a wide range of theories and concepts dealing with Third World development. World-systems theory, dependency theory, modernization theory, neoclassical trade and investment theories, and a variety of more specialized foci within economics, sociology, and political science have all been applied in attempts to understand the vicissitudes of Latin American and East Asian development. The interpretations derived from these theoretical perspectives often are misleading, however, because they are based on a selective and uneven reading of the evidence from the two regions. This volume attempts to close this gap through solid comparative research that uses the industrial experiences of these highly dynamic regions to explore different routes to industrial success in the contemporary world.

The perspective adopted in this volume is simultaneously cross-regional, multidisciplinary, and historical. The contributors are economists, sociologists, and political scientists by training. However many of the authors have found that they must move beyond their initial disciplinary vantage points to deal with the interplay between policy choices and development outcomes. Most chapters in this volume also focus on the historical contexts within which the Latin American and East Asian nations are situated in order to provide a broader baseline for generalizations about the development patterns that characterize the two regions.

The first part of this book provides a cross-regional overview of the development trajectories followed by the newly industrializing countries (NICs) in Latin America and East Asia. This section goes beyond the simplified concepts of inward-oriented and outward-oriented industrialization in order to highlight the interconnections between these apparently contrasting development paths. The second part of the book deals both comparatively and historically with the roles of different actors in Latin American and East Asian development, focusing primarily on foreign capital, local private firms, the state, and the popular sector. These chapters reveal substantial differences within, as well as between, these regions in terms of the sequences, implementation, and sociopolitical bases of distinct phases of industrial development in the NICs. The third part of this volume looks specifically at the impact of national development strategies in shaping industrial performance in the NICs. Two themes are particularly salient. The first is the degree to which governments lead or follow market forces in these countries and abroad, and the implications of these patterns for current debates about state intervention in the NICs. The second theme concerns the impact of current development strategies on the next stage of industrialization in each of these regions. In the fourth part of the book, new agendas for comparative development research at the global, regional, national, and local levels are highlighted.

This book has benefited from the generous support and guidance of numerous institutions and individuals. The Center for U.S.–Mexican Studies at the University of California, San Diego, played an instrumental role in hosting the initial workshop and subsequent conference on which this volume is based. This multiyear project was supported by grants to the Center for U.S.–Mexican Studies from the Rockefeller Foundation, the Ford Foundation, the William and Flora Hewlett Foundation, and the Institute of the Americas. A subsidy was provided to Princeton University Press by the Center for U.S.–Mexican Studies to facilitate the publication of a paperback edition of this book and to help cover the costs of preparing the final manuscript.

Wayne A. Cornelius, the director of the Center for U.S.–Mexican Studies, merits a tremendous debt of gratitude for his continual support of the efforts by Donald Wyman and myself to carry out this project. The varied participants at the Center's workshop and conference organized by Wyman and myself contributed a wealth of valuable comments that are reflected throughout the finished chapters of this volume. In addition, the staff at both the Center for U.S.–Mexican Studies at UCSD and the Department of Sociology at Duke University have given selflessly of their time and energy throughout the project's various stages. Christopher Ellison, who was the rapporteur at the conference and a coauthor of the volume's final chapter, deserves special thanks for his manifold intellectual inputs in helping to put the volume into its final form.

Completing an edited book is usually a happy occasion for all involved, but in this case it also is a time of sadness. Donald Wyman, my coeditor, died tragically of cancer at a young age in 1987. Don was an excellent scholar, a generous and insightful colleague, a warm friend, and a devoted family man. The suddenness of his death was a great shock to all who knew him. My sympathies, and those of the other contributors to this volume, go to Don's family: his wife, Barbara, and two children, Jamie and Meredith. In their honor and his, this volume is dedicated to Don's memory.

Gary Gereffi

PART ONE

A Cross-Regional Overview of National Development Trajectories

CHAPTER 1

Paths of Industrialization: An Overview

Gary Gereffi

INDUSTRIALIZATION has been the hallmark of national development in the twentieth century. Development studies in a variety of disciplines have focused on the determinants and consequences of the domestic changes that take place as agricultural and natural-resource-based societies have moved into the industrial world. The process of industrialization, although rooted in national societies, is also a global phenomenon, and it is shaped by the dynamics of the world-system.

The United States rose to a position of unparalleled economic and political dominance in the two decades after World War II. The postwar economic expansion of the United States was fueled by a decade of reconstruction in Europe and Asia. The revitalization of direct foreign investment (DFI) and international trade that followed reconstruction laid the groundwork for a new international division of labor, based on increasingly complex networks of industrial production and sourcing and new forms of geographical specialization (Fröbel et al., 1981; Gereffi, 1989a). A number of newly industrializing countries (NICs), which have been especially prominent in Latin America and East Asia, succeeded in significantly expanding their world share in the production and export of manufactured goods, which allowed them to penetrate key markets in the advanced industrial countries and rival the global dominance of manufacturing firms from these core nations (see OECD, 1979).

Industrial development in the Latin American and East Asian NICs is the central focus of this book. The timing, strategies, and consequences of industrial growth in the NICs have been uneven, however. The phrase "*newly* industrializing countries" actually is a misnomer when applied to Argentina, Brazil, and Mexico since they established their first major wave of import-substituting industries in the 1930s and 1940s in response to the international economic dislocations caused by the Great Depression and World War II (see Hirschman, 1968; Thorp, 1984). These Latin America NICs sought to deepen their industrialization in the mid-1950s by opening their doors to new waves of DFI from the United States, Western Europe, and eventually Japan. Whereas foreign investors in Latin America traditionally had concentrated on natural resource exports in the mining, oil, and agricultural sectors, postwar DFI emphasized

import-substituting investments in advanced manufacturing industries—
such as automobiles, chemicals, machinery, and pharmaceuticals—whose
output was destined primarily for the relatively large domestic markets in
Latin America.

The East Asian NICs (Hong Kong, Taiwan, South Korea, and Singapore) followed a contrasting sequence. Taiwan and South Korea did not
begin their rapid economic growth until the mid-1960s, after an extended
period of colonization by Japan prior to 1945 and with a heavy infusion
of American aid during the next two decades. All four of the East Asian
NICs pursued policies of outward-oriented industrialization in the 1960s
in order to generate foreign exchange via manufactured exports. During
this initial phase of export expansion, the rapid growth of these East
Asian nations was founded on light, labor-intensive industries like textiles, garments, and consumer electronics. In subsequent phases, however,
South Korea, Taiwan, and Singapore achieved success in much heavier
industries like steel, petrochemicals, shipbuilding, vehicle manufacture,
and computers that were further removed from their original factor endowments (i.e., limited raw materials, unskilled labor, and small markets).

The Latin American and East Asian NICs are now among the most industrialized nations in the developing world, but they have followed different paths of industrialization. In addition, their industrial growth has
had disparate economic and social consequences. During the 1980s, Latin
American nations found it difficult to maintain their previous levels of
economic expansion as they confronted staggering external debts, high
rates of inflation, shortages of investment capital, and the growing social
and economic marginalization of large segments of their population. In
the social realm as well, the East Asian nations have performed significantly better than their Latin American counterparts in terms of standard
indicators of development such as GNP per capita, income distribution,
literacy, health, and education (see World Bank, 1989a, tables 1, 28–30).

Their current differences notwithstanding, the NICs in both Latin
America and East Asia have been motivated by the principle of turning
their diverse initial comparative advantages into dynamic sources of competitive advantage. This book will explore how this has been accomplished, with an eye toward identifying the obstacles that have been overcome in these two regions and toward the challenges that lie ahead.

UNITING REGIONS AND DISCIPLINES

The cross-regional comparison of Latin America and East Asia raises a
number of critical issues about contemporary development. How did the
NICs in the two regions become so industrialized? In what ways are their

development trajectories similar and in what ways different? What role did government policies, domestic institutions, social actors, and cultural factors play in the development process? Is the current development crisis in Latin America a short-lived phenomenon, or is it symptomatic of profound structural problems that will require a major reorientation of these economies? Is the superior economic and social performance of the East Asian NICs in the 1980s a result of their outward-oriented development strategies or of unique historical and national conditions? Are the East Asian NICs models to be emulated by the rest of the developing world, or do they represent just one of a variety of viable paths of industrialization?

The essays in this volume seek to provide answers to these and other questions. The task is a daunting one, and it has led us to adopt an analytical approach with several distinctive characteristics. Our perspective is simultaneously cross-regional, multidisciplinary, and historical, since the global parameters within which national development is taking place are constantly shifting.

Cross-regional research is especially difficult. Although all national comparisons entail a variety of well-known problems, studies within a specific geographical region tend to be more tractable because the researcher is likely to encounter similar cultural backgrounds, related languages, and shared historical experiences. Cross-regional studies, on the other hand, demand the inclusion of a broader range of outcomes and possible explanatory variables, and the coverage of widely varying research literatures. In spite of these difficulties, we believe that a cross-regional perspective is invaluable because it affords greater theoretical payoff in trying to understand the diversity of development experiences in the world today.

The majority of the chapters in this volume are cross-regional studies of several countries in Latin America and East Asia. The essays that are not explicitly cross-regional compare nations within a single region. These regional chapters usually have been paired, however, so that the same topic is covered by different authors for both Latin America and East Asia. While the contributors to this volume certainly do not claim a mastery that would be required to do exhaustive cross-regional work, we believe that the effort to extend our analysis to include both the Latin American and the East Asian cases can help avoid the parochialism that often plagues the generalizations based on development research in just one country or a single region.

The essays in this volume are not only cross-regional, they also are interdisciplinary. This is because our examination of the determinants and consequences of the development paths followed by the Latin American and East Asian NICs covers a wide range of alternative explanations. The factors that will be analyzed include the comparative advantages of the

NICs in the two regions; the impact on regional and national development of major historical events, such as the Great Depression of the 1930s, World War II, the Chinese Revolution of 1949, the Korean War, land reform, the OPEC oil cartel, and the economic recession of the 1970s; the role played by geopolitical factors, including the hegemonic influence of the United States in the early postwar period and Japan's subsequent emergence as a premier world economic power; the legacy of distinct cultural heritages; the effect of domestic institutions and local class structures on the mobilization of protest and repression; the influence of government policies on economic outcomes; and the character of national political regimes.

The authors are trained as economists, sociologists, and political scientists, yet it would be difficult to identify any of their chapters with a narrow disciplinary perspective. All of the authors have felt compelled to be interdisciplinary in their treatment of development issues. It is precisely the connections between economic, social, and political factors that need to be understood in order to come up with a realistic appraisal of the accomplishments as well as the challenges facing the NICs.

The broad historical perspective of this volume, which is its third distinguishing feature, allows us to focus on three categories of comparative outcomes in the Latin American and East Asian NICs: (1) the similarities that characterize all of the NICs; (2) the cross-regional differences between the NICs in Latin America and East Asia; and (3) the sources of intraregional or national variation among the NICs.

The most striking commonalities among the NICs in the two regions have to do with their relatively high levels of economic growth, their industrial diversification, and their prominence as exporters, especially of manufactured goods. On the other hand, the Latin American and East Asian NICs frequently have been taken to represent two contrasting paths to industrialization: Argentina, Brazil, and Mexico are seen as having given primacy to an inward-oriented (import-substituting) mode of development, while the East Asian "Four Tigers" are associated with an outward-oriented (export-promoting) model. These countries vary not only in the timing and trajectories of their industrialization efforts but also in the ways they are linked to the world-system. Geopolitical alliances, foreign aid, DFI, international debt, and foreign trade have played very different roles in each region's development experience. Each of these factors will be analyzed in the chapters that follow.

While these regional patterns are of considerable importance in helping us understand Latin American and East Asian development, national diversity among the NICs often overshadows regional similarities. For example, Brazil, Mexico, and South Korea all have contracted substantial amounts of foreign debt, but Taiwan has not. Brazil, South Korea, and

Taiwan are major importers of oil, while Mexico is a major oil exporter. Mexico and Taiwan are similar to the extent that a single political party (the PRI and the KMT, respectively) has been dominant in each for the past four decades, while Brazil and South Korea share a common experience with more overt forms of military authoritarianism. Finally, there is substantial national variation in the industrial structure of the NICs in terms of the role played by foreign-owned firms, state enterprises, and different types of local private capital.

This introductory chapter will attempt to set the stage for the remainder of the volume. First, I will summarize the main economic achievements of the Latin American and East Asian NICs. This is the point of departure for all the essays, since the similar level of industrial development attained by the NICs in both regions serves as a baseline for their comparison. The main focus of the volume is on four countries: Mexico, Brazil, South Korea, and Taiwan. However, other nations are frequently dealt with in individual chapters in order to elaborate these comparisons.

Secondly, this chapter will identify the broad development patterns and strategies embodied in the historical trajectories of the Latin American and East Asian NICs. In contrast to the preceding emphasis on *what* the NICs have attained, the discussion in this section will indicate *how* their industrialization has taken place. Of concern here will be the timing and sequencing of distinct phases of inward- and outward-oriented development, the leading industries in each phase, and the changing constellations of domestic actors that assume primary responsibility for local industrialization.

Thirdly, I will outline the organization of the volume in terms of central questions, the comparative scope of each author, and the relationships between their chapters.

The Latin American and East Asian NICs that are the focus of this book frequently have been described as economic miracles. This metaphor, like all others, has the potential to mislead as well as enlighten. It is true that few observers looking at Mexico and Brazil in the 1930s, or South Korea and Taiwan in the mid-1950s, would have dared to predict that these nations were destined to become industrial powers several decades later. Nonetheless, these are not unadulterated success stories, nor should we accept the facile connotations of the term miracle.

The "manufacturing miracles" in the Latin American and East Asian NICs are no windfall achievements. They involved state planning, numerous entrepreneurial initiatives, and the sacrifices of millions of workers. Furthermore, economic growth in the NICs has gone hand in hand with authoritarian political regimes that often rose to power through military coups and the violent repression of dissident groups. Industrial progress in Latin America and East Asia, past and present, is not the result of divine grace, nor is its continuation inevitable. Rather, it is the product of the sweat, tears, and blood of the people who live in these nations. Only they can say whether they have been beneficiaries or victims of the miracle.

THE SETTING: THE SCOPE AND PACE OF INDUSTRIALIZATION IN THE NICs

The East Asian and Latin American NICs are a very heterogeneous group, with major differences in population, land area, resource endowments, cultural legacies, political regimes, social structures, per capita income, and economic policies. Nonetheless, these nations tend to have several dynamic features in common that lead them to be widely perceived as industrial success stories: rapid and relatively sustained economic growth based on a sharp increase in the manufacturing sector's share of total output and employment, a growing diversification of industrial production that permits each nation to make ever broader ranges of manufactured goods, and a fast expansion of exports with an emphasis on manufactures.

The Latin American and East Asian NICs are at similar levels of industrial development. They are all upper-middle-income countries by World Bank standards, although the average gross national product (GNP) per capita in 1987 was considerably higher in the East Asian nations: Hong Kong, $8,070; Singapore, $7,940; Taiwan, $5,550; South Korea, $2,690; Argentina, $2,390; Brazil, $2,020; and Mexico, $1,830. However, while the East Asian NICs grew rapidly during the 1980s, the Latin American NICs suffered an absolute as well as a relative decline. The 1981 GNP per capita figures highlight both trends (see table 1.1). The Latin American NICs had substantially *lower* per capita incomes in 1987 than six years earlier. The East Asian NICs, on the other hand, sharply raised their average incomes in the 1980s.

Manufacturing has been the cornerstone of development for the Latin American and East Asian NICs. The manufacturing sector's share of gross domestic product (GDP) in 1987 was 22 percent in Hong Kong; it ranged between 25 percent and 31 percent in Mexico, Brazil, Argentina, Singapore, and South Korea; and it reached a peak of 39 percent in Taiwan. The prominence of manufacturing activities in the NICs tends to be much higher than in the United States (20 percent) and many of the other advanced industrial economies, including Japan (29 percent). In all of the core nations, the service sector rather than manufacturing now accounts for the largest share of the economy.

TABLE 1.1
The East Asian and Latin American NICs: Basic Indicators

Country	Population (millions, mid-1987)	Area (thousands of square kilometers)	GDP (US$ millions)		GNP per capita		Distribution of Gross Domestic Product (percent)							
							Agriculture		Industry		Manufacturing[a]		Services, etc.	
			1965	1987	1981	1987	1965	1987	1965	1987	1965	1987	1965	1987
Taiwan	19.7	36	2,800	105,750	2,560	5,550	27	6	29	48	20	39	44	46
Hong Kong[b]	5.6	1	2,150	36,530	5,100	8,070	2	0	40	29	24	22	58	70
South Korea	42.1	98	3,000	121,310	1,700	2,690	38	11	25	43	18	30	37	46
Singapore	2.6	1	970	19,900	5,240	7,940	3	1	24	38	15	29	74	62
Brazil	141.4	8,512	19,450	299,230	2,220	2,020	19	11	33	38	26	28	48	51
Mexico[c]	81.9	1,973	20,160	141,940	2,250	1,830	14	9	27	34	20	25	59	57
Argentina	31.1	2,767	16,500	71,530	2,560	2,390	17	13	42	43	33	31	42	44

Sources: World Bank (1989a, pp. 165, 167, and 169); World Bank (1983, p. 149) for 1981 GNP per capita; and CEPD (1988, pp. 3–4, 23, 29, 41, and 199) for the data on Taiwan.

[a] Because manufacturing is generally the most dynamic part of the industrial sector, its share of GDP is shown separately.
[b] The most recent data for GDP and the sectoral distribution of GDP are for 1986. GNP per capita refers to GDP per capita.
[c] The sectoral distribution of GDP data are for 1986.

The Timing of Economic Growth

There is a stairstep pattern of economic growth in the Latin American and East Asian NICs. Mexico has the longest record of sustained economic progress. From the mid-1930s until the late 1970s, while experiencing uninterrupted political stability under its dominant party, the Partido Revolucionario Institucional (PRI), the Mexican economy grew at an average annual rate in excess of 6 percent, and manufacturing output rose approximately 8 percent a year. Mexico's real GDP increased most rapidly (about 9 percent per annum) from the mid-1950s until 1970, a period of considerable prosperity and price stability known as "stabilizing development" (Reynolds, 1970; Hansen, 1971).

The Brazilian economic "miracle" was just as impressive as Mexico's, although it peaked somewhat later. In the first three postwar decades (1945–1975), industrial growth averaged 8.8 percent a year; per capita income increased by 4 percent annually; and agricultural output showed a yearly increase of 5.6 percent—all in real terms. The decade following the military coup in April 1964 corresponds to the high point of the Brazilian economic cycle: real GDP grew at an average annual rate of 10.2 percent; there was a surplus in the balance of payments in every year from 1968 to 1973, thus providing ample resources to finance Brazil's chronic current account deficit; and the rate of inflation, although still high, had declined to around 15 percent (Malan and Bonelli, 1977; Fishlow, 1973).

South Korea, like Brazil, launched a major economic growth spurt on the heels of a military takeover. The 1950s in Korea were marked by a devastating war, extensive political corruption, and slow economic growth (about 4 percent annually in real terms). After General Park Chung Hee came to power in a coup in 1961, the economy became a central part of the regime's planning focus and of its legitimacy. During the 1960s and 1970s, GNP grew at an average rate of more than 10 percent a year, and per capita income tripled in real terms. The manufacturing sector was the star performer, growing at 18 percent annually in constant prices and increasing its share in the GNP from 14 percent to 30 percent, while at the same time, agriculture's share of the GNP fell from 40 percent to less than 25 percent. Exports skyrocketed, particularly of manufactured goods, with an average real rate of increase of 33 percent a year between 1961 and 1976 (Hasan and Rao, 1979; Mason et al., 1980).

Taiwan is, in many ways, the most successful of the NICs in terms of its economic performance. Gross national product grew at an average annual rate of 8.7 percent from 1953 to 1982, with a peak of 10.8 percent for the years 1963 to 1972, while industry's rate of expansion in the former period was even more spectacular, averaging 13.3 percent in real terms. Trade surpluses have been registered nearly every year since 1970, and the gross domestic savings rate has been above 20 percent of GNP ever since 1966 (Gold, 1986, pp. 4–5). All of this has been accomplished with negligible unemployment, nearly universal literacy, and an equitable income distribution record. Like Mexico, Taiwan has experienced a lengthy period of domestic political stability under the authoritarian one-party rule of the Kuomintang (KMT) from 1947 until the outbreak of popular antigovernment violence in the town of Chung-li in 1977, including a relatively smooth leadership transition after the death of longtime patriarch Chiang Kai-shek in 1975.

In summary, South Korea and Taiwan did not experience accelerated rates of economic growth until the mid-1960s, while Mexico and Brazil were already entering a second dynamic phase of import substitution by 1955. The East Asian NICs have been able to sustain their rhythm of economic growth into the 1980s, however, a far better performance than that of the Latin American NICS. While real GDP in the two East Asian NICs has grown at an average rate of about 9 percent between 1965 and 1987, Brazil's growth rate for this same period was 7.2 percent and Mexico's was 4.6 percent. The contrast is sharpest in the period from 1980 to 1987, when South Korea and Taiwan managed to grow at 8.6 percent and 7.5 percent, respectively, while Brazil's average real GDP increase was only 3.3 percent and Mexico struggled at 0.5 percent (see table 1.2).

These disparities in the timing of economic growth indicate that it would be extremely shortsighted to overemphasize the recent achievements of the East Asian NICs, as impressive as they might be, without considering them in their global context. Two features of this economic growth, however, make it especially noteworthy: the ability of the East

TABLE 1.2
Average Annual Growth Rates of Real Gross Domestic Product, 1955–1987

Years	Mexico	Brazil	South Korea	Taiwan
1955–1965	9.7	NA	5.1	8.1
1965–1980	6.5	9.0	9.5	9.8
1980–1987	0.5	3.3	8.6	7.5
1965–1987	4.6	7.2	9.2	9.0

Sources: IMF (1979, 1988) and World Bank (1989a, p. 167) for all countries except Taiwan. Figures for Taiwan are from CEPD (1988, p. 23).
NA = Not available.

Asian NICs to sustain it, even in the face of adverse circumstances, and its export-led nature.

The Export Drives of the NICs

The East Asian and Latin American NICs all have launched major export drives since 1965, when the overseas sales of the majority of these nations totaled between $1 billion and $1.6 billion, with Taiwan ($0.5 billion) and South Korea ($0.2 billion) lagging behind the others. Two decades later, the East Asian NICs had clearly established themselves as the Third World's premier exporters. Taiwan topped the list in 1987 with over $50 billion in exports, followed by Hong Kong and South Korea with export totals of approximately $48 billion each. Singapore and Brazil occupied a second tier with $28.6 and $26.2 billion of exports respectively, followed by Mexico ($20.9 billion) and then at a considerable distance Argentina ($6.4 billion) (see table 1.3). The three East Asian "superexporters" thus surged well ahead of the other NICs in export volume.

The NICs also vary considerably in the priority given to external trade. The East Asian nations are export-led economies in which exports in 1987 accounted for 48 percent and 39 percent of GDP in Taiwan and South Korea, respectively, and for 97 percent and 144 percent of GDP in the entrepôt city-states of Hong Kong and Singapore, respectively. This compares with export/GDP ratios of only 9 to 15 percent in the much larger Latin American NICs. To put these figures in a broader perspective, Japan, which often is seen as a model for its East Asian neighbors, had an export/GDP ratio of just under 13 percent in 1987, while the export ratio for the United States was only 6 percent. The East Asian NICs, partly because of their smaller size, thus are far more dependent on external trade than their Latin American counterparts or Japan.

The export drives of the East Asian NICs have been spearheaded by the phenomenal growth of their manufactured exports. In 1965, Taiwan led the NICs in both regions, with $207 million in manufactured exports, followed by Mexico ($170 million), Brazil ($124 million), and South Korea ($104 million). Ten years later, export revenues for manufactured goods from South Korea and Taiwan topped $4 billion for each country (a fortyfold increase for Korea and a more than twentyfold increase for Taiwan); Brazil's manufactured exports totaled almost $2.4 billion in 1975, while Mexico finished a distant fourth with $930 million in sales. The export drive of the East Asian NICs has continued to accelerate through the 1980s, with Taiwan earning an astounding $50 billion and South Korea close to $44 billion for manufactured export items in 1987. Brazil's overseas sales of manufactures grew very rapidly between 1975 and 1980, and reached a total of almost $12 billion in 1987. Mexico re-

TABLE 1.3
Exports by the East Asian and Latin American NICs, 1965 and 1987

| Country | Exports (US$ billions) | | Exports/GDP (percentage) | | Percentage Share of Exports[a] | | | | | | | |
| | | | | | Primary Commodities | | Textiles and Clothing | | Machinery and Transport Equipment | | Other Manufactures | |
	1965	1987	1965	1987	1965	1987	1965	1987	1965	1987	1965	1987
Taiwan	0.5	50.8	18	48	58	7	5	17	4	30	32	46
Hong Kong	1.1	48.5	51	97[b]	13	8	44	34	6	22	37	36
South Korea	0.2	47.2	7	39	40	7	27	25	3	33	29	34
Singapore	1.0	28.6	103	144	65	28	6	6	11	43	18	23
Brazil	1.6	26.2	8	9[b]	92	55	1	3[b]	2	17	6	25
Mexico	1.1	20.9	5	15	84	53	3	2[b]	1	28	12	17
Argentina	1.5	6.4	9	9	94	69	0	3	1	6	5	22

Sources: World Bank (1989a, pp. 190–91, 194–95). The 1965 export figures for all countries except Taiwan are from the IMF (1986, pp. 114–17). Taiwan's export total for 1965 is given in CEPD (1988, p. 208).
[a] Percentages may not add up to 100 percent due to rounding.
[b] 1986.

mained in fourth place among the Latin American and East Asian NICs, with nearly $10 billion in manufactured exports in 1987 (see table 1.4).

A major difference between the East Asian and Latin American NICs is that exports from the former are almost exclusively manufactured goods, while in Brazil and Mexico industrial products are still less than one-half of all exports. The Latin American NICs export a more diversified range of products, reflecting their more abundant supply of natural resources. The East Asian NICs, in response to growing protectionist pressures in some of their major overseas markets as well as rising domestic wages, have been shifting their manufactured exports in the direction of more technology-intensive (rather than labor-intensive) production. Even though the NICs in both regions have mounted successful export drives, they must continuously adapt their strategies in the face of economic and political trends and uncertainties.

Income Distribution

The contrast in terms of income distribution in the Latin American and East Asian NICs could hardly be more striking: Brazil and Mexico have among the most inequitable distributions of income in the world, while Taiwan and South Korea exhibit relatively egalitarian patterns of income distribution, especially by developing country standards. Data on the percentage distributions of household income show that the ratio between the top quintile and the bottom quintile of households is 33 to 1 in Brazil, 20 to 1 in Mexico, 8 to 1 in South Korea, 7.5 to 1 in the United States, 5 to 1 in Taiwan, and 4.3 to 1 in Japan (see table 1.5). A particularly dramatic example of the concentration of income in Brazil is the fact that in 1976 the top 1 percent of the population received a slightly larger slice of national income than the entire bottom 50 percent (Hewlett, 1982, p. 321).

In the East Asian NICs as well as Japan, the relatively flat profile of income distribution had its origins in events that can be traced back to the 1940s and 1950s: wars and foreign occupation made large segments of the population of these countries relatively poor, while land reform substantially benefited the cultivators by giving them land and placing restrictions on the size of land ownership. The resulting equalization of incomes in Taiwan constitutes, according to one observer, "a distribution revolution greater than any achieved under socialist or communist auspices and [it] was one of the main policies that fueled high-speed growth" (Johnson, 1981, p. 10). Brazil, on the other hand, never had a major land reform. And although there was an extensive and well publicized redistribution of land in Mexico in the late 1930s under President Lázaro Cárdenas, these measures were not effectively enforced or continued by sub-

TABLE 1.4
The Growth of Manufactured Exports, 1955–1987[a]

	Mexico		Brazil		South Korea		Taiwan	
	US$ Millions	Percent of Total Exports	US$ Millions	Percent of Total Exports	US$ Millions	Percent of Total Exports	US$ Millions	Percent of Total Exports
1955	76	12	11[b]	1[b]	3	16	13	10
1960	92	12	29	2	5	14	53	32
1965	170	15	124	8	104	59	207	46
1970	392	33	388	14	641	77	1,165	79
1975	931	31	2,371	27	4,147	82	4,441	84
1980	2,234	15	7,770	39	15,722	90	17,990	91
1987	9,774	47	11,750	45	43,579	92	50,290	94

Sources: United Nations (1985) for all countries except Taiwan up to 1965. From 1970 to 1987, the export data are from the World Bank (1989b, pp. 159, 355, 407). The data for Taiwan come from CEPD (1988), table 11-8.

[a] Manufactured exports for Mexico, Brazil and South Korea include the Standard International Trade Classification (SITC) sections 5, 6, 7 and 8, less chapter 68. For Taiwan, manufactured exports fall under the category of "Industrial Products" in CEPD (1988).

[b] 954.

TABLE 1.5
Patterns of Income Distribution

Percentile Groups of Households	Percentage Share of Household Income					
	Brazil (1972)	Mexico (1977)	South Korea (1976)	Taiwan[a] (1973)	Japan (1979)	United States (1980)
Lowest 20 percent	2.0	2.9	5.7	7.8	8.7	5.3
Second quintile	5.0	7.0	11.2	13.7	13.2	11.9
Third quintile	9.4	12.0	15.4	15.4	17.5	17.9
Fourth quintile	17.0	20.4	22.4	24.4	23.1	25.0
Highest 20 percent	66.6	57.7	45.3	38.7	37.5	39.9
Highest 10 percent	50.6	40.6	27.5	NA[b]	22.4	23.3
Ratio: Highest 20 percent/ Lowest 20 percent	33/1	20/1	8/1	5/1	4.3/1	7.5/1

Sources: World Bank (1989a, p. 223) for all countries except Taiwan. The figures for Taiwan are based on the author's calculations, using data in Fei et al. (1979, p. 306).

[a] The five quintiles correspond to the following percentile groups of families in Taiwan ranked according to their income: lowest quintile (19 percent); second quintile (the next 21 percent); third quintile (the next 19 percent); fourth quintile (the next 22 percent); and highest quintile (the top 19 percent).

[b] The top 5.7 percent of families in Taiwan accounted for 17.2 percent of total family income.

NA = Not available.

sequent administrations, and Mexican peasants became increasingly marginalized economically and socially.

A recent study of South Korea indicates that income inequality increased noticeably there in the 1970s, with the Gini index rising from 0.332 to 0.391 between 1970 and 1975 (Koo, 1984). The income distribution gains of the first decade of export orientation may have been eroding, therefore, in the second decade. One possible explanation is that the expansion of employment opportunities created by labor-intensive, export-oriented jobs was close to its maximum level by the early 1970s, thus diminishing the equity-promoting effect of export manufacturing. This interpretation is supported by the trend in the early 1980s for the tertiary sector (services) labor force to grow faster than the secondary sector (industrial) labor force.

DEVELOPMENT PATTERNS AND DEVELOPMENT STRATEGIES AS
    COMPARATIVE CONCEPTS

Our overview of the dynamic economic performance of the Latin American and East Asian NICs shows why they are standouts in terms of Third

World industrialization. In fact, their rapid rates of growth equal or exceed those attained by almost all of today's advanced industrial nations, even in the latter's periods of greatest economic expansion. This discussion does not tell us, however, how these NICs managed to achieve such impressive industrial development, nor does it indicate why the East Asian economies appeared to some to be better situated in the 1980s than their Latin American counterparts. To help answer these questions, we need to take a closer look at the principal phases of development of each of the four NICs. We also need to explore how government policies have shaped these economic outcomes.

Development Patterns

The development experience of the Latin American and East Asian NICs is complex. One way to conceptualize their trajectories is in terms of *development patterns* that are historically and structurally situated. These development patterns have three dimensions: (1) the types of industries that are most prominent in each phase of a country's economic development; (2) the degree to which these leading industries are inwardly or outwardly oriented (i.e., whether production is destined for the domestic market or for export); and (3) the major economic agents relied on to implement and sustain development.

Based on a broad historical view of industrialization in the Latin American and East Asian NICs, we can identify five main phases of industrial development. Three of these are outward-looking: a commodity export phase and primary and secondary export-oriented industrialization (EOI). The other two are inward-looking: primary import-substituting industrialization (ISI) and secondary ISI. The subtypes within the outward and inward approaches are distinguished by the kinds of products involved.

In the *commodity export* phase, the output typically is unrefined or semiprocessed raw materials (agricultural goods, minerals, oil, etc.). *Primary ISI* entails the shift from imports to the local manufacture of basic consumer goods, and in almost all countries the key industries during this phase are textiles, clothing, footwear, and food-processing. *Secondary ISI* involves using domestic production to substitute for imports of a variety of capital- and technology-intensive manufactures: consumer durables (e.g., automobiles), intermediate goods (e.g., petrochemicals and steel), and capital goods (e.g., heavy machinery). The two phases of EOI both involve manufactured exports. In *primary EOI* these tend to be labor-intensive products, while *secondary EOI* includes higher value-added items that are skill-intensive and require a more fully developed local industrial base.

Following this schema, the principal phases of industrial development in Mexico, Brazil, South Korea and Taiwan are outlined in figure 1.1 and

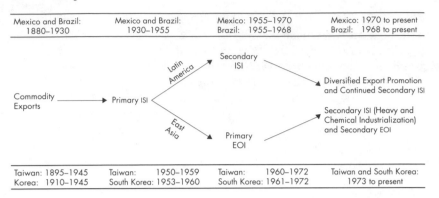

Mexico and Brazil: 1880–1930	Mexico and Brazil: 1930–1955	Mexico: 1955–1970 Brazil: 1955–1968	Mexico: 1970 to present Brazil: 1968 to present

Taiwan: 1895–1945 Korea: 1910–1945	Taiwan: 1950–1959 South Korea: 1953–1960	Taiwan: 1960–1972 South Korea: 1961–1972	Taiwan and South Korea: 1973 to present

FIGURE 1.1
Paths of Industrialization in Latin America and East Asia: Commonalities, Divergence, and Convergence.

(ISI = import-substituting industrialization; EOI = export-oriented industrialization.)

table 1.6. Each of the two regional pairs of NICs has followed a sequence of development strategies that closely approximates the ISI and EOI ideal types mentioned above, plus a "mixed" strategy in the most recent period. An analysis of these sequences, as shown in figure 1.1, suggests the following conclusions (see Gereffi and Wyman, 1989).

First, the contrast often made between the Latin American and East Asian NICs as representing inward- and outward-oriented development strategies, respectively, is oversimplified. While this distinction is appropriate for some periods, a historical perspective shows that each of these NICs has pursued *both* inward- and outward-oriented approaches.

Every nation, with the exception of Britain at the time of the Industrial Revolution, went through an initial stage of ISI in which protection was extended to incipient manufacturing industries producing for domestic markets. Furthermore, each of the NICs subsequently has combined both advanced ISI and different types of EOI in order to avoid the inherent limitations of an exclusive reliance on domestic or external markets and also to facilitate the industrial diversification and upgrading that are required for these nations to remain competitive in the world economy. Rather than being mutually exclusive alternatives, the ISI and EOI development paths in fact have been complementary and interactive.[1]

[1] Indeed, a previous period of import-substitution may have been a prerequisite for the successful adoption of EOI in East Asia based on national entrepreneurs (see Haggard and Cheng, 1987).

TABLE 1.6
Patterns of Development in Latin America and East Asia

| Development Strategies | Mexico and Brazil | | | |
	Commodity Exports	Primary ISI	Secondary ISI	Diversified Exports and Secondary ISI
Main Industries	Mexico: Precious metals (silver, gold), minerals (copper, lead, zinc), oil Brazil: Coffee, rubber, cocoa, cotton	Mexico and Brazil: Textiles, food, cement, iron and steel, paper, chemicals, machinery (Brazil)	Mexico and Brazil: Automobiles, electrical and nonelectrical machinery, petrochemicals, pharmaceuticals	Mexico: Oil, silver, apparel, transport equipment, nonelectrical machinery Brazil: Iron ore and steel, soybeans, apparel, footwear, transport equipment, nonelectrical machinery, petrochemicals, plastic materials
Major Economic Agents	Mexico: Foreign investors Brazil: National private firms	Mexico and Brazil: National private firms	Mexico and Brazil: State-owned enterprises, transnational corporations, and national private firms	Mexico and Brazil: State-owned enterprises, transnational banks, transnational corporations, and national private firms
Orientation of Economy	External markets	Internal market	Internal market	External and internal markets

(continued on page 20)

TABLE 1.6 (cont.)

Development Strategies	Taiwan and South Korea			
	Commodity Exports	Primary ISI	Primary EOI	Secondary ISI and Secondary EOI
Main Industries	Taiwan: Sugar, rice Korea: Rice, beans	Taiwan and South Korea: Food, beverages, tobacco, textiles, clothing, footwear, cement, light manufactures (wood, leather, rubber, and paper products)	Taiwan and South Korea: Textiles and apparel, electronics, plywood, plastics (Taiwan), wigs (South Korea), intermediate goods (chemicals, petroleum, paper, and steel products)	Taiwan: Steel, petrochemicals, computers, telecommunications, textiles and apparel South Korea: Automobiles, shipbuilding, steel and metal products, petrochemicals, textiles and apparel, electronics, videocassette recorders, machinery
Major Economic Agents	Taiwan and Korea: Local producers (colonial rule by Japan)	Taiwan and South Korea: National private firms	Taiwan and South Korea: National private firms, transnational corporations, state-owned enterprises	Taiwan and South Korea: National private firms, transnational corporations, state-owned enterprises, transnational banks (South Korea)
Orientation of Economy	External markets	Internal market	External markets	Internal and external markets

Note: ISI = import-substituting industrialization; EOI = export-oriented industrialization.

Second, the early phases of industrialization—commodity exports and primary ISI—were common to all of the Latin American and East Asian NICs. The subsequent divergence in the regional sequences stems from the ways in which each country responded to the basic problems associated with the continuation of primary ISI. These problems included balance-of-payments pressures, rapidly rising inflation, high levels of dependence on intermediate and capital goods imports, and low levels of manufactured exports.[2]

Third, the duration and timing of these development patterns vary by region. Primary ISI began earlier, lasted longer, and was more populist in Latin America than in East Asia. Timing helps explain these sequences because the opportunities and constraints that shape development choices are constantly shifting. The East Asian NICs began their accelerated export of manufactured products during a period of extraordinary dynamism in the world economy. The two decades that preceded the global economic crisis of the 1970s saw unprecedented annual growth rates of world industrial production (approximately 5.6 percent) and world trade (around 7.3 percent), relatively low inflation and high employment rates in the industrialized countries, and stable international monetary arrangements. The expansion of world trade was fastest between 1960 and 1973, when the average annual growth rate of exports reached almost 9 percent.

Starting in 1973, however, the international economy began to enter a troublesome phase. From 1973 to the end of the decade, the annual growth in world trade fell to 4.5 percent as manufactured exports from the developing countries began to encounter stiffer protectionist measures in the industrialized markets. These new trends were among the factors that led the East Asian NICs to modify their EOI approach in the 1970s.

Fourth, the development strategies of the Latin American and East Asian NICs show some signs of convergence in the 1970s and 1980s. To support this convergence thesis, it is necessary to distinguish two subphases during the most recent period. In the 1970s Mexico and Brazil began to expand both their commodity exports (oil, soybeans, minerals, etc.) and their manufactured exports, as well as to accelerate their foreign borrowing, in order to acquire enough foreign exchange to finance the imports necessary for furthering secondary ISI. This "diversified exports" approach was an important addition to their earlier emphasis on industrial deepening.

South Korea and Taiwan, on the other hand, emphasized heavy and

---

[2] The problems associated with ISI in Latin America are discussed in Baer (1972) and Hirschman (1968). For an account of similar problems in the East Asian countries, see Lin (1973, pp. 68–74) and Deyo (1987).

chemical industrialization from 1973 to 1979, with a focus on steel, automobiles, shipbuilding, and petrochemicals. The objective of heavy and chemical industrialization in East Asia was twofold: to develop national production capability in these sectors, justified by national security as well as import-substitution considerations, and to lay the groundwork for more diversified exports in the future. China's reentry into the international community, ushered in by its détente with the United States in the early 1970s, not only made South Korea's and Taiwan's domestic defense concerns more credible but also presented a long-term threat to labor-intensive industries in the region.

Thus, the Latin American and East Asian NICs coupled their previous strategies from the 1960s (secondary ISI and primary EOI, respectively) with elements of the alternate strategy in order to enhance the synergistic benefits of simultaneously pursuing inward- and outward-oriented approaches.

It is clear that neither inward-oriented nor outward-oriented development strategies are economic panaceas. Both are susceptible to systemic constraints or vulnerabilities such as recurring balance-of-payments problems, persistent inflation, and the disruption of key trading relationships.[3] However, the NICs in each region have adapted or switched development strategies in response to these problems, and thus they succeeded in moving to a more diversified pattern of export growth in the 1980s.

Development Strategies

The development phases outlined above are economic outcomes that themselves need to be explained. There are a multitude of determinants that could impinge on such an explanation (see Gereffi and Wyman, 1989). One could look at the comparative advantage of these economies in terms of natural resource endowments or market size, the kinds of economic policies pursued, the role of geopolitical considerations, the impact of diverse transnational economic linkages, elite policy preferences and levels of state intervention, social coalitions, cultural predispositions, and prevailing development ideologies. The reciprocal influence of these external and internal determinants are seen most clearly, however, when one tries to understand the major choices that are made by key actors during periods of transition from one development phase to another. The importance of choices, in turn, raises the issue of whether there are purposeful strategies that guide or facilitate the process of developmental change.

---

[3] The inherent limitations of both import-substituting and export-oriented development strategies in the NICs are outlined in Gereffi (1989b).

Development strategies can be defined as sets of government policies that shape a country's relationship to the global economy and that affect the domestic allocation of resources among industries and major social groups. This notion of development strategies links policies and production structures in such a way as to shed light on a country's relationship to international markets and resources and on its decisions about domestic economic growth and equity. A variety of policies may be used to establish a particular pattern of inward- or outward-oriented production, but the focus here is on the broad strategy itself rather than on policy oscillations or shifts within specific ISI or EOI approaches.

The question of whether governments have acted as leaders or followers in the industrial transformation of the Latin American and East Asian NICs is a key issue that various chapters in this volume will address. Our working hypothesis is that state-led industrialization has become the norm in the Latin American and East Asian NICs since the 1950s, although the motives, instruments, and consequences of this government involvement vary.

The essays in this volume, therefore, look at strategy choice as well as at the consequences of that choice. To see how this is accomplished, I will briefly review the focus of each of the chapters.

ANALYZING INDUSTRIALIZATION

Colin I. Bradford, Jr.'s chapter offers a new way to look at the role of markets and governments in development strategies. Rather than seeing inward- and outward-oriented development strategies as a dichotomous typology, Bradford argues that they actually form a continuum. Both the ISI and EOI development strategies range from market-oriented versions, where the government's role is very mild, to *dirigiste* versions, in which government intervention is quite substantial. The importance of this perspective is that it allows us to increase the range of policy choices associated with distinct development strategies. Bradford also reviews the main macroeconomic trends in the four principal Latin American and East Asian NICs from the mid-1960s to the mid-1980s, with an emphasis on their patterns of investment growth and adjustment, their export drives, and the external debt situation, thus supplementing the economic frame of reference provided in the introductory chapter.

The next five chapters deal with key economic, political, and social dimensions of industrialization in the Latin American and East Asian NICs. In chapter 3, Barbara Stallings looks at the role of foreign capital in the postwar economic development of the four major NICs in the two regions. Stallings frames her analysis in terms of two debates: the modernization-dependency debate about the positive and negative impact of foreign capital in national development and the statist-dependency debate, which is concerned with the ability of governments to shape the contributions of foreign capital in ways compatible with national interests. Her main argument is that the Latin American and East Asian NICs have had very different experiences with foreign capital. In the Latin American NICs, private foreign capital (direct foreign investment and private bank loans) has been very important, while in the East Asian NICs local private capital and the state have played a dominant role in recent years. The form of foreign capital that has been most important in Taiwan and South Korea is public bilateral and multilateral loans, especially in the 1950s and early 1960s. One of the reasons the dependency approach has been more prevalent in the studies of the Latin American NICs is that DFI and private foreign loans tend to be particularly conflictive in relations with the host countries.

In chapter 4, Gary Gereffi extends the analysis of Stallings by focusing on the relations between big business and the state in the Latin American and East Asian NICs. Gereffi shows that there are sharp regional contrasts in the composition and political impact of the big business sector. In Brazil and Mexico, the largest firms are transnational corporations and state-owned enterprises, while in the East Asian NICs, local private firms are the main economic actors. However, there are also important subregional differences. The role of state enterprises, for example, is more prominent in Mexico and Taiwan than in their regional counterparts. Furthermore, the size of local private companies varies greatly in the East Asian NICs. South Korea is characterized by the predominance of giant, vertically integrated industrial conglomerates (*chaebols*), whereas the industrial structure of Taiwan is composed mainly of small and medium-sized family-owned firms. These differences in the ownership, size, and sectoral distribution of big business in the NICs influence the autonomy of the state to formulate and implement effective industrial policies in these nations. They also affect their ability to internationalize their industries.

The chapters by Robert R. Kaufman and Tun-jen Cheng are cross-national studies of Latin America and East Asia, respectively, which identify major sources of intraregional variations in the transitions between distinct development strategies. Both authors share the same premise: namely, the first phase of ISI in Latin America and East Asia was a spontaneous "situational imperative" induced by the Great Depression of the 1930s (Latin America) or the breaking of colonial ties with Japan and associated postwar economic exigencies (East Asia). When confronted with the need to choose a subsequent strategy after the inevitable end of "easy" ISI, the governments in each of these countries assumed a far more explicit and directive role, notwithstanding the fact that the Latin American and East Asian NICs moved in divergent directions.

Kaufman examines six Latin American nations: the three large nations (Argentina, Brazil, and Mexico) and three smaller countries (Chile, Colombia, and Uruguay) in order to consider a fuller range of ISI experiences. His concern is with the patterns of alliance and conflict among four sets of actors: (1) the agricultural-mercantile groups in charge of export staples; (2) anti-oligarchical coalitions, composed of popular sector groups and rival agrarian interests; (3) state elites, especially military officers and civilian technocrats; and (4) industrial capitalists, national and international.

In exploring the two critical turning points of the Depression and the early 1940s, when first-stage ISI accelerated, and the two decades following the end of World War II, when secondary ISI was implemented, Kaufman finds substantial variation within the Latin American region. In the Southern Cone countries (Argentina, Chile, and Uruguay), the pressures were strongest for an inclusive form of ISI relying on old-style urban-based distributive politics. In Mexico and Colombia, more cautious fiscal and monetary policies were adopted in the face of considerably weaker distributive pressures. Brazil, which exercised the greatest degree of state control over the popular sector, moved furthest to consolidate a "triple alliance" based on foreign and national industrial capitalists and state enterprises, with the working class largely excluded from the benefits deriving from this arrangement.

In chapter 6, Cheng provides an original and carefully crafted analysis of the differences between South Korea and Taiwan in terms of political regime dynamics. He examines the initial transitions, implementation, and sociopolitical bases of the three main phases of postwar industrial development in the East Asian NICs: ISI, EOI, and EOI deepening. He finds that in general South Korea and Taiwan differ in their approaches to implementing development strategies: South Korea's approach is hierarchical, unbalanced, and command-oriented, while Taiwan has followed a contrasting path that is horizontal, balanced, and incentive-oriented.

This difference is reflected in each of the development strategies pursued by these two nations. With regard to ISI, South Korea followed a classic "rent-seeking" approach, while Cheng characterizes Taiwan's experience as "surplus-generating." In implementing EOI, South Korea's approach was "centralized" while Taiwan's was "decentralized." EOI in South Korea was supported by an alliance of accumulation between the military regime and the leading businesses, while the party state in Taiwan organized and supervised a loose distributional coalition consisting of technocrats, fragmented local capital, foreign investors, farmers, labor, and household savers. The contrast for EOI deepening was equally striking: South Korea's "big push" approach to heavy and chemical industrialization, in which the industries that were to be the new backbone of national exports were rapidly built on the basis of heavy foreign borrowing, versus Taiwan's "gradualist" approach based on decentralized industrialization that would preserve the key elements of the regime's broad distributional coalition.

In chapter 7, Frederic C. Deyo picks up some of the same themes raised by Kaufman and Cheng in his analysis of the popular sector in the Latin American and East Asian NICs. Deyo argues that the political role of the popular sector is mainly indirect—i.e., it opposes or encourages particular policies that flow from more general development strategies, and thus it can shape the implementation of these strategies in important ways. The polar opposite cases in Deyo's analysis are Taiwan (which has a strong state and a weak society) and Argentina (weak state and strong society), with Brazil and South Korea falling in between. The role of the popular sector generally has been stronger in Latin America than in East Asia. It is strongest in Argentina and weakest in Taiwan, which is the extreme case of top-down, guided, preemptive democratization. While political regimes provide the political opportunity for an insertion of popular class agendas in national policy-making, Deyo shows how socioeconomic structural factors such as employment concentration and the emergence of class-homogeneous communities can encourage popular sector mobilization and generate the capacity to create autonomous class organizations that allow popular sector groups to seize elite-sponsored opportunities in an effective manner.

Chapters 8 through 11 deal with the role of government policies in shaping the performance of the Latin American and East Asian NICs. The chapters by Gustav Ranis and Robert Wade offer differing viewpoints of the degree to which the government has taken a leadership role in East Asia's economic success, while the chapters by Chi Schive and René Villarreal focus on how current development strategies in the East Asian and Latin American NICs, respectively, are posing quite different problems for the next stage of industrialization in these regions.

The current interest in comparing East Asia and Latin America is testimony, according to Ranis, that policy choices can in fact make a good deal of difference in development outcomes. The key issue is whether the policy choices that confront nations in their development experience are explicit, debated, and negotiated; or implicit, clandestine, and imposed. Ranis sees explicit tax and expenditure policies as examples of "on the table" measures of the first type, while inflation and overvalued exchange rates are instances of "under the table" income transfers that are symptomatic of "governments' myopic need to solve short-run problems while putting off the social conflict consequences to a later point in time."

In chapter 8, Ranis looks at four medium-sized cases from the two regions: Taiwan, South Korea, Mexico, and Colombia. His analysis identifies two distinct regional patterns. The East Asian pattern is one in which the nations studied gradually but consistently shift away from "under the table" (or implicit) income transfers among groups toward "on the table" (or explicit) revenue and expenditure-related government policies. The Latin American pattern is characterized by liberalization/interventionist cycles in which the persistence of ISI is related in part to the ability of these nations to continue to pay for ISI through the ample availability of traditional natural resource revenues, and also to the governments' felt need to be viewed as solving all problems in order to forestall social conflict.

Wade traces in chapter 9 two different explanations of the role of the state in the East Asian NICs: the "self-adjusting market" theory, which holds that East Asian economic success is due to the vigor of private entrepreneurs operating in relatively open economies, and the "developmental state" theory, which holds that "East Asian governments (minus Hong Kong) have been active players in the market, able to influence the use of public and private resources in line with a vision of how the industrial structure of the country should be evolving." Wade dissects the experiences of Taiwan and South Korea in a variety of industrial sectors and concludes that in both these nations government has exercised a substantial amount of leadership in promoting industrial growth.

The mode of government leadership is quite different in the two cases, however. In Taiwan, leadership has been exercised through public enterprises or public research and service organizations. In South Korea, on the other hand, government leadership takes the form of pushing and prodding large private firms, which are backed by a considerable amount of direct and indirect state assistance. Although industrial policy in a government "followership" mode can still be worth pursuing, Wade asserts that economies whose governments have the capacity to intervene effectively in a "leadership" mode have greater potential for welfare-enhancing transformations.

In chapter 10, Schive examines the two most recent development strategies pursued in Taiwan and South Korea: secondary ISI, which aims to replace imported intermediate and capital goods with local production, and secondary EOI, which attempts to develop high-tech industries to substitute for conventional exports. With regard to secondary ISI, Schive shows that Korea is ahead of Taiwan in heavy industries, especially machinery, while Taiwan tends to be ahead of Korea in certain intermediate goods industries, such as chemicals, petrochemicals, petroleum, and coal.

To explore secondary EOI, which is ushering in the next stage of industrialization in these NICs, Schive highlights the production of very-large-scale integrated circuits (VLSI). In an analysis that recalls the industrial structural differences between the East Asian NICs outlined in chapter 4 and the distinction between the "big push" versus "gradualist" approaches to implementing secondary EOI mentioned in chapter 6, Schive shows that Taiwan and South Korea built their VLSI industries in contrasting ways: Taiwan first developed the technology, then moved into manufacturing, while Korea first established its manufacturing capacity, then acquired the needed technology. "The development of Korea's VLSI industry in a scant four years can be attributed not only to the enormous capital invested, but also to a heavy reliance on foreign technology." Taiwan, on the other hand, has had the capacity to design VLSI technology since 1985, but the ability to manufacture those designs remains a problem.

In chapter 11, René Villarreal focuses on the Latin American experience with ISI. Villarreal acknowledges that ISI has created an anti-export bias in Latin America. As a backdrop to his comparative analysis of ISI in Brazil and Mexico, however, Villarreal criticizes the neoliberal orthodoxy of the Southern Cone countries (Argentina, Chile, and Uruguay) as the wrong solution to the problem, since ultraliberalism in the Southern Cone has resulted in extensive deindustrialization and financial upheavals.

Like Schive, Villarreal paints contrasting portraits of the two leading NICs in his region, Brazil and Mexico. Brazil has advanced further down the path of secondary ISI than Mexico has, which is best exemplified by Brazil's capital goods industry, the strongest in Latin America. The energy crisis of the 1970s affected Brazil and Mexico in opposite ways: Brazil gave top priority to a fuller integration of its productive structure through ISI; Mexico became a prominent oil exporter, but in the process the structural integration of its economy took several steps backward. Villarreal provides a detailed discussion of the various stages of ISI in Mexico and concludes by advocating a three-dimensional industrial model for Mexico's future, involving a combination of endogenous growth, industrial exports, and selective ISI.

Fernando Fajnzylber and Ronald Dore call our attention to previously ignored variables and begin to chart new comparative research agendas based on their understandings of the forces influencing the Latin American and East Asian NICs. In Chapter 12, Fajnzylber begins to outline in a systematic way the argument that key aspects of the development patterns of South Korea and the three Latin American NICs are outgrowths of their efforts to emulate the Japanese and American experiences, respectively. The Japanese development pattern, like that of the East Asian NICs, can be characterized by the following traits: a strategic, long-term orientation toward economic affairs; a tendency toward high levels of saving; firms oriented toward the conquest of international markets; and relatively high levels of social integration, with top priority given to education in the system. The development pattern of the United States has a contrasting set of features: a preoccupation with short-term planning,

high levels of consumption, an emphasis on producing for large and secure domestic markets, and relatively low levels of social integration.

Fajnzylber demonstrates in a detailed empirical analysis that the Latin
American NICs have been attempting to reproduce the "American way of
life." In contrast to East Asia, the Latin American NICs have lower levels
of economic dynamism, consumption trends that are heavily skewed in
favor of urban elite groups, domestically oriented production structures,
lower international competitiveness, and less distributive equity. Whereas
Latin American nations have emphasized "showcase modernity," the
East Asian nations have given top priority to "endogenous modernity."

Dore observes in Chapter 13 that there has been relatively little attention given in this volume or in recent development literature as a whole
to the historically conditioned role of culture and ideas as they influence
development strategies and social institutions. Dore discusses a variety of
cultural dimensions in terms of their salience for cross-regional comparative research: the intensity of the will to develop; the sense of backwardness and its determinants; the centrality of national cohesion and the
sense of nationhood; the legitimacy of elites and political authority; values and economic achievement; and attitudes toward technological learning and technical change.

At a broader conceptual level, Dore stresses again the importance of
distinguishing between development "strategies" (i.e., the mixture of intentions and forecasts people have when they take policy decisions) and
development "patterns," which are sequences of events or economic and
social outcomes. The main contribution of a focus on development "patterns" is the development of typologies that can aid us in providing explanations as well as clarifying our value judgments about the kinds of
outcomes we find desirable.

The last chapter, by Christopher Ellison and Gereffi, seeks to order
some of the conclusions arrived at in the volume along two broad dimensions: first, the level of their explanatory variables (world-system factors,
the role of national, institutional, and organizational forces, development
strategies, and grounded interpretations of networks, culture, and historical events) and, secondly, the scope of the generalizations that the authors
make in interpreting their findings. Ellison and Gereffi organize the findings from the chapters into three sets of outcomes: (1) patterns of development that are common to the NICs in both Latin America and East
Asia, (2) development outcomes that vary between the two regions but
are basically similar for the NICs within each region, and (3) aspects of
the development experience in Latin America and East Asia where there
is sharp intraregional variation or distinctive national traits. Ellison and
Gereffi also seek to identify some promising areas for the next wave of

development research and emphasize the emerging importance of social networks at the global, national, and local levels.

It is not the intent of this volume to extol the virtues of either the Latin American or the East Asian paths of development, nor to try to advocate the adoption of "correct" economic policies or institutional arrangements. Historically conditioned patterns cannot be repeated, and policies or institutions that work well in one national setting may have quite different consequences elsewhere. Countries obviously are capable of learning from each other, and highly selective adaptation or emulation may prove successful. Whatever is "learned," however, must be adapted to particular historical, cultural, and political circumstances. The goals, needs, and resources of the Latin American NICs are quite different from those of the East Asian NICs. Comparative research is most helpful if it combines good history and good theory, and both lead to a better appreciation of the constraints as well as the possibilities of the present.

REFERENCES

Baer, Werner. 1972. "Import Substitution and Industrialization in Latin America: Experiences and Interpretations." *Latin American Research Review* 7:95–122.
CEPD (Council for Economic Planning and Development). 1988. *Taiwan Statistical Data Book, 1988*. Taipei.
Deyo, Frederic C., ed. 1987. *The Political Economy of the New Asian Industrialism*. Ithaca, N.Y.: Cornell University Press.
Fei, John C. H., Gustav Ranis, and Shirley W. Y. Kuo. 1979. *Growth with Equity: The Taiwan Case*. New York: Oxford University Press.
Fishlow, Albert. 1973. "Some Reflections on Post-1964 Brazilian Economic Policy." In *Authoritarian Brazil: Origins, Policies, and Future*, edited by Alfred Stepan. New Haven: Yale University Press.
Fröbel, Folker, Jürgen Heinrichs, and Otto Kreye. 1981. *The New International Division of Labor*. New York: Cambridge University Press.
Gereffi, Gary. 1989a. "Development Strategies and the Global Factory: Latin America and East Asia." *Annals* of the American Academy of Political and Social Science, no. 505, pp. 92–104.
———. 1989b. "Industrial Restructuring and National Development Strategies: A Comparison of Taiwan, South Korea, Brazil and Mexico." In *Taiwan: A Newly Industrialized State*, edited by Hsin-Huang Michael Hsiao, Wei-Yuan Cheng, and Hou-Sheng Chan. Taipei: Department of Sociology, National Taiwan University.
Gereffi, Gary, and Donald Wyman. 1989. "Determinants of Development Strategies in Latin America and East Asia." In *Pacific Dynamics: The International Politics of Industrial Change*, edited by Stephan Haggard and Chung-in Moon. Boulder, Colo.: Westview Press.
Gold, Thomas B. 1986. *State and Society in the Taiwan Miracle*. Armonk, N.Y.: M. E. Sharpe.

Haggard, Stephan, and Tun-jen Cheng. 1987. "State and Foreign Capital in the East Asian NICs." In Deyo, ed., *Political Economy.*

Hansen, Roger D. 1971. *The Politics of Mexican Development.* Baltimore: Johns Hopkins University Press.

Hasan, Parvez, and D. C. Rao. 1979. *Korea: Policy Issues for Long-Term Development.* Baltimore: Johns Hopkins University Press.

Hewlett, Sylvia Ann. 1982. "Poverty and Inequality in Brazil." In *Brazil and Mexico: Patterns in Late Development*, edited by Sylvia Ann Hewlett and Richard B. Weinert. Philadelphia: Institute for the Study of Human Issues.

Hirschman, Albert O. 1968. "The Political Economy of Import-Substituting Industrialization in Latin America." *Quarterly Journal of Economics* 82:2–32.

IMF (International Monetary Fund). 1979, 1986, 1988. *International Financial Statistics Yearbook.* Washington, D.C.: IMF.

Johnson, Chalmers. 1981. "Introduction—The Taiwan Model." In *The Taiwan Experience, 1950–1980*, edited by James C. Hsiung. New York: Praeger.

Koo, Hagen. 1984. "The Political Economy of Income Distribution in South Korea: The Impact of the State's Industrialization Policies." *World Development* 12, no. 10, pp. 1029–37.

Lin, Ching-yuan. 1973. *Industrialization in Taiwan, 1946–72.* New York: Praeger.

Malan, Pedro S., and Regis Bonelli. 1977. "The Brazilian Economy in the Seventies: Old and New Developments." *World Development* 5, no. 1/2, pp. 19–45.

Mason, Edward S., Mahn Je Kim, Dwight H. Perkins, Kwang Suk Kim, and David C. Cole. 1980. *The Economic and Social Modernization of the Republic of Korea.* Cambridge: Harvard University Press.

OECD (Organization for Economic Co-operation and Development). 1979. *The Impact of the Newly Industrializing Countries on Production and Trade in Manufactures.* Paris: OECD.

Reynolds, Clark W. 1970. *The Mexican Economy: Twentieth-Century Structure and Growth.* New Haven: Yale University Press.

Thorp, Rosemary, ed. 1984. *Latin America in the 1930's: The Role of the Periphery in the World Crisis.* Oxford, England: Macmillan.

United Nations. 1985. *International Trade Statistics Yearbook.* New York: United Nations.

World Bank. 1989a. *World Development Report 1989.* New York: Oxford University Press.

———. 1989b. *World Tables*, 1988–89 ed. Baltimore: Johns Hopkins University Press.

———. 1983. *World Development Report 1983.* New York: Oxford University Press.

CHAPTER 2

Policy Interventions and Markets: Development Strategy Typologies and Policy Options

Colin I. Bradford, Jr.

THE PURPOSE of this chapter is to explore different types of development strategies over time and between countries to better understand the most effective means of achieving dynamic development. Three major dimensions are of interest: the relationship between the relative roles of the state and the private sector, the interaction between external conditions and economic policies and patterns, and the evolution and sequence of dominant policy regimes in dynamic economies over time. The paper will compare economic policies, patterns, and performance of South Korea, Taiwan, Brazil, and Mexico from 1966 to 1984.

This analysis seeks to increase the range of policy choices associated with distinct development strategies and redefine the frequently asserted dichotomies between import substitution versus export orientation, intervention versus liberalization, and the public sector versus the private sector to emphasize effective combinations of these elements rather than mutually exclusive choices between them.

DEVELOPMENT STRATEGY TYPOLOGIES

The highly dynamic export performance of the developing economies in Pacific Asia has aroused a discussion about the virtues of inward- versus outward-oriented growth strategies. The East Asian and Latin American NICs have frequently been cited as contrasting examples of export orientation and import substitution, respectively. Part of the controversy undoubtedly derives from the use of loosely fashioned phrases that sound like dichotomous typologies when in fact more rigorous specification of meaning would reveal that they define different points along a spectrum of policy regimes rather than stark alternatives. What follows is an attempt to attach differentiated meaning to commonly used labels that are often used as substitutes for one another.

The results are summarized in table 2.1 and reveal a continuum from autarky to export promotion, which hopefully captures a variety of con-

The able research assistance of George Wozencraft is gratefully acknowledged.

TABLE 2.1
Development Strategy Typologies: A Continuum

		Dirigisme
Autarky	No trade "Delinking" Self-reliance	
Import Substitution	a. Discriminates against all imports through controls EERm > EERx[a] b. Selective discrimination c. Mild and limited applications	
Inward Orientation	Priority to the domestic economy	Markets
Outward Orientation	Priority to exports	Markets
Open Economy	Internal liberalization EERx = EERm[a] a. Tradable goods b. (a) + nontradable goods c. (a) + (b) + macro variables	
Export Push	a. Uniform subsidies for all exports EERx > EERm[a] b. Selective subsidies Industrial policy Import substitution	
		Dirigisme

[a] EERx and EERm are the real effective exchange rates for exports and imports, respectively.

figurations of elements defining development strategies. The table illustrates, for example, that outward orientation as a highly general category includes both a market-oriented version (internal liberalization) and a government interventionist version (export push). Import substitution may be only mildly interventionist and indeed could be supportive of export promotion rather than antithetical to it. As described below, these typologies are meant to break down the stereotyped links between orientation, openness, and degree of intervention by illustrating different possible combinations. No attempt is made here to identify particular countries with specific development thrusts, but it is hoped that by differentiating the categories and conceptualizing them as elements on a spectrum, the varieties of policy experience may be thought about more clearly than by applying the dichotomous framework conventionally used.

Before examining the categories in the table in detail, it is necessary to distinguish between the importance of trade in an economy as an empirical matter and the degree of policy openness of an economy. The terms *closed* and *open* often carry policy content describing the bias of policies toward import substitution or export promotion. In this rendering, it is helpful to have designations that empirically identify the importance of trade in the economy. A closed economy is defined here as one in which trade (exports plus imports) as a share of GDP is low, that is, less than 5 percent. It may be that this ratio is low because of deliberate policies, but it may also be due to size, the abundance of natural resources, the similarity of country endowments to world endowments, or other factors. As used here, the term *closed economy* does not describe a policy, as it does in much of the literature, but rather it depicts a state of affairs; it is one in which trade is a minor factor in the economy.

A *trade economy* is its opposite. It is a category in which exports are a large share of GDP, say above 10 to 15 percent. The phrases *export-led* or *open economy* are more frequently used. However, *export-led* implies some empirical substantiation of a cause-effect relationship from exports to economic growth, when in fact high GDP growth may drive exports by generating a supply surplus. The term *open economy* associates internal liberalization (the removal of import controls, tariffs, etc.) with trade as a large share of GDP. Abstracting for the moment from the direction of the causality or the degree of this association, the phrase *trade economy* attempts to convey the importance of exports in an economy that is necessarily embodied in a high export share of GDP. The term *trade economy* is meant to be policy neutral. There remains the question of whether exports are driven by external demand, and thereby induce internal growth, or are supply-determined, resulting in export push. Both the terms *closed economy* and *trade economy* identify endogenous economic outcomes rather than policy inputs in this classification scheme.

Referring to table 2.1, inward versus outward orientation are helpful as the most general categories under which a variety of development strategies can be classified. They imply simply a difference in emphasis, as between the domestic market (not imports) and trade (especially exports) as the main sources of economic growth. They appear, then, at the midpoint of the spectrum between autarky and export promotion rather than necessarily being identified with the extremes in the type of development strategy.

Autarky means no trade and would derive from a severe government decision to "delink" from the world economy in order to achieve some measure of self-reliance or the appearance thereof.

An *import substitution* strategy is a set of deliberate policies that discriminates against those imports that compete with existing or nascent domestic sources of production. Import substitution does not necessarily imply a low volume of imports, since capital goods imports may be essential to establish the industries necessary to achieve future self-sufficiency in the designated range of activities. Normally, import substitution strategies discriminate against imports through the use of import controls, tariffs, multiple exchange rate systems, or other policy devices. Import substitution is not a set policy; the scope and degree of the bias against imports may vary considerably. In the extreme case, it is the dominant policy, in which case the development strategy is fundamentally associated with it. In a more limited case, policies may be applied only to selected sectors with the bulk of the economy otherwise being relatively "open" to free trade. It is also possible that selective import substitution policies may be part of an outward orientation, in which industrial policy is used to sustain an export promotion strategy.

The other large category of strategies is *outward orientation*, which carries the meaning of priority to exports in the policy of the country. In its mildest manifestation, exports may be responsive to external demand and grow rapidly due to the intrinsic competitiveness of the economy or, at a minimum, of the tradable goods sectors. On the other hand, there may be a deliberate policy to liberalize the economy, ranging from a limited case of liberalization only in the tradable goods sector, to a more inclusive case of liberalization across the economy as a whole, even incorporating macroeconomic variables such as interest rates. In this case, an open economy trade strategy meshes with an orthodox macroeconomic adjustment policy. Internal liberalization is labeled here as an *open economy* strategy. In most of the literature, open economy is synonymous with outward orientation, and the two terms are used interchangeably as if they exhaust the policy possibilities for trade promotion.

In the formulation here, open economy is delineated as only one type of outward oriented strategy, that associated with internal liberalization. The open economy–internal liberalization strategy implies that the incentives to export are equivalent to the incentives to import or, as Anne Krueger (1985, p. 21) puts it, "there is as much incentive to earn as to save foreign exchange." This in effect means, as Jagdish Bhagwati (1978) has emphasized, that the effective exchange rate for exports "is not significantly different" from the effective exchange rate for imports. Curiously, Bhagwati labels this an export promotion strategy (EP) which has a potentially quite different meaning than the characterization of the term to be set forth here. In Bhagwati's formulation the absence of discrimination against exports is the major achievement and is seen to provide sufficient incentives for export "promotion." A policy of equivalent incentives for imports and exports would be a free trade optimality point in Ronald Findlay's (1981) ingenious formulation on the subject.

Finally, the most dirigiste form of outward orientation is designated here as *export push*. In this strategy category, the state plays a major role in goal setting and policy implementation to achieve the goals. Variation can exist under an export promotion strategy. A mild form, for example, would be illustrated by uniform export subsidies across the range of exports rather than favoring some export sectors over others. A more interventionist form of export promotion would be linked to an industrial policy that sets sectoral priorities for investment, credit, foreign exchange, imports, and/or subsidy allocations to make the structure of production conform to the export strategy. Import substitution policies could run simultaneously with and support this style of development strategy. Under this strategy category, the effective exchange rate provides more incentives for exports than for imports, in effect subsidizing exports and shielding import competing industries. As a result, exports are promoted beyond the range of optimality leading to what Findlay (1981) calls "right wing deviations."

These typologies of development strategies differentiate among categories in the economic literature that are frequently lumped together. The often portrayed dichotomy between inward- versus outward-oriented growth strategies, in this framework, becomes more a gradual gradation of approaches to development policy composed of different clusters of elements. Rather than once-and-for-all categorizations, different countries would be expected to fall at different places on the continuum at different moments in time.

EXPORT PUSH

This section will highlight some of the distinctions between the unbiased or neutral concept of export promotion and of the export biased concept labeled here as export push. The neutral version remains the dominant version and the one most clearly identified with the East Asian NICs. In a recent volume surveying current thinking on development strategies, Jagdish Bhagwati has written:

> Let me first clarify that, by EP strategy, the literature now simply means a policy such that, on balance, the effective exchange rate for exports (EERx) is not significantly different from that for imports (EERm), so that the EERx is roughly equal to EERm. . . . This as it were minimalist definition of EP conforms closely to the actual experience of the successful East Asian export promoters. (Bhagwati, 1986, pp. 92–93)

The case studies referenced by Bhagwati in this paragraph are the National Bureau of Economic Research studies summarized in part in Bhagwati (1978). The data and country experience referred to is for the pre-1973 period (Bhagwati, 1978, table 7.1, pp. 185–90). Subsequent literature puts this interpretation of the NIC experience out of phase with the historical reality, which during the 1970s entailed more government involvement in export promotion (Bradford 1986). Bhagwati does go on to say in the 1986 article, however, that "perhaps we need to distinguish between EP regimes where EERx roughly equals EERm and the 'ultra'-EP regimes where, instead, EERx is substantially greater than EERm" (Bhagwati, 1986, p. 93).

An alternative theory of the successful export strategies of the NICs finds a major role for the state in using economic policy instruments to affect the productive structure of the economy and the volume and composition of exports (Bradford, 1987). There is evidence of a strong association between rates of structural change and rates of growth in value added in manufacturing between 1965 and 1980, on the one hand, and criteria used to identify NICs, such as the volume and rate of growth of exports of manufactures, on the other. There is also evidence in most transitional economies of considerable change in the composition of exports according to factor intensities following a general pattern from natural resource intensive exports to unskilled labor intensive exports to physical and human capital intensive exports. These patterns of dynamic structural change internally and externally seem to suggest a strong role for the state in accelerating these dimensions of the development process. In most cases, the state also has had a sectorally specific strategic design to promote structural change internally and externally and has marshalled policy instruments and engaged the private sector to achieve it.

Not surprisingly, the principal instrument variable for affecting these supply-side changes is investment. There is evidence based on data from the United Nations International Price Comparison Project (Kravis, Heston, and Summers, 1982) that investment goods prices are lower than government and consumption goods prices within transitional economies and lower in transitional than in nontransitional economies. This seems to suggest that underpricing investment goods (which would be expected to accelerate the structural changes identified with the NICs above) is associated with the high growth and dynamic export performance of the NICs (Bradford 1987). As a result, monetary and fiscal policies affecting interest rates become important elements supporting the export push development strategy of the NICs.

From this conceptual framework emerges a pattern of investment-led structural change leading to dynamic supply-side "export push" in which the state has played the crucial catalytic role in achieving the development success associated with the NICs. The overall effect has been to produce a bias toward exports (EERx > EERm), which is consistent with the extraordinary export growth rates of the NICs in the 1970s and 1980s. This state-led, structural change, export-push theory of dynamic development stands in contrast to the open economy, internal liberalization version of outward orientation in which competitive exports are responsive to and driven by world demand.

The trade regimes adopted by all four countries examined in this chapter closely fit the export push model during much of the period covered, more than either the import substitution regime attributed to the Latin American NICs or the open economy regime attributed to the East Asian NICs. Some controversy continues to surround these interpretations. This is true in part because of divergent patterns and performance in the two regions especially in the 1980s. The rest of this chapter compares and contrasts trends in South Korea, Taiwan, Brazil, and Mexico over the last two decades, with a view to keeping an open mind both about development strategy typologies and the regional character of policy behavior.

EXPORT DRIVES, 1966–1984

Looking at the economic record of South Korea, Taiwan, Brazil, and Mexico for the years 1966 to 1984 reveals an interesting blend of commonality and variety in policy and performance. The crucial interactions are between the trade balance and investment. These interactions in the NICs are fundamental in determining both the growth drive in the 1970s and the adjustment experience in the 1980s. The growth drive was fueled by investment, which depends on capital goods imports made possible by either exports or debt. The adjustment experience, on the other hand, required an export surplus, which in turn forced an internal adjustment that fell largely on a contraction of investment.

This section traces the changes in trade as a share of GDP over the entire 1966–1984 period. The subsequent two sections examine the patterns of investment growth from 1966 to 1979 and the patterns of adjustment and macroeconomic trends in the following period, 1980–1984.

The export drives of the NICs as measured by exports as a share of GDP (table 2.2) occurred at different phases and in different rhythms. Each of the four NICs achieved a more than doubling in its export-GDP share from 1966 to 1984. South Korea experienced two spurts, one in the early 1970s and one in the early 1980s. The first was accompanied by a major jump in imports as a share of GDP facilitating industrialization for export growth. The import-GDP share stabilized from the mid-1970s to mid-1980s, facilitating adjustment. Taiwan experienced a more continuous increase in the export-GDP share from 1966 to 1979, with imports trailing exports in lockstep with a spurt in trade shares from 1971 to 1973. The unique aspects of the Taiwan experience were the continuity of the export drive and the fact that it began in the 1960s and was complete by the end of the 1970s with export and import shares above 50 percent of GDP.

TABLE 2.2
Export Drives, 1966–1984 (percent of GDP)

		Exports	Percent Change		Imports	Percent Change
	1966–1971	10.4–15.3	+ 4.9	1966–1972	20.3–22.4	+ 2.1
South	1971–1973	15.3–29.1	+13.8	1972–1975	24.3–35.3	+11.0
Korea	1973–1979	29.1–27.3	− 1.8	1975–1979	33.2–34.5	+ 1.3
	1979–1984	27.3–37.5	+10.2	1979–1984	34.5–37.1	+ 2.6
	1966–1970	21.3–29.6	+ 8.3	1966–1970	21.0–29.7	+ 8.7
Taiwan	1970–1973	29.6–46.7	+17.1	1970–1973	29.7–41.4	+11.7
	1976–1979	47.4–54.6	+ 7.2	1976–1979	45.1–54.0	+ 8.9
	1967–1973	5.8– 8.3	+ 2.5	1969–1975	6.2–11.4	+ 5.2
Brazil	1973–1981	8.3– 7.6	− 0.7	1975–1980	11.4–10.6	− 0.8
	1981–1984	7.6–13.9	+ 6.3	1980–1984	10.6– 8.4	− 2.2
	1967–1976	8.7– 8.5	− 0.2	1967–1976	9.4– 9.9	+ 0.5
Mexico	1976–1979	8.5–11.2	+ 2.7	1976–1979	9.9–12.5	+ 2.6
	1981–1984	11.9–19.5	+ 8.4	1981–1984	13.6– 9.4	− 4.2

Source: IMF (1985).

Brazil's export drive began in the famous boom period from 1967 to 1973, when increasing manufactured exports was a deliberate policy backed by export subsidies and other arrangements. Mexico, while exporting a sufficient volume of manufactured exports by 1976 to qualify as a NIC, increased its export-GDP share with oil exports only in the 1976–1979 period. Imports as a share of GDP led, rather than followed, the export-GDP share and increased proportionately with exports. The second surge in export-GDP shares for Brazil and Mexico came in the 1980s under pressure from debt service requirements.

There are differences among the four countries in the timing, sequence, and magnitude of the growth of trade as a share of GDP, which need to be explored more fully. There is also a clear difference between the experience through the end of the 1970s—when exports in effect financed import growth, especially capital goods imports for investment—and the 1980s, when exports financed debt service payments. The sections that follow will examine patterns of investment growth in the four NICs from 1966 to 1979 and patterns of adjustment from 1980 to 1984.

PATTERNS OF INVESTMENT GROWTH, 1966–1979

For investment as a share of GDP to increase, it is a matter of straightforward arithmetic that consumption and/or government GDP shares must decline or that net imports as a share of GDP must increase. If the shift in the net trade balance is less than the increase in the investment-GDP share, then either the consumption or the government-GDP shares or both must drop. Given the four NICs' general pattern of import-GDP shares increasing with export-GDP shares, we can anticipate a relatively high potential for investment growth.

The period 1966–1973—which was a time of export drive in South Korea, Taiwan, and Brazil—was also a period in which the investment-GDP share increased significantly in these three countries (see table 2.3). Mexico's investment-GDP share increased only moderately. In all four countries, the net trade balances provided virtually none of the "space" for investment growth (in South Korea and Taiwan, in fact, the trade balance improved). Therefore, contraction in the consumption-GDP share was the offset to increasing investment-GDP shares in both sets of countries. It is also interesting to note that the lion's share of the shift in the investment-consumption shares occurred by 1970 in these four countries.

TABLE 2.3
Patterns of Investment Growth, 1966–1979 (percent of GDP)

South Korea	1966–1973	1973–1975		1976–1979	Total
Investment	+4	+4		+6	+14
Consumption	−10	+2		−8	−16
Government	−2	+1		0	−1
Net Imports	+7	−6		+2	+3
Taiwan	1966–1973		1973–1979		Total
Investment	+13		+3		+16
Consumption	−11		0		−11
Government	−2		+1		−1
Net Imports	+4		−4		0
Brazil	1966–1973	1973–1975		1976–1979	Total
Investment	+4	+5		−10	−1
Consumption	−4	−2		+9	+3
Government	0	0		−1	−1
Net Imports	−1	−3		+2	−2
Mexico	1966–1973		1974–1979		Total
Investment	+2		+4.5		+6.5
Consumption	−4		−6		−10.0
Government	+2		−1.5		+3.5
Net Imports	−1		0		−1.0

Source: IMF (1985)

South Korea and Brazil managed to continue to increase their investment-GDP shares in 1974 and 1975, with some help from the net trade balance in these years. Taiwan and Mexico had a more continuous adjustment in 1974 and 1975.

From 1973 to 1979, Taiwan's export drive continued with the investment-GDP share rising and net exports falling. Mexico's oil boom in this period was accompanied by an increase in the investment-GDP share and a commensurate decline in the consumption-GDP share. South Korea's trade shares stabilized in the late 1970s, while the investment share increased at the expense of consumption. In Brazil the reverse occurred, with the investment share falling dramatically from 1976 to 1979 and the consumption share gained by the same proportions (table 2.3).

The general patterns for the 1966–1979 period seem to reveal that investment growth is used to sustain the export drive by channeling investment to export industries. As a result, exports grow faster than GDP, thereby increasing their GDP share. Imports of capital goods are financed by rapid export growth. The trade share shift both is fueled by and fuels investment growth. Consumption growth in absolute terms is higher during the export drive than in other periods, but it is slower than GDP growth during the export drive, thereby providing room for high investment growth.

Constrained consumption growth is the important adjustment variable for rapid investment growth, not the net trade balance. The export drive not only sustains investment growth through increasing capital goods imports, but also investment growth generates the capacity to supply exports. These patterns then are consistent with the export push structural change theory of dynamic development in which changes in productive structure through investment create capacity to supply exports at faster rates than growth rates in world demand. The East Asian and Latin American NICs are more similar to each other than previously thought; they adopted broadly comparable export push development models.

These patterns both establish the basis for and contrast with the patterns of adjustment in the early 1980s, when the need to run trade surpluses relied on the installed capacity in export industries and the compression of investment to generate the surplus of goods and savings required to finance debt service payments.

PATTERNS OF ADJUSTMENT, 1980–1984

Based on the similarities in achieving dynamic industrialization and manufactured export growth in the 1970s, it might be expected that South Korea, Taiwan, Brazil, and Mexico would have similar patterns of adjustment in the 1980s. Trends in macroeconomic variables would be anticipated to be quite similar deriving from their similar development strategies. On the other hand, if the East Asian NICs have indeed shown greater capacity to implement the export push development model than the Latin American NICs, then economic performance in the 1980s might be poorer in Latin America, even though the main lines of economic direction were similar in the 1970s.

Since the second oil shock and the interest rate shock in 1979, most economies and the world economy itself experienced major adjustment. South Korea, Taiwan, Brazil, and Mexico have shown a striking shift in their trade balances of between 9 and 14 percentage points of GDP since 1979 (see table 2.4). This is a major shift of GDP shares in a relatively short period. For South Korea, Brazil, and Mexico, growth in export shares were between two and three times more important than contraction in import shares of GDP in correcting the trade balance. South Korea began with a trade deficit of 7 percent of GDP in 1979 and 1980, while the other three NICs had trade deficits of 1 to 2 percent of GDP in that interim. By 1984, South Korea had achieved trade balance, and the others had obtained sizable trade surpluses: Taiwan 11.6 percent, Brazil 5.5 percent, and Mexico 10.1 percent of GDP. The one divergence from the general patterns characteristic of the four NICs in this period is that Taiwan achieved its massive trade surplus more through restricting imports than expanding exports. Nevertheless, all four countries registered export growth rates of between 13 and 23 percent.

To move from a trade deficit, in which a surplus of goods is available to the domestic economy through imports, to a trade surplus, in which a surplus of goods is supplied to the world economy through exports, requires an offsetting internal adjustment. Table 2.4 shows that in the four NICs the burden of the internal adjustment was largely borne by a contraction of the GDP share of investment. There is essentially a common pattern as between the two East Asian and the two Latin American NICs. Instead of a classic case of overheating with excess demand triggering an adjustment that requires contraction in consumption and government spending, the NIC pattern is one of adjustment through shifts in the key instrument variable in the NIC development model, namely investment.

This pattern in the 1980–1984 period reverses the common NIC pattern discerned for the 1974–1979 period (Bradford, 1982; Sachs, 1981; Díaz-Alejandro, 1984; Van Wijnbergen, 1984). The NIC pattern in the earlier period was one in which investment growth outpaced GDP growth, pulling in capital goods imports from the Organization for Economic Cooperation and Development (OECD) countries for industrialization and export capacity, with the resulting current account deficits being financed by recycling the Organization of Petroleum Exporting Countries (OPEC) petrodollar surplus. Whereas savings as a share of GDP increased in East

TABLE 2.4
NIC Adjustment Patterns, 1980–1984 (percent shifts in GDP shares)

	(1) Exports/ GDP 1979–84	(2) Imports/ GDP 1980–84	(3) Total Shift in Trade Balance [(1) + (2)]	(4) Investment/ GDP 1980–84	(5) Government Consumption/ GDP 1980–84	(6) Total Internal Adjustment [(4) + (5)] (percent of Trade Balance [(6)/(3)]
South Korea	10.4	3.5	13.9	6.7	1.2	7.9 (57)
Taiwan	4.1	8.1	12.2	12.8	0.0	12.8 (105)
Brazil	7.1	2.2	9.3	6.1	1.5	7.6 (82)
Mexico	8.3	4.2	12.5	7.9	3.1	11.0 (88)

Source: IMF (1985, summary of country data).

Asia and Latin America in the adjustment period following the first oil shock, the investment share increased even more rapidly with the gap being filled by external savings. In this period, external adjustment facilitated internal transformation in economies with strong public policy commitments to industrialization and exports. In the wake of the 1979 shocks, these patterns reversed themselves with the adjustment in the external accounts forcing a dramatic contraction in investment.

Nevertheless, this contraction did not disrupt the capacity to generate an export surplus. In fact, evidence of supply-push export capacity by these NICs is shown by the fact that the export growth rates for the 1980–1984 period for the four NICs are well above the average export growth rates for developing countries and for industrial countries in addition to being well above the average growth in world trade. The average annual growth rate of exports was 12.6 percent for South Korea, 14.2 percent for Taiwan, 13.3 percent for Brazil, and 23.2 percent for Mexico—as compared to 4.3 percent for developing countries as a whole and 3.4 percent for industrial countries. The NIC adjustment pattern in the 1980–1984 period was achieved through expansion of exports and the contraction of investment, whereas it was determined by capital goods imports and external savings in the 1974–1979 period.

MACROECONOMIC TRENDS: 1980–1984

Differences in economic performance would be expected to reveal themselves in the macroeconomic trends in the four countries. Even though the basic pattern and underlying dynamic may be similar, as between the East Asian and Latin American NICs, there may well be differences in economic performance that may be due to factors other than differences in the trade regimes adopted in the two regions. The macroeconomic trends reviewed below reveal further similarities and differences between the four countries.

South Korea and Taiwan, with growth rates in the 7-to-7.5-percent range, were able to sustain dynamic growth during the early 1980s, when the rest of the world was growing at 2 to 2.5 percent. Brazil and Mexico, on the other hand, suffered massive downturns in their growth rates from 1981 to 1983, with an average performance from 1981 to 1984 of between 0.5 and 1.5 percent, well below the rest of the world. South Korea and Taiwan were able to correct the trade balance and achieve high real rates of GDP growth, whereas Brazil and Mexico were able to correct their trade balances, but at the cost of GDP growth.

In Mexico the fiscal deficit increased to over 15 percent of GDP by 1982, with growth rates in the money supply and domestic credit equal to or greater than nominal GDP growth from 1979 to 1982. Real GDP growth was sustained through 1981. Inflation increased while the exchange rate remained relatively fixed with a commensurate deterioration in both the trade balance and the current account, especially in 1981. In 1982 a massive devaluation of over 260 percent turned around the trade balance, improved the current account and triggered a recession. From this data, Mexico appears to be a classic case of an overheating economy in this period.

Brazil presents a similar but somewhat more mixed picture. The data on the fiscal deficit do not include public enterprises and therefore do not give a full picture of the impact of government deficits on the economy. Examination of the change in public and private sector shares of domestic credit from 1979 to 1984 in the four countries reveals that credit to public enterprises as a percentage share of domestic credit in Taiwan in 1979 was 19 percent, compared to 10.3 percent in Brazil and 2.4 percent in Mexico. This confirms what other literature suggests, namely that public enterprises play a relatively large role in Taiwan. However, the public sector share of domestic credit remained relatively constant in Taiwan and South Korea between 1979 and 1984, whereas it mushroomed in Brazil, from 10.3 percent in 1979 to 28.8 percent in 1984, and increased to 10 percent in Mexico by 1984 from 2.4 percent in 1979 with proportionate declines in the share of domestic credit going to the private sector. Crowding out is evidenced in Brazil and Mexico, whereas the private sector share of domestic credit declined only marginally in South Korea and Taiwan.

Domestic credit growth in Brazil was greater than or equal to nominal GDP growth in four of the six years between 1979 and 1984, consistent with growing pressure from the public sector. Inflation accelerated. The exchange rate was adjusted and the trade balance actually improved beginning in 1981, but the current account deteriorated with a sharp increase in the current account deficit in 1982. A maxidevaluation followed in 1983 with major improvements in both the current account and the trade balance in 1983 and 1984.

South Korea took major adjustment measures much earlier than Brazil and Mexico. For a variety of reasons, South Korea's external position had deteriorated in the late 1970s. On top of this, its president was assassinated in late 1979. In January 1980, the exchange rate was devalued significantly, and a stabilization program was put into effect. The result was a drop in the real rate of GDP growth from 7.3 percent in 1979 to minus 3 percent in 1980. This slump caused Korean policymakers to adopt an expansionary policy in 1981 and 1982, with the fiscal deficit rising to over 3 percent of GDP and the growth rates in the money supply and domestic credit running ahead of nominal GDP growth. Growth performance rebounded, but the external accounts were slow to improve until more contractionary monetary and fiscal policies were adopted in 1983 and 1984. The rate of inflation dropped continuously over the period and exchange rate adjustment kept pace with the inflation rate after 1980.

Taiwan presents a very different case indeed. The external accounts were in surplus throughout the period, with the minor exception of a slight deficit in the current account in 1980. Inflation was high in 1980 and 1981 but was brought immediately under control in 1982 with an accompanying drop in the real GDP growth rate to 3.3 percent. Moderately expansionary fiscal and monetary policies were adopted in 1982 and 1983 to bring up the growth rate.

Taiwan is unique among the four countries in a number of related respects. There is smooth and balanced adjustment to changing international circumstances. The external balance improved markedly in Taiwan to sizable surpluses in both the current account and the trade balance. Taiwan achieved this more by cutting imports than by expanding exports, unlike the other three NICs. Domestic monetary and fiscal policy and performance were kept on track. The exchange rate was adjusted with the inflation rate, which itself declined to the vanishing point. Taiwan is a case of smooth autonomous adjustment without significant recourse to external financing.

The general pattern of the other three NICs seems to be that the oil and interest rate shocks from 1979 onward were caused in each case by a mushrooming of current account deficits (1981 in Mexico, 1982 in Brazil, and to a lesser extent 1980 in South Korea) followed by or occurring concurrently with a major devaluation (1982 in Mexico, 1983 in Brazil, 1980 in Korea). The year of the devaluation is the year in which the major portion of the adjustment in investment as a share of GDP occurs in Mexico, Brazil, and South Korea. Capital goods imports undoubtedly contracted with the devaluation while oil imports increased as proportion of total imports.

The other common pattern seems to be that the interest rate shock drove debt service payments significantly above new loans (increments to debt) (table 2.5) such that the external payments imbalance forced both a trade and a savings surplus. The need for a savings surplus beyond the trade surplus due to the increase in debt service payments put pressure on the government deficit and the money supply.

Ex post, the following identity must hold:

$$(M - X) + R = Se = I - Sn$$

or the current account equals external savings, which equals the internal saving-investment gap,

TABLE 2.5
New Loans and Debt Service (US$ billions)

	1980	1981	1982	1983	1984	1982–1984
			Korea			
Loans	6.9	5.2	4.6	3.1	2.3	10.0
Debt service	4.4	5.5	5.8	5.7	6.8	− 18.3
			Brazil			
Loans	3.3	34.6	11.3	8.3	8.6	28.2
Debt service	7.9	16.7	19.5	14.4	12.2	− 46.1
			Mexico			
Loans	4.3	41.4	10.0	5.7	3.1	18.8
Debt service	7.6	8.5	19.4	21.6	16.1	− 57.1

Sources: Korea, Aghovli and Marquez-Ruarte (1985); Brazil and Mexico, IDB (1982, 1984, and 1985). Comparable data not available for Taiwan.

where M = imports
X = exports
R = net factor payments (interest payments largely)
Se = external savings
I = total investment
Sn = national savings = private savings and governmental savings

As interest payments (R) rise and external savings (Se) fall (because banks are less willing to lend), pressures build for the trade balance to generate a surplus and for investment to be reduced below the level of national savings. This is the pattern we have seen in the adjustment of all four NICs. If external savings becomes negative, an export surplus and a savings surplus must be generated to meet debt service obligations in excess of new loans. This creates strain on the entire system, ultimately putting pressure on the government to close the savings gap through taxation, which is recessionary, or through domestic credit creation, which is inflationary.

Therefore, the fact that debt service payments exceeded new loans—by $18 billion in the case of Brazil for 1982 to 1984, (table 2.5) and by nearly $40 billion for Mexico in the same interval—indicates the pressure that the external sector has put on the domestic economy and the vulnerability to external change of macroeconomic variables in these economies. In South Korea the difference between debt service and new debt is $8 billion. Comparable figures are not available for Taiwan, but we know that Taiwan has accumulated a large foreign exchange surplus. As a result, the differences in economic performance between Mexico and Brazil, on the one hand, and South Korea and Taiwan, on the other, appear to be rooted in the vulnerability of macroeconomic policy variables to external shocks. Indeed, both Mexico and Brazil have been praised for having taken strong adjustment measures during this period in the midst of adverse circumstances (Morgan Guaranty, 1984b; 1984c). South Korea and Taiwan seem to have been more able to keep macroeconomic policy consistent with and supportive of the development thrust, while Brazil and Mexico, despite having a similar thrust, were unable to keep macropolicy harnessed to it due to external economic and, undoubtedly, internal political pressures. Differences in economic performance seem to have relatively less to do with stylized differences between regions in development strategies, trade regimes, and macroeconomic adjustment policy designs than with the social, political, and institutional context within which broadly similar plans and intentions were adopted (see chaps. 5, 6, 7, 9, this volume).

Development Policy Regimes: Some Conclusions

To fully analyze the development patterns and policies in two East Asian and two Latin American economies over the last twenty years would require more than is possible here. Nonetheless, based on the foregoing analysis, it is possible to draw some tentative conclusions and to conceptualize some overall understandings.

First, each of the four countries has an individual development pattern with some unique feature(s) not shared by the others. Taiwan is determined to avoid accumulating significant external debt and as a result has run a trade surplus in thirteen of the nineteen years between 1966 and 1984. This alone drives the development strategy and supporting macropolicy in a different way from other countries. By contrast, South Korea didn't run a trade surplus in a single year between 1966 and 1984 (IMF, 1986). South Korea's pattern of external debt accumulation is more similar to Mexico and Brazil than to Taiwan. Another unique feature that illustrates differences within regions is the presence of large reserves of oil in Mexico, which obviously had a major influence on its development patterns, differentiating it in a significant way from Brazil.

These examples lead to a second conclusion: it does not seem possible to identify separate East Asian or Latin American models of development strategies and patterns that are clear-cut and not distorting constructs. Not only is the variety of country experience too great for the regional models to mean anything, but the commonalities between NICs in East

Asia and in Latin America make the stylized contrasts embodied in most versions quite exaggerated.

Third, the interaction of the world economy with these dynamic economies has been a major source of policy change, but the policy responses show as much variety as they do similarity. Taiwan and Brazil had export drives that began in 1966 or 1967 whereas South Korea's first export surge began in 1971 and Mexico's in 1976. The oil price shock in 1974 and 1975 appears to have prompted more severe adjustment in South Korea and Brazil than in Taiwan and Mexico. Taiwan and Mexico, for different reasons, experienced high growth in their trade shares in 1976 to 1979, whereas South Korea and Brazil did not. In the period after the second oil shock in 1979 and the interest rate shock in the early 1980s, the U.S. trade deficit elicited a surge in exports from South Korea, Brazil and Mexico but not from Taiwan, which achieved adjustment largely through compressing imports.

As one examines each of the four countries over the last two decades, one sees a different set of interactions between individual country economic and trade patterns and the international context. The response of each country is different, illustrating a range of policy possibilities in different countries in similar international contexts. As just noted above, the sequence of national policy shifts has been highly individual, with as many similarities and differences within the two East Asian and two Latin American countries as between them. Stylized versions highlighting once-and-for-all choices between outward versus inward orientation, intervention versus liberalization, and public versus private sector dominance that abstract entirely from the prevailing conditions in the world economy do not appear to effectively capture the essential elements characterizing policy regimes in these interactive, highly dynamic, interdependent countries.

REFERENCES

Aghevli, Bijan B., and Jorge Marquez-Ruarte. 1985. *A Case of Successful Adjustment: Korea's Experience during 1980–84*. Occasional Paper 39. International Monetary Fund, Washington, D.C.: International Monetary Fund.

Arida, Persio, and Edmar Bacha. 1984. "Balance of Payments: A Disequilibrium Analysis for Semi-Industrialized Economies." *Pesquisa e Planejamento Econômico* 14, no. 1, pp. 1–58. Also in *International Trade, Investment Macro Policies and History: Essays in Memory of Carlos F. Díaz-Alejandro*, edited by P. Bardhan, A. Fishlow, and J. Behrman. Amersterdam: North-Holland.

Balassa, Bela. 1984. "Adjustment Policies in Developing Countries: A Reassessment." *World Development* 12, no. 9, pp. 955–72.

Bhagwati, Jagdish. 1986. "Rethinking Trade Strategy." In *Development Strategies Reconsidered*, edited by John P. Lewis. New Brunswick, N.J.: Transaction Books.

Bhagwati, Jagdish. 1978. *Foreign Trade Regimes and Economic Development: Anatomy and Consequences of Exchange Control Regimes.* New York: National Bureau of Economic Research; and Cambridge: Ballinger Publishing Company.

Bradford, Colin I., Jr. 1987. "Trade and Structural Change: NICs and Next Tier NICs as Transitional Economies." *World Development* 15, no. 3, pp. 299–316.

———. 1986. "East Asian Models: Myths and Lesson." In *Development Strategies Reconsidered*, edited by John P. Lewis. New Brunswick, N.J.: Transaction Books.

———. 1982. "The NICs and World Economic Adjustment." In *The Newly Industrializing Countries: Trade and Adjustment*, edited by Louis Turner et al. London: George Allen & Unwin.

Bradford, Colin I., Jr., and William H. Branson. 1987. "Patterns of Trade and Structural Change." In *Trade and Structural Change in Pacific Asia*, edited by Bradford and Branson. Chicago: National Bureau of Economic Research and University of Chicago Press.

Bryant, Ralph C. (1985) "Financial Structure and International Banking in Singapore," *Brookings Discussion Papers in International Economics*, Washington, D.C.: Brookings Institution.

———. 1980. *Money and Monetary Policy in Interdependent Nations.* Washington, D.C.: Brookings Institution.

Buiter, William H. 1985. "Macroeconomic Responses by Developing Countries to Changes in External Economic Conditions." Paper for Yale University and NBER. December. Mimeo.

De Castro, Antonio Barros, and Francisco Eduardo Pires de Souza. 1985. *A Economia Brasileira em Marcha Forcada.* São Paulo: Paz e Terra.

Díaz-Alejandro, Carlos. 1984. "Latin American Debt: I Don't Think We Are in Kansas Anymore." *Brookings Panel on Economic Activities.* Vol. 2. Washington, D.C.: Brookings Institution.

Findlay, Ronald. 1981. "Comment." In *Trade and Growth of the Advanced Developing Countries in the Pacific Basin.* edited by Wontack Hong and Lawrence B. Krause. Seoul: Korean Development Institute Press.

Hong, Wontack. 1987. "Export-Oriented Growth and Trade Patterns in Korea." In *Trade and Structural Change in Pacific Asia*, edited by Colin I. Bradford, Jr., and William H. Branson. Chicago: National Bureau of Economic Research and University of Chicago Press.

IDB (Inter-American Development Bank). 1982, 1984, and 1985. *Economic and Social Progress in Latin America.* Washington, D.C.: IDB

IMF (International Monetary Fund). 1985. *International Financial Statistics*, November. Washington, D.C.: IMF.

———. 1986. *International Financial Statistics Yearbook.* Washington, D.C.: IMF.

Keohane, Robert O. 1984. *After Hegemony: Cooperation and Discord in the World Political Economy.* Princeton: Princeton University Press.

Khan, Mohsin S., and Roberto Zahler. 1983. "The Macroeconomic Effects of

Changes in Barriers to Trade and Capital Flows: A Simulation Analysis." *IMF Staff Papers*, 30, no. 2, pp. 223–82.

Killick, Tony, Graham Bird, Jennifer Sharpley, and Mary Sutton. 1984. "The IMF: Case for a Change in Emphasis." In *Adjustment Crisis in the Third World*, edited by Richard E. Feinberg and Valeriana Kallab. Washington, D.C.: Overseas Development Council; and New Brunswick, N.J., and London: Transaction Books.

Krasner, Stephen D. 1985. *Structural Conflict: The Third World against Global Liberalism*. Berkeley: University of California Press.

Kravis, Irving B., Alan Heston, and Robert Summers. 1982. *World Product and Income: International Comparisons of Real Gross Product*. Baltimore: Johns Hopkins University Press for the World Bank.

Krueger, Anne O. 1985. "Import Substitution Versus Export Promotion." *Finance and Development* 22, no. 2, pp. 20–23.

Morgan Guaranty Trust Company of New York. 1984a. "Korea: Adjustment Model for the 1980s?" *World Financial Markets*, March.

———. 1984b. "Mexico: Progress and Prospects." *World Financial Markets*, May.

———. 1984c. "Stabilization Policies in Brazil." *World Financial Markets*, July.

Nelson, Richard R., and Sidney G. Winter. 1982. *An Evolutionary Theory of Economic Change*. Cambridge: Belknap Press of Harvard University Press.

Sachs, Jeffry D. 1985. "External Debt and Macroeconomic Performance in Latin America and East Asia." *Brookings Papers on Economic Activity*, pp. 523–73.

———. 1981. "The Current Account and Macroeconomic Adjustment in the 1970s." *Brookings Papers on Economic Activity*, pp. 201–82.

Van Wijnbergen, Sweder. 1984. "The Optimal Investment and Current Account Response to Oil Price Shocks under Putty-Clay Technology." *Journal of International Economics* 17.

PART TWO

Key Economic, Political, and Social Dimensions of Development in the Latin American and East Asian NICs

CHAPTER 3

The Role of Foreign Capital in Economic Development

Barbara Stallings

ONE OF THE most controversial topics in development theory and policy has been the role of foreign capital. Looking back over the post–World War II era—the period in which governments actually began to devise development policies and strategies in the Third World—debates on the advantages and disadvantages of foreign resources have often been at center stage. Is foreign capital the principal vehicle for the promotion of development or the central cause of underdevelopment? Do Third World governments have any bargaining leverage with multinational firms, or do the latter simply impose conditions? What are the relative advantages of direct investment versus loans? Who are the main winners and losers from foreign capital inflows?

Many of the important questions about foreign capital can be grouped into two interrelated debates. One focuses on the positive or negative effects of foreign capital in Third World countries, juxtaposing the theories or approaches known as "modernization" and "dependency."[1] The other debate deals with the relative power of foreign actors and Third World governments in determining rules for investment and the distribution of benefits. This second debate also involves dependency theory, but in this case it is pitted against "statist" theories or approaches.[2]

In evaluating these theories, comparisons between Latin America and East Asia provide several advantages. First, such comparisons offer greater empirical variation in experiences with foreign capital than can be found in a single region. Of course, these very differences also complicate the task of comparison, as Gary Gereffi indicates in the introductory chapter. Second, looking at both regions leads us to broaden our theoretical inquiry. That is, the modernization-dependency debate has been focused primarily on Latin American countries, while the statist-depen-

---

[1] There has been an extensive debate as to whether these bodies of literature are really theories, as opposed to more general frameworks or approaches. Use of Thomas Kuhn's term, *paradigm*, is also common. For a discussion of this issue, focusing on the dependency literature, see Palma (1978). An interesting related work, dealing with economic paradigms in East Asia, is Yusuf and Peters (1985).

[2] The approach referred to here as "statism" is closely related to, although broader than, Gereffi's "dependency management" (1989).

dency debate has been more prevalent in analyses of East Asia. Since both are clearly important and interrelated, it is useful to consider them together. Third, East Asian experts typically have come down on the more positive side of both debates (arguing for the validity of modernization and statism), while Latin Americanists have supported the opposite view. A comparative study provides the opportunity to see if objective conditions justify the respective positions.

Like most other chapters in the volume, this one concentrates on the two largest developing countries in each region: Brazil and Mexico in Latin America, and South Korea and Taiwan in East Asia. The time period is the postwar years, generally starting in the mid-1950s. The chapter consists of five sections. The first briefly outlines the two theoretical debates on foreign capital and the questions to be explored in the chapter. The second looks at some quantitative data on foreign capital in the four countries, focusing on changes over time. The third asks how the quantitative differences across countries and regions might be explained. The fourth examines some qualitative data on the role of foreign capital by concentrating on a particular question: what was the relationship between foreign capital and choice of development strategy in the two regions? Finally, the concluding section returns to reconsider the two debates in light of the evidence presented in the chapter.

Two Debates on Foreign Capital

The dependency-modernization debate has been going on in Latin America for several decades. Criticisms of foreign capital have been prominent at least since the 1949 Economic Survey of Latin America, produced by the UN Economic Commission for Latin America (ECLA). ECLA's moderate critique, which focused mainly on international trade as an impediment to development, was followed in the 1960s by more radical attacks that concentrated on foreign capital and especially multinational corporations. By the early 1970s, the so-called dependency paradigm was dominant both in Latin America and in U.S. studies of Latin America. Major problems identified by dependency analysts included profit outflows exceeding new capital inflows, elimination of jobs through use of capital-intensive technology, and marginalization of poorer regions and income groups; in general, it was claimed that dependency and development were incompatible. Early works of this genre tended to attribute most problems in Latin America to the United States, whether through political manipulation by the CIA or economic manipulation by multinational corporations and their home governments.[3] The widespread acceptance of the

[3] The best-known works in the early dependency tradition include Baran (1957), Frank (1967), and dos Santos (1970).

dependency critique, however, led to more sophisticated versions that concentrated on the interaction of foreign and domestic actors, the role of ideology, and the contradictory effects of foreign capital with respect to development.[4]

The modernization approach, by contrast, has focused on the positive aspects of foreign capital as well as foreign trade. Characteristics such as new resource inflows, employment generation, access to technology, and entry to foreign markets have been emphasized as ways that foreign capital promotes development. While this approach was being relegated to obscurity in Latin America, it was alive and well in East Asia. Indeed, the best-known studies (in English) of South Korea and Taiwan have been carried out within this paradigm.[5] International openness in both trade and capital flows was accepted as the optimal policy stance. The questions, then, became what type of capital was most advantageous and how it could be attracted. To be sure, there have been critiques of foreign capital in East Asia, but they have tended to be less sophisticated and more easily refuted than in Latin America. There has been more of an emphasis on direct U.S. and/or Japanese domination and even conspiracy theory. In many ways, criticisms of foreign capital in East Asia have resembled the early dependency analyses of Latin America.[6]

The statism-dependency debate is of more recent origin. Just as the dependency approach has emphasized the negative effects of foreign capital, it has also posited the inability of Third World governments to avoid these negative effects. Host governments have been portrayed as extremely weak vis-à-vis multinational corporations, international banks, and foreign governments. It has been argued that they are unable to establish rules for investment or profit remittance and that they are compelled to provide incentives to foreign investors. Recently, it has been claimed that they were forced by international bankers to borrow money during the lending wave of the 1970s and early 1980s. To some extent, this argument about the power of foreign capital has also been modified

[4] The most important of the later Latin American studies is Cardoso and Faletto (1979). This book was written in the mid-1960s and first published in Spanish in 1969. Other examples include Evans (1979), Gereffi (1983), Newfarmer (1985), and Bennett and Sharpe (1985).

[5] The most prominent of the East Asian studies using the modernization approach are those jointly sponsored by the Harvard Institute for International Development and the Korean Development Institute. See, for example, Krueger (1979), Kim and Roemer (1979), and Mason et al. (1980). On Taiwan, see Jacoby (1966), Galenson (1979), and Kuo et al. (1981). A useful comparative volume is Galenson (1985). Berger (1986) provides a general justification of this approach.

[6] On East Asia, see Long (1977), Sunoo (1978), and Landsberg (1979). Similar tendencies elsewhere in Asia are described in Thanamai (1985, pp. 9–12). Two recent exceptions to this unsophisticated approach are Gold (1981) and Lim (1982). For a discussion of the "lessons" that East Asia offers for dependency theory, see Evans (1987).

by the more sophisticated versions of the dependency approach, and increasing attention has been placed on the role of domestic protagonists. Nevertheless, foreign actors have remained central to the analysis, and the new focus has been on how the state, local capital, and foreign capital come together to produce "dependent development."[7]

In East Asia, by contrast, authors on all sides of the ideological spectrum have concentrated the bulk of their attention on domestic groups rather than foreign actors. In particular, emphasis has been placed on the economic role of the state, although the domestic private sector has been singled out as well. "Dirigisme," "etatisme," and the "developmental state" have been the concepts used to attack dependency theory from the East Asian perspective. The state's role in providing credit, channelling investment into particular industries, subsidizing export products, protecting the domestic market, and attracting new technology has been considered far more important than foreign capital in accounting for political and economic developments in East Asia. The state has been portrayed as capable of using foreign capital, rather than the other way around.[8]

These debates have aroused intense controversy within the two regions, so trying to evaluate them across regions is a daunting task. I will proceed by focusing on the proposition that the newly industrializing countries (NICs) of Latin America and East Asia have had very different experiences with foreign capital. These different experiences, in turn, would be expected to produce different interpretations in the literature. To examine this general proposition, two specific hypotheses will be tested. From the dependency-statism debate, the hypothesis is that foreign capital has been less important in East Asia than in Latin America; conversely local capital and the state have been more important. An initial test of this hypothesis can be carried out by comparing foreign capital with aggregates such as gross domestic investment (GDI). A key aspect will be changes in the ratios over time. A second hypothesis, from the modernization-dependency debate, is that foreign capital has played a more positive role in East Asia than in Latin America. This hypothesis is harder to operationalize since the term *positive* is clearly a normative one. In this study, *positive* will be defined along two dimensions: relatively easy terms for servicing foreign capital and a relatively high degree of decision-making autonomy provided to the host government. Central to the investigation of this second

---

[7] See especially Cardoso (1973) and Evans (1979). A work on Latin America that takes a line somewhat similar to that of the statists in East Asia is Becker (1983).

[8] See, for example, Amsden (1979), Barrett and Whyte (1982), Wade (1984), and Luedde-Neurath (1984). Perhaps the person who has argued most consistently and extensively for a statist rather than a dependency approach in interpreting the East Asian cases is Stephan Haggard (see Haggard, 1983, 1986; Haggard and Moon, 1983; and Haggard and Cheng, 1987).

hypothesis will be the composition of foreign capital and its change over time.

CHARACTERISTICS OF FOREIGN CAPITAL

A necessary first ingredient in evaluating the debates is basic descriptive information on the characteristics of foreign capital in the four countries. For purposes of this initial discussion, foreign capital is defined very broadly to include direct foreign investment, grants and long-term loans by public (bilateral and multilateral) agencies, long-term loans by private banks, and short-term capital exclusive of official reserves. In balance of payments categories, then, foreign capital inflow—or foreign savings—is equivalent to the current account minus unrequited transfers. Using this latter definition for convenience of calculation, it is possible to compare the volume of foreign capital inflow for Brazil, Mexico, South Korea, and Taiwan as a percentage of each country's gross domestic investment (GDI).[9]

Figure 3.1 shows these percentages for the period 1957–1987 and suggests some regional similarities. South Korea and Taiwan started with extremely high ratios in the 1950s; an average of 55 percent of domestic investment in the two countries was financed by foreign capital between 1956 and 1960. From then on, however, there was a sharply *decreasing* trend in the importance of foreign capital in the two East Asian nations. Brazil and Mexico, by contrast, began with much lower ratios, less than 14 percent. But from the mid-1950s to the mid-1970s, they experienced gradually *increasing* capital inflows, when calculated as a percentage of GDI.

Between the mid-1970s and the onset of the international debt crisis in late 1982, foreign capital inflows for South Korea and the two Latin American countries converged at around 20 to 25 percent of GDI, while Taiwan continued its capital *export* that began in the early 1970s (reflected in negative percentages in figure 3.1). After the debt crisis, Mexico also became an (involuntary) capital exporter, and Brazil's capital inflows dipped significantly too. As of 1986, South Korea began to repeat the Taiwanese pattern, with large merchandise surpluses easily outweighing profit remittances and interest payments to create a current account surplus. The counterpart of a current account surplus, of course, is net capital export and/or the accumulation of reserves.

Having seen the differing aggregate importance of foreign capital in the four countries, we can turn to the differences and similarities in the com-

[9] The trend over time of foreign capital as a percentage of GDP for the four countries is very similar to that of foreign capital as a share of GDI.

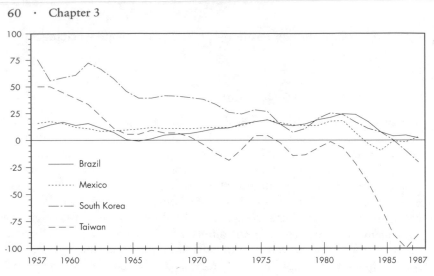

FIGURE 3.1

Net Foreign Capital as Percentage of Gross Domestic Investment, 1957–1987 (three-year moving averages).

(Three-year moving averages are more appropriate than annual data since we are mainly interested in long-term trends rather than yearly fluctuations. Five-year moving averages would be preferable to three-year figures but their use would involve loss of more data. *Sources: International Financial Statistics; Taiwan Statistical Data Book.*)

position of foreign resources. Figure 3.2 and table 3.1 show a rough breakdown of four types of long-term capital: bilateral public-sector loans, multilateral loans, private bank loans, and direct foreign investment.[10] Figure 3.2 summarizes the data for the period 1961–1986, while table 3.1 provides a breakdown by five-year intervals since there has been substantial variation over time. Once again it is possible to discern Latin American and East Asian patterns, but the notion of a dichotomy should not be pushed too far. Interesting cross-regional similarities as well as intraregional differences have also occurred.

The composition of foreign capital in Latin America has emphasized private-sector funds, especially direct foreign investment (DFI) and loans from private banks. In Brazil private capital flows constituted 86 percent

[10] For the period prior to the World Bank's *World Debt Tables*, these data are rough approximations. The published data in *World Debt Tables* begin with 1967, but the World Bank considers that figures prior to 1970 are not completely comparable to later ones. The Interamerican Development Bank has calculated series for Latin American countries from 1961, and these are used in this chapter for 1961 to 1969. For the East Asian countries, a combination of country sources, the IMF's *Balance of Payments Yearbook*, and the OECD's *Geographical Distribution of Financial Flows to Developing Countries* have been used. It is probable that some grant aid is included in these figures.

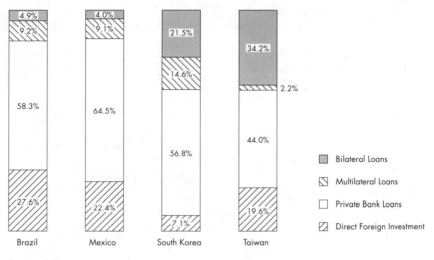

FIGURE 3.2
Types of Long-Term Net Foreign Capital, 1961–1986.

(Percentages reflect distribution of total foreign capital for 1961–1986, except Taiwan, where the data are for 1961–1983, since the repayment pattern from 1984 to 1986 would significantly distort the percentage. *Sources: International Financial Statistics; Taiwan Statistical Data Book.*)

of the total, while for Mexico they represented 87 percent. For both countries, DFI accounted for about one quarter of all foreign capital. Public-sector capital can be broken down into bilateral and multilateral sources. The former provided 4 to 5 percent for the two nations, while the latter was 9 percent of total capital inflows in each case. In Brazil and Mexico, bilateral funds were nonconcessional loans, mostly guaranteed export credits from the U.S. Export-Import Bank and similar institutions in Europe and Japan.

The East Asian pattern has had a much heavier emphasis on public-sector funds. For both South Korea and Taiwan, bilateral and multilateral loans together constituted over one third (36 percent) of capital inflows in the 1961–1986 period. In each case, the bulk of the public funds were bilateral loans: 22 percent of total foreign capital in South Korea and 34 percent in Taiwan. Multilateral loans, then, accounted for 14 and 2 percent respectively. Although less so than in the 1950s, some of the bilateral loans in the 1960s were still of the concessional ("aid") variety.[11] In terms

[11] Inclusion of grants in the data in table 3.1 would greatly increase both the role of bilateral sources and the United States as providers of foreign capital. Throughout the period 1962–1976, but especially in the 1960s, South Korea was still receiving about $100 million per year in economic assistance grants from the U.S. government; Taiwan received about

TABLE 3.1
Types of Long-Term Net Foreign Capital in Four Countries, 1961–1986

Period	Bilateral (percent)	Multilateral (percent)	Private Banks (percent)	DFI (percent)	Average Amount ($ millions)
			Brazil		
1961–1965	57.1	7.8	−3.2	38.3	316.2
1966–1980	15.1	16.2	29.0	39.6	544.8
1971–1975	5.3	8.1	52.0	34.6	2834.4
1976–1980	3.0	4.4	66.7	25.9	6701.0
1981–1982	5.2	6.1	61.2	27.5	8570.3
1983–1986	2.1	20.2	54.9	23.0	5018.0
			Mexico		
1961–1965	7.3	14.3	36.4	42.0	352.8
1966–1970	7.4	16.7	34.1	41.8	555.1
1971–1975	3.0	8.1	66.1	22.8	2064.8
1976–1980	1.7	5.5	72.6	20.2	5469.6
1981–1982	4.1	7.3	70.2	18.3	11160.4
1983–1986	11.9	24.7	33.1	30.2	1857.5
			South Korea		
1961–1965	84.0	1.8	12.6	1.6	259.7
1966–1970	39.7	1.7	55.1	3.5	369.7
1971–1975	34.9	14.9	38.7	11.5	854.1
1976–1980	18.1	16.3	60.4	5.2	2026.8
1981–1982	19.6	18.0	59.3	3.1	2748.0
1983–1986	6.0	14.6	67.6	11.8	1783.3
			Taiwan		
1961–1965	77.8	0.5	8.9	12.8	98.1
1966–1970	23.7	11.1	39.4	25.8	138.0
1971–1975	35.6	16.2	30.2	18.0	287.6
1976–1980	37.9	−3.3	47.2	18.2	581.2
1981–1982	19.1	−3.2	61.3	22.8	757.5
1983–1986	−42.9	−3.6	−97.3	43.8	−580.5

Sources: *External Financing of the Latin American Countries*; *World Debt Tables*; *Balance of Payments Yearbook*; *Geographical Distribution of Financial Flows to Developing Countries*; *Major Statistics of the Korean Economy*; *Taiwan Statistical Data Book*.

of private capital, differences have also appeared in the two East Asian cases. Bank loans represented 53 percent of Korean foreign capital but only 44 percent for Taiwan. An even more striking difference occurred with respect to direct foreign investment. DFI was a miniscule 7 percent of the total for South Korea, while in Taiwan it accounted for 20 percent of foreign capital.

These, then, are the intraregional similarities: In Latin America, there was a concentration on private capital, with a predominance of bank loans but also an important role for DFI. In East Asia, there was more emphasis on public capital and on loans in general (whether from bilateral sources or private banks). Despite these regional contrasts, however, there have also been similarities across the two regions. One similarity in all four cases was the relative lack of importance of multilateral loans, an average of less than 10 percent among the four. This contrasts with many African countries, where World Bank and other multilateral loans have constituted a major portion of foreign resources. Other similarities have tended to link three countries, thus isolating the fourth as a deviant case. In the two Latin American countries and South Korea, for instance, well over half of total foreign capital inflow was in the form of private bank loans, while Taiwan stood apart with only 44 percent in this category. The other side of the latter comparison was that Taiwan had a much larger percentage of foreign capital as bilateral loans. Finally, South Korea stood out among the four for its very small share of direct foreign investment.

Table 3.1 provides more detail on these patterns. Perhaps its most interesting feature is some tendency toward convergence of patterns over time—until the debt crisis struck in 1982. In general, private bank loans became more important for all four countries in the 1970s and early 1980s, while DFI and bilateral loans came to play a lesser role. Multilateral loans also became less significant for all countries except South Korea. Since 1982, important new differences have emerged. Taiwan has begun to pay off its debt, so that only DFI flows remain positive in net terms. South Korea was relatively unaffected by the debt crisis, with its foreign capital pattern continuing the same tendencies as before 1982. What the table does not show is that, as of 1986, South Korea also began repaying its debt to all three types of lenders. Both Brazil and Mexico saw a drop in private bank loans and some increase in loans from multilateral

$10 million per year. For Brazil and Mexico, the comparable figures were $40 million and $4 million respectively. It should also be noted that military aid was very important in East Asia. Again in the 1962–1976 period, Korea received an average of $379 million per year and Taiwan $141 million. Figures for Brazil and Mexico were $31 million and $1 million. Data are from U.S. Overseas Loans and Grants, 1976.

sources after 1982. DFI has assumed greater importance in three of the countries; for Brazil it has fallen, but only slightly.

A final descriptive contrast is illustrated in figure 3.3, which focuses on the country origin of foreign lenders and investors. Because of difficulties in assembling comparative data, a shorter period (1971–1986) is represented. If a longer time span were included, the most important variation would be greater dominance by the United States.[12] The main interregional difference, and the main basis of regional patterns, involves the relative importance of Japan and the United States. In the East Asian cases, there has been a dual origin of foreign capital, which reflects the overall dual hegemony of the two countries in the region. Although the United States has been very important, Japan has provided a significant counterweight. Indeed, in South Korea, Japanese capital has outweighed that of the United States (44 and 30 percent respectively), while in Taiwan Japanese funds have been three quarters of the U.S. total (39 and 51 percent). In the two Latin American countries, by contrast, no single nation has been able to challenge the weight of the United States, which has provided 65 percent of total foreign capital for Mexico and 41 percent for

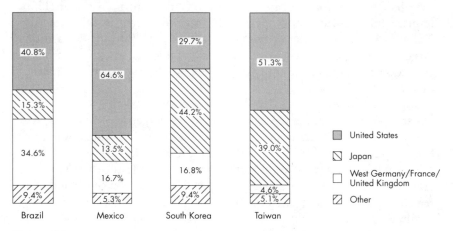

FIGURE 3.3
Country Origin of Long-Term Net Foreign Capital, 1971–1986.

(Percentages reflect the distribution of the total amounts of foreign capital by country of origin in 1978–1986. *Source: Geographical Distribution of Financial Flows to Developing Countries* [1973–1988].)

[12] The United States was virtually the only source of bilateral funds before the early 1960s. For the period 1953–1961, the U.S. government provided average annual economic aid (loans and grants) to the four countries as follows: $322 million to Korea, $122 million to Taiwan, $39 million to Brazil, and $5 million to Mexico (*U.S. Overseas Loans and Grants*, 1976). The vast majority of direct foreign investment in this period was also from the United States.

Brazil. This situation is congruent with the general political-economic dominance of the United States in Latin America.

Despite these intraregional similarities—and surely the dual hegemony issue is more important in qualitative terms than these quantitative figures reveal—some interesting cross-regional similarities also emerge in figure 3.3. For example, Mexico and Taiwan have relied especially heavily on the United States. Although the reasons have been different—Mexico's geographical proximity and Taiwan's international isolation—the two countries in some ways have been more similar between themselves than to their regional "partners." Brazil and South Korea have had a more varied structure of lenders and investors. South Korea's diversification has been based on balance between the United States and Japan, but Europe and other countries together represented almost one quarter of total capital inflows. It will be remembered that multilateral funds were also increasingly important in South Korea, which furthered the diversification process. The United States has represented less than half of Brazil's foreign capital, while Japan and three European nations (Britain, France, and West Germany) accounted for 50 percent.

A number of implications for the debates derive from these characteristics of foreign capital in the four countries. First, the overall importance of foreign capital has fallen over time in the two Asian countries. In fact, both are now paying off their foreign debts although DFI continues to come in at a moderate rate. This declining trend has increased both the actual and perceived autonomy from foreign economic domination. In the Latin American countries, by contrast, foreign capital's importance rose from the 1960s until the early 1980s. The post-1982 situation, in which net capital inflows have become negative in Mexico and very small in Brazil, has been involuntary and fueled the view that foreign capital is prejudicial to development in the Latin American region.

Second, the differences in composition of foreign capital have at least two significant implications. On the one hand, the East Asian countries have had a lower reliance on DFI, the type of foreign capital that has created the greatest friction in Third World countries. On the other hand, the mix of lenders has led to easier repayment terms for East Asia. A greater share of East Asian borrowing was from public-sector lenders, who provide lower interest rates and longer maturities than their private-sector counterparts.

Third, the country distribution among foreign lenders and investors has also favored Taiwan and Korea. The fact that Japan and the United States have both been heavily involved has provided greater room for maneuver than in Latin America (especially in Mexico). With both countries interested in East Asia, a possibility has existed for playing the two off against each other. Brazil and Mexico have tried to follow a similar strategy, but with less success.

SOME EXPLANATIONS FOR DIFFERENCES IN FOREIGN CAPITAL

Understanding the reasons for the differences just described is an important part of evaluating the two debates about foreign capital. Four components of an overall explanation will be explored briefly in this section: (1) the general supply conditions with respect to types of foreign capital during the 1950–1985 period; (2) the views of those in control of foreign capital about the four countries as investment sites; (3) the preferences of the governments of the four countries in terms of foreign capital; and (4) alternative sources of capital.

The general supply conditions can be estimated by looking at foreign capital flows to all developing countries during the period in question. Unfortunately, these data are not easy to find. Table 3.2 uses U.S. data as

TABLE 3.2
Net Flow of Foreign Capital to Developing Countries, 1950–1985

Year	Bilateral (percent)	Multilateral (percent)	Banks (percent)	DFI (percent)	Total Amount ($ millions)
1950[a]	53.8	9.7	2.7	33.9	1,181 (1,473)[b]
1955[a]	51.8	8.3	12.0	27.9	2,483 (2,732)
1961	31.0	12.2	14.2	42.6	4,303 (4,114)
1965	35.3	11.3	11.2	42.2	5,851 (5,276)
1970	30.3	9.0	21.7	39.0	9,463 (6,999)
1975	23.8	10.6	35.9	29.7	34,806 (18,514)
1980	19.3	15.9	47.7	17.0	59,609 (22,367)
1982	15.3	17.3	52.6	14.8	69,122 (22,240)
1985	13.1	32.0	33.4	21.5	35,748 (10,305)

Sources: *Survey of Current Business* and *World Bank Annual Report* (for 1950–1955); *World Debt Tables* and *Development Cooperation* (for 1961–1985).
[a] Figures for United States and World Bank only.
[b] Figures in parentheses are constant (1958) dollars.

a proxy for the early part of the period, since the United States was by far the largest capital exporter during the 1950s. Beginning in the 1960s, when Europe and Japan became more important, they are added in. The table shows two trends. First, there was a large increase in total capital flows, from $1.2 billion in 1950 to a high of $69.1 billion in 1982; in constant (1958) dollars, the figures were $1.5 billion and $22.2 billion.[13] After the debt crisis, there was a sharp decline to only $35.7 billion by 1985 ($10.3 billion in 1958 dollars). Second, the relative importance of different types of capital flows varied considerably. Bilateral loans and direct foreign investment were the main type of foreign funds in the 1950s and 1960s, while private banks surpassed all other sources in the 1970s and early 1980s. Multilateral funds became more important in the later years, but they never played a major role.

This first explanation, based on overall capital flows, is an extremely partial one and merely provides an indication of general proclivities on the part of the groups, public and private, in control of foreign resources. Not surprisingly, none of the four countries closely followed the overall pattern. During the 1950s and 1960s, the East Asian countries relied on one of the major sources available (bilateral loans), while the Latin American nations took advantage of the other (direct foreign investment). In the 1970s, by contrast, all four followed the general trend toward private bank loans, although Taiwan did so less extensively than the other three.

To understand why these deviations from the overall norm occurred, we must look at both suppliers' views of individual countries and the preferences within the recipient countries themselves. With respect to the former, an appropriate starting place is with the largest source of foreign capital in the early postwar period—bilateral lenders and especially the United States. For reasons of national security, U.S. government officials were disposed to provide large-scale loans and grants to South Korea and Taiwan. The destruction from World War II and the Korean War had left the two countries unable to provide their own foreign exchange requirements, and the resulting void was seen as dangerous in terms of possible communist expansion in the region. Thus, an extensive aid program was devised. By the early 1960s, however, the two countries were perceived as able to operate on their own to a much greater extent (Jacoby, 1966; Krueger, 1979). It was precisely at this point that bilateral aid to Latin America, through the Alliance for Progress, assumed greater salience, with Brazil as one of the major beneficiaries. Mexico, as will be discussed below, had been able to take advantage of its geographical proximity to

---

[13] The increase is slightly exaggerated by the exclusion of Europe and Japan in the 1950–1960 period, but little capital was coming from those regions since they were rebuilding their own economies.

gain access to U.S. private bank funds at an earlier time than other Third World countries. By the 1970s, U.S. bilateral funds were being phased out in general, although some of the resulting gap was filled by similar loans from Europe and Japan (*Geographical Distribution of Financial Flows to Developing Countries*, 1971–1986).

Direct foreign investors were favorably inclined toward the two Latin American countries from the beginning of the postwar period because of historical tradition as well as geographical proximity to the main investors. Mexico, in particular, had been a primary site of U.S. direct foreign investment since the nineteenth century. The main change in the 1950s and 1960s was a sectoral shift from mining/petroleum and public utilities into industry (Díaz-Alejandro, 1970). Brazil's location meant that it was somewhat less familiar to U.S. investors, but the country's size and natural resources made it increasingly attractive to them. An important advance came with the Kubitschek government in the 1950s, which offered many incentives to foreign investors (Skidmore, 1967; Baer, 1983).

The Asian countries, by contrast, were not very appealing to foreign direct investors, at least until their economies had been reconstructed and political conditions stabilized. The phaseout of U.S. aid was an indication that these prerequisites had been accomplished. At that point, Taiwan began to obtain more direct investment although a fairly substantial part was from "overseas Chinese."[14] South Korea generally did not get much DFI. Some possible reasons for its low level of DFI are suggested by a survey that asked foreign investors about perceived obstacles. The most-often-cited problems were difficult bureaucratic procedures and lack of support by domestic banks (each with 23 percent of responses). These were followed by low labor productivity (17 percent) and the small size of the domestic market (16 percent). Less important obstacles were said to be political instability (9 percent), insufficient social infrastructure (7 percent), and cultural or communications difficulties (5 percent).[15] The low level of DFI in South Korea was also a function of South Korean government preferences, as will be discussed below.

Multilateral institutions have made fewer distinctions among borrowing countries than have other sources of foreign capital, since their mandate is to provide resources to all member countries. Nevertheless, those countries that are best able to design sophisticated projects are most likely to get large sums of money from the multilateral agencies. This criterion

[14] "Overseas Chinese" investors are people of Chinese descent who do not reside in Taiwan; more than half of them come from Hong Kong. On overseas Chinese investment, see Gold (1983).

[15] The survey data are reported in Cha (1983). The survey was conducted in 1980 and included executives from 521 corporations with headquarters in Japan, the United States and Korea. The percentage from each country is not provided.

includes all four countries being considered here. Three of the four—South Korea, Mexico, and Brazil—have indeed gotten substantially larger shares than their populations would predict. South Korea's share of World Bank loans through 1985 was four times its population share, Mexico's 2.8 times, and Brazil's 2.5 times.[16] Taiwan, by contrast, has received no multilateral loans since the late 1970s, when it was replaced in those institutions by the People's Republic of China. Since it continued to repay its earlier loans, Taiwan has had a negative flow from multilateral sources.

Once the private banks began to move toward large-scale lending to the Third World, all four nations became prime borrowers, since it was precisely the newly industrializing countries that were most attractive to the banks. In general the private banks did not become major lenders until the early 1970s, but Mexico was the exception. As early as the mid-1960s, it had begun to obtain a substantial volume of loans from U.S. banks (Green, 1976). Brazil and Korea then followed in the early 1970s. These three countries alone held 41 percent of total private bank debt to the Third World at the start of the debt crisis in 1982 (calculated from *World Debt Tables*, 1986). Taiwan's lower volume of loans was a function of government preferences and alternatives rather than the banks' willingness to lend. Most of Taiwan's investment needs could be financed through its growing trade surplus, which was considered preferable to borrowing and building up future debt-service obligations.

Moving, then, to the preferences of the four governments, some complementary insights can be added to the supply-side explanations. In general, it would seem that all four wanted as much foreign capital as possible. The main exception was Taiwan during its period of capital export after 1970; South Korea seems to be moving in the same direction now. The differences occurred with regard to types of foreign capital and how they fit into the various development strategies. This topic will be discussed at greater length in the next section, but a brief introduction will be useful here. The main point to be considered at a general level is the relative importance attached to the public versus the private sector as the motor of growth and accumulation, since the public/private division has implications for types of foreign capital.

Loans of all kinds—bilateral, multilateral, and private—were of particular relevance for development strategies dominated by the public sector because most loans were made to governments. Direct foreign investment, by contrast, was compatible in situations where the private sector

[16] Figures are calculated from the *World Bank Annual Report* for 1986. They exclude China, a recent member, since its inclusion would greatly skew the results.

dominated.[17] Thus the strong government role in the South Korean and Taiwanese economies from the beginning of the postwar period meant that loans were especially attractive, regardless of whether import substitution or export promotion predominated. In Latin America, the greater emphasis on the private sector during the 1950s and 1960s led to a strong role for DFI. The increasing economic activity of both the Brazilian and Mexican governments in the 1970s increased the appeal of loans, in this case from the private banks.

Finally, alternative sources of capital need to be considered. Table 3.3 provides data to compare the four countries' ability to mobilize domestic resources.[18] The last column shows the ratio of domestic savings to GDP. If we make a first cut at analyzing the data by taking a simple unweighted average for the entire 1956–1986 period, it turns out that the two Latin American countries had similar savings ratios—18.8 percent for Brazil and 18.5 percent for Mexico. Korea's average was slightly lower at 17.9 percent, while Taiwan's was considerably higher at 23.8 percent. A more sophisticated approach would look at the ratios over time. Not surprisingly, all four countries increased their savings ratios during the three decades covered in the table. In addition, all reached a peak in the 1970s and then fell off to some extent. The Brazilian ratio peaked in the early 1970s at 25 percent and then fell to 16 percent in the early 1980s. The other three countries reached a savings peak in the second half of the 1970s: Mexico at 23 percent, South Korea at 26 percent, and Taiwan at 34 percent. All declined in the early 1980s, but savings in the Asian countries have now surpassed the earlier levels. Finally, we can compare savings performance in the most recent period. Focusing on the last decade reveals an important difference between Latin America and East Asia. The former saved between 18 percent (Brazil) and 22 percent (Mexico) of gross domestic product in the period 1976–1986, while the latter saved between 26 percent (South Korea) and 34 percent (Taiwan).

Turning to the first column of table 3.3, we find a similar pattern for the role of domestic savings in financing investment. On average over the entire period 1956–1986, domestic savings in the two Latin American

[17] The distinction is somewhat less clear in practice because of joint ventures and because governments can relend borrowed money to the private sector. The latter is especially important in South Korea, given the close relationship between the government and the private conglomerates (*chaebols*).

[18] Net domestic savings, of course, is the flip side of the trade balance. This can be seen in the basic economic identity $(G - T) + (I - S) \equiv (M - X)$, where G is government expenditure, T is taxes, I is investment, S is savings, M is imports, and X is exports. Thus a surplus in domestic savings (public and private) will be reflected in a trade surplus which, in principle, will render foreign capital unnecessary. In reality, there are other reasons that foreign capital might be sought, such as changing the maturity structure of domestic capital or obtaining access to technology.

TABLE 3.3
Role of Foreign and Domestic Savings, 1956–1986 (percent)

	Finance of Gross Domestic Investment				
Period	Domestic Savings	Public Savings	Private Savings	Foreign Savings	Gross Domestic Savings ÷ GDP
	Brazil[a]				
1956–1960	86.7			13.3	13.5
1961–1965	97.2			2.8	16.9
1966–1970	94.9	(21.2)	(73.7)	5.1	21.9
1971–1975	83.5	(17.0)	(66.5)	16.5	24.6
1976–1980	82.9	(10.8)	(72.1)	17.1	20.1
1981–1982	75.0	(3.2)	(71.8)	25.0	15.9
1983–1986	92.7			7.3	16.5
	Mexico				
1956–1960	85.6	(21.6)	(64.0)	14.4	13.5
1961–1965	90.4	(22.8)	(67.6)	9.6	16.2
1966–1970	87.7	(24.2)	(63.5)	12.3	18.2
1971–1975	84.1	(8.6)	(75.5)	15.9	18.7
1976–1980	84.6			15.4	23.1
1981–1982	80.3			19.7	20.6
1983–1986	106.1			−6.1	20.9
	South Korea[b]				
1956–1960	34.8	(−21.7)	(43.5)	65.2	4.2
1961–1965	45.8	(0.0)	(33.3)	54.2	6.4
1966–1970	61.0	(19.5)	(37.7)	39.0	17.4
1971–1975	69.1	(9.3)	(60.3)	30.9	19.0
1976–1980	82.9	(18.3)	(64.5)	17.1	25.9
1981–1982	79.4	(22.6)	(56.9)	20.6	22.4
1983–1986	98.1	(23.5)	(74.6)	1.9	29.1
	Taiwan				
1956–1960	54.5	(9.0)	(45.5)	45.5	9.1
1961–1965	85.7	(14.3)	(71.4)	14.3	16.2
1966–1970	96.2	(32.1)	(64.1)	3.8	23.8
1971–1975	97.7	(33.7)	(64.0)	2.3	30.7
1976–1980	106.1	(40.9)	(65.2)	−6.1	33.6
1981–1982	112.1	(40.5)	(71.6)	−12.1	31.1
1983–1986	181.0	(56.6)	(124.4)	−81.0	35.2

Sources: *International Financial Statistics*; *Economic Statistics Yearbook* (South Korea); *Taiwan Statistical Data Book*; *A Economia Brasileira e suas Perspectivas*; Fitzgerald (1977).

[a] Public enterprises are included in private savings.
[b] Figures do not add because of statistical discrepancy.

countries financed 89 percent of their investment (with the remainder coming from foreign savings). South Korea was much lower at 65 percent, and Taiwan was higher at 102 percent. Focusing on the last decade puts South Korea in a more favorable light, but Mexico continued to have a higher rate. In part, the latter was due to differences in the percentage of GDP devoted to investment in the two countries. The Mexican share dropped off substantially in the 1980s, while the opposite occurred in South Korea.

For all four countries, the private sector has provided the majority of domestic savings, generally in the range of 65 to 70 percent. Taiwan has been especially successful in promoting household savings, although corporate savings have also been important. Some underlying characteristics of the country are thought to have encouraged household savings: the lack of an extensive system of social security and medical insurance, the payment of annual bonuses, the requirement for a large down payment to purchase a house, and the emphasis on (expensive) higher education. In addition, Taiwan has followed a policy of high interest rates, differing from most Third World countries, where negative interest rates are common. South Korea generally shares Taiwan's structural characteristics, and it has followed a similar interest rate policy during certain periods (Scitovsky, 1985; Wade, 1985). Mexico's attempt to stimulate household savings centered on the authorization of dollar savings accounts (prior to their conversion into pesos as part of the 1982 bank nationalization), while Brazil's main innovation involved indexation to deal with its traditionally high inflation rate (Maxfield, 1986). Neither Latin American country, however, has been as successful as East Asia in promoting savings.

The other component of domestic savings is savings by the public sector, which is equivalent to the current balance of the government and public enterprises. In South Korea, after an initial period of large budget deficits, the government contribution to the finance of domestic investment has increased steadily from the early 1970s. This increase has been at the expense of foreign, not private domestic, savings. The same tendency has occurred in Taiwan, but the government share has been much larger in the latter case. Together, domestic public and private savings in Taiwan have made it possible to eliminate completely the need for foreign savings, and the country has accumulated a volume of reserves second only to Japan's. In Brazil and Mexico, the trend in public savings has been the opposite of Taiwan and Korea; public savings have fallen as budget deficits have increased. Budget deficits have been especially large in Mexico because of three factors: the unwillingness or inability to increase tax rates from their historically low level; the decision to use public enterprises to subsidize the private sector and, at some points, the government itself; and the increased expenditures of public firms and central government. Since 1982 an attempt has been made to remedy these problems but with limited success. Brazil has done a better job of eliminating central government deficits, but those of the public enterprises remain large (Maxfield, 1986).[19]

The explanations for the characteristics of foreign capital in Latin America and East Asia are especially relevant to the debate over who determines the flow of foreign capital. We saw that no direct extrapolation was possible from the overall pattern of capital flows to those of Mexico, Brazil, Korea, and Taiwan, but the question remains as to whether supply or demand factors were more important in determining the deviations. Although the next section will further clarify this issue, some points can be made now.

First, despite the lack of a close fit between the overall pattern of capital flows and those of the four countries, the former constitutes a kind of institutional constraint on the process at any given time. That is, financial institutions (including companies engaging in direct investment) must exist and have the willingness and capacity to send capital abroad in order for Third World governments to tap them. Thus private bank loans were not a viable option in the 1950s and early 1960s. Likewise, before the early 1960s, the priority of the multilateral institutions was reconstruction of Europe rather than Third World development. Second, the objective conditions of a country at a particular time may make it impossible to attract certain kinds of foreign capital, especially from the private sector. For the public sector, by contrast, these objective conditions may be overcome by geopolitical considerations, such as occurred with East Asia in the 1950s and Mexico after 1982. Third, taking a more dynamic approach, it may be possible over time to change the objective conditions and to induce new sources of capital to participate. It is to these issues that we now turn.

[19] In addition to the points discussed in the text, it should be added that the impact of foreign savings is often limited by the problem of capital flight. That is, under certain circumstances, capital inflows may be substantially offset by capital outflows, often illegal. Thus foreign funds may contribute nothing to domestic investment, but merely facilitate money being shipped abroad. Figures published by Morgan Guaranty Trust (*World Financial Markets*, March 1986) illustrate the magnitude of this problem. Of the countries discussed in this chapter, Mexico has by far the worst problem with an estimated $53 billion in capital flight between 1976 and 1985, compared with a net increase in foreign capital of $86 billion. South Korea is said to have experienced capital flight of $12 billion out of $40 billion in capital inflow. Brazil has been much more successful in this respect, losing "only" $10 billion while taking in $100 billion in new capital. Taiwan, as a net capital exporter, is not included in the study. The Morgan figures are very controversial. For a general discussion of capital flight and a comparison of different estimates of its size, see Cumby and Levich (1987).

FOREIGN CAPITAL AND DEVELOPMENT STRATEGIES

To understand more completely the nature of the relationship between foreign capital and Third World governments, it is useful to look at some concrete historical data. In this section, we will examine a particular type of interaction involving choice of development strategy. Who determined such choices—governments or external structures and actors? What were the mechanisms involved? The basis for the discussion is the timing sequence set out in the introductory chapter to this volume. Since the data presented earlier refer only to the post–World War II period, the focus will be on the shift from primary to secondary import-substitution industrialization (ISI) in the mid-1950s in Brazil and Mexico, and the later decision in the early 1970s to move toward diversified export promotion. In the case of South Korea and Taiwan, the emphasis will be on the adoption of export-oriented industrialization (EOI) in the early 1960s, the expansion into secondary ISI (or heavy and chemical industrialization) in the early 1970s, and an overlapping shift to secondary EOI in the 1980s.

The first case in chronological order was the shift from primary to secondary import substitution in Mexico and Brazil in the mid-1950s. According to most analyses, primary ISI dated from the 1930s in the large Latin American countries and had begun to "exhaust" itself by the mid-1950s. This meant that, given the prevailing distribution of wealth and income, producers of basic consumer goods could no longer count on rapidly increasing demand (Fishlow, 1972; Villarreal, 1977). Gereffi and Evans (1981) suggest that 1955 marked the turning point as the Korean War boom petered out and various domestic difficulties, such as inflation and balance-of-payments problems, confronted the two economies. "The clear message from both the external and the internal sectors was that a shift in development strategy was necessary. Policymaking elites in Brazil and Mexico made the decision at this juncture to replace horizontal [primary] ISI with vertical [secondary] ISI" (p. 39).

Although it is doubtful that things were as clear at the time as they may appear with the benefit of hindsight, the presidency of Juscelino Kubitschek did represent an important shift in Brazil. The problem that Kubitschek faced in his desire to accelerate Brazil's industrialization was that production of more sophisticated goods demanded technology and finance that were not available locally. Thus he threw off Getúlio Vargas's restrictions on foreign capital and invited multinational firms to invest. The most important incentive was Instruction 113, issued by the monetary authority in early 1955. According to Brazilianist Werner Baer (1983, p. 71), it was designed mainly to attract DFI by providing special facilities for the import of machinery. The Tariff Law of 1957 increased protection for domestic industry, including foreign firms producing in Brazil (Leff, 1968; Bergsman, 1970).

In Mexico, similar processes were under way. After the large devaluation of the peso in 1954, President Adolfo Ruiz Cortines changed his policy stance to try to attract more foreign investment into the industrial sector. Again special incentives were offered. In 1955, the Law for New and Necessary Industries allowed exemptions from certain taxes, and Rule 14 of the General Tariff Law provided a subsidy for duties on the import of capital equipment. Like Brazil, Mexico also increased protection for locally based industry (Villarreal, 1977; Weinert, 1977; Story, 1986).

Total foreign capital as a share of GDI declined in Brazil from the late 1950s to the late 1960s and stayed about constant in Mexico, but the share of DFI was at its peak in this period (see figure 3.1 and table 3.1), and almost all of it was going into manufacturing. As a consequence, by 1972, half of the largest three hundred manufacturing firms in the two countries were controlled by foreign corporations. The share was even higher in the most dynamic sectors, such as chemicals, transportation equipment, and other machinery. Only food and textiles were safe for domestic firms (Newfarmer and Mueller, 1975).

Thus, we had a situation in the mid-1950s where the economic, and perhaps the political, conjuncture produced pressures for some kind of change. It could have been toward export promotion, but the large size of the market in the two countries and the inefficiency of the ISI firms militated against that choice. (See Kaufman, chap. 5, this volume, for further discussion of why export promotion was not adopted.) The option selected does not appear to have been pushed by foreign capital, but foreign capital was perceived to be a necessary part of the development strategy. In particular, DFI was sought and policies were devised to attract it into target sectors. The large volume of foreign capital needed to implement the secondary ISI strategy meant that the chosen vehicles, multinational corporations, increased their already substantial political and economic power in the two countries. Local capital was generally unable to compete, and the state had great difficulty in regulating foreign firms.

The next case in chronological order was the East Asian countries' move toward export-oriented industrialization (EOI) in the early 1960s. This was the case where foreign capital probably had the greatest influence; the extreme nature of the circumstances suggests that such influence is likely to be rare indeed. There is a general consensus that the South Korean and Taiwanese economies could not have survived in the 1950s without U.S. aid. A variety of figures are cited to support the claim. Aid financed 40 percent of investment in Taiwan and 80 percent in South Korea. Likewise, concessional capital flows covered 70 percent of imports in Korea and 85 percent of the balance-of-payments deficit in Taiwan (Jacoby, 1966; Cole, 1980). Even authors defending the independence of decision-making in the two countries admit that "dependence on aid was high" (Haggard and Cheng, 1987, p. 87). U.S. aid of this magnitude could not continue indefinitely, and the intention to phase it out was announced in the late 1950s. The question was where the two countries would obtain needed foreign exchange, once the aid flows ceased. U.S. aid officials apparently lobbied for a strategy that would have two prongs: a greater role for exports, thus replacing the ISI strategy followed during the 1950s, and more openness to private capital and especially direct foreign investment.

Without a detailed historical study, it is hard to be sure about the causal relations. On the one hand, Asia specialist Bruce Cumings (1984, p. 27) says flatly: "In both countries the export-led program was decided by the United States."[20] On the other hand, Stephan Haggard and Tun-jen Cheng (1987, p. 111) speak merely of "intellectual inspiration" from AID and the IMF. Furthermore, economic as well as political pressures pushed in the same direction. With small markets, import substitution had mainly exhausted its early phase. Moving into intermediate industry would have required a great deal of already-scarce foreign exchange, and the small market size that caused existing problems also militated against the secondary ISI path that Brazil and Mexico had chosen.[21]

Regardless of the actual role of U.S. officials in the decision to adopt export-oriented industrialization, it was clear that foreign capital had to participate in order to make it a success. There were four minimum requirements for EOI: large quantities of unskilled labor, modest technology, a relatively small amount of capital, and access to foreign markets. The East Asians themselves would obviously provide the labor, and they could also provide a substantial share of the capital and technological requirements. (This contrasted with the much larger needs under secondary ISI.) Foreign firms were important for links with international markets and for some capital and technology. As a result of this particular configuration, foreign capital took two main forms. One was direct investment, often in export processing zones (EPZs) that provided tax incentives and exemptions on import duties as long as output was exported (Grunwald and Flamm, 1985). The other form was marketing, typically through subcontracting arrangements with international retail chains (Sharpston, 1975).

[20] Cumings's case relies on quotes from Edward Mason, director of the Harvard Institute for International Development, and Oxford economist Ian Little. The quote from Little, however, is misinterpreted, thus weakening Cumings's argument.

[21] Korea and Taiwan actually experimented briefly with secondary ISI, but their lack of success became part of the case for moving toward EOI. See Cheng, chap. 6, this volume.

Both the South Korean and Taiwanese governments were strong, centralized institutions, which used a combination of incentives and regulations to deal with foreign capital. The South Koreans had a more top-down approach and privileged loans over DFI since loans gave them greater control. The Foreign Capital Inducement Law of 1960 and its subsequent amendments set out procedures and guarantees for attracting foreign loans. Direct investors were also offered tax incentives, but they were never really encouraged in this period (Frank, 1975, chap. 7; Haggard and Moon, 1983). In addition, the South Koreans were especially sensitive to the issue of dependency on the United States, and the normalization of relations with Japan in 1965 provided an opportunity to play off South Korea's two most important international allies (Cole, 1980). The KMT government in Taiwan was more willing to let foreigners acquire equity participation in the economy. Much of this was initially carried out through EPZs, the first of which was established at Kaohsiung in 1965. Nevertheless, the government maintained substantial control by ownership of key upstream industries, including banking, and by targeting chosen sectors for investment (Wade, 1984; Gold, 1986; Haggard and Cheng, 1987). In both countries, the governments used their power to protect the interests of local firms as well as to regulate foreign participation.

The third case, again moving in chronological order, was the Latin American turn toward "diversified export promotion" in the early 1970s. Although it pales by comparison with the East Asian countries, the Latin American shift was significant in its own context. Total exports in Brazil and Mexico, for example, grew at average annual rates of 22 and 49 percent respectively between 1970 and 1980 (calculated from *International Financial Statistics Yearbook*, 1984). Within the diversified export strategy, the emphasis was on manufactured products, although primary exports retained a significant role. For Brazil, industrial exports (manufactured and semimanufactured) increased at 33 percent per year for 1970–1980, rising from 24 to 58 percent of total exports during that period (World Bank, 1983). For Mexico, the trend began at a similar pace and was aided by introduction of the "border industrialization program," comparable in some ways to the East Asian EPZs (Grunwald and Flamm, 1985, chap. 4). By the late 1970s, however, exports in Mexico were increasingly dominated by petroleum. In 1980 over 75 percent of exports were oil, and other products atrophied as petroleum took command of the economy (Unger, 1985; Beckerman, 1986).

As was the case in the mid-1950s, the more recent shift in development strategy was stimulated by economic problems, especially the balance of payments. These problems became worse for Brazil after the two oil shocks. The issue was not a push by multinational corporations (MNCs) for exports, but how to get them to export more of their output. Gereffi and Evans (1981, p. 42) report that reduced profits in the United States and Europe made it possible to gain their cooperation, but this overlooks much of what was happening in Brazil and Mexico during the 1970s. The importance of MNCs was greatly reduced, as both countries became eager to obtain private bank loans rather than direct foreign investment. In this way, it was thought, foreign capital could be acquired and the state could better control the use of the funds.

Some of the bank loans did go to increase exports although a substantial part went to further ISI. Frieden (1985) provides data on the big borrowers in the two countries. In Mexico, other than the state oil company Pemex, the major users were the electricity commission (CFE), the steel plants, the development bank (Nafinsa) that lends to domestic industrial firms, and the central government itself. In Brazil, the main borrowers were the energy companies; the petroleum firm (Petrobrás); the steel companies; telecommunications, mining, and railway firms, and banks. The Mexican and Brazilian governments saw what seemed to be a tremendous opportunity during the 1970s—not with the MNCs but with the private banks. The banks were eager to lend, so it appeared to be a happy coincidence of interests, and the debt of the two countries rose rapidly. In Brazil, long-term debt to private banks increased from less than $1 billion in 1970 to $40 billion in 1982; comparable figures for Mexico were $2 billion and $44 billion (*World Debt Tables*, 1986).

Unfortunately for the Latin Americans, the opportunities of the 1970s turned into the nightmares of the 1980s. Debt problems arose for these countries because, even with the new stress on exports, they did not increase fast enough to keep up with rising interest payments and amortization. First Mexico and then Brazil fell into major debt crises by 1982 and 1983. The behavior of foreign capital itself was an important component of the crises. As can be seen in table 3.1, foreign capital inflows fell dramatically with private bank loans most affected. Although some new loans have been arranged in connection with rescheduling agreements, they have mostly gone to service existing debt.

Among the results of the debt crisis has been renewed influence of foreign actors, especially the IMF and World Bank, but also private bankers and investors. In both countries, these groups have acquired a role in decision-making that is second only to the situation in East Asia during the early postwar era. Interestingly, the same policies are again being pushed: more exports and a more positive stance toward direct foreign investment. The Mexican government has been eager to follow the advice, and it has been successful in attracting DFI, especially to the border-area assembly plants (*maquiladoras*) that are specifically designed for export. Partly as a consequence, industrial exports have again resumed the

growth that petroleum had sidetracked, but overall economic performance remains dismal. Brazil's situation is even worse since the new civilian government has been unable to chart a consistent course. Industrial
exports have stagnated, and attempts to attract foreign capital have foun-
dered. A politically controversial agreement with the IMF is probably a
necessary but not sufficient condition for renewed foreign capital flows.
(For further discussion of Mexico and Brazil since the 1970s, see Villarreal, chap. 11, this volume.)

Finally, we turn to the second East Asian transition in development
strategy—toward secondary ISI in the 1970s and secondary EOI in the
1980s.[22] As with the other cases discussed, this shift was closely related
to problems in being part of the world economy. For East Asia in the
1970s, protectionism became a hindrance to rising exports. So did competition from countries with even lower wages than South Korea and Taiwan themselves. For South Korea, an additional problem was balance-of-
payments deficits deriving from the heavy import content of its exports.
An apparently obvious solution was further industrialization to include
sectors that were not viable in the early 1960s. A number of factors made
such an approach seem feasible as well as necessary. First, the domestic
market for industrial goods had expanded. Second, import substitution
could prevent supply bottlenecks that had been building up. Third, defense considerations made heavy industry attractive. Fourth, some heavy
industries were being abandoned by the advanced industrial nations, thus
creating new trade opportunities (Cheng, chap. 6, this volume).

As a result of these push and pull factors, both South Korea and Taiwan launched so-called heavy and chemical industrialization (HCI)
schemes in 1973. Target industries included iron and steel, petrochemicals, oil refining, shipbuilding, machinery, electronics, and cement
(Schive, chap. 10, this volume). Protection was reimposed in these sectors, and state resources were allocated for investment. Tax and financial
incentives were established to bring the private sector into the process,
but the plan was heavily dependent on foreign capital and technology.
South Korea, in particular, still preferred to use foreign loans rather than
DFI, and its long-term debt to the banks consequently increased from less
than $200 million in 1970 to $9.7 billion in 1982. Taiwan's debt went
from $34 million to $2.1 billion in the same period (*World Debt Tables*,
1978, 1986; OECD, 1986). DFI was also involved to a lesser extent, and
its composition shifted from light to heavy industry. Foreign investors

[22] This shift, of course, is in the direction of the Latin American strategy and perhaps gives
some hint of an eventual convergence for all NICs. A key characteristic of such nations may
become the presence of a fully developed industrial structure at home, together with sufficient export revenue to support it. For similar comments, suggesting the possibility of a
convergence of development strategies, see Gereffi (1988).

were pressured to expand local purchases as a means to involve domestic capital.

The South Korean version of the shift toward HCI was very rapid and ran into trouble despite some significant successes. Technology and finance were particular problems, which resulted in slowed growth and increased inflation by the end of the decade. With the new government of Chun Doo Hwan in 1980, some modifications were made toward concentration on upgrading sectors in which Korea already excelled. At the same time, there was a move toward some liberalization and privatization, including liberalization of private investment rules. Taiwan's HCI program was more judicious, with the state playing a greater organizing role and investing in infrastructure as well as production facilities. Incentives were expanded for foreign firms, with the latter encouraged as a way to combat Taiwan's increasing international isolation. In fact, some argue that Taiwan's search for DFI was mainly designed to acquire political allies, but the production of more sophisticated goods also required the technology that foreign firms could provide (Haggard and Cheng, 1987).

The post-1982 debt crisis did not have much impact in East Asia, although the world recession did slow exports and thus growth. The slowdown in the major industrial countries, in turn, increased pressure on South Korea and Taiwan to open their economies and revalue their currencies. To a limited extent, both were done. A related phenomenon was that the two countries began to repay their foreign debts. Taiwan initiated the process in 1984, and South Korea followed in 1986, when it moved into a large trade surplus. In the South Korean case, in particular, the motivation is said to have been reducing the dependency that a large foreign debt is seen to imply (Balassa and Williamson, 1987, p. 40).

This brief look at the relationship between foreign capital and choice of development strategy furthers the discussion in the previous section of the relative power of foreign capital and the state in Third World countries. In its extreme version, the issue at stake is whether the state's choice of development strategy determines the role of foreign capital or whether foreign capital determines development strategy.

The evidence in the four cases examined suggests that choice of development strategy goes a long way toward defining the requirements for foreign capital, both type and amount. The contrast was most stark in the early options for secondary import-substitution and export-oriented industrialization. Secondary ISI required enormous long-term investments and thus significant economic and political incentives to acquire foreign participation. EOI was much more amenable to lower foreign participation although the marketing link was crucial. In the 1970s, both Latin American and East Asian strategies required large amounts of foreign capital, but the banks were so eager to lend that special incentives were usually unnecessary. The difference came in terms of capacity to service the resulting debt. The prior export orientation of the East Asian countries made their debts manageable, while the Latin Americans have experienced great difficulties.

Nevertheless, the relationship between development strategy and foreign capital has not been unidirectional. Foreign capital has also had an impact on choice of strategy; the problem is to specify the nature of the impact. Only in the early East Asian case did foreign capital, conceptualized as a group of individuals, have a dominant role in decision-making (although such influence has increased recently in Latin America). In general, international influence has been more important in indirect ways. First, the international economy created problems that provoked decisions to change economic policies and strategies. Second, the availability of certain types of foreign resources could make strategies viable that would not otherwise have been so. Once foreign capital was present, however, especially if it came in large quantities for crucial roles, it then tended to constrain the options of the very governments that invited it in.

CONCLUSIONS

To conclude the discussion, we return to reconsider the two debates introduced at the beginning of the chapter. These were the modernization-dependency debate, which looks at the impact of foreign capital, and the statist-dependency debate, which focuses on the question of control over economic decisions. The basic proposition investigated in the chapter was that Latin America and East Asia have had different experiences with foreign capital, and that this variation in experience has been reflected in the literature. Two specific hypotheses were that foreign capital has been less important in East Asia than Latin America and that the impact has been more positive.

Investigation of the relative importance of foreign capital leads to some potentially contradictory results. On the one hand, the dominant role of foreign capital in the East Asian countries in the early postwar years was never matched in Latin America. During that period in South Korea and Taiwan, virtually all investment was financed by foreign savings, while Brazil and Mexico relied on domestically generated funds. On the other hand, the trends over time suggest an alternative interpretation that outweighs the previous one. In Latin America, reliance on foreign capital gradually *increased* during the period under consideration, while in East Asia the role of foreign savings *decreased* dramatically. South Korea and Taiwan have even begun to repay their debts in the last few years. This declining trend increased both the ability of the East Asian governments to "manage dependency" (see Gereffi, 1989) and the perception that foreign capital was a positive influence.

Concurrently with the discussion of *volume* of foreign capital, we also need to look at its *composition*. Averages for the postwar period show that private capital was dominant in Latin America, while public capital had a greater role in East Asia. These averages are important because they affect capacity to service the debt resulting from capital inflow. In particular, public-sector lenders provide softer terms than their private-sector counterparts. The effect can be seen by examining the terms on the debt. The average interest rate of South Korean loans on the eve of the debt crisis was 11.3 percent, for example, while the figures for Brazil and Mexico were 12.7 and 14.5 percent respectively. Maturities were also longer for Korea. In addition, while Brazil and Mexico had 70 and 77 percent of their debt on floating interest rates, South Korea had only 41 percent, so South Korea was more sheltered from international interest rate increases in the past decade (*World Debt Tables*, 1986). Comparable figures are not available for Taiwan, but that country's small foreign debt makes the issue less relevant.

The trends over time in the composition of foreign capital were even more important than the averages, since they led to very different dynamics in the two regions. In Latin America during the 1950s and 1960s, the dominant source of foreign capital was direct foreign investment. As implied by the term itself, investors maintained direct control over their assets. This control, when combined with the particularly crucial role of foreign investment in secondary ISI, meant that foreign capitalists acquired a great deal of economic and even political power vis-à-vis the state and local capital. Although the Brazilian and Mexican governments attempted to regulate the behavior of foreign investors, they lacked the power to enforce key decisions on investment and balance-of-payments policy. Moreover, small local firms encountered major difficulties in competing with the giant multinationals.

In South Korea and Taiwan during the same period, the main source of foreign capital was bilateral aid from the United States. This was money that went directly to the two governments, which used it to increase their own power. Both the KMT in Taiwan and the Syngman Rhee and later military regimes in South Korea were highly centralized from the start, but the channeling of resources through them exacerbated this characteristic. Initially the resources went into primary ISI development strategies; later the shift to primary export promotion took place. While the latter was accompanied by a greater opening to private foreign capital as U.S. aid was scaled back, the requirements for foreign capital were limited, so the governments were able to maintain their own control and to promote and protect local firms.

The appearance in the 1970s of a glut of money in the international capital markets led all four countries toward this new resource. In each case, private bank loans became the dominant source of foreign capital, but the circumstances under which the new development occurred were not the same. On the one hand, there was a difference in the capacity of the various governments to manage the loans. This included assuring the productive use of funds, avoiding capital flight, and limiting the volume of loans to a viable amount. A spectrum of management capacity existed, with Taiwan in the strongest position and Mexico in the weakest; South Korea and Brazil were in between. Substantial "overborrowing" took place in Mexico and Brazil, and possibly in South Korea as well. Large projects were begun in all three countries that later turned out to be of dubious value. Capital flight was especially heavy in Mexico, but it also occurred in Brazil and Korea. On the other hand, there was differing ability to service the loans that had been acquired. The high level of export revenue in the East Asian countries meant that debt service was not an insurmountable problem, while Latin America's greater import-substitution emphasis exacerbated payments difficulties, once international conditions turned negative. Debt-service ratios summarize the difference. Debt service as a share of export revenues in 1982 was 5.9 percent in Taiwan, 13.1 percent in South Korea, 33.9 percent in Mexico, and 43.0 percent in Brazil (*World Debt Tables*, 1986; OECD, 1986).

The post-1982 circumstances in the two regions provide a dramatic *denouement* to the differing historical trajectories of foreign capital. The East Asian economies have continued their rapid development, coming to rival the advanced industrial countries in many sectors. Latin America, by contrast, has fallen into the deepest recession of the postwar era, and it is not clear when or how it will recover. Despite the differences in performance, the situation with respect to foreign capital appears similar: Brazil, Mexico, and South Korea all seem to have followed Taiwan in running current account surpluses, thus ending their need for foreign capital.[23] The apparent similarity, however, is quite deceptive. South Korea has indeed embarked on the Taiwanese balance-of-payments path, but Brazil's and Mexico's lesser reliance on foreign capital is not by choice. Both countries have been forced to run large merchandise surpluses in order to continue at least partial debt service, and the decline in capital inflow has been an important cause of their enormous economic and political problems. Overall, the last eight years have been basically positive for Taiwan and South Korea (which have grown rapidly and begun to escape prior economic dependency relations), while the period has been

[23] A balance-of-payments deficit is not the only reason for seeking foreign capital. Obtaining foreign technology and access to markets were other reasons for both South Korea and Taiwan. Indeed, there is some evidence to suggest that the importance of foreign capital in the East Asian NICs is increasing—despite balance-of-payments surpluses—as they move into production of high-tech goods (Haggard and Cheng, 1987).

extremely negative for Brazil and Mexico (which are mired in recession and have witnessed greater foreign intrusion into their domestic affairs than at any time since the 1920s).

These differing trends over time, toward a lesser need for foreign capital in East Asia and a greater ability to control it, add up to an objective set of reasons for East Asian specialists to be more positive than their Latin Americanist counterparts about the role of foreign capital. (Of course, they would be unwise to be completely sanguine.) The key to understanding the different experiences centers on the issue of host country autonomy, an issue that also links the two debates being considered. Regardless of its form—direct investment, private bank loans, or public-sector credits—the purpose of foreign capital is to further the interests of those who provide it. Development of the host country is a fortuitous side effect at best, which will only come about if the host government maintains enough autonomy and control to guarantee that the benefits are shared between providers and recipients of foreign capital. Taiwan and South Korea have been more successful than Brazil and Mexico in retaining this control. The reasons are multiple. They include historical-structural variables such as colonial heritage, domestic political power relations, geographical location, and natural resource availability. Policy choices on mobilization of domestic savings, promotion of local capital, selective use and regulation of foreign capital, and sequencing of development strategies have also been important.

Scholars interested in theory concerning the role of foreign capital and practitioners offering advice to policymakers have to place these historical and structural distinctions at the center of their analysis. Assuming that the same theories and the same policy advice will work in both regions can be misleading at best and dangerous at worst. Perhaps the most obvious examples of ignoring such distinctions are economists who suggest that, if Latin America would only emulate East Asia, its problems would be solved. While few would deny that Latin America has lessons to learn from East Asia, direct adoption of East Asian policies will not work under very different historical-structural circumstances. More generally, lessons in either direction can never provide "quick fixes," but only small advances in our understanding that may one day lead to improvements in East Asia as well as Latin America.

REFERENCES

Books and Articles

Amsden, Alice. 1979. "Taiwan's Economic History: A Case of Etatisme and a Challenge to Dependency Theory." *Modern China* 5, no. 3, pp. 341–79.
Baer, Werner. 1983. *The Brazilian Economy*, 2d edition. New York: Praeger.

Balassa, Bela, and John Williamson. 1987. *Adjusting to Success: Balance of Payments Policy in the East Asian NICs*. Washington, D.C.: Institute of International Economics.

Baran, Paul. 1957. *The Political Economy of Growth*. New York: Monthly Review Press.

Barrett, Richard, and Martin King Whyte. 1982. "Dependency Theory and Taiwan: An Analysis of a Deviant Case." *American Journal of Sociology* 87, no. 5, pp. 1064–89.

Becker, David. 1983. *The New Bourgeoisie and the Limits of Dependency: Mining, Class and Power in 'Revolutionary' Peru*. Princeton: Princeton University Press.

Beckerman, Marta. 1986. "Promoción de exportaciones: Una experiencia latinoamericana, el caso de Brasil." *Comercio Exterior* 36, no. 5, pp. 424–33.

Bennett, Douglas, and Kenneth Sharpe. 1985. *Transnational Corporations Versus the State*. Princeton: Princeton University Press.

Berger, Peter. 1986. *The Capitalist Revolution*. New York: Basic Books.

Bergsman, Joel. 1970. *Brazil: Industrialization and Trade Policies*. London: Oxford University Press.

Cardoso, Fernando Henrique. 1973. "Associated-Dependent Development: Theoretical and Practical Implications." In *Authoritarian Brazil*, edited by Alfred Stepan. New Haven: Yale University Press.

Cardoso, Fernando Henrique, and Enzo Faletto. 1979. *Dependency and Development in Latin America*. Berkeley: University of California Press.

Cha, Dong-Se. 1983. *Analysis of the Effects of Foreign Capital Inflow*. Seoul: Korean Institute for Industrial Economics and Technology (in Korean).

Cole, David. 1980. "Foreign Assistance and Korean Development." In *The Korean Economy—Issues of Development*, edited by David Cole et al. Berkeley: University of California Press.

Cumby, Robert, and Richard Levich. 1987. In *Capital Flight and Third World Debt*, edited by Donald R. Lessard and John Williamson. Washington, D.C.: Institute for International Economics.

Cumings, Bruce. 1984. "The Origins and Development of the Northeast Asian Political Economy: Industrial Sectors, Product Cycles, and Political Consequences." *International Organization* 38, no. 1, pp. 1–40.

Díaz-Alejandro, Carlos. 1970. "Direct Foreign Investment in Latin America." In *The International Corporation*, edited by Charles Kindleberger. Cambridge: MIT Press.

Dos Santos, Theotonio. 1970. "The Structure of Dependence." *American Economic Review* 60, no. 2, pp. 231–36.

Evans, Peter. 1987. "Class, State, and Dependence in East Asia: Lessons for Latin Americanists." In *The Political Economy of the New Asian Industrialism*, edited by Frederic C. Deyo. Ithaca: Cornell University Press.

———. 1979. *Dependent Development: The Alliance of Multinational, State, and Local Capital in Brazil*. Princeton: Princeton University Press.

Evans, Peter, and Gary Gereffi. 1982. "Foreign Investment and Dependent Development: Comparing Brazil and Mexico." In *Brazil and Mexico*, edited by Sylvia Ann Hewlett and Richard Weinert. Philadelphia: ISHI.

Fishlow, Albert. 1972. "Origins and Consequences of Import Substitution in Brazil." In *International Economics and Development*, edited by Luis Eugenio di Marco. New York: Academic Press.

FitzGerald, E.V.K. 1977. *Patterns of Saving and Investment in Mexico: 1939–76.* Working Paper no. 30. Cambridge: University of Cambridge, Centre of Latin American Studies.

Frank, Andre Gunder. 1967. *Capitalism and Underdevelopment in Latin America.* New York: Monthly Review Press.

Frank, Charles, et al. 1975. *Foreign Trade Regimes and Economic Development: South Korea.* New York: Columbia University Press.

Frieden, Jeffry. 1985. "Studies in International Finance: Private Interests and Public Policy in the International Political Economy." Ph.D. diss., Columbia University.

Galenson, Walter, ed. 1985. *Foreign Trade and Investment: Economic Growth in the Newly Industrializing Asian Countries.* Madison: University of Wisconsin Press.

———, ed. 1979. *Economic Growth and Structural Change in Taiwan.* Ithaca: Cornell University Press.

Gereffi, Gary. 1989. "Rethinking Development Theory: Insights from East Asia and Latin America." *Sociological Forum* 4, no. 4, pp. 505–33.

———. 1988. "Industrial Structure and Development Strategies in Latin America and East Asia." Paper presented at the Latin American Studies Association International Congress, New Orleans.

———. 1983. *The Pharmaceutical Industry and Dependency in the Third World.* Princeton: Princeton University Press.

Gereffi, Gary, and Peter Evans. 1981. "Transnational Corporations, Dependent Development, and State Policy in the Semiperiphery: A Comparison of Brazil and Mexico." *Latin American Research Review* 16, no. 3, pp. 31–64.

Gold, Thomas. 1986. *State and Society in the Taiwan Miracle.* Armonk, N.Y.: M.E. Sharpe.

———. 1983. "Differentiating Multinational Corporations: American, Japanese and Overseas Chinese Investors in Taiwan." *Chinese Journal of Sociology* 7: pp. 267–78.

———. 1981. "Dependent Development in Taiwan." Ph.D. diss., Harvard University.

Green, Rosario. 1976. *El Endeudamiento público externo de México, 1940–1973.* Mexico: Colegio de Mexico.

Grunwald, Joseph, and Kenneth Flamm. 1985. *The Global Factory: Foreign Assembly in International Trade.* Washington, D.C.: Brookings Institution.

Haggard, Stephan. 1986. "The Newly Industrializing Countries in the International System." *World Politics* 38, no. 2, pp. 343–70.

———. 1983. "Pathways from the Periphery: The Newly Industrializing Countries in the International System." Ph.D. diss., University of California, Berkeley.

Haggard, Stephan, and Tun-jen Cheng. 1987. "State and Foreign Capital in East Asian NICs." In *The Political Economy of the New Asian Industrialism*, edited by Fred Deyo. Ithaca: Cornell University Press.

Haggard, Stephan, and Chung-In Moon. 1983. "The South Korean State in the International Economy: Liberal, Dependent, or Mercantile?" In *The Antinomies of Interdependence*, edited by John Gerard Ruggie. New York: Columbia University Press.

Jacoby, Neil H. 1966. *U.S. Aid to Taiwan: A Study of Foreign Aid, Self-Help and Development*. New York: Praeger.

Kim, Kwangsuk, and Michael Roemer. 1979. *Growth and Structural Transformation*. Cambridge: Harvard University Press.

Krueger, Anne O. 1979. *The Developmental Role of the Foreign Sector and Aid*. Cambridge: Harvard University Press.

Kuo, Shirley, et al. 1981. *Taiwan Success Story*. Boulder: Westview Press.

Landsberg, Martin. 1979. "Export-Led Industrialization in the Third World: Manufacturing Imperialism." *Review of Radical Political Economics* 11, no. 4, pp. 50–63.

Leff, Nathaniel. 1968. *The Brazilian Capital Goods Industry, 1929–64*. Cambridge: Harvard University Press.

Lim, Hyun-Chin. 1982. "Dependent Development in the World-System: The Case of South Korea, 1963–79." Ph.D. diss., Harvard University.

Long, Don. 1977. "Repression and Development in the Periphery: South Korea." *Bulletin of Concerned Asian Scholars* 9, no. 2, pp. 26–41.

Luedde-Neurath, Richard. 1984. "State Intervention and Foreign Direct Investment in South Korea." *IDS Bulletin* 15, no. 2, pp. 18–25.

Mares, David. 1985. "Explaining Choice of Development Strategies: Suggestions from Mexico, 1970–1982." *International Organization* 39, no. 4, pp. 667–97.

Mason, Edward S., et al. 1980. *The Economic and Social Modernization of the Republic of Korea*. Cambridge: Harvard University Press.

Maxfield, Sylvia. 1986. "The Internationalization of Finance and Macroeconomic Policy: Mexico and Brazil Compared." Paper presented at APSA Annual Meeting, Washington, D.C.

Newfarmer, Richard, ed. 1985. *Profits, Progress, and Poverty: Case Studies of International Industries in Latin America*. Notre Dame: University of Notre Dame Press.

Newfarmer, Richard, and Willard Mueller. 1975. *Multinational Corporations in Brazil and Mexico: Structural Sources of Economic and Non-economic Power*. Report to the U.S. Senate, Committee on Foreign Relations, Subcommittee on Multinational Corporations.

OECD (Organization for Economic Co-operation and Development). 1986. *Financing and External Debt of Developing Countries, 1985 Survey*. Paris: OECD.

Palma, Gabriel. 1978. "Dependency: A Formal Theory of Underdevelopment or a Methodology for the Analysis of Concrete Situations of Underdevelopment." *World Development* 6, nos. 7/8, pp. 881–924.

Scitovsky, Tibor. 1985. "Economic Development in Taiwan and South Korea." *Food Research Institute Studies* 19, no. 3, pp. 215–64.

Sharpston, Michael. 1975. "International Sub-contracting." *Oxford Economic Papers* 27, no. 1, pp. 94–135.

Skidmore, Thomas. 1967. *Politics in Brazil*. London: Oxford University Press.

Stallings, Barbara. 1987. *Banker to the Third World: U.S. Portfolio Investment in Latin America*. Berkeley: University of California Press.

Story, Dale. 1986. *Industry, the State, and Public Policy in Mexico*. Austin: University of Texas Press.

Sunoo, Harold H. 1978. "Economic Development and Foreign Control in South Korea." *Journal of Contemporary Asia* 8, no. 3, pp. 322–39.

Thanamai, Patcharee. 1985. "Patterns of Industrial Policymaking in Thailand: Japanese Multinationals and Domestic Actors in the Auto and Electrical Appliances Industries." Ph.D. diss., University of Wisconsin.

Unger, Kurt. 1985. "El comercio exterior de manufacturas modernas en México." *Comercio Exterior* 35, no. 5, pp. 431–43.

Villarreal, René. 1977. "The Policy of Import-Substituting Industrialization, 1929–1975." In *Authoritarianism in Mexico*, edited by José Luis Reyna and Richard Weinert. Philadelphia: ISHI.

Wade, Robert. 1985. "East Asian Financial Systems as a Challenge to Economics: Lessons from Taiwan." *California Management Review* 27, no. 4, pp. 106–27.

———. 1984. "Dirigisme Taiwan-Style." *IDS Bulletin* 15, no. 2, pp. 65–70.

Weinert, Richard. 1977. "The State and Foreign Capital." In *Authoritarianism in Mexico*, edited by José Luis Reyna and Richard Weinert. Philadelphia: ISHI.

Westphal, Larry, et al. 1981. *Korean Industrial Competence: Where It Came From*. Staff working paper no. 469. Washington, D.C.: World Bank.

World Bank. 1983. *Brazil: Industrial Politics and Manufactured Exports*. Washington, D.C.: World Bank.

Yusuf, Shahid, and R. Kyle Peters. 1985. *Capital Accumulation and Economic Growth: The Korean Paradigm*. Staff working paper no. 712. Washington, D.C.: World Bank.

Periodical Publications

A Economia Brasileira e suas Perspectivas. Rio de Janeiro: APEC.

Balance of Payments Yearbook. Washington, D.C.: IMF.

Country Profile (for Brazil, Mexico, South Korea, and Taiwan). London: Economist Intelligence Unit.

Country Report (for Brazil, Mexico, South Korea, and Taiwan). London: Economist Intelligence Unit.

Development Cooperation. Paris: OECD.

Economic Statistics Yearbook (Korea). Seoul: Bank of Korea.

External Financing of the Latin American Countries. Washington, D.C.: Interamerican Development Bank.

Geographical Distribution of Financial Flows to Developing Countries. Paris: OECD.

International Financial Statistics. Washington, D.C.: IMF.

Major Statistics of the Korean Economy. Seoul: Economic Planning Board.

Survey of Current Business. Washington, D.C.: Department of Commerce.

Taiwan Statistical Data Book. Taipei: Council for Economic Planning and Development.

U.S. Overseas Loans and Grants. Washington, D.C.: Agency for International Development.

World Bank Annual Report. Washington, D.C.: World Bank.

World Debt Tables. Washington, D.C.: World Bank.

World Financial Markets. New York: Morgan Guaranty Trust.

CHAPTER 4

Big Business and the State

Gary Gereffi

THE LATIN AMERICAN and East Asian newly industrializing countries (NICS) frequently have been taken to represent two contrasting development orientations: Mexico, Brazil, and Argentina are seen as having given primacy to an inward-oriented (import-substituting) mode of development, while Taiwan, South Korea, Hong Kong, and Singapore are associated with an outward-oriented (export-promoting) model. While these regional contrasts help us to understand many features of Latin American and East Asian development, national diversity among the NICS often overshadows regional similarities.

One form of subregional variation that tends to have been ignored in previous studies is industrial structure. There are two sets of indicators related to industrial structure: (1) the characteristics of a country's leading firms and (2) aggregate concentration measures that show how important big business is within the national economy. At the firm level, the three main features of industrial structure are: size, ownership, and industrial sector. At the aggregate level, the most convenient way to measure industrial concentration is to see what share of a country's gross domestic product (GDP) is accounted for by a certain number of the biggest firms. We will use both kinds of indicators in this chapter.

Taiwan and South Korea have sharply contrasting industrial structures in terms of the characteristics of their leading business enterprises. Taiwan has a predominance of small and medium-sized firms, often family-owned, while Korean industry centers around huge economic conglomerates (*chaebols*). Although local private companies predominate in both East Asian countries, state-owned enterprises are still quite important in Taiwan. They are relatively insignificant in South Korea, however. Foreign-owned firms play a limited role in both economies, with a focus on select export industries. Even there, local companies account for the vast majority of export sales. Although both Taiwan and South Korea have strong textile and electronics industries, they differ in the prominence of

Previously published as "Big Business and the State: East Asia and Latin America Compared," in *Asian Perspective* 14, no. 1 (1990), pp. 5–29. The author would like to thank Frederic Deyo, Christopher Ellison, Stephan Haggard, and Lynn Nonnemaker for their helpful comments on this chapter.

their other leading sectors. Taiwan has given considerable emphasis to petrochemicals and plastics, while South Korea has emerged as a world power in heavier industries, such as steel, shipbuilding, and motor vehicles (see Haggard and Cheng, 1987).

The Latin American NICs, on the other hand, are extensively penetrated by transnational corporation (TNC) subsidiaries. Foreign firms and state-owned enterprises are clustered at the top of the industrial pyramid in each country. Mexico, to a greater extent than Brazil, has promoted joint ventures between foreign and local investors. As a result, local private capital has a somewhat larger role in the Mexican economy. The automobile complex has been central to the industrialization efforts of the Latin American NICs, but they differ in the relative importance of other leading industries. The capital goods sector in Brazil is the most advanced in Latin America. An export-oriented armaments industry and the local production of computers are top priorities for Brazil as well. Mexico's economy revolves around oil and petrochemicals, but a wide array of other industries from the booming labor-intensive *maquiladora* (bonded processing) export plants along the U.S. border to high-tech computer exports also are playing growing roles (see Gereffi, 1989a; 1989b). Whereas Mexican industries are becoming ever more tightly integrated to the U.S. market, Brazil is growing into a regional economic power with expanding investment and trade ties with Western Europe and Japan.

This chapter will explore the impact that these differences in industrial structure have on the *paths* of industrialization in the Latin American and East Asian NICs. The nature of each country's industrial structure also is a key determinant in understanding the choice, implementation, and consequences of the government's main economic *policies*.

Different industrial structures help us understand why the same broad industrial path may have distinctive characteristics within a region. Heavy and chemical industrialization (HCI) in South Korea and Taiwan in the 1970s, for example, had a contrasting pace and sectoral profile in each country. There is a similar contrast in the process of secondary import-substituting industrialization (ISI) in Mexico and Brazil, which began in the late 1950s. Industrial structure not only mediates the consequences of development trajectories, but it also helps to shape their design. In the 1980s South Korea has been pursuing a strategy that combines high value-added manufactured exports with aggressive (although still relatively limited) overseas investments and marketing efforts by the Korean *chaebol* groups in the United States and other developed country markets. This type of internationalization is beyond the capability of the smaller Taiwanese companies.

In the Latin American countries, foreign investors play a similar organizational role to the *chaebols* by utilizing their global networks to facilitate industrial integration across national boundaries. Transnational automobile companies in Mexico, relying on the country's proximity to the U.S. market and its plummeting labor costs due to recent peso devaluations, have converted Mexico into a major platform for automotive exports to the United States in the 1980s. A large proportion of these exports are intrafirm sales between related TNC units that directly link Mexican suppliers to their buyers in the United States and elsewhere. Japanese and American companies now are rushing to expand their manufacturing capacity in the Mexican industry. The Brazilian automobile industry is also strong and export-oriented, but the structure of its global integration is distinctive because of its geographical location and the relatively greater prominence of West German and Japanese auto firms there. Attention to industrial structure will allow us to better understand these and other national variations in development among the NICs.

BIG BUSINESS: NATIONAL VARIATIONS IN OWNERSHIP, SECTORAL DISTRIBUTION, AND SIZE

The ten largest industrial enterprises in Mexico, Brazil, South Korea, and Taiwan are listed in table 4.1. This provides us with a glimpse into some of the most salient firm-level differences in industrial structure in the Latin American and East Asian NICs.

First, there are clear regional contrasts. The largest firms in Mexico and Brazil are state-owned enterprises or foreign subsidiaries of TNCs. Local private companies, on the other hand, are without question the dominant firms in South Korea, and together with state enterprises they share industrial leadership in Taiwan. A closer look, however, also reveals some important subregional differences in industrial structure.

There is a rather consistent division of labor in the roles played by foreign, state, and local private capital in the Latin American NICs (see Gereffi and Evans, 1981; Newfarmer, 1985). Foreign firms have been central to the development of certain industries: electrical and nonelectrical machinery, motor vehicles, tires, rubber, chemicals, and pharmaceuticals, among others. State enterprises are concentrated in the natural resource industries, such as oil and minerals, transportation and communication, and steel production. Local private capital is quite diversified, but it is a more prominent actor in Mexico than Brazil. This has to do in part with Mexico's long-standing policy of promoting joint ventures in which domestic capitalists are involved.

We can see in table 4.1, for example, that local private capital has a substantial minority share in two of the largest state firms in Mexico (Telefonos de México and Compañía Mexicana de Aviación). Eleven of the top twenty-five industrial companies in the country are majority-owned

TABLE 4.1
The Ten Largest Companies in Mexico, Brazil, South Korea, and Taiwan, 1987

Rank/Company	Main Industry	Sales[a] (US$ millions)	Employees	Ownership[b]
Mexico				
1. Petróleos Mexicanos	Petroleum	13,115.7	210,157	State
2. Chrysler de México	Motor vehicles	1,216.6	15,412	Foreign
3. General Motors de México	Motor vehicles	1,129.6	9,793	Foreign
4. Teléfonos de México	Communications	1,081.1	44,700	State[c]
5. Ford Motor Company	Motor vehicles	1,054.4	5,344	Foreign
6. Altos Hornos de México	Iron and steel	816.1	24,963	State
7. Gigante	Commerce	681.1	20,680	Local private
8. Volkswagen de México	Motor vehicles	644.9	12,855	Foreign
9. Cia. Mexicana de Aviación	Transportation	629.0	14,052	State[d]
10. Celanese Mexicana	Synthetic fibers and resins	549.3	8,263	Local private[e]
Brazil				
1. Petrobrás	Petroleum	12,492.4	50,000	State
2. Petrobrás Distribuidora	Petroleum	4,690.8	4,300	State
3. Shell Brasil	Petroleum	2,952.1	3,200	Foreign
4. Esso Brasil	Petroleum	1,877.3	1,350	Foreign
5. Eletropaulo	Electric power	1,755.3	20,600	State
6. Cia. Vale do Rio Doce	Minerals	1,736.4	23,673	State
7. Cia. Energetica São Paulo	Electric power	1,528.3	15,157	State
8. Texaco	Petroleum	1,464.9	1,313	Foreign
9. Cia. Brasileira Distribucão	Commerce	1,429.7	49,000	Local private
10. Furnas Centrais Eletricas	Electric power	1,385.3	9,101	State
South Korea				
1. Samsung	Electronics	21,053.5	160,596	Local private
2. Lucky-Goldstar	Electronics	14,422.3	88,403	Local private
3. Daewoo	Electronics	13,437.9	94,888	Local private

TABLE 4.1 (*cont.*)

Rank/Company	Main Industry	Sales[a] (US$ millions)	Employees	Ownership[b]
4. Sunkyong	Petroleum refining	6,781.6	17,985	Local private
5. Ssangyong	Petroleum refining	4,582.7	16,870	Local private
6. Korea Explosives	Chemicals	3,563.8	18,291	Local private
7. Pohang Iron and Steel	Iron and steel	3,533.2	19,329	State
8. Hyundai Motor	Motor vehicles	3,437.4	29,000	Local private
9. Hyosung	Textiles	3,257.8	24,000	Local private
10. Hyundai Heavy Industries	Transportation equipment	2,964.5	48,200	Local private
Taiwan				
1. Chinese Petroleum	Petrochemicals and plastics	5,491.0	20,700	State
2. Taiwan Tobacco and Wine Monopoly Bureau	Food and beverages	2,277.1	13,495	State
3. Nan Ya Plastics	Petrochemicals and plastics	1,423.7	11,883	Local private
4. China Steel	Steel	1,287.8	9,476	State
5. Formosa Plastics	Petrochemicals and plastics	946.8	5,352	Local private
6. Ret-Ser Engineering	Construction	852.0	13,358	State
7. Tatung	Electronics	836.2	14,139	Local private
8. Formosa Chemicals and Fiber	Textiles and dyeing	702.9	8,377	Local private
9. Yue Loong Motor	Motor vehicles	687.4	3,782	Local private
10. San Yang Industry	Motor vehicles	600.9	3,637	Local private

Sources: Mexico: *Expansión* (1988); Brazil: *Visão* (1988); South Korea: *Fortune* (1988); and Taiwan: *CommonWealth* (1988).

[a] The following annual average exchange rates for 1987 were used for converting company sales figures from the domestic currency into U.S. dollars: Mexico—1,378.2 pesos per $1.00 (IMF, 1988, p. 364); Brazil—39.229 cruzados per $1.00 (IMF, 1988, p. 132); and Taiwan—31.975 NT$ per $1.00 (calculated as an average of year-end exchange rates for 1986 and 1987, CEPD, 1988, p. 199). The sales totals for South Korean companies were initially given in U.S. dollars.

[b] Ownership designations indicate a majority share. The classifications for Mexico, Brazil, and Taiwan come from the sources cited, while the ownership categories for South Korea have been supplied by the author using a variety of secondary sources.

[c] Teléfonos de México; 51 percent state-owned, 49 percent local private capital.

[d] Compañía Mexicana de Aviación: 56 percent state-owned, 44 percent local private capital.

[e] Celanese Mexicana: 60 percent local private capital, 40 percent foreign capital.

by local private capital, compared with a total of seven foreign and seven state firms among the top twenty-five (*Expansión*, 1988). In Brazil, on the other hand, local private businesses account for only five of the top twenty-five industrial enterprises, while twelve state companies and eight TNC subsidiaries make up the remainder of the list (*Visão*, 1988). Although foreign firms have a similar level of importance in the two Latin American NICs, the difference lies in the greater role for state enterprises in Brazil and for the local private sector in Mexico.

In the East Asian nations, local private firms are the main industrial actors. Nine of the ten largest companies in South Korea are privately held domestic conglomerates; the only exception is Pohang Iron and Steel, a state-owned enterprise that is ranked seventh (see table 4.1). Each of the private South Korean conglomerates is involved in a wide range of industries and has a staggering number of affiliates. The Lucky-Goldstar group, for example, contained sixty-two companies in 1988; Samsung was made up of thirty-seven related firms, while Hyundai had thirty-four, and Daewoo twenty-eight (Clifford, 1988).

In Taiwan, as in South Korea, there are no TNCs among the top ten companies and only three foreign-owned firms in the top twenty-five. The upper level of Taiwan's industrial pyramid is relatively evenly divided between four state enterprises and six local private companies in the first ten, although four of the six biggest firms in Taiwan are government-owned (see table 4.1). Fourteen of the top twenty-five companies in Taiwan and twenty-nine of the top fifty are local private businesses, while government and foreign-owned firms account for ten and eleven, respectively, of Taiwan's fifty biggest enterprises (*CommonWealth*, 1988). The state enterprise sector in Taiwan is more diversified than in the other NICs, with wide-ranging interests that include petrochemicals, plastics, steel, shipbuilding, construction, fertilizer, food, and beverages.

Just as significant as these regional and subregional variations in ownership and sectoral emphasis are differences among the NICs in the size of their leading industrial enterprises. South Korea's industrial structure is dominated by giant *chaebol* groups. The biggest Korean conglomerate, Samsung, had a sales total of $21 billion for 1987, which is nearly 40 percent larger than the sales of all of Taiwan's top ten companies in 1987 *combined*. Samsung's 160,000 employees exceed by more than 50 percent the total employment of the ten biggest companies in Taiwan.

The largest enterprises in Brazil and Mexico are their state-owned oil companies, Petrobrás and Pemex (Petróleos Mexicanos), with 1987 sales of $17.2 billion (including Petrobrás Distribuidora) and $13.1 billion, respectively. Once we move beyond these industrial leaders, however, the next largest Brazilian company is Shell Brasil, whose annual sales total of $2.95 billion for 1987 would place it just behind South Korea's tenth-ranking company (Hyundai Heavy Industries, with $2.96 billion in sales). Mexico's second largest firm, Chrysler de México, had a 1987 sales total of $1.2 billion, which is only two fifths that of Korea's tenth-ranking company, Hyundai Heavy Industries (see table 4.1). South Korea had eleven companies in *Fortune*'s list of the five hundred largest non-U.S. industrial firms in 1987. There were six Brazilian companies on the list, three companies from Taiwan, and two from Mexico (*Fortune*, 1988).

The differing levels of industrial concentration in the Latin American and East Asian NICs are indicated by the share of the ten largest companies in the GDP of each country (see table 4.2). South Korea's top ten firms accounted for 63.5 percent of the country's GDP in 1987, compared to concentration ratios of 14.7 percent for Mexico, 14.3 percent for Taiwan, and 10.5 percent for Brazil. The striking disparities that exist between the size of the largest companies in South Korea versus the other three NICs may be overstated somewhat because the listings for Taiwan, Mexico, and Brazil take firms rather than economic groups as the unit of analysis. The Korean *chaebol* that appear in *Fortune*'s "International 500" are in fact diversified enterprise groups, and similar kinds of economic groupings exist in each of the other countries as well.

A recent analysis of enterprise groups in East Asia compares six major intermarket groups (*kigyo shudan*) and ten large independent industrial groups (*keiretsu*) in Japan, the fifty biggest *chaebol* in Korea, and the top ninety-six business groups (*jituanqiye*) in Taiwan. The number and size of affiliated firms in each group vary markedly. Japan's business groups include the largest number of firms, with an average of over 112 companies for each of the six intermarket groups, and about thirty-three firms for each of the ten independent *keiretsu*. South Korea's *chaebol*, in con-

TABLE 4.2
GDP Shares of the Ten Largest Companies, 1987 (US$ millions)

Country	Sales of the Top Ten Companies	Gross Domestic Product	Top Ten Companies/ GDP (percent)
Mexico	20,917.8	141,940	14.7
Brazil	31,312.5	299,230	10.5
South Korea	77,034.7	121,310	63.5
Taiwan	15,105.8	105,750	14.3

Sources: Sales of the top ten companies for each country are from table 4.1; gross domestic product figures for 1987 are from the World Bank (1989, p. 169) and CEPD (1988, pp. 23, 199).

trast, are composed on average of about eleven firms each, while Taiwan's business groups are smaller still, typically having only about eight affiliated firms each. Overall sales also differ sharply, with Japanese business groups representing an extraordinary total of $871 billion (U.S.) in 1982, South Korea's fifty *chaebol* earning $68 billion in 1983, and Taiwan's ninety-six business groups selling $16.5 billion in 1983 (Hamilton et al., 1987, pp. 82–83). Thus even if we include business groups rather than individual firms as our unit of analysis for Taiwan, the gap between the two East Asian NICs is still very significant, with the average *chaebol* being eight times larger in terms of sales than the average Taiwanese business group.

The Political Impact of Big Business

This analysis raises a key question about the political impact of these variations in industrial structure among the Latin American and East Asian NICs. How are the government's economic policies affected by the different character of big business in each country? The Latin American and East Asian NICs each have authoritarian states that have strongly supported industrial growth, often at the expense of the agricultural sector. The capitalist class in these countries plays a major role, not so much in formulating development strategies but, even more importantly, in implementing them (see Deyo, chap. 7, this volume). Development strategies must be carried out by a distinct constellation of big business interests in each nation, and this influences what can be achieved.

In the East Asian NICs, although the state actively participates in the public and private spheres of the economy, a good deal of this involvement is indirect (e.g., government-controlled credit, government regulation of the purchase of raw materials, energy, and foreign exchange, and price controls for selected commodities; see Wade, chap. 9, this volume). In South Korea, the *chaebol* are crucially important in the implementation of the government's economic policies. This was especially true during the phase of HCI in the 1970s, when the steel, shipbuilding, automobile, petrochemical, and heavy machinery industries were the focus of the government's "big push" approach, which was predicated on an unprecedented concentration of capital in the *chaebol* groups (see Cheng, chap. 6, this volume). The normative or authority structure that underlies this pattern of interfirm relations is what might be called a principle of *corporate patriarchy*, in which "these huge industrial empires are the property of an authoritarian individual and his designees who manage them not by consensus, but by centralized command supported by the state" (Hamilton et al., 1987, p. 102).

The link between the government and business groups in South Korea is quite direct. These vertical pressures cannot be easily countered, because intermediate or independent local institutions are weak, repressed, or absent. A homogeneous and very nationalistic big business class thus is available in South Korea to carry out the government's objectives in terms of domestic and overseas investments and external trade.

Taiwan, in sharp contrast to South Korea, is characterized by a decentralized pattern of industrialization, a low level of firm concentration, and a predominance of small and medium-sized family businesses. Whereas there are strong pressures for vertical integration in Korea's *chaebols*, Taiwan's business groups resemble loosely knit agglomerations in which firms tend to be organizationally separate from other firms, with no unified management structure. Instead of a formal system of command, one finds a highly flexible management arrangement that relies on networks generated by personal relationships based on reciprocal trust, loyalty, and predictability (Hamilton and Kao, 1987). The underlying social principle here is that of the *patrilineal network*, since "the Taiwanese business groups do not express the will of a single patriarch but rather the interests of an extended family" (Hamilton et al., 1987, p. 102).

While South Korean patriarchs may direct their business empires even in the absence of a corporate position, Taiwanese business leaders simultaneously hold multiple executive posts to reinforce their authority. The strategy of expansion typically is to start new companies, even if it is in the same or a closely related product line, rather than enlarging the size of the original firm. This pattern of opportunistic diversification helps explain the existence of numerous small and medium-sized firms.

How does this configuration of interfirm relations in Taiwan affect state planning in the economy? Gary Hamilton and Nicole Biggart (1988) argue that while there is state planning in both South Korea and Taiwan, the difference in the role of the state resides in the fact that Taiwan's government has no real implementation procedures. Furthermore, in regard to the export business sector, the Taiwan government is said to promote "virtually free trade conditions," which leaves the export sector plenty of latitude to work out its own preferences.

This interpretation seems to ignore the fact that state enterprises continue to operate in a wide range of economic areas, and that they are disproportionately represented among Taiwan's biggest companies (see table 4.1). The state, in fact, has tended to discourage the creation of large private firms. An alternative explanation for this pattern is that there is a strong ethnic cleavage in Taiwan between the Mainlander-dominated political elite that arrived on the island in the late 1940s (and which runs state enterprises) and the Taiwanese-based economic elite. This situation makes it very difficult for Taiwan's government to have an effective industrial policy, because the state cannot count on the unqualified support of a subordinate capitalist class to compete with the large, vertically integrated Japanese and South Korean conglomerates and general trading companies. This has led to Taiwan's "gradualist" approach in implementing large-scale projects like HCI (see Cheng, chap. 6, this volume) and to its difficulty in penetrating external markets in capital- and technology-intensive industries associated with export-oriented industrialization (EOI), other than through short-term subcontracting relationships with big foreign buyers.

The Latin American NICs have very different industrial structures from their East Asian counterparts, as we have seen. Transnational corporations have been an integral part of the industrialization process in Mexico and Brazil, especially since the secondary ISI phase that began in the 1950s. In contrast to the familial basis of East Asia's leading businesses, which led to patrimonial and patrilineal interfirm networks, TNCs have tied the Latin American NICs to the rest of the world economy according to two very different principles of global economic organization: (1) during the ISI period of the 1950s and 1960s, TNCs, at the behest of national governments, followed a principle of *national segmentation*, in which the foreign companies set up parallel national industries to supply highly protected domestic markets; and (2) during the turn to diversified EOI in the 1970s and 1980s, TNCs followed the logic of *transnational integration* in reuniting the Latin American NICs to global markets through export promotion schemes that often were heavily subsidized by the host governments. While manufactured exports during the import-substitution phase were based on the utilization of existing excess capacity, new highly automated export-oriented plants began to be built at or above the minimum efficient scale in Mexico and Brazil during the 1970s and 1980s, with the export market increasingly seen as the main outlet for production.

Foreign firms in the postwar period typically came to establish new industries (like automobiles, petrochemicals, and electrical and nonelectrical machinery) to supply the domestic market, or they sought to modernize certain traditional industries (like textiles or food-processing), which resulted in the displacement of many of their domestic rivals. Family ties and personal networks play virtually no role in this setting. Foreign companies were authorized by the state to enter certain segments of the domestic market where local capital was relatively weak or absent. The subsequent bargaining that took place between TNCs and the host governments usually revolved around how to incorporate changing national priorities into the TNCs' global decision-making framework.

Mexico and Brazil enlisted foreign firms to help make the shift in the 1970s and 1980s from ISI to a diversified EOI strategy, while simultaneously restructuring domestically oriented industries by lifting the mantle of permanent protectionism and privatizing many public enterprises in order to push local companies to higher levels of competitiveness. The trend toward economic liberalization and a reduced governmental role in the Latin American NICs, when coupled with the relative weakness of their local private sectors and an overwhelming external debt burden, meant that foreign economic and political actors had increased leeway to shape development patterns in the region. Bargaining between TNCs and host governments during the EOI phase centered around renegotiating the form of insertion of the NICs in the world economy in response to new patterns of international production and trade that were redefining the spatial location of integrated global industries (see Gereffi, 1989a). As a *quid pro quo* for increased exports, the TNCs demanded and frequently got significant policy shifts from the Mexican and Brazilian governments with regard to the relaxation of local content requirements, reduced import tariffs on inputs, and very attractive packages of export incentives.

The presence of TNCs as major industrial actors in the Latin American NICs has posed both opportunities and constraints for the formulation and implementation of state development strategies. As long as the domestic market was expanding, the Mexican and Brazilian governments had a significant degree of bargaining power over foreign investors. Nonetheless, TNCs inevitably are guided by a global rather than a national perspective, and their ability to shift their investments elsewhere meant that nationalistic governments had to be cautious in what they demanded. The financial controls that proved to be an effective lever of influence for East Asian governments in dealing with local private capital have little or no effect over TNCs since they have multiple sources of financing available to them. Since TNCs continue to be the major exporters in the Latin American NICs, their access to global markets through integrated production and export networks gives the TNCs the upper hand in their dealings with Latin American governments pursuing export-promotion strategies. Conversely, in the East Asian NICs, governments have the advantage as they induce their local private exporters to adopt a mercantilistic approach to global markets where overseas sales are equated with enhanced national security and prestige.

THE INTERNATIONALIZATION OF BIG BUSINESS: THE CASE OF AUTOMOBILES

So far, our analysis of industrial structures in the Latin American and East Asian NICs has emphasized the ownership, sectoral distribution, size, and concentration of the largest companies in each country, and some of the implications of these patterns for the formulation and implementation of industrial policy by the state. Another angle from which we can compare the NICs is to look at how industrial structure has affected the internationalization of their industries. The case of the automobile industry will be examined to illustrate this point.

The fascination of Latin American countries with the automobile industry as the centerpiece for secondary ISI probably resulted in large part from their desire to emulate the industrialization experience of the United States. In the 1970s and 1980s, however, the international motor vehicle industry underwent a profound change. The oil price rises of 1973 and 1979, coupled with the rapid growth of the Japanese automotive industry since the 1960s and the decline in the demand for motor vehicles in the main producing countries, led to a major restructuring in the motor vehicle industry, which required massive new investments at a time of very low profitability (see Jenkins, 1987, chaps. 9–11).

This restructuring has significantly advanced the internationalization of capital and fostered the creation of a truly global industry. The three primary blocs of North America, Europe, and Japan are becoming much more closely integrated in trade, cross-investments, and joint production arrangements. The leading automotive TNCs, especially from the United States, increasingly view their operations as an integrated whole and have developed "world component supply strategies" to fit their concept of the world car. Finally, there is a tendency toward market homogenization as the main regional motor vehicle producers supply similar cars using similar production techniques in auto factories around the world (Jenkins, 1987, pp. 170–84).

The restructuring of the international motor vehicle industry has given a new importance to peripheral economies as production sites for the integrated operations of auto producers. The state's role in the NICs has been to persuade locally established carmakers and parts suppliers to take advantage of these new export opportunities. In Mexico and Brazil, the state in the 1970s and 1980s tried to exploit the increased competition between the automotive TNCs in order to generate more exports. In return, the TNCs were granted a battery of incentives, ranging from one half to two thirds of the value of auto exports in the 1970s, and reductions in the level of local content required in the production of vehicles for the protected domestic markets (Jenkins, 1987, pp. 190–94, 215–16). Mexico announced at the end of 1989 that its high tariffs on imported vehicles would be virtually eliminated by the beginning of 1991, on the condition that only auto firms already established in and exporting from Mexico be allowed to import vehicles. This practice of tying import licenses to success in exporting has long been a part of industrial policy in South Korea, and it marks a further step in the dismantling of the traditional ISI regime in the Latin American NICs.

The politics of export production in the South Korean motor vehicle industry were based on inducing the local industry leader, Hyundai Motor Company, to spearhead a spectacular export drive that increased South Korean motor vehicle exports more than tenfold between 1984 and 1987 (from 52,350 units to 546,310 units) (MVMA, 1989, p. 94). In 1988, however, motor vehicle exports (576,134 units) grew at only about one half the rate of total production (5.5 percent versus 10.6 percent, respectively) (Ward's Communications, Inc., 1989, pp. 79, 110). Strikes and slowdowns by South Korean auto workers, which closed car factories for more than two months in 1989, contributed to a 36 percent fall in exports, to 370,000 vehicles, compared to the industry's original target shipment for 1989 of 650,000 units. Domestic labor costs have roughly doubled since 1987, thus trimming the price advantage South Korean carmakers have enjoyed in export markets to $1,000 or less (down from $2,000 three years ago) (Clifford, 1989). As a result of increased worker militancy, higher labor costs, and slumping U.S. car sales, the domestic market is likely to become a much more important source of growth for South Korea's automotive industry in the near future.

Unlike the other three NICs, Taiwan does not export a substantial quantity of finished automobiles, although this remains a priority for government officials and industry executives alike (see Arnold, 1989). However, Taiwan has succeeded in establishing an export niche for itself as a supplier of auto parts. In 1985 the automotive parts industry had overseas sales of $450 million, double the export volume of three years earlier. Whereas Taiwan's auto assembly industry employed around ten thousand people in the mid-1980s, its parts industry provided fifty thousand jobs (Tank, 1986). To assure the continued growth of auto-related exports, Taiwan's government has begun to radically cut protectionist barriers in an effort to force local carmakers and component manufacturers to become internationally competitive. The philosophy behind Taiwan's bid to become a world center for auto parts was articulated by Dick Mou, director of market development at the China External Trade Development Council: "The goal is to be part of the international division of labor rather than developing a fully integrated industry. We take a global view" (Tank, 1986, p. 30).

A comparison of motor vehicle production trends in Latin America and East Asia reveals some interesting regional and subregional differences (see table 4.3). The Brazilian and Mexican motor vehicle industries were far larger than their East Asian counterparts throughout the 1970s and early 1980s. There was an enormous leap in South Korea's motor vehicle production to over 600,000 units in 1986, up 59 percent from 1985. South Korea and Brazil both topped the 1 million units mark in motor vehicle output in 1988, a plateau that Brazil first surpassed in each of the three years from 1978 to 1980. The severe slump that hit the Brazilian

TABLE 4.3
Motor Vehicle Production, 1965–1988 (thousands of units)

Year	Mexico	Brazil	South Korea	Taiwan
1965	97	185	0.1	3
1970	193	416	29	9
1971	211	517	23	20
1972	230	622	19	22
1973	286	750	26	24
1974	351	906	30	29
1975	361	930	36	31
1976	325	987	48	31
1977	281	921	83	44
1978	384	1,064	156	77
1979	444	1,128	204	116
1980	490	1,165	123	133
1981	597	781	134	138
1982	473	859	163	134
1983	285	896	221	158
1984	344	865	265	171
1985	398	967	378	160
1986	341	1,056	602	184
1987	395	920	980	224
1988	513	1,069	1,084	250

Sources: Mexico, Brazil, and South Korea—MVMA (1989, pp. 11, 13); Ward's Communications, Inc. (1989, p. 79) for 1988 production figures only. Taiwan—CEPD (1988, p. 94); Ward's Communications, Inc. (1989, p. 79) for 1987 and 1988 production figures.

economy in 1981 caused auto production to decrease by one third in a single year (from 1,165,000 units in 1980 to 781,000 units in 1981). Mexico's total vehicle production of 513,000 units in 1988 was the highest since 1981, when it peaked at almost 600,000 units. Taiwan's output of 250,000 units represented significant growth from the early 1980s, but still placed it far behind the other three NICs.

There have been distinct patterns of internationalization in the automotive industry in each of the NICs. During the course of the 1970s and 1980s, the motor vehicle industry in Mexico and Brazil became progressively more integrated into the world industry, but the exact form of this integration varied between the two countries. Export expansion in the Mexican automotive industry has been based on a component-supplier role characterized by ever-closer links to the United States, with an emphasis on TNC-made exports of parts and components for incorporation in vehicles built in the TNCs' U.S. plants (similar to the pattern that has occurred in Canada since the mid-1960s). Brazil, on the other hand, has stressed exports of finished vehicles as well as parts to a variety of international markets, with Brazil playing a regional power (or "subimperialist") role as an export base for foreign companies like Volkswagen and Ford to serve their customers in neighboring Latin American and other Third World countries. These different forms of national integration into the global motor vehicle industry are reflected in the fact that finished vehicles accounted for 58 percent of Brazil's automotive exports between 1972 and 1982, while 78 percent of Mexico's automotive exports during the same period were parts and components, particularly engines and gearboxes (Jenkins, 1987, pp. 210–11).

Automakers and suppliers from Japan and Europe as well as the United States have accelerated their efforts to export from plants in Mexico, lured by wage rates below a dollar per hour, an extremely favorable dollar/peso exchange rate, and close proximity to the U.S. market. Automotive-related shipments to the United States nearly tripled, from $460 million in 1981 to $1.3 billion in 1984, and then tripled again to $3.9 billion in 1988 (Winter, 1989, p. 27). American TNCs have taken the lead in auto exports from Mexico, with Chrysler (38.5 percent) in front of the field in 1987, followed by Ford (31.7 percent), General Motors (19.8 percent), and Nissan (9.9 percent) (*Latin American Weekly Report*, 1988). Despite skyrocketing exports to the United States, export sales as a percentage of total motor vehicle production in Mexico dropped from 41 percent in 1987 to 34 percent in 1988. Slower inflation, along with domestic consumer price freezes that in effect dropped the price of cars in Mexico by at least 20 percent in 1988, helped spur domestic automotive sales to their highest level in almost a decade (Ward's Communications, Inc., 1989, pp. 115, 117).

While the internationalization in Mexico's automobile industry has emphasized components production, this has been a weak link in Brazil's automotive complex. Inflation-ravaged suppliers have not been able to make components fast enough, and a critical parts shortage developed in 1986, causing thousands of cars and trucks to be stockpiled in holding yards awaiting installation of missing components. Seeking efficiencies of scale, Brazil's first and third largest automobile manufacturers—Volkswagen do Brasil (40.5 percent of the market) and Ford Brasil (20.3 percent)—merged their car operations in Brazil and Argentina into Autolatina, owned 51 percent by Volkswagen (*Ward's Automotive Yearbook*, 1987, pp. 84–85). Brazilian automotive production for 1988 increased 16.2 percent over 1987, although exports were down by 7.3 percent. Despite exorbitant taxation on autos, the growth in domestic sales reflects two basic trends in the Brazilian automobile industry: Brazilians are very car hungry, with only 12 million cars in a country of 140 million people, and cruzado/dollar export exchange shortfalls continue to make life very difficult for exporters (Ward's Communications, Inc., 1989, p. 115). Thus, although the auto industry in the Latin American NICs is becoming more export oriented, the domestic market remains an important source of industry growth.

South Korea emerged as one of the world's major motor vehicle competitors in the mid-1980s. South Korean automobile companies began to aggressively target the U.S. market for export sales and eventually foreign direct investments in Korean manufacturing subsidiaries, a pattern that even Brazil has not tried to follow. The ability of South Korea to internationalize its automobile industry in this way undoubtedly is related to the size and marketing capability of its *chaebols* in this sector (Hyundai, Daewoo, and Kia). Hyundai Motor Company, South Korea's leading auto manufacturer, was Canada's top importer with over 85,000 vehicles in 1985, and it set a record with sales of 168,000 subcompact Excel cars in the U.S. market in just 10 months in 1986. Unlike Hyundai, South Korea's other two automakers have utilized joint venture partnerships to get ahead in the volatile environment of the auto industry. Daewoo Motor Company is owned 50 percent by General Motors, while Kia Motors Corporation, which produces only trucks and buses, has issued a 10 percent share of its stock to Ford and 8 percent to Japan's Mazda Motor Corporation (itself partially owned by Ford).

Taiwan's limited achievements in motor vehicle exports reveal the constraints faced by its relatively small firms (Yue Loong and Ford Lio Ho), which must upgrade their production efficiency before they can mount major export drives. Yue Loong, the largest automaker with 33 percent of Taiwan's car market in 1986, has not had significant overseas sales to date. Ford Lio Ho began exporting its Mazda-based Tracer to Canada in the fall of 1986, and Toyota has now begun producing in Taiwan as well with an annual capacity of sixty thousand Coronas and Corollas (Ward's Communications, Inc., 1987, pp. 75, 77). With Taiwan's rising per capita income (over $5,500 in 1987), the domestic sales of subcompacts and larger cars is likely to show a sizable increase. To encourage additional foreign investments, the government has dropped its requirement that foreign firms export 50 percent of their production, and it has relaxed its former policy of insisting that auto manufacturers use at least 70 percent locally made parts.

Taiwan has been far more successful in fostering a competitive domestic auto parts industry that has considerable export potential. There are problems here as well, however. Most of Taiwan's two thousand auto parts firms in the mid-1980s are family businesses that are able to respond quickly to shifting consumer demand, but they are less able to invest in research and expensive production machinery needed to improve their design capability and technological sophistication. Most of Taiwan's auto exports are add-on accessories or spare parts sold in the after-market; relatively few of Taiwan's auto parts exporters have major original equipment manufacturer (OEM) contracts. Taiwan also is heavily dependent on the U.S. market, which accounted for nearly 60 percent of its auto exports in 1985 (Tank, 1986, pp. 30–31). This makes auto exports vulnerable to retaliatory protectionist legislation.

In sum, this brief overview of the motor vehicle industry in the Latin American and East Asian NICs shows how the common pressures toward internationalization in both production and trade have produced distinct results in each country. South Korea and Brazil both have stressed exports of finished vehicles, but these are based on different kinds of corporate strategies and structures. South Korea's large, integrated domestic auto companies have the resources to fund both long-term investment and product development at home and overseas, while Brazil's auto exports are the result of the global sourcing strategies of American, Japanese, and European TNCs. Taiwan and Mexico, on the other hand, have tended to emphasize a component-supplier role in the global auto industry, with close ties to the U.S. market. Whereas Mexico has implemented this strategy through TNC intrafirm supply networks, Taiwan has relied heavily on the efforts of small domestic auto parts companies who do not have major captive markets. Thus these differences in the mode of incorporation of each of the NICs into the global automotive industry are a product of variations in industrial structure at the national level, the competitive strategies of the leading manufacturers in the global automobile industry, and the role of automobiles in secondary ISI and EOI.

CONCLUSIONS

Foreign capital, private and public, has played very different roles in the Latin American and East Asian NICs (see Stallings, chap. 3, this volume). The TNCs that came into Mexico and Brazil to help implement secondary ISI initially were satisfied to supply protected domestic markets, while some of these same firms entered the newly established export processing zones in Taiwan and South Korea in the late 1960s and early 1970s to produce manufactured items for export. The lesson here would seem to be that economically powerful TNCs, under the right conditions, can be induced to contribute to either ISI or EOI development objectives.

Brazil and Mexico had some success in the 1970s requiring foreign automobile manufacturers to generate increasing export revenues as a condition for continuing to supply their domestic markets (Gereffi and

Evans, 1981). Transnational corporations substantially expanded their export efforts in the 1980s in response to the economic imperatives created by the reorganization of the global motor vehicle industry and the fiscal incentives offered by the Brazilian and Mexican governments to promote increased automotive exports. Brazil has made fewer concessions than Mexico in terms of reductions in local content requirements for car producers, which helps explain why Brazil has managed to run a sizable positive trade balance for its automotive industry since 1975, while Mexico has had an alarming growth in its trade deficit in this sector since the early 1970s (see Jenkins, 1987, p. 217).

In terms of the predominant role played by local private capital in East Asia, South Korea seems to have a key organizational edge over Taiwan. Both countries remain very dependent on the U.S. market for nearly half of their exports. Thus American protectionist pressures are a real threat to their continued economic prosperity. In South Korea's case, the *chaebols* have the capability to jump over these protectionist barriers by adopting an aggressive investment and marketing strategy overseas. In Taiwan, however, the main channel for exports (with the exception of the auto parts industry) has been OEM procurement contracts with big foreign buyers, mainly in the United States. A relatively conservative estimate would place OEM sales at 60 to 70 percent of Taiwan's total exports, and this figure is probably higher in selected industries (like footwear). In the OEM market, Taiwan suppliers are basically selling components or generic finished goods to clients who put their own brand names on these products when they reach their final destination. If these buyers decide to shift their orders elsewhere (e.g., because of rising labor costs in Taiwan), Taiwanese producers may not have sufficient international marketing networks and skills to succeed on their own.

There are different levels at which one can compare national development experiences. One can emphasize commonalities among the NICs, or alternatively one can focus on interregional or intraregional differences. This chapter has focused on intraregional variations among the four main Latin American and East Asian NICs. Industrial structure has been our central concern. At this level, each one of the Latin American and East Asian NICs is quite distinctive. Although this variety in industrial structures does not allow easy generalizations applicable to all the NICs or even to the regional pairs, it is at the level of economic institutions that much of what is useful to other countries can be learned.

REFERENCES

Arnold, Walter. 1989. "Bureaucratic Politics, State Capacity, and Taiwan's Automobile Industrial Policy." *Modern China* 15, no. 2, pp. 178–214.

CEPD (Council for Economic Planning and Development). 1988. *Taiwan Statistical Data Book, 1988.* Taipei.

Clifford, Mark. 1990. "The Engine Is Straining: South Korea's Carmakers Run into Difficulties." *Far Eastern Economic Review*, January 18, pp. 35–38.

———. 1988. "Breaking Up Is Hard to Do: South Korean Chaebol Still Thrive Despite Official Disapproval." *Far Eastern Economic Review*, September 29, p. 32.

CommonWealth. 1988. "The 1,000 Biggest Manufacturing Companies in Taiwan" (in Chinese). Taipei. July 1, pp. 111–12.

Expansión. 1988. "Las empresas individuales mas importantes de México." Mexico City. August 17, pp. 98–101.

Fortune. 1988. "The International 500." August 1, pp. D7–D31.

Gereffi, Gary. 1989a. "Development Strategies and the Global Factory." *Annals of the American Academy of Political and Social Science*, no. 505, pp. 92–104.

———. 1989b. "Rethinking Development Theory: Insights from East Asia and Latin America." *Sociological Forum* 4, no. 4, pp. 505–33.

Gereffi, Gary, and Peter Evans. 1981. "Transnational Corporations, Dependent Development, and State Policy in the Semiperiphery: A Comparison of Brazil and Mexico." *Latin American Research Review* 16, no. 3, pp. 31–64.

Haggard, Stephan, and Tun-jen Cheng. 1987. "State and Foreign Capital in the East Asian NICs." In *The Political Economy of the New Asian Industrialism*, edited by Frederic C. Deyo. Ithaca, N.Y.: Cornell University Press.

Hamilton, Gary G., and Nicole Woolsey Biggart. 1988. "Market, Culture, and Authority: A Comparative Analysis of Management and Organization in the Far East." *American Journal of Sociology* 94, Supplement on Organizations and Institutions, pp. 52–94.

Hamilton, Gary G., and Kao Cheng-shu. 1987. "The Institutional Foundations of Chinese Business: The Family Firm in Taiwan." Unpublished manuscript.

Hamilton, Gary G., Marco Orrú and Nicole Woolsey Biggart. 1987. "Enterprise Groups in East Asia: An Organizational Analysis." *Financial Economic Review* (Tokyo), no. 161, pp. 78–106.

IMF (International Monetary Fund). 1988. *International Financial Statistics.* Washington, D.C.: IMF. August.

Jenkins, Rhys. 1987. *Transnational Corporations and the Latin American Automobile Industry.* Pittsburgh, Pa.: University of Pittsburgh Press.

Latin American Weekly Report. 1988. "Slim Mexican Auto Industry Boosts Exports: Foreign Sales Soar While Local Market Shrinks Further." May 12, p. 52.

MVMA (Motor Vehicle Manufacturers Association of the United States). 1989. *World Motor Vehicle Data*, 1989 ed. Detroit: MVMA.

Newfarmer, Richard, ed. 1985. *Profits, Progress and Poverty: Case Studies of International Industries in Latin America.* Notre Dame, Ind.: University of Notre Dame Press.

Tank, Andrew. 1986. "Made in Taiwan: Will Taiwan Be Asia's Next Automotive Powerhouse?" *Automotive News*, September 29, pp. 29–31.

Visão. 1988. "Quem é quem na economia brasileira—as 200 maiores." São Paulo, Brazil. August 31, pp. 54-59.

Ward's Communications, Inc. 1989. *Ward's Automotive Yearbook 1989*. Detroit: Ward's Communications, Inc.

———. 1987. *Ward's Automotive Yearbook 1987*. Detroit: Ward's Communications, Inc.

Winter, Drew. 1989. "The Land of Great Promise Opens Up: Mexico Soon Could Become a Major Player." *Ward's Auto World*, June, pp. 26–29.

World Bank. 1989. *World Development Report 1989*. New York: Oxford University Press.

CHAPTER 5

How Societies Change Developmental Models or Keep Them: Reflections on the Latin American Experience in the 1930s and the Postwar World

Robert R. Kaufman

EVER SINCE the societies of Latin America began to expand their role as exporters of primary products in the late nineteenth century, issues related to inward- and outward-oriented models of development have been an important feature of that region's political life. This chapter examines two turning points in the conflicts surrounding these models: (1) the Depression and early 1940s, a watershed period in the acceleration of import-substituting industrialization (ISI), and (2) the first several decades after the end of World War II, from 1945 to the 1960s, a time in which ISI objectives were articulated as explicit components of state development policy. Although the changes unfolding in these decades can obviously be analyzed from a number of different angles, the emphasis here will be on the way that developmental paths were influenced by variations in the state initiatives and political coalitions that emerged within the region. On the one hand, we will look at the political forces influencing the ways in which ISI accelerated in the 1930s and 1940s. On the other, we will examine the reasons why, during a postwar period of expanding international trade, the emphasis continued to be on the diversification of "inward-looking" models of development.

Six countries will serve as the main empirical points of reference. Argentina, Brazil, and Mexico—the countries with the largest domestic markets—will receive the most extensive treatment. In addition we will refer to Chile, Colombia, and Uruguay. Inclusion of the smaller economies will enable us to consider a fuller range of ISI experiences and to explore the influence of factors not directly related to size.

Despite major differences in economic parameters and political histories, these six societies were the earliest and most extensive ISI industrializers in the region. Prior to the Depression, export-led growth in each of these countries had already generated substantial domestic markets and urban-based manufacturing sectors. This in turn provided the basis for roughly comparable periods of industrialization after 1929: a more or less "spontaneous" substitution of consumer nondurables in the 1930s;

a more deliberate extension of this pattern from about 1945 to 1955; and (in every case but Uruguay) movement into consumer durables and producers goods during the 1950s and 1960s. In every country—even those with very small domestic markets—both policy emphasis and economic outcomes remained primarily inward-oriented until the late 1960s. Such parallels offer a broad ground of comparison against which we can trace patterns of alliance and conflict among four sets of actors: (1) the agricultural-mercantile groups in control of the principal export staples; (2) "anti-oligarchical" coalitions, based in popular sector groups and rival agrarian interests; (3) state elites—the military officers and civilian technocrats within the state apparatus; and (4) national and international industrial capitalists, which began to acquire increasing political importance from the 1940s onward.

Discussion of the role played by these forces in the shaping of development models will be organized under three broad headings:

The first portion of the chapter will focus on the political and economic responses to the shocks of the Depression. Far from providing an economic basis of inclusionary politics, ISI was frequently sponsored during this period by conservative governments in societies still dominated by agro-exporting interests. On the other hand, post-Depression conflicts over distributive politics were conditioned in important ways by the differences in the kinds of balances struck between export interests and government officials, as well as by the way the ruling coalitions dealt with perceived threats from the popular sector.

The second section of the chapter traces cross-national variations in the way ISI models were consolidated and extended after World War II. Although I will refer briefly to the bureaucratic-authoritarian (BA) experiences of the 1960s and 1970s, the primary emphasis will be on the years between 1945 and 1960, when a series of pivotal policy choices regarding inflation and the overvaluation of exchange rates had an important impact on the overall political and economic effects of ISI models.

The last section of the chapter explores the question of an alternative choice that might have been made during the postwar period: namely, the possibility of a turn toward export-oriented industrialization (EOI) that eventually became the hallmark of the Asian NICs. Since authoritarian controls have been important concomitants of EOI models in both Asia and Latin America, it is not at all clear that the failure to shift in such a direction was necessarily a bad thing. On the other hand, in the Asian version of this shift—unlike the drastic neoconservative experiments that later surfaced in Argentina and Chile—state promotional policies and credit inducements were pivotal in allowing the Asian economies to capitalize on the expanding world trade opportunties of the 1960s (Haggard and Moon, 1983; Haggard and Chen, 1987). Perhaps if Latin American industrializers had also moved earlier along similar lines, they could have avoided some of the shocks and dislocations of subsequent decades (Geisse and Kim, 1988). Either way, the EOI option deserves to be considered as an important road not taken.

A brief chapter such as this one obviously has no hope of providing definitive statements about such issues for so many countries over such a long period of time. Nevertheless, the overviews and explanatory sketches provided in the pages below do highlight some general themes that can be advertised briefly in advance:

1. The shift to ISI models marked certain important broad changes in the *context* of political struggles. It implied a new framework of tense interdependence between industrial and agro-exporting sectors; a growing power for state elites emerging within this framework; and an increasing use of the state's regulatory apparatus to protect organized interests.

2. On the other hand, the long-term implications of these changes (with respect to growth, equity, political stability, etc.) were shaped by broad conflicts that had been unfolding since early in the century over oligarchic concentrations of power.[1] Put differently, the effects of ISI depended on distributive politics as much as (or more than) an underlying logic of state interests, accumulation, or dependency relations.

3. There were important differences in economic outcomes *within* the framework of ISI models that were attributable in part to the way coalitional politics varied cross-nationally and over time. Indeed, the differences in performance between, say, an Argentina and a Brazil suggest the ongoing need to explain differences within as well as between broad developmental models.

4. Because the assumptions underlying ISI models did allow state officials to respond to a wide variety of short-term interests, a shift toward a new strategy—even before the 1970s—could only have been produced by a major concentration of state power and at a very high sociopolitical cost.

THE TURN TO ISI IN THE 1930s

Although the shocks of the 1929 Depression provide a useful point of departure for a comparative discussion of a shift in economic models, it is important to reiterate that many key components of contemporary political-economic systems had begun to crystalize well before that time. As suggested in the introduction, the acceleration of export-led growth during the latter part of the nineteenth century had already stimulated a significant process of social modernization—including the growth of domes-

---

[1] For possible contrasts to the East Asian cases, see Chen, chap. 6, this volume. For a useful discussion of the state's role in development see Evans et al. (1985).

tic markets, the development of a transport and communications infrastructure, and the emergence of a nucleus of domestic manufacturing firms. In addition, the oligarchic states of the pre-Depression era had also experienced major political transformations, involving both the growth of new military and governmental bureaucracies and the rise of popular-sector movements (Collier and Collier, forthcoming, chap. 3). By 1929, for example, middle-class based movements had dominated Argentina and Uruguay for fifteen years or more; Chile's parliamentary oligarchy had been displaced by Arturo Alessandri and Carlos Ibáñez; and the Porfiran state in Mexico had been shattered by two decades of civil war and revolutionary consolidation.

But if the modern histories of the ISI countries did not begin with the Depression, the shocks of that era did alter the course of their development in several important ways. First, the drastic deterioration in external terms of trade during the 1930s did stimulate new shifts of investment and labor resources into home industries, which produced important changes in the structure of the economy. Manufacturing growth led the expansion of GDP as a whole, usually for the first time; and while the ratio of imports to GDP dropped substantially, the share of import-substituting industries expanded[2] (see table 5.1). The depression also encouraged an

TABLE 5.1
Changes in Industrial and Trade Structure, 1929–1947

	Industrial Output as percent GDP			Imports as percent GDP		
	1929	1937	1947	1929	1937	1947
Argentina	22.8	25.6	31.1	17.8	13.0	11.7
Brazil	11.7	13.1	17.3	11.3	6.9	8.7
Chile	7.9	11.3	17.3	31.2	13.8	12.6
Mexico	14.2	16.7	19.8	14.2	8.5	10.6
Colombia	6.2	7.5	11.5	18.0	12.9	13.8

Source: Furtado (1970, p. 111).

[2] Industrial growth rates in Brazil and Colombia were especially high, averaging over 6 and 8 percent respectively (as compared with overall GDP rates of about 4 percent). The averages were between 4 and 5 percent in Chile and Uruguay. In Argentina, which adopted relatively restrictive policies in the 1930s, industrial growth rates were only around 3 percent, but still above the 2 percent figure for GDP as a whole (Díaz-Alejandro, 1984, pp. 38–44). In Mexico, where there is a lively debate about the timing of the initial ISI phase, Enrique Cárdenas (1984, p. 233) calculates that "real industrial output increased an average of 6.1% from 1932–1940, accounting for 38 percent of the growth in GDP as a whole."

expansion of the state's economic role—an expansion that both spurred and reflected the structural changes in the economy. Finally, the Depression intensified sociopolitical conflicts evolving since the late 1800s, setting into motion processes of coalition-formation and political rivalries that varied markedly from one country to the next.

This section reviews the way these processes of state-building and sociopolitical realignment interacted with the shifts toward ISI. As background to the discussion of subsequent periods of choice, I would like to highlight several paradoxical aspects of these processes: one was the interplay between the expansion of the scope of the state's economic responsibility and the limited, reactive character of the policy measures that underlay this expansion. The state apparatus that emerged was larger than before, and perhaps more powerful, but still lacking in the capacity for independent, long-term developmental initiatives. The second aspect emphasizes contradictory tendencies in the course of underlying sociopolitical conflicts—on the one hand, the convergence of conflicting sociopolitical forces around specific countercyclical measures; on the other, the exacerbation of unresolved conflicts over political participation and material distribution.

State Expansion in the Depression Era

Among the governments of the ISI countries, the sudden contraction in external financing and export revenues inaugurated an era of emergency experimentation with exchange controls, tariffs, and fiscal deficits. Although by the mid-1930s, there was some awareness that such measures might produce lasting changes in the economy, the overriding concern of state officials was not to promote ISI but to stave off the balance of payments crisis, to maintain public employment, and to defend the interests of politically important constituencies. Nevertheless, as is well known, these measures had crucial countercyclical effects and were pivotal steps in promoting the acceleration of ISI. Carlos Díaz-Alejandro has suggested that the most important effects were produced by the decision to end convertibility of the local currency in the early 1930s, since by raising the costs of imports, the resulting depreciation ratified the worldwide shift of relative prices in favor of nontradable goods.[3] At the same time, of course, by engaging in such steps, governments within the ISI countries were also significantly expanding their own regulatory authority. By the end of the decade, there had been a marked increase in the scope of such activities,

---

[3] In the countries under consideration, the real value of the local currency declined from 30 to 90 percent against the dollar between 1929 and 1934 (Díaz-Alejandro, 1984, p. 24).

as well as in the range of manufacturing, financial, and landowning groups seeking some form of public protection.

For the purpose of understanding the state's role in subsequent choices about economic models, several features of this political transition need to be underlined.

First, on the eve of the Depression, there was wide intraregional variation in the capacity of states to undertake the relatively simple emergency measures described above. The smaller states of the Caribbean and Central America, tied almost totally to the U.S. financial system, followed orthodox policies throughout the Depression era—as did larger enclave economies such as Cuba, Peru, and Venezuela (Thorp and Londono, 1984; Bulmer-Thomas, 1984). In the six ISI countries, countercyclical responses to the shocks of the Depression were made possible by earlier growth of state decision-making structures with some capacity to resist external economic pressures and to regulate trade and finance.

Unfortunately, the converging sources of these pre-1929 patterns of state development can only briefly be indicated here. In several societies, efforts to modernize and elaborate a state apparatus were undertaken by local oligarchies themselves, at times in collaboration with foreign technical advisers linked closely to international financial capital.[4] This was the case, for example, with a number of central banking institutions established during the post–World War I era. Orginally intended to eliminate political influence over currency issues and exchange rates, these institutions provided the locus of major new regulatory activities during the Depression (Falcoff and Dolkart, 1975; Platt and Di Tella, 1985; Topik, 1980). Local military establishments often played an even more important role. In Argentina and Brazil, independent and increasingly professionalized military elites had shared considerable political authority with political oligarchies ever since the founding of their modern states in the 1870s and 1880s. By the turn of the century, nationalist currents within the armed forces constituted the most important domestic pressure group favoring state-sponsored industrialization. Finally, in Chile and Mexico, where foreign mining interests were major components of the agro-export sector, earlier anti-oligarchic struggles were important factors in the growth of state power. Especially in Mexico, the degrees of freedom acquired by state elites during the Depression era depended quite directly on the popular support mobilized during the revolutionary civil wars of the 1910–1920 period (Cardoso and Faletto, 1979). To the extent that such convulsive state-building processes were preconditions for the accelera-

---

[4] A seminal line of analysis about the constraints on foreign-owned enclave economies is presented by Fernando Henrique Cardoso and Enzo Faletto (1979, pp. 101–26, 143–48).

tion of ISI in the 1930s, it seems quite misleading to characterize the early phases of the process as "easy."

On the other hand, for state organizations that (however painfully) had already crossed relatively low thresholds of institutional development and international independence, the emergency responses to the shocks of the Depression could be undertaken without extensive changes in existing administrative capabilities. Indeed, the most critical government measures—for example, devaluations, deficit spending, tariffs—primarily affected the aggregate parameters of the local economy, leaving extensive scope within these parameters for private market decisions. Politically, moreover, it was obviously far more convenient to adopt exchange controls and tolerate fiscal deficits than to resist the demands for emergency relief that often came from the most powerful sectors of society.

For these reasons, the Depression-era growth in state authority was on the whole noncontroversial, and occurred in the context of a wide variety of conservative and reformist political coalitions. In virtually every case, the agrarian oligarchy was a major beneficiary of the devaluations mentioned above, as well as of much of the anticyclical fiscal expenditures that helped to maintain domestic demand. At the same time, by the middle of the Depression era, it was becoming increasingly clear that such measures could also advance the goals of nationalist military currents and of the industrial groups—owners and workers—that were emerging by the time of World War II.

What does this imply about the state's role in this and subsequent periods of economic change? I do not wish at this point to enter the thicket of debates in the "state theory" literature over autonomy and instrumentalism. Nevertheless, the familiar patterns reviewed above do imply the need for caution in drawing grand conclusions. By the 1940s and 1950s, the "easy" ISI of the Depression years had provided the basis for widespread efforts at state-led development, rationalized and legitimated by postwar doctrine of the Economic Commission on Latin America (ECLA). But we must proceed cautiously in delineating the actual power and independence of the states that assumed these responsibilities. A good deal depends on the angle of vision from which the issue is approached.

At one level, state elites—that is, civilian technocrats and military officers—had certainly gained influence as individuals and as pressure groups. By the late 1940s, state civilian and military elites in Brazil, Mexico, and Argentina had become the most important source of pressure behind industrializing initiatives—well ahead of the emerging manufacturing class itself (Bennett and Sharpe, 1980; Evans, 1979; Whittaker, 1976). As suggested, even relatively limited concerns with protecting the balance of payments reflected state interests in insulating authority against the uncertainty of market forces (Krasner, 1985).

On the other hand, private groups offered little resistance to the general expansion of this role. Indeed, most such groups—oligarchical interests foremost among them—actively sought public resources and protection as a means to preserve or extend their distributive share of the national income. For this reason, it may be useful to distinguish between state elites—admittedly powerful as pressure groups—and the state apparatus as a whole. As just suggested, the initiatives of the former were extremely important in setting economic changes into motion. Yet the state apparatus could only rarely be fully and coherently mobilized behind such initiatives. Indeed, as this apparatus expanded in size, it became an extremely porous arena of distributive conflict, through which state elites formed a wide variety of alliances with contending groups based in civil society. In the remaining portion of this section, we survey the way such alliances unfolded during the Depression era. In the following section, we will then suggest some ways in which these conditioned variations in ISI models during the 1940s and 1950s.

Patterns of Political Coalition

Before as well as after the Depression, political conflicts within civil society turned primarily on issues of political power and distribution, rather than on the questions of accumulation implied in models of development. But the Depression tended to exacerbate these conflicts. On the one hand, with the collapse of export-based prosperity, it helped to strip away oligarchical claims to hegemony, making it clear that the narrow interests of agro-exporters could no longer be conflated with the interests of society as a whole. This in turn opened the way for accelerated attempts to mobilize middle- and working-class forces behind new ideologies, to capture existing political organizations or to create new ones. Yet even in the face of such mobilizations, agro-exporting oligarchies typically remained economically dominant and politically powerful throughout the Depression and the first several postwar decades, frequently competing with state elites themselves for control of the political system.

Discussion of the ways in which these conflicts unfolded in specific national situations can be organized in terms of three basic patterns: a shift toward reformist governments in Mexico and Colombia; a concentration of state power in Brazil; and more conservative projects of economic modernization in Argentina, Chile, and Uruguay.

In Mexico and Colombia, Depression-era politics were marked by a turn toward the left. In Colombia, the 1930 presidential election brought the Liberals to power for the first time in fifty years. And although coffee and mercantile interests dominated both traditional parties, the Liberal party became a platform from which reform politicians began to reach out for popular support—a process that reached a high-water mark during the administration of Alfonso López (1934–1938). In Mexico, a far more convulsive period of popular mobilization, land reform, and oil nationalization under Lázaro Cárdenas (1934–1940) brought about a much more extensive sociopolitical reorganization of the regime. By the end of the 1930s, a restructured ruling party, now based on organized worker and peasant sectors, helped to consolidate the control of governmental elites over the political system. As we shall see in the next section, this provided an important basis for the kinds of ISI policies adopted in the 1940s. Interestingly, however, despite its later association with nationalism and distributive politics, ISI did not figure directly in attempts to construct new reform-oriented coalitions during this period. On the contrary, the Colombian government under Alfonso López actually initiated a stabilization program in an attempt to bring governmental spending under control; while in Mexico direct concern focused almost exclusively on rural reform and political reorganization, with very little attention to the politics of the industrial sector (Villarreal, 1976; Reynolds, 1970). Thus, as was the case with more conservative regimes elsewhere, the shift to ISI was a largely unplanned and unintended process—the effect of exchange control measures adopted for other purposes. Not until the 1940s, as politics were shifting in more conservative directions, did ISI become an official component of governmental policy.

In Brazil, the 1930 revolution against the Old Republic placed civilian officials and military elites in a position to arbitrate the conflicts between the Paulista coffee planters, their regional landowning rivals, and middle-class groups in the more modernized southern states. By the late 1930s, especially after the *golpe* that established the Estado Novo, the overall balance of power within the system had shifted clearly toward the state elites who controlled the federal government. On the other hand, all upper-class groups gained from the government's efforts to demobilize and control recurrent labor militancy—an objective sought through a considerable application of force in the mid-1930s, and subsequently through the institution of the corporatist labor framework in 1937. Moreover, after an aborted attempt at counterrevolution in 1932, a process of reconciliation between Getúlio Vargas and the Paulistas permitted the latter to recoup much of the political ground it had lost in 1930 vis-à-vis other landed groups and the civilian middle sector.

In this context, import-substitution processes were initiated by a highly conservative constellation of oligarchical and governmental forces. During the 1930s, industry grew at an average rate of over 6 percent a year—one of the highest of the countries under study (Díaz-Alejandro, 1984). But the agro-exporters continued to be the most important beneficiaries of the measures that stimulated this process—for example, the massive government expenditures on coffee stockpiles. And most government officials, including Vargas himself, continued throughout the decade to warn against the risks of changing Brazil's "natural" role as a producer of raw materials (Wirth, 1970; Skidmore, 1967; Dean, 1969).

In Argentina, Chile, and Uruguay, finally, ISI of the Depression era was marked by an even more pronounced shift toward the right. In all three societies, representatives of the old agro-export oligarchies assumed leading positions in the rise of conservative governments seeking to roll back the institutional gains achieved by popular organizations during preceding decades. To understand the sociopolitical implications of the ISI occurring in this context, we need to consider two sets of observations about these governments.

On the one hand, in the context of highly modernized and politically complex Southern Cone societies, even governments with close links to the traditional oligarchy had to incorporate a comparatively wide range of urban-based interests, representing party elites, state officials, and military nationalists, as well as groups of middle-class government workers and some manufacturing interests. In Argentina, foreign industrial companies established in the 1920s not only served as a major force behind Depression-era import substitution, but as an important political ally of some relatively large-scale local manufacturing firms that were also already on the scene. Under these circumstances, political considerations of coalition maintenance, as well as the types of economic incentives referred to above, may have played a role in inducing agro-exporters to accept ISI as a part of a larger conservative project (Falcoff and Dolkart, 1975). In Argentina, as early as 1933, the powerful agriculture minister was already arguing that, through industrialization, "the country should look to itself . . . with its own resources . . . for relief of the present difficulties" (Díaz-Alejandro, 1984, p. 40). And notwithstanding the controversial Roca-Runciman agreements of 1934, leading government officials continued to express such views throughout the Depression era.

But the adaptability implied by these conservative projects of modernization did not extend to the issues of political participation or material distribution that had served as the bases of early popular challenges to oligarchic control. On the contrary, by attempting to suppress such issues, the conservative governments of the 1930s set the stage for new waves of popular mobilization that surged in post-Depression decades. In Chile and Uruguay, constitutional institutions and well-organized centrist political parties placed some constraints on the amplitude of these swings—there were limits to both the conservative retrenchments of the 1930s and subsequent distributive protests. But in Argentina, the exclusionary policies practiced by post-1930s conservative governments—policies that bore a considerable resemblance to those later practiced under

Juan Carlos Onganía—were very much the antecedents of the radical populism that characterized the first part of the Perón era during the middle and late 1940s.

POSTWAR PATTERNS: CROSS-NATIONAL VARIATIONS

The expanding volume of international trade that followed World War II, like the very different kinds of shock produced by the Depression, grafted a new set of choices about economic models onto these ongoing conflicts over distribution of material resources and political power. We can consider these choices in terms of three broad courses of action. First, despite the structural and political changes of the preceding decade, one possibility was to return to models based exclusively on comparative advantage in natural resources. This view was still pressed by unreconciled fractions of the agro-exporting sectors, notwithstanding their earlier acquiescence to Depression-era ISI. Another option might conceivably have been the promotion of exports based on the labor-intensive industries established in the preceding decades. In fact, during the 1940s, Brazilian and Argentine textiles had already had some success in regional markets (see table 5.2). Nevertheless, as we shall discuss more extensively below, EOI models had little serious support until at least the late 1960s. Finally, there was the option of protecting existing manufacturing firms and extending the ISI process into consumer durables and capital goods—the model that actually evolved in the region from the 1940s until the 1960s.

As we shall see more extensively in the next section, a host of international and domestic factors operated during the 1940s and 1950s to weight the scales against the first two of these options and in favor of the third. Shifts toward outward-oriented models were discouraged, among

TABLE 5.2
Exports of Manufactured Goods in Argentina and Brazil

Argentina: Exports of Nontraditional Manufactured Products (annual averages at 1954 prices)		Brazil: Cotton Cloth Exports (kilos)	
1934–1936	15.5	1933	86,807
1937–1939	21.5	1937	686,687
1940–1944	107.1	1940	1,981,734
1945–1946	158.9	1943	25,168,682
1947–1949	46.2	1945	24,246,510
1950–1954	37.2	1947	16,678,215
1955–1959	21.4	1950	1,361,359

Sources: For Argentina, Díaz-Alejandro (1970, p. 263); for Brazil, Stein (1957, p. 194).

other things, by the influence of the ECLA doctrine among nationalist state technocrats[5] and by the region-wide shift in the balance of power away from agro-export interests and toward foreign and domestic industrial capitalists interested in preserving or gaining access to protected markets. Finally, the increasing mobilization of mass groups into politics was an important factor behind decisions to allow increases in domestic prices to outpace exchange rate adjustments—a policy that both subsidized capital imports of import-substituting industries and transfered resources out of the export sector.

But precisely because ISI could be "appropriated" by a wide range of interests, struggles over the implementation of the strategy implied major choices about income distribution, intersectoral relations, and the role of foreign capital and the state. Cross-national variations in the outcome of such struggles occurring "within" the ISI model were thus at least as important as the implications of the export roads not taken. Accordingly, we concentrate here on describing some of the key differences among the three categories of countries already discussed in the preceding section. In each of the three sets of cases, ISI experiences of the 1940s and 1950s were shaped by reactions to the patterns of distributional struggle established during the Depression era.

The Southern Cone: Argentina, Chile, and Uruguay

Predictably, distributive pressures were strongest during the postwar period in the countries dominated most thoroughly by conservative coalitions during the 1930s. The strong waves of broadly based populism that displaced these coalitions in the 1940s reflected reformist claims that had accumulated during the Depression era, as well as the worldwide spread of egalitarian expectations that had emerged at the end of World War II.

As already implied, the distributive surge went farthest in Argentina—the country where earlier oligarchic rule had been particularly transparent. Under Juan Perón, nationalist military officers and government technocrats became somewhat reluctant junior partners in a coalition that attempted to mobilize working-class interests and to link them with small business and white-collar groups. In Uruguay and Chile, where urban-based party elites had played a more extensive role in the conservative Depression-era governments, the swing in populist directions was both less convulsive and less complete. An important turning point in Chile was the brief ascendency of the Popular Front coalition in the early 1940s; in Uruguay, it was marked by a partial resurgence of the reformist,

[5] Interestingly, however, Raúl Prebisch (1984) began to advocate more export-manufacturing sectors by the mid-1950s.

Batllista wing of the Colorado party and by the further extension of the state as a source of employment and patronage.

The common theme in all of these experiences, despite different emphases and varied forms of institutional expression, was the adoption of ISI models as a new basis for an old style of urban-based distributive politics. Argentine blue-collar workers made dramatic gains in income shares during this period, as did the white- and blue-collar bases of the Uruguayan welfare system.[6] Tariff and credit policies also gave strong preferences to national over international manufacturing companies (Díaz-Alejandro, 1970, pp. 265–66). In Chile, where the power of working-class political movements was far more precarious, the situation was more ambiguous. Industrialization policies of the 1940s and 1950s were associated, at least on an ideological plane, with the material aspirations of the white-collar and unionized constituency of the Left and the Radical parties; but in this case, the real gains were more limited and tended to come primarily at the expense of the unorganized urban and rural underclasses (Foxley, 1976).

In all of these cases, a particularly extensive use of overvalued exchange rates and subsidized interest rates (Sheahan, 1980; 1987) was also a reflection in part of the increased political marginalization of agrarian classes that had been in the ascendency in the 1930s. The result economically was recurrent crises produced by external bottlenecks and increasing inflationary pressures. Politically, such crises in turn stimulated periodic efforts to reconstitute antipopulist alliances, linking declining agrarian interests with new centers of transnational manufacturing capital.

Mexico and Colombia

As in the Southern Cone countries, governments of Mexico and Colombia pursued ISI models based on the protection of home industries and the diversion of agro-export earnings toward capital-goods imports. From the 1940s through much of the 1960s, however, the main differences lay in more cautious fiscal and monetary policies, implemented in the context of considerably weaker distributive pressures. From the 1940s through the mid-1950s, the Mexican government actively promoted commercial agriculture and suppressed wages—the exact opposite of the course then being followed under Perón. Both the Colombian and the Mexican governments also attached a high priority to containing domestic inflation (Berry, 1983; Reynolds, 1970). And as John Sheahan

[6] For a recent intepretation emphasizing the post-1955 durability of Perón's redistributive policies, see Ascher (1984).

(1980; 1987) suggests, compared to the Southern Cone, both countries tended to adopt relatively conservative interest rate and trade policies during the 1950s (see table 5.3). For the most part, overall growth curves also tended to be higher in the two "northern" countries during the 1940s and 1950s.

Historical-geographical circumstances provide an important part of the explanation for these contrasts. Colombia's macroeconomic conservatism, for example, stems in part from memories of the runaway inflation experienced during the Thousand Days War, which had an traumatizing effect similar to Germany's post–World War I hyperinflation. Fear of the recurrence of this episode strongly shaped the policies of both the populist governments of the 1930s and the more conservative administrations of later years (Ocampo, 1984, pp. 125–26). In Mexico, the need to avoid capital flight across the long border with the United States imposed a special incentive to stabilize prices and exchange rates and to maintain relatively high domestic rates of interest. The stabilization and devaluation measures of the late 1940s and early 1950s were clearly influenced by such considerations and contributed to the long period of "stabilizing development" that stretched into the late 1960s. At the same time, public investments in rural roads and irrigation during the 1940s stimulated agricultural export production, which grew at or above the rate of GDP throughout the 1940s and much of the 1950s (Gomez, 1964; Herrera, 1955).

TABLE 5.3
Selected Postwar Economic Indicators

	Annual GDP Growth (1945–1960)	Annual Inflation (1955–1960)	Avg. Tariff on Semi-Manufacturing and Consumer Durables (1957–1959)	Excess Rate of Inflation Over Interest Rates (1958–1960)
Argentina	2.1	22.0	139	17.5
Chile	3.3	38.0	96	8.4
Uruguay	2.1	10.0	—	—
Brazil	5.7	17.0	143	21.0
Mexico	6.2	8.0	58	2.0
Colombia	4.2	9.0	48	3.5

Sources: For growth and inflation, Kaufman (1979, pp. 218–19); for tariff and excess rate, Sheahan (1980, p. 270).

On the other hand, the capacity to pursue such objectives, problematic in the best of circumstances, depended as well on the changing balance of domestic political forces. One important contrast with the Southern Cone cases concerns the timing of these domestic struggles relative to changing international opportunities. In the Southern Cone, the opening of international trade opportunities during the 1940s coincided, as we have seen, with a swing toward the anti-oligarchical popular movements. In Mexico and Colombia, postwar import substituting policies were imposed in the context of a swing toward the right—away from the distributive regimes installed in the second half of the 1930s and toward far more conservative administrations. While the underlying investment priorities of these governments remained similar to those of the Southern Cone, there were fewer political inhibitions in forcing urban popular sector groups to bear the costs of controlling the inflation-overvaluation impediments to traditional exports.

Finally, the economic patterns established in the postwar era were also facilitated by the kinds of party systems that had emerged from political struggles of earlier decades. In Mexico, the popular mobilizations under Cárdenas consolidated the role of the governing party, the PRI, as the legitimating base of the political system, providing state officials with the leverage to alter the economic orientations of the regime. By 1940, Cárdenas's successors could move toward political and economic accommodation with commercial agricultural and mining interests in the reformed agrarian sector—much of which had now come under the control of the politico-military leaders who had fought in the civil wars.

In Colombia, the traditional party system encouraged similar patterns of intersectoral accommodation, although in very different ways. Although the Liberal reforms of the 1930s did help to provide some opening to popular sector forces, it also led to profound ideological splits within the Liberal party itself, and from there to the murderous interparty *violencia* of the 1940s and early 1950s (Wilde, 1978). On the other hand, because the coffee elites exercised such important positions within both major parties, the interparty violence tended to be directed away from distributive issues—and indeed, toward a reinforcement of grassroots loyalties toward the traditional parties themselves. Thus, even during the worst periods of political polarization, moderate elites at the apex of the party and governmental structure controlled economic decision-making. The National Front agreements of the late 1950s consolidated this control, reinforcing an already established pattern of steady growth rates and low levels of inflation. During the late 1960s, these conditions in turn made it easier for government officials to experiment with minidevaluations and other incremental policy adjustments that allowed Colombia to become the first country in the region to promote the expansion of industrial exports (Berry, 1983; Morawitz, 1981).

State Power in Brazil

To understand the political basis of Brazil's postwar policy, we must refer back to several characteristics of the complex balancing of social forces that facilitated the growth of the central state during the 1930s. As noted in the preceding section, after 1932, the Paulista coffee elite did begin to gain ground against its regional rivals. But this could be accomplished only with the assistance of federal officials and military officers whose mediating role gave them an increasing measure of independence from any of the competing regional oligarchies. In contrast to the oligarchic resurgence in Argentina, therefore, Paulista control over the state apparatus itself continued to decline.

This shift in the balance of power between state elites and conflicting oligarchic groups, in turn, also facilitated greater state control over the popular sector. The institutional cornerstone of this control was the labor code of the Estado Novo, which provided for state financing and supervision of the union movement (Collier, 1982; Erickson,1977). Until the end of the Depression years, the corporatist structures established under this legislation were used primarily to repress and demobilize an independent union movement that had become increasingly militant in the mid-1930s. With the establishment of a competitive electoral process in the mid-1940s, however, state officials allied with Vargas also began to use public resources as a means of mobilizing popular support from above (Skidmore, 1967).

The economic policies of the postwar republic reflected these balances of power, with military elites and civilian technocratic factions operating as the dominant centers of shifting alliances among populist and anti-populist social forces. Even under the economically liberal Eurico Gaspar Dutra administration (1946–1951), the power exercised by state authorities tended to place export interests at a disadvantage. During the first several years of his administration, Dutra did dismantle import controls established under the Estado Novo, presumably as a reflection of his commitment to market-oriented policies. On the other hand, his administration sustained an increasingly overvalued exchange rate, which of course proved to be a bonanza for importers and upper-middle class consumers. The moment of truth came with the predictable foreign exchange crisis of 1947, when the government decided to reimpose import controls rather than to devalue. The primary impulse for this decision, as with so many others before and since, appears to have been the inclination of state elites to expand their administrative control when market uncertainties threaten to undermine their authority. It was an incremental defense of institutional interests, whose long-term consequences for either overall questions of state power or other social forces were not fully understood. Nevertheless, it marked an important point of consolidation for a pattern that was to persist for several more decades, reaffirming the threatened position of import-substituting industries and continuing the high implicit tax on the export sector (Leff, 1968, pp. 9–35; Skidmore, 1967, pp. 69–71).

At the same time, in contrast to Argentina, state enterprises and private industrial capitalists—rather than workers—were the principal beneficiaries of this tax on exports. By the mid-1950s, the "tri-pe" alliance described so well by Peter Evans had already been consolidated as the basis of the move into "deeper" forms of import-substitution during the Kubitschek years, 1956–1960 (Evans, 1979). Conversely, as in the Estado Novo period, the combination of corporatist control and military force continued to circumscribe the scope of populist appeals, with upsurges of distributive mobilization contributing to the ouster of Vargas himself in 1954 and to the much more drastic imposition of a bureaucratic-authoritarian regime a decade later.

ROADS NOT TAKEN: WHY NO TURN TO INDUSTRIAL EXPORT MODELS?

From the 1940s through the 1960s, all of the industrializing countries of the region followed a trajectory roughly parallel to the one just described for Brazil. During the early postwar years, the primary emphasis was on extending the "light" industrial phase of ISI, although in some instances there was also considerable public investment in infrastructure and in intermediate products such as steel. When the opportunities for the substitution of consumer nondurables declined in the early 1950s, attempts were then made to move into consumer durables and capital goods investment by foreign companies and state enterprises. These import-substituting choices implicitly precluded industrial export models of the sort later adopted in Asia.

Since such models were not pursued, of course, we can only speculate about their viability or potential consequences. Despite the brief surge in Argentine and Brazilian regional textile exports during the mid-1940s, there is no way to know whether such manufactures could have penetrated U.S. or European markets before the trade liberalization agreements of the 1960s.[7] Even if this had been possible, it is not at all clear

[7] For a pessimistic assessment of the prospects for postwar agricultural exports, see Fodor (1975). On the other hand, Carlos Díaz-Alejandro (1970, pp. 263–64) suggests that even without the war, Argentina did appear to some to be poised on the brink of a substantial increase in manufacturing exports. He cites U.S. trade and government publications in the

that countries like Brazil and Mexico would have been able to improve on their extremely impressive growth performances during that period. Yet even as early as the mid-1950s, some scattered but important international voices—among them Raúl Prebisch (1984)—had begun to attach greater emphasis to the importance of industrial exports. And by the middle of the 1960s, full-fledged export-led growth strategies were already beginning to show important signs of success in Asia. So, the question remains: why the continuation of Latin American ISI models for so long into the 1960s and 1970s?

Some of the cross-regional comparisons with the East Asian cases included in this volume suggest that contrasting developmental choices may be explained in part by interregional differences in the relation between state and social forces.[8] In South Korea and Taiwan, local dominant classes had been battered by colonialism, war, and foreign occupation. After 1945, this opened the way for the consolidation of highly concentrated and autonomous systems of state power that were capable of responding to expanding export opportunities. In Latin America, as we have already suggested, the development of national states coincided in the late nineteenth century with the formation of strong, oligarchic class systems. And although Latin American state officials frequently did acquire some independence for maneuver, their degrees of freedom to alter economic models were continually constrained by the need to deal both with powerful economic classes and their challengers.

Within this context, several other factors also appear relevant to a full explanation of the contrasts: (1) the symbiotic connections between Asian governments and local industries, rather than the arms-length relations that typically prevailed in Latin America; (2) a relatively restricted role for direct foreign investment in Asia, along with more extensive state control of credit flows; (3) a very high Asian dependence on the economically liberal U.S. hegemon for military security and (until the late 1950s) direct economic assistance; and (4) the greater strength of populist movements in Latin America as compared with Asia.

Since it is beyond the scope of this paper to pursue such cross-regional comparisons at length, I will use them as backdrops against which to discuss two related aspects of the unfolding political scene within Latin America itself: (1) the coalitional patterns of ISI discussed in the preceding section and (2) in the context of these underlying coalitional patterns, the

---

late 1930s, for example, predicting significant increases in such products as leather goods and shoes. He also indicates (p. 509) that there were possible opportunities for cotton cloth and other nontraditional products.

[8] Especially relevant contributions are Stallings, chap. 3, and Deyo, chap. 7, both this volume. Also helpful were oral comments by Sung Joo-Han (1986). For an excellent general discussion of issues, see Haggard (1986).

implications of the kinds of incremental decision-making processes that underlay the earlier expansion of the role and power of state authority.

Coalitional Opportunities

To understand the coalitional spaces that conditioned the choices described above, it is important to emphasize the pivotal role played by the agro-export sectors as generators of foreign exchange. As long as traditional commodities provided the basis of crucial industrial imports, ISI was a model that could serve as a useful framework for struggle and coalition among other key socioeconomic interests operating within the system. This, as Gustav Ranis has observed, provides an important point of contrast with the resource-poor East Asian cases, where more restricted commodity export opportunities limited the possibilities of extending the ISI process beyond the "easy" phase and increased the pressure to diversify into industrial exports (Ranis, chap. 8, this volume). But within both regions, of course, the role played by traditional export commodities also depended on the characteristics of the staple itself and on the historic conflicts within and between industrial and export sectors. Regarding Latin America, this argument can be carried farther by using observations sketched in the preceding sections to distinguish between two types of situations: (1) the relatively enduring coalitions of interests that permitted traditional agro-export sectors to underwrite a relatively sustained pattern of ISI growth in Mexico, Colombia, and Brazil; and (2) the more zero-sum distributional struggles of the Southern Cone, characterized by recurrent and severe external bottlenecks.

Among the countries in the first set of cases, the viability of traditional exports (and hence of extended ISI models) was conditioned by at least three sets of interrelated factors operating in the 1940s through the 1960s: First, through very different historical pathways, political conflicts between agro-exporters and urban-based elites were relatively low. A second factor was the low supply elasticity of coffee production in Brazil and Colombia. This meant that unfavorable policies were less likely to have an immediate impact on levels of production.[9] Finally, in all three countries the organization of the state or party structures discouraged competing segments of the elite from attempting to mobilize populist pressures against the export sector.

The foreign exchange generated under such conditions, while subject to recurrent scarcity, nevertheless facilitated processes through which industrial investments and distributional alliances could be sustained

---

[9] Nathaniel Leff (1967) notes that Brazil maintained its share of the world coffee market during this period, while other agricultural and nontraditional exports suffered.

within an inward-oriented growth framework. As long as they could obtain the necessary capital inputs, both national firms and multinational subsidiaries had clear preferences for operating within the context of protected home markets—rather than assuming the risks of entering new markets and/or competing with subsidiaries established elsewhere. Such a system of alliances, as just noted, presupposed considerable control of the popular sector and was arguably suboptimal from the point of view of employment-generation. Still, the expansion generated by this type of ISI did create the material resources for systems of patronage that could be extended to organized white- and blue-collar interests within the Colombian and Mexican parties and to the constitutencies of Brazil's more diffuse populist movements. Finally, I suspect that even for traditional agro-export classes, the costs of overvaluation (which could be diffused among *all* producers of exportable goods) was preferable to more selective taxes directed specifically at them (Hirschman, 1971, p. 118).

In these societies, in other words, ISI models were sustained primarily because they worked well for the capitalist, military, and technocratic groups and political elites that dominated their respective political systems. An important indication of this is the continuing inward-oriented emphasis adopted by the tri-pe alliance of state, multinational, and large-scale local capital that dominated Brazil's exclusionary BA regime in the period after 1964 (Foxley, 1983). The economic decision makers of this period did, it is true, attempt to address chronic foreign exchange shortages by minidevaluations and export subsidies. In the late 1960s, this led to a significant diversification into manufacturing and other nontraditional exports (Kaufman, 1979). But the turn toward the outside was deliberately cautious and partial—more appropriately characterized as "export-adequate" than "export-led" growth (Fishlow, 1985). Even after the late 1960s, the Brazilian economy remained primarily inward-oriented, with the main emphasis on the production of consumer durables and capital goods for the domestic market. Tariff barriers were kept much higher than was later the case in Argentina and Chile, and the role of the state enterprise sector continued to expand dramatically. As late as 1973, manufactured exports represented less than 5 percent of total industrial output, whereas the figures for South Korea, Singapore, and Taiwan ranged between 40 and 50 percent (see table 5.4).

In the Southern Cone countries, different combinations of domestic conflicts and staple characteristics implied more severe balance-of-payments constraints on the postwar extension of ISI. First, the political antagonisms of the Depression era exacerbated sectoral conflicts, creating particularly significant pressure on exportable agricultural products. Second, in Argentina and Uruguay grain and livestock producers could (in contrast to the coffee producers in Brazil and Colombia) respond quite

TABLE 5.4
Share of Manufactured Exports in Total Manufacturing Output

	1960	1966	1973
Argentina	0.8	0.9	3.6
Brazil	0.4	1.3	4.4
Chile	3.0	4.1	2.5
Colombia	0.7	3.0	7.5
Mexico	2.6	2.9	4.4
South Korea	0.9	13.9	40.5
Singapore	11.2	20.1	42.6
Taiwan	8.6	19.2	49.9

Source: Belassa (1975, p. 36).
Note: Data for Uruguay not available.

quickly to changing price signals—by reducing investment or diverting products into home markets.[10] Finally, in all three Southern Cone societies, popularly-based organizations and parties were more independent than in Mexico, Colombia, and Brazil and in a much stronger position to extend or protect their distributive share of resources. It is not too difficult to imagine why sociopolitical coalitions formed in such circumstances tended to be relatively unstable or why distributive conflicts within the ISI framework might escalate to very high levels. And it is, in turn, precisely for this reason that it was so difficult to find a political formula for altering the basic ISI model, even in the context of increasingly severe foreign exchange and stagflation crises. In the cases of Mexico, Brazil, and Colombia, fairly stable patterns of intersectoral political relations reduced the incentive to alter relatively successful experiences with ISI. In the Southern Cone, on the other hand, political antagonisms made it difficult to do so.

To explore this further, it may be useful to consider the kinds of coalitional struggles that unfolded in Argentina from 1949 to 1951, after the depletion of wartime reserves undermined the ISI model that sustained Perón's original coalition of labor and local business, and military nationalists. Guillermo O'Donnell provides an important interpretation of the

[10] This was obviously not the case with Chile's copper industry, where high fixed costs made it difficult to adjust production to price fluctuations in the short term. On the other hand, the Chilean wheat and livestock producers occupied an analagous position to their Argentine and Uruguayan counterparts. For a seminal discussion of the political implications of export staples, see Hirschman (1981).

stop-go cycles that followed, basing his analysis on the periodic formation and reconstitution of two types of coalitions: (1) an expansionist coalition—formed around the interests of urban wage workers, small local industrialists, and an "upper bourgeoisie" comprised of large-scale national industrialists and multinational companies—which eventually ran up against external bottlenecks to the continued importation of capital equipment and industrial raw materials; and (2) a "devaluation/stabilization" alliance between the upper bourgeoisie and the Pampean oligarchy, which lasted until the contractions caused by the transfer of resources away from local markets reduced balance of payments pressures and allowed the upper bourgeoisie to shift its support back to policies based on an expansion of domestic demand (O'Donnell, 1978).

What prevented one of these coalitions—or some alternative one—from moving instead toward industrial export promotion? On the national populist side, a combination of economic interests and historic political antagonisms served as important impediments: during upswings of the ISI cycle, national capitalists had little incentive to undergo the painful readjustments that would have been necessary to compete internationally; and on downswings, the Pampean oligarchy and the upper bourgeoisie were in a far better position to control the transfer of resources produced by devaluations. On the other hand, despite their liberal orientations, the alternative alliances formed by these groups lacked the interest or the staying power necessary to back a turn toward industrial export models. For the Pampean oligarchy, devaluations were a means to reorient production toward traditional international specialization. For the upper bourgeoisie, still oriented primarily toward the domestic market, support for devaluation/stabilization packages persisted only through short-term crisis situations. In the absence of strong state initiatives and incentives, they thus tended to withdraw from the coalition well before it had time to sustain a realignment of the economy.

The failure of Argentina's first bureaucratic-authoritarian attempt to sustain such initiatives illustrates how difficult it was for state elites to break out of such coalitional stalemates. Under Juan Carlos Onganía (1966–1970), an exclusionary alliance of technocrats and large industrialists confronted *both* popular sector groups and the agrarian oligarchy by imposing a major devaluation and a high direct tax on traditional exports. For a few years, these measures did encourage a significant surge in industrial exports—although as in Brazil, the primary orientation of the model continued to point inward. But by 1969, authorities had alienated not only the popular sector, but smaller industrialists, the agrarian oligarchy, and much of the military establishment itself. Worker and student protests in the city of Córdoba during 1969 and 1970 dramatized the regime's increasing political isolation; and although the protests themselves were put down, the authoritarian project collapsed when the military itself decided it was unwilling to increase the level of coercion needed to maintain Onganía in power (O'Donnell, 1982).

Processes of Choice and the Role of the State

This brings us to the role of the state elites who so often operated at the center of these coalitional conflicts. What factors impeded their capacity to undertake more dynamic and sustained initiatives to change economic models? To what extent were Argentine- and Chilean-style repressions "necessary" components of attempts to overcome such impediments? Although there is, of course, no way to answer such questions conclusively, the incrementalist patterns built into earlier processes of economic choice do offer a basis for some speculative conclusions.

The most important aspect of the earlier ISI choices—one frequently obscured by broad discussion of ideologies and structures—is that the development and maintenance of economic models were largely the by-products of short-term improvisations rather than the direct outcome of grand designs. This was particularly true from the Depression to the end of the 1940s. Key decisions involving the shift to ISI—to end convertibility in the early 1930s and to place exchange controls on overvalued currencies in the postwar years—were made in response to immediate balance-of-payments pressures, without a clear understanding of their long term consequences. Of course, as noted above, considerations of economic nationalism and state control did broadly influence the direction of such choices, as did the anticipated reaction of key social interests. But, if I can use a distinction more familiar in other contexts, this was more a reflection of a "mentality" than of a coherent and driving set of beliefs about the need for state-directed development (Linz, 1964). The 1950s and 1960s did, of course, witness the fuller articulation of "developmentalist" ideologies, along with an increasingly sophisticated application of economic theory to policy choices. But the developmentalist ideologies were themselves constructed as more systematic extensions of activities already initiated in earlier decades. And even as economic policy grew more self-conscious and "strategic," it typically built extensively on earlier decisions—as we saw, for example, in the case of the first bureaucratic-authoritarian experiences of the 1960s. Finally, we should not ignore the fact that even after the 1950s, crisis management, miscalculation, and experimentation continued to play an important role in the development of economic policy.

One important point to be drawn from these considerations is that it is difficult to lay the "blame" for the failure to shift to EOI predominately at the door of ideological rigidity, or on a statist impulse to economic control (Leff, 1968). Even in the 1950s and 1960s, well after state-sponsored "developmentalism" had become a part of the political scene, it is doubtful that such factors constituted overwhelming impediments to a change of course. During the early 1950s, for example, even Juan Perón was willing to abandon his economic nationalism for a more "liberal" approach (Skidmore, 1977).

The problem—if it can really be called that—was not too much state ideology, but too much pragmatism in selecting policies that most clearly reflected the converging short-term interests of state officials themselves and of their key constitutencies. And most of these interests—including those of the "liberal" agro-exporters and multinational industrialists— were framed in the context of tense interdependence of new home manufacturers and old commodity exports. Incrementalism and pragmatism, it appears (Wade, chap. 9, this volume), also guided much of the decision-making in the Asian cases as well. But in Asia, as I have indicated above, state elites evidently operated in the context of less pressure from conflicting business, labor, and agrarian interests, and with greater leverage for channeling private investment decisions (Wade, forthcoming; Zysman, 1983). This made it possible over time for relatively limited choices to cumulate into significant reorientations of the economic system. In Latin America, where state elites were more vulnerable to cross-cutting sectoral and class pressures, incremental decisions were more likely to offset each other—or at least to limit the scope and degree of systemic change.

The overall consequences of such a pattern depended very much on the larger political balances of forces sketched above. In situations like the one described in Argentina, short-time horizons in the implementation of ISI policies had severe long-term costs, particularly when it was so frequently intermixed with strident confrontations and exclusionary practices at other levels of the political system. On the other hand, well before the 1970s, a major change of economic models implied a drastic restructuring of state and societal relations—with costs potentially far higher than the ones involved in the shifts to and maintenance of ISI.

In the first place, for governments in relatively high-growth ISI countries (and this meant Brazil, Mexico, and Colombia from the 1950s through much of the 1970s), efforts to engineer a major shift in economic models implied replacing something that already appeared to be working relatively well—a task for philosopher kings not politicians. But even in societies that experienced bitter zero-sum struggles during the 1950s and 1960s, state-induced changes in economic models faced problems very different from the ones in the Depression era. In the 1930s, governmental measures frequently met the immediate needs of groups with different long-term objectives. In the postwar decades, state officials seeking to stimulate a move toward EOI had to pursuade competing groups to supersede conflicting short-term distributional interests in order to realize potential longer-term collective benefits. For groups asked to take such risks—as well as for government officials who sought to deflect their oppositions—it was generally more prudent to stick with the known evils of existing developmental models.

It is also plausible that instead of shrinking the state's economic role, a shift toward EOI would have involved considerable new strains on officials' capacity for economic administration. In his classic study of import-substitution, Albert Hirschman (1971) has pointed generally to the need for new forms of public assistance to induce private sector firms out of protected home markets. Colin Bradford's (1984; plus chap. 2, this volume) studies of the Asian cases have emphasized the pivotal role played by supply-side "micro-policies" in credit, research and development, and marketing. And although the drive toward industrial exports was more limited in Latin America in the late 1960s, supply-oriented pressures and inducements played a crucial role in important cases involving multinationals (Bennett and Sharpe, 1985). Of course, a shift away from ISI might also have involved an arrest (or shrinkage) of the state's growing role in other areas (for example, exchange controls and selective protection). But there is no way to tell in the abstract whether the net change would have been in the direction of more or less state activism—particularly since many of the key ISI policies involved no more than the manipulation of a few broad fiscal and monetary instruments. All this, of course, leaves aside the question of the mobilization of new coercive resources that might well have been necessary to deal with the "transitional" disruptions.

Finally, given the strength of the organized business and labor interests rooted in the ISI model, a shift to EOI would have required a major ideological transformation among state elites—not simply the adoption of new economic policies but an uncompromising commitment to impose broad social changes regardless of the cost. It was precisely this sort of transforming zeal that distinguished Chile's "Chicago boys" and the neoconservative technocrats in Argentina from the authoritarian rulers of previous decades (Foxley, 1983; Canitrot, 1980). The latter in some measure accommodated the inward-oriented business and military sectors that backed their rise to power. The Chicago boys, on the other hand, operated on principles that seemed to bear a much closer resemblance to the "totalitarian" assumptions imputed to their Leninist enemies. Like Leninists, their revolutionary mission rested on a claim to scientific knowledge that allowed them, and them alone, to decide on appropriate directions of social change. This assumption, in turn, allowed neoconservative technocrats as well as Leninists to justify the use of repression to root out the bad habits engrained under the old system and to compel people to act rationally in their own best interests.

REFERENCES

Amsden, Alice H. 1985. "The State and Taiwan's Economic Development." In Evans et al. (1985).

Ascher, William. 1984. *Scheming for the Poor*. Cambridge: Cambridge University Press.

Balassa, Bela. 1978. "Export Incentives and Export Performance in Developing Countries: A Comparative Analysis." *Weltwirtschaftliches Archiv* 114, no. 1, p. 36.

Bennett, Douglas, and Kenneth Sharpe. 1985. *Transnational Corporations Versus the State: The Political Economy of the Mexican Auto Industry*. Princeton: Princeton University Press.

———. 1980. "The State as Banker and Entrepreneur." *Comparative Politics*, pp. 165–89.

Berry, Albert. 1983. *Essays on Industrialization in Colombia*. Temple: Center for Latin American Studies, Arizona State University.

Bradford, Colin I., Jr. 1984. "Trade and Structural Change: NICs and Next Tier NICs as Transitional Economies." Paper presented at NBER Conference on The Global Implications of Trade Patterns of East and Southeast Asia, Kuala Lampur, Malaysia, January 4–6.

Bulmer-Thomas, Victor. 1984. "Central America in the Inter-War Period." In Thorp (1984).

Canitrot, Adolfo. 1980. "Discipline as the Central Objective of Economic Policy: An Essay on the Economic Programme of the Argentine Government since 1976." *World Development* 8, no. 11, pp. 913–28.

Cárdenas, Enrique. 1984. "The Great Depression and Industrialization: The Case of Mexico." In Thorp (1984).

Cardoso, Fernando Henrique, and Enzo Faletto. 1979. *Dependent Development in Latin America*. Berkeley, London, and Los Angeles: University of California Press.

Collier, Ruth Berins. 1982. "Popular Sector Incorporation and Political Supremacy: Regime Evolution in Brazil and Mexico." In *Brazil and Mexico: Patterns in Late Development*, edited by Sylvia Ann Hewlett and Richard S. Weinert. Philadelphia: Institute for the Study of Human Issues.

Collier, Ruth Berins, and David Collier. Forthcoming. *Shaping the Political Arena: Critical Junctures, Trade Unions, and the State in Latin America*. Princeton: Princeton University Press.

———. 1984. "Unions, Parties, and Regimes in Latin America: An Introduction." Rutgers University Political Science/Political Economy Workshop, March.

Dean, Warren. 1969. *The Industrialization of São Paulo, 1880–1945*. Austin and London: University of Texas Press.

Díaz-Alejandro, Carlos F. 1984. "Latin America in the 1930's." In Thorp (1984).

Díaz-Alejandro, Carlos F. 1970. *Essays on the Economic History of the Argentine Republic*. New Haven and London: Yale University Press.

Erickson, Kenneth P. 1977. *The Brazilian Corporative State and Working Class Politics*. Berkeley and Los Angeles: University of California Press.

Evans, Peter B. 1979. *Dependent Development: The Alliance of Multinational, State, and Local Capital in Brazil*. Princeton: Princeton University Press.

Evans, Peter B., Dietrich Rueschemeyer, and Theda Skocpol, eds. 1985. *Bringing the State Back In*. Cambridge: Cambridge University Press.

Falcoff, Mark, and Ronald H. Dolkart, eds. 1975. *Prologue to Peron: Argentina in Depression and War, 1930–1943*. Berkeley, London, Los Angeles: University of California Press.

Finch, M. H. J. 1981. *A Political Economy of Uruguay since 1870*. New York: St. Martin's Press.

Fishlow, Albert. 1985. "The State of Latin American Economies." Stanford-Berkeley Occasional Papers in Latin American Studies.

Fodor, Jorge. 1975. "Perón's Policies for Agricultural Exports, 1946–1968: Dogmatism or Common Sense?" In *Argentina in the Twentieth Century*, edited by David Rock. Pittsburgh, Pa.: University of Pittsburgh Press.

Foxley, Alejandro. 1983. *Latin American Experiments in Neoconservative Economics*. Berkeley: University of California Press.

———. 1976. *Income Distribution in Latin America*. Cambridge: Cambridge University Press.

Furtado, Celso. 1970. *Economic Development of Latin America: Historical Background and Contemporary Problems*. Cambridge: Cambridge University Press.

Geisse V., Guillermo, and Hyung Kook Kim. 1988. "The Political Economy of Outward Liberalization: Chile and Korea in Comparative Perspective." Duke University Program in International Economy, working paper no. 35.

Gomez, Rodrigo. 1964. "Estabilidad y Desarollo: El Caso de Mexico," *Banco Nacional de Comercio Exterior*, November, pp. 778–82.

Haggard, Stephan. 1986. "The Newly Industrialized Countries in the International System." *World Politics* 38, no. 2, pp. 343–70.

Haggard, Stephan, and Tun-jen Cheng. 1987. "State and Foreign Capital in the East Asian NICs." In *The Political Economy of the New Asian Industrialism*, edited by Frederic C. Deyo. Ithaca: Cornell University Press.

Haggard, Stephan, and Chung-in Moon. 1983. "The South Korean State in the International Economy: Liberal, Dependent, or Mercantile?" In *The Antimonies of Interdependence*, edited by John G. Ruggie. New York: Columbia University Press.

Han, Sung-Joo. 1986. Oral comments to the Conference of Development Strategies in Latin America and East Asia. Center for U.S.-Mexican Studies and Institute of the Americas, San Diego, Calif., May 4–6.

Herrera, Alberto Norriega. 1955. "Las Devaluaciones monetarias de Mexico, 1938–1954," *Investigacion Economia* 15, no. 1, pp. 149–77.

Hirschman, Albert. 1981. "A Generalized Linkage Approach to Development,

With Special Reference to Staples." In his *Essays in Trespassing, Economics to Politics and Beyond.* Cambridge: Cambridge University Press.

———. 1971. "The Political Economy of Import-Substituting Industrialization." In his *A Bias for Hope, Essays on Development and Latin America.* New Haven and London: Yale University Press.

Kaufman, Robert R. 1979. "Industrial Change and Authoritarian Rule in Latin America: A Concrete Review of the Bureaucratic-Authoritarian Model." In *The New Authoritarianism in Latin America*, edited by David Collier. Princeton: Princeton University Press.

Krasner, Stephen D. 1985. *Structural Conflict: The Third World against Global Liberalism.* Berkeley, Los Angeles, and London: University of California Press.

Leff, Nathaniel H. 1968. *Economic Policy-Making and Development in Brazil, 1947–64.* John Wiley and Sons.

———. 1967. "Export Stagnation and Autarkic Development in Brazil." *Quarterly Journal of Economics* 81, no. 2, pp. 286–301.

Linz, Juan J. 1964. "An Authoritarian Regime: Spain." In *Cleavages, Ideologies, and Party Systems*, edited by E. Allardt and Y. Littune. Helsinki: Westermarck Society.

Morawitz, David. 1981. *Why the Emperor's New Clothes Are Not Made in Colombia: A Case Study in Latin American and East Asian Manufactured Exports.* Oxford University Press for the World Bank.

Ocampo, Jose Antonio. 1984. "The Colombian Economy in the 1930's." In Thorp (1984).

O'Donnell, Guillermo. 1982. *El Estado Bureaucratico Autoritario, 1966–1973: Triunfos, derrotas y crisis.* Editorial Belgrano.

———. 1978. "State and Alliances in Argentina, 1955–1976." *Journal of Development Studies* 15, no. 1, pp. 3–33.

Platt, D. C. M., and Guido Di Tella, eds. 1985. *Argentina, Australia, and Canada: Studies in Comparative Development, 1870–1965.* New York: St. Martin's Press.

Prebisch, Raúl. 1984. "Five Stages in My Thinking." In *Pioneers in Development*, edited by Gerald M. Meier and Dudley Seers. Oxford University Press for the World Bank.

Reynolds, Clark Winton. 1970. *The Mexican Economy: Twentieth Century Structure and Growth.* New Haven: Yale University Press.

Sheahan, John. 1987. *Patterns of Development in Latin America: Poverty, Repression, and Economic Strategy.* Princeton: Princeton University Press.

———. 1980. "Market-Oriented Economic Policies and Political Repression in Latin America." *Economic Development and Cultural Change*, no. 28, January.

Skidmore, Thomas E. 1977. "The Politics of Economic Stabilization in Post War Latin America." In *Authoritarianism and Corporatism in Latin America*, edited by James M. Malloy. Pittsburgh, Pa.: University of Pittsburgh Press.

———. 1967. *Politics in Brazil, 1930–1964: An Experiment in Democracy.* London, Oxford, and New York: Oxford University Press.

Stein, Stanley J. 1957. *The Brazilian Cotton Manufacture: Textile Enterprise in an Underdeveloped Area, 1850–1950.* Cambridge: Harvard University Press.

Thorp, Rosemary, ed. 1984. *Latin America in the 1930's: The Role of the Periphery in World Crisis.* New York: St. Martin's Press.

Thorp, Rosemary, and Carlos Londono. 1984. "The Effect of the Great Depression on the Economies of Peru and Colombia." In Thorp (1984).

Topik, Steven. 1980. "State Intervention in a Liberal Regime: Brazil, 1889–1930." *Hispanic American Historical Review* 4, no. 60, pp. 593–616.

Villarreal, René. 1976. *El Desequilibrio externo en la industrializacion de Mexico, 1929–1975.* Mexico City: Fondo de Cultura.

Wade, Robert. Forthcoming. "The Role of Government in Overcoming Market Failure: Taiwan, South Korea, and Japan." In *Explaining the Success of East Asian Industrialization* (tentative title), edited by Helen Hughes et al.

Whittaker, Arthur P. 1976. *The United States and the Southern Cone, Argentina, Chile, and Uruguay.* Cambridge: Cambridge University Press.

Wilde, Alexander M. 1978. "Conversations among Gentlemen: Oligarchical Democracy in Colombia." In *The Breakdown of Democratic Regimes: Latin America*, edited by Juan J. Linz and Alfred Stepan. Baltimore and London: Johns Hopkins University Press.

Wirth, John D. 1970. *The Politics of Brazilian Development, 1930–1954.* Stanford, Calif.: Stanford University Press.

Wynia, Gary W. 1978. *Argentina in the Post-War Era: Politics and Economic Policy-Making in a Divided Society.* Albuquerque: University of New Mexico Press.

Zysman, John. 1983. *Governments, Markets, and Growth: Financial Systems and the Politics of Industrial Change.* Ithaca and London: Cornell University Press.

CHAPTER 6

Political Regimes and Development Strategies: South Korea and Taiwan

Tun-jen Cheng

THE "EAST ASIAN MODEL" is not of a piece. Despite many commonalities among the East Asian newly industrializing countries or NICs (Deyo, 1987), it is important to understand the variations within them. This chapter identifies differences between two major NICs in East Asia, South Korea and Taiwan, with respect to their developmental processes. It seeks to demonstrate that the distinct patterns of development are fundamentally shaped by regime dynamics. Three questions are central in this essentially political analysis: First, how were developmental transitions made? Second, how were developmental strategies executed? And finally, in each case how did the sociopolitical consequences of a particular approach to development affect future strategies?

These questions are especially salient in light of a more general comparison between the East Asian and Latin American NICs. On the one hand, an economic comparison of these two sets of NICs draws attention to major regional differences in economic orientation, "inwardness" in Latin America and "outwardness" in East Asia, as well as distinct pathways to development (Gereffi, chap. 1, this volume). On the other hand, differences in political regime type cut across regional lines. Taiwan and Mexico have been ruled continuously by a dominant party, and both possess a long revolutionary tradition. In South Korea, Brazil, and Argentina, bureaucratic authoritarian rule (BA) has replaced earlier relatively competitive politics, and each regime is now challenged by new or revived democratic tendencies.

The economic and political differences highlighted by a general regional comparison of NICs suggest that developmental sequences do not co-vary with political regime changes. A careful specification of regime dynamics—the gaining or losing of political legitimacy, the weakening or reconsolidation of political power—is necessary to assess how political variables impinge on development processes. Because Taiwan and South

Thanks are due to Colin Bradford, Peter Evans, Manuel Antonio Garreton, Gary Gereffi, Steph Haggard, Sung-Joo Han, Liz Norville, Gustav Ranis, Tibor Scitovsky, and Don Wyman for their comments on this chapter. Research for this article was supported by a Pac Rim research grant from the University of California.

Korea possess similar background conditions—they share the same Confucian cultural traits, economic preconditons, geopolitical setting, and history of incorporation in and withdrawal from the international capitalist system—the cases provide a good opportunity to undertake a paired comparison (between two most similar cases) of political regime dynamics that controls for factors generic to the region.

The developmental sequences in the East Asian NICs as designated by the market destination and factor composition of production have been clearly delineated (Fei, Ohkawa, and Ranis, 1985). Since the turn of the century the East Asian NICs, like Japan before them, moved through various developmental phases, shifting production sequentially from land-intensive to capital-intensive industries and decisively turning from domestic to international market in the early sixties. The pursuit of export-oriented industrialization (EOI) is widely acknowledged to account for the hypergrowth of the East Asian NICs. Out of the literature emerged a laudable, perhaps stereotyped, East Asian model of development with two defining features: brief (less entrenched) and light (less costly) import substitution industrialization (ISI) and sustained EOI.

This general model, however, skips the discussion on developmental transitions and obscures important differences between the two NICs. This chapter analyzes the major turning points in the developmental trajectory for South Korea and Taiwan, and uncovers the profound divergence between them, veiled in the East Asian model. First, a three-part argument about developmental processes is outlined. Second, three postwar developmental stages in South Korea and Taiwan are discussed in detail: ISI, EOI, and EOI deepening. A political explanation is offered to explain why different approaches were selected to pursue the same developmental strategy. Finally, the economic implications of this basically political analyses are extrapolated.

THE PROCESS OF DEVELOPMENT IN EAST ASIA

The study of development in Korea and Taiwan has been well told in economic terms. Similar to Japan, these two NICs simultaneously passed through five phases of industrial development: primary commodity export in the colonial era; ISI for consumer goods based on *land* surplus and aid in the 1950s; EOI based on unskilled *labor* since the 1960s; EOI deepening based on more use of *capital* and selective use of ISI since the early 1970s; and finally an ongoing stage of EOI diversification into *technology*-based production. Intellectual discourses on this "East Asian model" center on the assessment of each developmental stage. Disagreement arises as to whether Japanese colonization basically distorted or laid down groundwork for development (Suh, 1978; Ho, 1978; Myers and Peattie, 1984). There are debates on the necessity, utility and costs of ISI, either pursued in whole or in part (Lin, 1973; Scott, 1979). Interpretation of EOI is a consensual one: EOI underlay the hypergrowth of East Asian NICs. These analyses, however, all take developmental shifts as a given.

Initiating a Development Strategy

A developmental transition requires a new policy package, a revamping of basic incentive schemes, and often a trade-off between favored and less-favored sectors, hence it must be understood in its political context. According to Raúl Prebisch's logic, the pursuit of ISI in the 1950s was a desirable and a well-calculated move to retreat from an international system that had eroded the terms of trade and precluded national industrial competitiveness for the Third World (ECLA, 1950). In Gustav Ranis's view, however, EOI is the most rational and promising strategy for small-size, resource-poor, yet labor-abundant economies (Ranis, 1979).

If economic inwardness was purported to insulate a national economy from systemic constraints, then economic outwardness provided a way to exploit systemic opportunities by realizing national factor advantage. However, the state, the national goal-setter in a "catch-up economy," is not always a strategic thinker. Moreover, the state's political capacity to steer national development is often questionable. In reality, the course of development is shaped more by numerous improvised decisions or ad hoc policy change than by some premeditated national grand designs.[1] And the process is replete with political battles.

The history of postwar development in South Korea and Taiwan did prove to closely reflect the changing pattern of national comparative advantage. Additionally, state leadership in both cases was able to override social interests during the transitions. The sequencing of postwar developmental phases, however, does not imply a "rational" state making value-maximizing choices. ISI in South Korea and Taiwan was not a conscious choice, but rather grew out of decolonization and postwar economic control. The turn to EOI was largely a consequence of transnational persuasion, if not pressure, after the ISI deepening ran aground. The EOI deepening began as a defensive measure for reducing vulnerability to external economic conditions. The suggestion that the move to new stages of development in the East Asian NICs was in any way a "strategic choice" is, it is here argued, a post facto conceptualization. However, once nudged in a new direction, the state elite in Taiwan and post-1961 Korea *did* follow a development strategy. A highly coherent set of policies was devised to shape a particular pattern of economic activities (a key and lock relationship).[2]

[1] I am indebted to Peter Katzenstein for this point.

[2] To what extent a strategy is responsible for economic success is a different issue beyond the scope of this chapter (see Wade, chap. 9, this volume).

Implementing a Development Strategy

The second issue in this paper concerns the implementation of a development strategy. There are several ways to implement a strategy. I contend that the selection of a particular approach to a strategy is less attributable to economic constraints than to the coalitional base of the regime constructed during the process of political change. Taiwan and post-1961 South Korea designed two different policy packages to effectuate identical developmental objectives. For ISI, Taiwan funneled aid to agriculture and then extracted surplus from farms to subsidize industry. In contrast, Korea had no integrated policy measures: the rural sector was neglected and its aid-dependent ISI was at best irregular, at worst a waste of resources. In the pursuit of EOI, South Korea centralized various policy instruments, in particular, the power to allocate domestic and foreign credit. Taiwan, on the other hand, employed a more decentralized approach using fiscal incentives and attracting foreign direct investment. In EOI deepening, South Korea intensified its highly discretionary industrial policy to transform itself into a heavy-industry based economy (a "big push" approach), while Taiwan strengthened the existing light industries.

Aside from their differing agricultural-industrial balance, specificity of industrial policy, and light-heavy industrial mix, the two NICs also differ in macroeconomic emphasis: South Korea has tolerated price instability for growth while the reverse is true for Taiwan (Cheng, 1978; Keran, 1983; Cole and Park, 1983; Scitovsky, 1985). The logic of the Korean approach—hierarchical, unbalanced, and command-oriented—calls for the intensive use of resources to foster a highly select and obedient big business sector to carry out the specific tasks the leadership may assign. The logic of the Taiwan approach—horizontal, balanced, and incentive-oriented—implies the extensive use of resources to allow a more pluralistic economy within the broad parameters delimited by the state. The divergences between the two are both profound and uniform.

Different economic conditions characterizing the two NICs—notably South Korea's less favorable agricultural environment, lower national savings, and relative lateness in economic takeoff—certainly contribute to national propensity for a particular approach to development. But the difference in economic conditions is a matter of degree, and not of kind. Both NICs have similar policy instruments and could find an economic rationale for alternative approaches. What actually determines their selection between the two approaches is their different regime dynamics.

Postwar South Korea and Taiwan have experienced two different types of authoritarian regime. South Korea has possessed a strong bureaucracy, either civil or military, sustained by a state-business alliance and a visible, coercive apparatus, while Taiwan has been ruled by a dominant party that maintains tight control over the state, a quasi-corporatist structure in the society, and initially a large public sector in the economy. Approximating the bureaucratic-authoritarian regimes of Latin America, regimes in postwar South Korea have never managed to institutionalize political power. In Juan Linz's words, the regimes were constantly in "authoritarian situations" (Linz, 1973, p. 235) and periodically in need of reconsolidation. A historical factor specific to postwar South Korea is the early formation of a capitalist class in and for itself. Low in capacity for political co-optation and mobilization, the regime in Korea must ensure economic performance and secure ample political funds in order to acquire legitimacy. The grip over the economy and businesses is thus necessarily tight, direct and heavy. The main challenge for the dominant party regime in Taiwan is to retain its hegemony in a capitalist system. The party regime requires the business sectors for accumulation, but needs to regulate them to justify its organizational dominance and ideological leadership. An additional factor peculiar to Taiwan is that the separation between political power and wealth roughly parallels the subethnic cleavage between the Mainlanders and the Taiwanese. Hence policy choices inevitably favor those measures that would fragment business, disperse economic power, and expand the latitude for economic distribution in order to buttress the state's power bases in society.

The origin of the two different patterns of regime dynamics has important implications. Like many other Third World countries, South Korea and Taiwan were "endowed" with an "overdeveloped" state machinery, built by the colonial regime to extract, coerce, and penetrate the society. Theoretically, a postcolonial regime will be born strong, given that the preexisting state machine and the available economic resources are instrumental to various tasks the state leadership later may define (Alavi, 1974; Saul, 1974). Postwar Taiwan followed this pattern, but in postwar South Korea the political regime was actually weakened during decolonization. The critical factor in determining regime formation is not colonial inheritance per se, but how the leadership appropriates the state machine and economic resources. In the process of decolonization, the Kuomintang (KMT) regime centralized state power, established its hegemony over the society, and, in particular, subdued a previously recalcitrant capitalist class. In contrast, the Rhee regime in South Korea (1948–1960) disbanded its mass mobilizational organizations and, due in large measure to American influence, privatized the economy, fostering first a dependent, but later a powerful, capitalist class. The Rhee regime also introduced, yet took pains to violate, a democratic system. This postwar political structure remained intact despite efforts to transcend it by the subsequent military regimes.

The Sociopolitical Bases of Development Strategies

The third issue of the chapter follows from the second one: Different approaches to ISI and EOI resulted in different sociopolitical consequences that further constrain the way a development strategy is pursued in the following stage. Development is a cumulative process: once the policy pattern is set in motion, it tends to sustain itself and, in the event of a regime change, to repeat itself. Different sets of policy tend to shape, and then become anchored in, a particular social structure. This process is particularly evident during the stage of EOI deepening, a period when social change was quick-paced in the wake of rapid economic growth. The South Korean approach to development results in a society with distinct classes capped with a highly concentrated capitalist class. The Taiwan approach leads to a society characterized by fused and fluid social classes, a substantial overlapping between workers and farmers, and a sizeable small and medium business sector. This social consequence of development conditions political action when distribution competes with growth on the national political agenda.

ISI: RENT-SEEKING VS. SURPLUS GENERATING

Latin American decolonization in the mid-nineteenth century did not mark a transitional point in economic terms. Although the Spanish colonial power had receded, the dominance of agrarian-export interests continued to sustain an outward-oriented economy. In contrast, after the colonial era ended, Taiwan and South Korea embarked on ISI in consumer goods industries. The shift from primary commodity exports to ISI was abrupt rather than cumulative, different from Latin America where ISI began at the turn of the century and accelerated after the onset of the great depression (Kaufman, chap. 5, this volume). Some rudimentary import substitution industries were installed in the late colonial era of South Korea and Taiwan, but as a wartime measure, they mainly produced intermediate goods. Decolonization permitted national decision makers in Taiwan and South Korea to start the "easy" phase of ISI.

The Transition to ISI

The move to ISI in both South Korea and Taiwan was neither a consequence of coalitional politics, nor a strategic choice of state elites, but was rather a response to a situational imperative associated with the breaking of colonial ties and postwar economic exigencies. The power of the landlord class—the most sizeable vested economic interest—was neutralized during land reform, while the dominance of Japanese *zaibatsu* during the colonial period precluded the development of strong, indigenous commercial interests or industrial capitalists. No social interest existed to hinder or advocate ISI. Previously protected export markets for primary commodities were severed while the option for industrial exports was not yet open. Meanwhile, postwar economic exigencies—notably, high inflation and foreign exchange shortages—dictated economic control, a condition conducive to ISI. As the economy became more stabilized (foreign aid arrived, prices dropped, and the balance-of-payments difficulties eased), ISI emerged as an objective in itself. Many temporary measures were maintained and became key ISI policies. Foreign exchange control, import restriction and an overvalued currency were kept as policy tools while commodity rationing and price fixing terminated. Meanwhile economic control boards were transformed into the developmental institutions vested with the new function of economic planning. Two additional factors also pointed in the direction of ISI. First, the domestic consumer market was already fostered during the colonial era, thus providing ample opportunity for local industry to develop once import was restricted. Second, foreign aid such as raw cotton was also compatible with ISI. In essence, ISI in both Taiwan and South Korea was embedded in the postwar recovery and was as unintended in the East Asian NICs as it was in Latin America.

Once it "slipped" into ISI, Taiwan actively pursued this strategy, while South Korea simply drifted along the course delimited by economic conditions. Two policy moves underlined the strategic thinking of Taiwan's technocrats. First, the principle of developing agriculture to support industry was quickly established and firmly adhered to. Agriculture and farm-supporting industries received 21.5 percent of foreign aid funds, while industry received only 15 percent (Jacoby, 1966, pp. 50–51). Agricultural surplus was then siphoned off through low grain prices, compulsory purchase, grain-fertilizer exchange, and state controlled exports in order to finance industry. Also agricultural exports based on limited barter deals were reopened to Japan, a move originally initiated by the technocrats but accomplished only with the assistance of American authorities in Japan (Chou, 1979, pp. 153–57). Second, the protection and subsidies were systematically extended to selected light industries in spite of the criticism from some state elites (who were concerned about corruption) and neoclassical economists (who disliked the infant industry argument). Most notable and controversial was the promotion of the textile industry; the state supplied initial capital and raw materials, and then purchased the output. It is within the above context—systematic resource extraction and transfer between sectors and industrial targeting—that one can identify ISI qua *strategy* in Taiwan.

In South Korea, the only strategy that existed was aid-maximization

(Kuznets, 1980, p. 63). After land reform, its agricultural sector was simply neglected (Ban et al., 1979) and the reopening of trade with Japan, a main market for Korean agricultural products, was categorically ruled out by an anti-Japanese regime. The position of the elite toward industrial development was ambivalent, oscillating between the regime's aspiration for capital goods industries and the necessity of consumer goods industries during the period of reconstruction. Economic plans sponsored by aid agencies were never accepted, while no plans were written by the regime itself until the late 1950s. While ISI gradually generated surplus in Taiwan, it was reduced to a pervasive rent-seeking activity (defined below) in South Korea. This resulted in a much lower level of economic performance in Korea: a 4 percent annual growth rate (1954–1960), which was below the world average of 5 percent (Bairoch, 1975, p. 184) and certainly below Taiwan's 7.2 percent (1952–1960).

Implementing ISI

Different ISI outcomes reflected the divergent state capacity to implement ISI policies. This in turn was a function of state structure and the makeup of social interests. Since the colonial structure was much the same, what matters are distinct patterns of decolonization. Postcolonial South Korea was turned over to the American military government (AMG) and then managed by exiled South Korean leaders while Taiwan fell to a full-blown KMT party, developed on a continental size but soon compressed into an island. The difference in the composition of leadership, the political situation within which leadership assumed control over the state machinery, and the role the hegemon played in the process of decolonization resulted in two kinds of state structure: in Taiwan, a state dominated by a Leninist party with a mobilizational capacity and a strong presence in the economy; while in South Korea, a bureaucratized, underinstitutionalized regime facing a large private sector. Decolonization weakened the state in South Korea while it strengthened the state in Taiwan.

The most decisive factor for the making of a capitalist class in South Korea was the privatization of the immense property that the colonial government left behind.[3] Privatization was originally not intended by the

---

[3] During the Japanese period, local entrepreneurs were discriminated against and were only a residual category. The small group of capitalists was composed of merchants and landlords. There is no proven link between the landed class and the newly emerged capitalist class. Clive Hamilton (1984) asserted that numerous landlords bypassed land reform through private land sale and became the commercial capitalists thriving during and after the Korean War, and subsequently went into import substitution industry. Jones and Sakong (1980) mention that many landlords directly turned into industrialists. Kim (1975) argues that landlords were only lured by the access to, not actually compensated by, industrial

newly formed South Korean state. In fact, having just struggled with communist political forces, the Rhee regime had acquired a socialist bent in its economic thinking, which was evident in its 1948 constitution, which stressed economic planning, and state control of heavy industry, public utilities and foreign trade. But because of two factors, most of the enterprises appropriated from Japan were liquidated. First, the South Korean state lacked economic managers. This allowed the United States to press for private capitalism. Second, the confrontation with socialist North Korea led the Rhee regime to take an unmistakable stand in the revised 1954 constitution.

Under a South Korean–American agreement in 1954, Rhee committed himself to relinquishing state-owned enterprises (SOEs) and state-owned banks. Subsequently more than fifty major industrial enterprises were privatized (Choy, 1971, p. 348; Yi, 1983). Then in 1957 the commercial banks were sold, and the Bank of Korea was made autonomous of the Ministry of Finance (Cole and Park, 1983: pp. 50–53). The United States, with the leverage of aid funds, was the main impetus for these moves. The Rhee regime did not easily submit to American pressure. The bilateral relations were fraught with conflicts (Steinberg, 1984). Although the Rhee regime chose the aid recipients, the United States determined the level and content of the aid (Cole, 1980). While the United States often lost control over the actual operation of the aid program, its position on the institutional framework of the South Korean economy was not open to compromise. The autonomous status of the Central Bank was more or less maintained—at least it shared power and was not subservient to the Ministry of Finance—and the privatization of state enterprises was throughly carried out. Given this sort of institutional restructuring of the economy, it is arguable that the United States acted as a catalyst for the formation of a capitalist class in South Korea.

The divestment of SOEs gave rise to the first crop of capitalists in postwar South Korea, a pattern of development found in early Meiji Japan. Most purchasers of SOEs were shrewd merchants and ex-managers, previously appointed to run factories. The transfer of many undervalued SOEs, usually based on political acquaintances, resulted in a close association between the state and businesses. The massive liquidation of SOEs also shaped the structure of the business sector. As in Meiji Japan, here the beneficiaries turned into leading firms that "never lost the lead they were given" (Smith, 1955, p. 87). Close to political power and with ample capital resources, the newly emerged capitalists were in a position to reap

---

holdings. In any event, land reform and the privatization of industry did not go hand in hand and various land bonds allotted to landlords were nonnegotiable and quickly devalued. One can thus contend that by and large the landlord class was economically eliminated.

further economic gains. Later when the state sold banks, they were acquired by those industrial transferees. As the American aid flowed in for
post–Korean War reconstruction and ISI, the very same group of capitalists exploited and responded to new economic opportunities (Kim, 1976).

While the capitalists steadily grew, the political regime under Rhee
gradually lost its capacity to rule. The weakening of this political regime
was attributable to a combination of two factors: the failure of the original "mobilization leadership" to institutionalize its political power and
the existence of a democratic, albeit often abused, political framework.
The first factor was an outcome of political dynamics among state elites
upon decolonization. The second factor reflected American influence, direct and indirect.

The victory of the Allies in 1945 brought home anticolonial activists,
which created an oversupply of political entrepreneurs. In South Korea,
two groups of political elites were important contenders for state power:
one under the charismatic (quickly degenerating into autocratic) leadership of Syngman Rhee, previously based in the United States, and the
other under the leadership of organizational mobilizers, previously based
in China. The state machinery was, however, controlled by colonial Korean police and bureaucrats, who were rehired by the AMG to keep administration functioning. Like the landlords who prospered in the colonial era, these state functionaries were branded collaborationists, and
they guarded their vested interests carefully. The exiled anti-Japanese
leaders had nationalist credentials and the skill of social mobilization.
Despite internal conflicts and tension, the bureaucratic-agrarian interests
and various nationalist leaders formed an anticommunist alliance under
Rhee. After the communist threat abated, this tactical alliance disintegrated and the collapsing Rhee was "rescued" by the unexpected Korean
War.

To consolidate political power, Rhee initiated a party by subsuming
social organizations that the other nationalists had earlier cultivated and
by recruiting the bureaucratic elite. Among the social organizations, the
youth corps (including many hoodlums and urban unemployed) was the
largest and most action prone (Oh, 1968, pp. 42, 45). Instrumental to
Rhee's electoral victory and constitutional revision in 1953 (which re-
leased the presidency from the yoke of the Diet), the youth corps was not
under Rhee's control however. Rhee disbanded it and turned to the police
and money to manage future elections (Han, 1974, p. 21). As such, machine politics with a strong dose of patrimonialism replaced party organizations as the main mechanism for ensuring political power. The rule
by one displaced the rule by few. The once dynamic ruling party steadily
lost the functions of political co-optation, penetration and mobilization.

In Robert Tucker's (1961) words, a "movement-regime" had become extinct.

The rule by one, however, was constrained by a democratic political framework. The adoption of democratic institutions had to do with, ironically, the education of Rhee (a Princeton Ph.D. in government under Woodrow Wilson) and the American occupation (which had already implanted a democracy in Japan). A constitution by itself obviously did not ensure democracy. As Bruce Cumings (1984, p. 480) argues, the Americans actually "[played] midwife to a Japanese gestation [viz., an autocracy], rather than [brought] forth their own Korean progeny [viz., a democracy]." And as James Palais (1973) demonstrates, political praxis under Rhee deviated from every single democratic norm and rule. However, political space at the national level was kept open; political contests, though tempered, were intense, and opposition parties, though often suppressed, remained legal and active. As Linz (1973, p. 239) aptly put it, political symbols and promises that accompany the birth of an authoritarian regime limit the degree of freedom of the regime in trying to institutionalize authoritarian rule. Repeated revisions of the constitution to perpetuate personal rule imposed political costs, as manifested in the deteriorating electoral outcome. Anticommunism and national unification provided an excuse for organized violence, but they were not an alternative political formula for a type of rule such as corporatism.

American influence on the South Korean political structure was also reflected in the civil-military relationship of the regime. Built by the United States as a strictly professional institution, the South Korean military was beyond the control of the ruling party, although its top leadership was often manipulated by Rhee. Twice the United States vetoed the proposals to install a party component, such as the commissar system or the national youth corps, in the military (Han, 1974, p. 49; Kim, 1975, pp. 133–34). Moreover, field operation power of the military was vested with the (more precisely, the U.S.) Command. The military elite was beyond the reach of the regime. The coercive power of the Rhee regime was limited to the police, and the autonomous military became an alternative source of authoritarianism.

The formation of a capitalist class at the expense of state capital and the decline of a "movement regime" in South Korea stand in dire contrast to the making of a strong party state in Taiwan. Several factors contributed to the effective consolidation of political power in Taiwan. First, the indigeneous elite was never strategically positioned in the state machinery. The colonial government recruited fewer local elite in Taiwan than in South Korea for two reasons: South Korea had a violent nationalist movement and was nominally merged with rather than ceded to Japan. Upon Japan's defeat, a large contingent of KMT expatriates quickly displaced colonial administrators in Taiwan. And an island-wide revolt in 1947 caused by the mismanagement of a corrupt KMT governor decimated the local elite.

Second, the defeat of the KMT regime on the mainland motivated and ironically facilitated a thorough political reform by which the party state acquired a high degree of organizational capacity and a semblance of corporatist structure. Upon its arrival in Taiwan, the KMT purged factional leaders (many had already fled abroad), built a commissar system in the army, and extended organizational arms into all levels of government. Following the land reform, and defining its social base as the masses, the KMT penetrated every corner of the society; it organized the youth corps, recruited leading farmers and prevented (if impossible, contained through sponsorship) labor unions—all through leadership control and exclusive representation.

Third, because of regime relocation, political space was conveniently foreclosed and was gradually reopened at the subnational level (Lerman, 1978). Removed from their mainland constituencies, the KMT-controlled national assemblies that chose and legitimated political leadership were indefinitely exempted from reelection. Opposition parties disintegrated during their retreat to Taiwan and survived on the subsidies from the KMT. Subnational political contests were introduced only after the KMT had established its organizational hegemony in the society and could encapsulate competitive politics.

In the economic domain, the KMT state also predominated, primarily due to the colonial inheritance. Except for four corporations divested in 1953 to compensate landlords, all industrial enterprises inherited from colonial Japan remained state-owned and state-run. The financial sector was almost a state monopoly. Equally significant, the KMT as a party also acquired a dozen enterprises and was thus financially self-sufficient (KMT, 1957). Due to the existence of a critical mass of economic bureaucrats, as well as to the necessity to trim and place a superfluous state elite, the KMT regime repeatedly rejected Agency for International Development (AID) advice on transfering the SOEs to the private sector.

The direct state control of vast economic resources drastically altered the KMT-capitalist relationship. In its mainland era, a war-fighting (hence revenue short) KMT regime was neither a captive nor a captor of the capitalists, especially those based in the foreign enclave of Shanghai. The KMT refused to grant organized business a veto power to prevent the government from fiscal abuses, and political coercion over financiers to dispense government bonds had only limited success (Coble, 1980). The regime also never elicited enough support for an industrial development program and, after the war with Japan began, for industrial relocation. On Taiwan, the private sector fractionalized, as financial capitalists perished following the loss of the mainland (most Shanghai industrialists migrated to Hong Kong rather than to Taiwan). Controlling agrarian export earnings and aid funds as well as half the industrial production, the state itself was the major capitalist in Taiwan. Partly due to AID sponsorship and partly due to the oversized SOEs, the state began to nurse some private import substitution industries. This the state did with a high degree of efficiency, when compared to South Korea.

The Sociopolitical Bases of ISI

The making of a political capitalist class and the cost of maintaining a bureaucratic regime were two critical variables that led ISI in Korea to degenerate into a rent-seeking exercise that diverted and wasted already existing value rather than creating added value. Raising funds to perpetuate autocracy in a democratic setting was the most critical task for the Rhee regime. This the regime did through collecting political contributions from the capitalists selected to receive U.S. aid funds. Multiple exchange rates and the shortage of capital supply allowed the state to charge arbitrary prices for access to dollars. To "entrepreneurs," the entry costs—the expenses for hiring the expediters, cultivating political connections, buying information, and clearing other blockades in order to gain access to incredibly underpriced foreign exchange—were high (Krueger, 1974). But the payoff far exceeded the costs: a permit to import any materials or any finished consumer goods (especially for sugar refining, cotton spinning, and flour milling—the "three whites" industries) meant an instant windfall profit (Earl, 1960, pp. 170–71).

Rent-seeking does not necessarily impede economic growth. First, rent-seeking would diminish if entry barriers are open and hence prices are allowed to fall to their market level (Buchanan, 1980, p. 9). Second, rent as a sort of arbitrarily assigned profit could be a stimulant for entrepreneurship (Hirschman, 1971, pp. 109–10) if it could be channeled to industrial investment (North and Thomas, 1973). These two conditions were not met in South Korea under Rhee. Qualifications for holding foreign exchange and import licenses were largely based on the strength of political ties. The resources flowed to the highest bidders for political contributions, but entry to bidding was limited to the selected few. Moreover, political capacity to specify the use of resources was lacking. For the privileged businesses, imports, the resale of foreign exchange, the leasing of licenses, or any other speculative activities were significantly more profitable than actual investment in production. This is vividly illustrated by the continuous decisions to overimport and overprice chemical fertilizers, instead of establishing a fertilizer industry (Earl, 1960).

The ability to extract rent from *individual* businesses, while at the same time the regime was unable to direct the use of resources by the business *sector*, denoted the structural dependency of political power on the capitalist class. Controlling the aid fund enabled the Rhee regime to manipulate business by providing economic favors in exchange for political financing. In due course, the regime became a captive of the mechanism it created. The privileged businesses fostered by the regime were eventually able to penetrate political power for four reasons. First, business was a critical link or a conduit through which aid funds were translated into political money, an indispensable agent in rent collection. Second, as Rhee's charismatic power dissipated, the cost of running the political machinery increased. Third, the privatization of the commercial banks in 1957 allowed business to tap domestic capital sources and control at least one third of their financial flow (Cole and Park, 1983, p. 55). Ownership of banks gave business operational freedom. Fourth, after 1957 AID imposed stabilization policies on the Rhee regime, which consequently became more dependent on businesses for funding and on the police for rigging elections. As the political crisis deepened, the principal-agent relationship between the Rhee regime and private business was almost reversed.

Under the hegemonic KMT regime in Taiwan, rent-seeking ISI was minimized. As mentioned above, the KMT was financially autonomous and organizationally strong, hence not in need of a huge amount of economic resources for its political machinery to win elections. The import substitution industries were made to work without having to pay political dues, while the technocrats, constantly under the scrutiny of party ideologues, had to justify their "special favors" to the industry by economic performance. The allocation of raw materials, capital funds and import privileges were determined by a priority list for industrial development, and rents went to those who invested. Also, the expanding agricultural surplus alleviated the demand pressure for capital supply.

Three key import substitution industries were promoted through the use of economic aid. In chemical fertilizers, the most crucial input for agriculture, the state monopolized imports and distribution and linked its supply of this material to the compulsory purchase of a large portion of (but not all) grain output. However, the state as the exclusive rent seeker here also actively established fertilizer plants. The plastics industry, also promoted by the state, was open to any entrepreneurs. With the aid funds, the state built several plastic plants, protected the market, and advertised them for transfer, but it found no buyers for the plants (Li, 1976). The state was compelled to plead for takeover by promising all sorts of lucrative support. Meanwhile new entrants were not prohibited. Finally in the textile industry, credit and raw materials were extended to a select few who certainly received unearned profit. But the privilege was contingent upon investment and actual production.

EOI: Centralized vs. Decentralized

With ISI reaching its limits, Taiwan (between 1958 and 1960) and South Korea (between 1963 and 1965) shifted to EOI to further economic growth. This watershed economic change reduced import control, which was then gradually replaced by tariffs; redressed the overvalued currency, which was then more realistically maintained; gave export industries various incentives; and, in the case of Taiwan, froze state capital while unleashing private entrepreneurship. Agriculture was pushed into the background, now more a provider of an industrial workforce than a production base, although in Taiwan agrarian exports such as sugar and mushrooms remained valuable until the late 1960s. Though ISI policies were still selectively applied, ISI protection was clearly superceded by export promotion. Tax and tariff burdens on export items were systematically offset, hence the manufacturers for domestic market were purposively discriminated against (Chou, 1985, pp. 150–54). The state's commitment to a comprehensive and well integrated policy package that sustained an EOI strategy reduced the degree of uncertainty and information costs and ensured a political and economic setting conducive to long-term investment (Lim, 1981, chap. 4; Bradford, 1982, pp. 21–22).

The Transition to EOI

The transition to EOI in the East Asian NICs was exceptional, for a less developed country (LDC) with some natural resource base tends to perpetuate ISI, a path of least resistance that avoids the pains of dismantling vested protected interests, both private and bureaucratic (Ranis, 1977, p. 32). For a small, resource-poor yet labor-surplus economy, the turn toward EOI rather than a deepening of ISI or an acceleration of primary exports is the most desirable and economically logical choice. Yet what is desirable is not necessarily imperative; abundant labor was a permissive, not a determining, factor of growth, and the intensive use of labor is not an automatic process (Kindleberger, 1967, p. 4). In Taiwan, the transition to a new developmental strategy was mediated by economic reforms that involved persuasion and pressure, while in South Korea, the regime change also accompanied the transition. During the transition no battle was waged between the state and social interests in Taiwan, while the ISI interests were brought under control by the 1961 military coup in South Korea. Within the KMT state, however, reformist technocrats clashed with other state elites, while the military junta in South Korea did not immediately break with ISI.

This developmental transition also took place within a changing international context. During the late 1950s, the United States as the aid-giving hegemon redefined the purpose of its assistance to East Asian allies from one of defense support to development, altered the major content of aid from grants to loans, and in the 1960s decided to phase out the aid altogether (Jacoby, 1966, chap. 3). These contextual changes created pressure for policy change. However, the role of U.S. AID in the process of transition should not be seen as simply an application of foreign leverage. In Taiwan AID's influence was vicariously exercised by expatriate economists and local technocrats, while in South Korea its influence became significant only after the onset of an economic crisis. And in both cases, ISI deepening had been attempted, the burden of which added to the suasion of EOI that economic reformers were advocating.

Beginning in 1954 Taiwan experimented with some ad hoc measures such as export subsidies to foster exporters within an ISI system. These piecemeal tactics were ineffective since profits to be reaped in a protected market were much more attractive than the cost of exploring world markets. As the domestic market was being saturated, the pressure for production or price cartels rose. Given the land reform that was just completed, another social redistribution would not significantly broaden the domestic market. Cartels, however, weakened the technocrats' position within the state as party ideologues began to question the unearned profits of the collusive private capitalists. The technocrats then tried ISI deepening: automobile assembling plants were built and a large steel mill conceived, all justified on national security grounds. However, the cost inefficiency of ISI, still unfavorable external payments, and an increasingly acute problem of surplus labor finally enabled two noted Chinese economists—S. C. Tsiang and T. C. Liu, then affiliated with the International Monetary Fund (IMF)—to persuade the technocrats of the desirability of economic reform (Tsiang, 1980).

The 1958–1960 economic reform liberalized exchange rates, adopted a nineteen-point policy plan (which included measures to rationalize the fiscal system, monitor military spending, and liquidate SOEs), and enacted an investment promotional act. Assuring the political feasibility of this economic reform in Taiwan meant selling a new policy package to the state elite rather than neutralizing the possible opposition from society. Both agrarian interests and import substitution industrial interests were weak and unpersuasive. The state, as mentioned above, monopolized major agrarian exports such as rice and sugar. Given its low import content, farm produce had a higher value of foreign exchange earning than labor intensive goods (Tang and Liang, 1973, p. 136). Export markets for agrarian products could fluctuate wildly, however, and had a low demand elasticity in comparison to manufactured goods. Accelerated agrarian exports were not the key to further growth and more employment. Like agrarian interests, ISI interests had no case to make and no influence on policy-making. ISI enterprises would be the primary beneficiaries under EOI if their production was targeted at world markets. And they were too young to be entrenched in the political process.

While social interests were submissive, several institutional interests within the state hesitated to endorse economic reform. Leading state bankers assumed that the deregulation of foreign exchange and imports would rekindle inflation, and they were pessimistic about exports and the balance-of-payments condition (Ho, 1988). The SOEs obviously were averse to the idea of their self-liquidation. The military disliked the effect of EOI on economic self-sufficiency and war preparedness (Amsden, 1985). Bureaucrats in local government were concerned with the industrial use of rural land that might upset the land tenure system. Some party ideologues warned that re-creation of private capitalists would obliterate the fruits of land reform. If coalesced, these interests might have blocked the reform.

How the reformers prevailed is still not documented. However, three factors were crucial: the political weight of academic arguments, a modest policy compromise, and AID's support. Inspired by expatriate economists and AID, Chinese technocrats in development institutions initiated the reform (Jacoby, 1966, pp. 134–35; Wang, 1978, pp. 58–59; Ho, 1988). The economic theory-based assurance on the avoidance of inflation enabled technocrats to convince political leaders. The political leadership used AID to silence the dissenting voice within the state. Leading state bankers who doubted (but could not propose any alternative to) the reform were replaced and the foreign exchange system was revamped. The military might be vocal, but it was subordinated to party leadership. The military was, after all, a consumer rather than a producer, a user rather than a saver, and a beneficiary rather than a generator of economic development. However, the political leadership did not privatize the SOEs, a decision compatible with the KMT's ideological views on restraining private capital in some form. Finally AID added bonus funds to smooth the transition, introduced Taiwan to international banking and transnational corporations, and incorporated Taiwan into U.S. overseas investment insurance and tax deferral schemes (Schreiber, 1970, chap. 2).

The transition in South Korea was carried out from 1963 to 1965, after the military regime flirted with the idea of self-sufficiency between 1961 and 1963 and after the incessant advice by AID (the fresh experience of Taiwan stood as a reference point). The military had centralized state power: it purged and colonized the civil bureaucracy (Lee, 1981, p. 84) and began to recruit well-trained academics to staff the newly created developmental institutions. The voice of technocrats was still weak, and there appeared to have been no policy debate among state elites on the alternative courses of development. Vested social interests were either nonexistent or weakened. Agrarian exports were insignificant. The 1961 military coup, though staged for political reasons, bridled ISI interests that might have hindered if not precluded the developmental transition. After the coup, the military nationalized the banks and threatened to confiscate industrial capital.

The first five year plan or FFYP (1962–1966) under the military regime was adapted from an earlier plan that stressed ISI deepening to achieve an integrated industrial structure (Nam, 1965). Although the FFYP emphasized both export expansion and import reduction to achieve trade balance, only agrarian-mineral exports were emphasized (Cole and Nam, 1969, pp. 26–27). Sustained economic growth based on industrial exports was not contemplated. However, structural weaknesses of the economy and situational factors forced a drastic departure from the course of ISI. Low domestic savings—a result of a decade-long financial repression and lackluster agricultural growth, an obsession with ISI, and a low credit rating—locked South Korea into dependence on U.S. aid and sponsorship for foreign borrowing. The confluence of a number of adverse economic events aggravated the structural difficulties of the South Korean economy. The deviation from a stabilization policy in 1961, the failure of a currency reform in 1962 (based on a wrong assumption that idle cash was massively hoarded), and a severe harvest shortage in 1962–1963 rekindled inflation and the balance-of-payments (BOP) crisis. Food imports jumped 250 percent (Kuznets, 1977, p. 203), inflation rates rose from 10 percent in 1960 to 35 percent in 1964 (Cole and Park, 1983, p. 251), and the current BOP deficits dipped to a new low point. As Nam Duck Woo (deputy prime minister, 1974–1978) noted, by 1963 the FFYP was no longer relevant and the pressing task was again to cope with inflation and BOP deficits (Nam, 1965, p. 523).

This economic crisis compelled the leadership to embrace reform measures, mostly prescribed by the IMF or American advisory teams (Cole and Lyman, 1971, p. 179; Lim, 1967). These included currency devaluation in 1964, interest rate reforms in 1965, tax reform, and export promotion (but not liberalization, which came only after the BOP improved and South Korea joined the GATT in 1967). The government was cautious in predicting the effect of the outward turn. While the original FFYP overestimated the growth of heavy industry (a project that was shelved for lack of capital), the revised FFYP grossly underestimated the volume of industrial exports. The shift toward EOI was not led by the planners but by market forces to which entrepreneurs responded (Lim, 1981). The initial, unanticipated success, then, led the state to sustain EOI.

Implementing EOI

Whether induced by transnational technocrats or impelled by economic crisis, Taiwan and South Korea by the mid 1960s had reoriented their economies toward world markets for light industrial goods. However, in pursuing the same developmental strategy, these two NICs followed two distinct approaches: a centralized one in South Korea and a decentralized one in Taiwan. These two approaches differed in three critical aspects: the principal incentive scheme, industrial planning, and the policy toward foreign capital.

To induce entrepreneurship, Korea mainly relied on credit allocation while Taiwan depended on fiscal incentives (Sakong, 1981; Hong and Park, 1986; Westphal, 1978; Hsing, 1971, 222–25). Capital sources were diverted away from consumption and commerce to support industrial export in Taiwan, but target lending was avoided. Tax breaks and tariff rebates for industry were also available in South Korea, but that nation's most powerful stimulant for investment was access to soft credit.

Indicative planning existed in both countries. Yet sectoral industrial policy was only a South Korean phenomenon, as manifested in the pervasive use of policy loans for specific industries, as well as in the integrated industrial estates clustered around two metropolitan areas, Seoul and Pusan. In Taiwan, light industry was broadly promoted, and its twenty-four industrial estates were scattered around the island.

With U.S. aid being phased out in both countries, foreign capital was secured to fill the gap between national investment and domestic savings. But South Korea preferred foreign borrowing to foreign direct investment (FDI), and in the case of the latter, joint ventures were preferred to wholly owned subsidiaries. The reverse was true for Taiwan, which opened the door to, but guided, FDI through trading tax privileges for regulations on investment categories, the export ratio, profit levels and local sourcing. In brief, Taiwan basically used a "field manipulation" mode of market intervention while Korea heavily relied on "discretionary control" to foster industrial growth[4] (Jones and Sakong, 1980, chap. 4).

The Korean approach had the effect of fostering the existing business firms for well specified economic tasks, while the Taiwan approach let new entrants in for broad industrial production. Unlike fiscal incentives, credit rationing was a discretionary method of directing corporate invest-

---

[4] However, both of these were what Chalmers Johnson called "market conforming" interventions. They did not displace private investment decisions.

ment decisions (Zysman, 1983, pp. 103–4). While in South Korea cheap credit for capital investment was allocated to privileged leading industrial firms, tax benefits reached most business firms in Taiwan. Export credit for working capital was comprehensive in both Taiwan and South Korea. It was automatically extended to all export firms, but other factors discriminated against new and small-medium firms in South Korea. The slow lifting of restrictions on new factories, and favorable provisions on depreciation, facilitated the expansion of the existing firms rather than encouraging new entrants. Reliance on foreign debt rather than FDI also allowed the leading firms to grow large. In contrast, Taiwan's small and medium industries were not discriminated against, though not purposely promoted either (Ho, 1982). Fiscal incentives in Taiwan forced a choice between an attractive tax holiday for new undertakings and a depreciation allowance for the established firms, a choice leading to the proliferation of new but small-medium firms. The reinvestment restriction of the Company Act in Taiwan dissuaded firms from branching out.[5] The influx of FDI was conducive to the emergence of small and medium component manufacturers (as opposed to big domestic assemblers in South Korea).[6] Finally, widely located industrial estates also contributed to the spread of small rural industry.

With a monopoly of banks, a well-developed economic planning body, and a high degree of autonomy vis-à-vis social interests, the state in both Taiwan and post-1961 South Korea had the capacity to enforce either approach to EOI. There was some economic rationale for the choice between the two. With a low level of national savings and investable funds, South Korea was tempted to massively introduce foreign capital and to ration credit. Better capital supply allowed a more hands-off approach to industrial promotion in Taiwan. But the difference of capital supply between the two NICs was one of degree, not kind. And such a difference did not explain why South Korea favored debt over FDI and why scarce and thus valuable credit was rationed so cheaply to selected firms. We therefore need to turn to political variables.

The Sociopolitical Bases of EOI

Different approaches to EOI reflected different coalitional bases for growth. What underlay EOI in South Korea was an alliance of accumulation between the military regime and the leading businesses. This sword-

[5] Until its recent revision, the Company Act in Taiwan was very restrictive in the scope of business operation as well as the interfirm equity flow. This had the effect of dissuading industrial integration.

[6] Several studies show that FDI stimulated indigenous component supply, especially in the consumer electronics industry.

won alliance was an unholy one, forged after their confrontation and at the expense of the interests of farmers and small-medium businesses. The military—with its rural background, moral orientation, and low social prestige—had harbored an antiurban bias and vowed to punish the leading businessmen. Upon seizing power, the military junta instantly relieved farmers of their private debt, reset the terms of trade for farm produce, and allotted investable funds to small-medium business and rural sectors (Cole and Park, 1983, pp. 56–58). This politically motivated policy had economic virtue, much in line with the proposal by Yale economists John Fei and Gustav Ranis that recommended EOI be based on farm surplus and labor-absorbing small industries (Nam, 1965, p. 530; Cole and Nam, 1969, pp. 27–28). Yet this policy was also costly, as long as Public Law 480 imports were available. The social partnership between the new regime and the farmers-small businessmen alliance soon became defunct, as the military pardoned the leading businessmen in exchange for economic cooperation and chose growth over redistribution as the basis of political legitimacy.

The collective action of the leading businesses was the most decisive factor in the state-capital alliance. Political change forced businesses to organize themselves to protect their property rights by acting on behalf of the interests of the political elite. Organized business drafted its version of economic plans, designed industrial estates, and volunteered to secure international capital (Han, 1974, pp. 163–70; FKI, 1983, pp. 166–79). To the military regime, organized business was a junior partner of development willing to redeem its previous sin and amenable to new policy. Promoting an organized business sector for economic performance was not only a timely and handy device for political legitimacy, it was also justifiable in terms of economic nationalism. Moreover, as the military regime failed to institutionalize itself, the sword-*won* alliance became indispensable to political power. In the name of revolution, the military had attempted to build "a mobilizational political party" with devoted cadres and a grassroots organizational network. But the expansion of a coercive organ (the South Korean CIA, initially a countercoup device, which became a society-wide control machine) and factional politics within the military soon demolished such a mobilizational party (Kim, 1975, pp. 271–72). As a result, economic performance displaced rather than complemented organizational capacity as the keystone of political legitimacy and stability.

The KMT's linkage to the masses (farmers, labor, and the youth) and the fragmented, dependent import substitution industry precluded an explicit alliance between the state and capital (Chen, 1977, p. 180). To pursue EOI, the party state organized and more importantly "supervised" a loose developmental coalition, consisting of technocrats and local and foreign capital. In appearance, the party itself was relegated to a logistical position, preventing the labor movement, capping rural discontent, and depoliticizing the issue of development in subnational elections. However, the KMT also exercised its ideological influence over the economic structure through personnel power, the debate over policy, especially that related to ownership patterns, and the initiation of preliminary welfare schemes.

Given that state capital was restrained, the concern now focused on the structure of private capital, specifically the prevention of big capital. The way to guard against the rise of big capital was not, however, through nationalization or antitrust law, but by keeping entry barriers low and the incentive system universal across industries. This political position was compatible with the logic of neoclassical economics, which prescribed minimal interference with the market. The Taiwan approach to EOI was also conditioned by electoral politics at the local level. The KMT regime used local elections to co-opt and compromise local political aspirants. The policy of dispersing industrial estates was more a design to balance local interests than a carefully considered industrial plan.

Under EOI, economic performance in Taiwan and South Korea was equally phenomenal: growth rates averaged 10 percent a year and prices were stable, 2 percent for Taiwan (1961–1970) and 7 percent for South Korea (1965–1970). Divergent approaches to EOI, however, resulted in two types of social structure. Emerging in South Korea was a society with distinct social classes and economic sectors. In contrast, a society with "class fluidity" and overlapping economic sectors was evolving in Taiwan. The degree of industrial concentration and the degree of role differentiation between labor and farmers are two key variables that define these two structures. By these measures, South Korea and Taiwan stood on opposite sides of the spectrum.

Although the major input factor of EOI was labor, heavily subsidized credit encouraged the use of capital in South Korea, as evidenced by a higher degree of capital intensity in export products and a lower degree of employment creation as compared to Taiwan (Hong, 1980, p. 373). Given this, and the negligence toward the agricultural sector, rural labor outflow in South Korea was more a push than a pull phenomenon. Most of those departing rural areas were nonfarming households, agricultural laborers, and petty farmers. Reentry to the farming sector is difficult for labor without access to land (Ban et al., 1980, p. 376). The concentration of industrial estates and the predominance of large enterprises had the effect of crowding out small- and medium-sized firms and precluded the development of rural industry. Seasonal movement between agricultural and manufacturing sector employment was not prevalent, as the low level of off-farm income of rural households indicated. While farmers tend to exit to become full-time industrial workers, the latter tend to reproduce themselves (see Deyo, chap. 7, this volume). As the existing firms benefited more from the South Korean approach to EOI than new firms, the turnover and growth rates of small and medium firms were low. The workers, blue- or white-collar, thus seldom quit to become self-employed.

Social classes in Taiwan were identifiable, yet interconnected, even fused. Primarily due to the pervasive rural industry, a large percentage of farmers were part-time workers employed in the assembly factories throughout the island. The labor flow to industry was more due to the pull factor (employment creation) than the push factor (rural deprivation). Most workers still kept land holdings, even continued to farm on a part-time basis. We may describe labor in Taiwan as "landed" labor in that workers could reenter farming and had a strong stake in agricultural policy change. Labor flow from big factories to small shops as apprentices and eventually self-employed owners was also common, given low entry barriers to small industry. Factory labor in Taiwan was thus a transitory class situated between farming and small business sectors, coming from the village and always ready to quit (Gates, 1979). A parallel pattern of social mobility also existed for many highly educated rural youth who after acquiring some working experience in business firms would initiate their own firms, usually in the export sector.

In sum, rapid EOI in South Korea gave rise to a social structure with only unidirectional mobility (from farmers to workers) while Taiwan's structure afforded multiple-directional mobility (among farmers, workers, and self-employed). Different social structures had different political implications. Labor was more volatile and the issue of wealth disparity more easily politicized in South Korea than in Taiwan. Policy prescriptions for a deprived rural sector in Taiwan had a "multiplier effect." All these factors would constrain the way EOI was deepened.

EOI DEEPENING: BIG PUSH VS. GRADUALIST

The initiation of EOI was based on the use of abundant labor as the major input factor and on exploiting the export market. In the early 1970s, these two crucial factors could no longer be taken for granted. Both Taiwan and South Korea were facing a three-dimensional pressure: from below, the second tier NICs; from above, creeping protectionism in the West; and inside, the shrinking labor pool, hence rising wage levels, especially in Taiwan. Moreover while EOI proved to be a successful strategy for growth, its risk for small economies—their sensitivity and vulnerability to external economic conditions—was also high. Rapid EOI has drastically increased the two NICs' dependence on the world market, as indicated in their high foreign trade–GNP ratio. These new economic parameters compelled a strategic rethinking about the future course of development.

The Transition to EOI Deepening

The major stimulant for change was export market restrictions rather than supply-side conditions. Surplus labor did not evaporate abruptly and the use of capital as an equally critical input factor was a long-term trend. The challenge from the demand side was, however, clear and imminent, underlined by a series of shocking events. Both Taiwan and South Korea were for the first time requested to "voluntarily" curb their cotton textile export in a 1971 agreement with the United States, and both signed the multifiber arrangements (MFA) to moderate their synthetic fiber exports in 1973. Comprehensive export restraints on textiles, the products most crucial to an industrializing LDC, questioned the very rationale of pursuing an EOI strategy to transcend the size and resource limits of a small economy.

Market restrictions and the vulnerability of their national economies, however, did not lead these two NICs to lapse into an inward-oriented process of development for several reasons. First, as the largest employment generator, the major foreign exchange earner, and the leading sector for growth, industrial exports were nonsubstitutable. Second, although the postwar economic system was unstable, only the Bretton Woods monetary regime had collapsed. The GATT regime was still maintained, albeit weakening. New protectionism is sector or even product specific, intrinsically different from either the old mercantilism or the trade wars of the 1930s. Third, textile exports were limited by quantity rather than ad valorem, thus leaving exporting nations the latitude to go up-market. The central issue therefore was not the reversal, but the improvement of, the existing developmental strategy.

Forward linkages, such as diversifying production from cotton textiles to high-grade garments, could minimize the constraints on the demand side. This is the Hong Kong solution. South Korea and Taiwan, however, showed a strong impulse toward backward linkages as well. The underlying assumption here is that the economy has not just encountered market restrictions and hence is in need of flexible adjustment, but more critically, the economy has reached a transitional point where an industrial restructuring is both necessary and possible. First, domestic demand for industrial input has become large enough to sustain scale-economy production for capital and intermediate goods. Second, import substitutes may not be competitive enough, but they will ensure the supply that is so crucial to a small and open economy (Triffin, 1960, p. 249). This is particularly true in the case of the petrochemical industry as the supply shortage of imported material in 1970 nearly suffocated downstream exports from Taiwan and South Korea. Third, defense considerations urged the two NICs to go into heavy industries, especially steel and heavy machinery. Fourth, the industrially advanced countries were losing competitiveness in the shipbuilding industry and abandoning pollution-causing industries. For these reasons, in 1973 both South Korea and Taiwan launched heavy and chemical industrialization (HCI) to upgrade their industrial structures. Import protection was thus reimposed (Kim, 1986, p. 3; Scott, 1979, p. 336) and capital resources were funneled into these sectors. Such an ISI was selective, rather than systemic, and designed to sustain rather than to supplant national exports as the basis for growth.

Implementing EOI Deepening

Taiwan and South Korea deepened their EOI in different ways. Essentially South Korea undertook a big push approach while Taiwan followed a gradualist approach to industrial transformation. Korea aimed to turn HCI into the new backbone of national exports while Taiwan strengthened existing industries. Both attempted to balance the protection of upstream import substitution industries with the export competitiveness of downstream industries, but the conflict between these two goals was resolved more in favor of the former in South Korea while the reverse was true for Taiwan. This is most evident in the machinery industry, which was massively promoted in South Korea while only receiving token support in Taiwan (Jacobsson, 1984). This difference between South Korea and Taiwan was further underscored by the way they coped with the first oil crisis. At a macroeconomic level, South Korea expanded and inflated while Taiwan contracted and stabilized (Cheng, 1978); at the industry level, Taiwan scaled down the HCI projects while South Korea speeded them up (Westphal, 1979, p. 256; Bank of Taiwan Quarterly, 1978).

Economic parameters (especially the wage level and domestic capital supply) in Taiwan were more conducive to an early and thorough industrial transition than those in South Korea. As early as 1965, technocrats in Taiwan, citing Stalin's Soviet Union and Ikeda's Japan as a model, had urged HCI, a temptation resisted by the state leadership until 1973 (Wang, 1981, pp. 1–53). In contrast, South Korea had incorporated several heavy industrial projects such as steel mills ever since its first five year plan. And in the early 1970s, when capital supply was still low and surplus labor was still available, the military leadership in South Korea bypassed doubtful technocrats to make a quick and complete industrial transition. What was the logic that lay behind this "perverted" pattern of EOI deepening?

The drive for a massive HCI in South Korea was often seen as a response to two worsening environments, trade and security (Kim, 1984, pp. 9–10). However, while the trade environment was identical for the four East Asian NICs, only South Korea attempted a great leap forward in industrial upgrading. Security concerns—a military buildup in North Korea and the planned retrenchment of U.S. forces in South Korea—did motivate South Korea to augment its defense capability through an accelerated industrial transformation. External threats, perceived or real, have been a critical variable in explaining the big push for industrialization in Meiji Japan and Stalin's Soviet Union. However, in facing a similar security challenge—forced withdrawal from the United Nations and the loosening of political and military ties with the United States—Taiwan did not allow military considerations to override the economic rationale. Fewer defense-related projects existed in Taiwan and the size of its armed forces and defense spending was trimmed in the 1970s.

The issue is not the security environment per se, but how the state elite interpreted it. Technocrats were given autonomy to conduct EOI in the 1960s, while party ideologues in Taiwan and the military in Korea retreated to the second line. The escalation of the security threat gave the South Korean military a new task by which the technocrats' economic advice was often overruled. In contrast, the party leadership in Taiwan reigned over the military; party ideologues recognized the security problem, but focused more on economic distribution.

The Sociopolitical Bases of EOI Deepening

Even more important than the institutional response to the altered international security setting was the timing and direction of political reconsolidation in the midst of rapid socioeconomic change. The very success of EOI brought forth new social forces and a new developmental agenda that tested the political capacity of the authoritarian regime. Labor, the nouveaux riches, and the middle class quickly emerged, and they possessed various forms of political resources such as votes, funds, and political skill. Two issues, wealth disparity and political participation, were added to the national agenda, which was hitherto dominated by economic growth. Because of land reform and EOI, distribution was not as serious a problem in East Asian NICs as it was in the ISI-oriented Latin American NICs. Still, it was a salient and politicizable issue because some social sectors lost ground or believed they had, and the reference point for relative deprivation tends to be domestic rather than international. The demand for political participation primarily came from the middle class, which assessed a regime by the yardstick of economic effectiveness *and* political acceptability.

Regime dynamics were basically a function of political battles over the issues of distribution and participation. The democratic movement in both South Korea and Taiwan intensified since the early 1970s, capitalizing on the issue of distribution and attempting to bring about social mobilization (Gold, 1986, chap. 7; Caiden and Jung, 1981). But the two regimes responded to societal pressure in opposite ways: the military regime in South Korea sealed up political space while the KMT regime, for the first time in postwar Taiwan, gradually opened up national politics for limited competition.

Political enclosure in South Korea was a once-and-for-all solution to the erosion of political power of the military regime, as highlighted by the near defeat of the leadership in the critical 1971 presidential election (Han, 1985). The political eclipse of the military regime has often been attributed to the neglect of the agricultural sector and hence the alienation and defection of farmers, especially those in southwestern Korea. More fundamental, however, was the failure of the military regime to institutionalize its power to preempt an urban "distributional coalition" that subsumed various political oppositions and threatened the survival of the regime.

Major components of political opposition, including students, the church and opposition parties, were of long standing in South Korean politics but had acted quite independently of one another and, except for the 1960–1961 democratic interval, were ineffective. At the turn of the 1970s, however, they each attained an internal qualitative breakthrough and began to converge. The principal opposition party in postwar South Korea, the New Democratic Party (NDP), had been fragmented and power- rather than policy-oriented. However, under Kim Dae Jung's leadership in 1971, the NDP clearly espoused the mass-line doctrine and attempted social mobilization under a mass-oriented "ideology" (Hahn, 1975, p. 86; Cole and Lyman, 1971, pp. 230–35; Kim, 1985). Students, congregated in the national capital, have been a formidable political force, but they had largely marched on behalf of grand issues concerning the political framework such as democracy and national unification. With the spurt of EOI, the students now examined the socioeconomic system, criticized the "unjust, corrupt and foreign capital dependent" economy, and demonstrated for or with workers (Han, 1980, p. 155). The church had been defending the cause of human rights and political freedom (Clark, 1986). But the 1968 Medellín Catholic conference of the Latin American church, a milestone meeting that justified the political action of the clergy, inspired the South Korean church to link religious attainment to social justice, especially pertaining to labor and industrial issues (Choi, 1983, pp. 125–26). Taken together, this resulted in the synchronized radicalization of the political opposition.

The military regime predictably tried to circumscribe any social alignment. It did this by prohibiting students and the church from political activities and relocating or segregating schools. However, the sheer existence of a blatant state-capital alliance conveniently, if not automatically, aggregated the opposition elements into a loose "distributional coalition." This coalition cannot be defined in terms of its concerted action for specific and pooled economic gains. Nor can it be denoted by collective violence based on shared economic grievances and suffering. Rather the coalition was united by a common position vis-à-vis the state-capital alliance. Students, the church, and opposition parties are not economic sectors per se, but they were mostly drawn from urban middle and lower classes and, more importantly, lent support to labor (Oh, 1975, p. 136; Choi, 1983, pp. 119–20). In the Latin American sense, they represented the broad interests of the "popular sector" to which they also belonged. This coalition posed a potent threat to the military regime. On the one hand, the regime was ill-equipped to co-opt the oppositional leadership. On the other hand, high labor density and an overstrained urban infrastructure rendered labor accessible to the persuasion of this "distributional coalition." The regime, with high capacity in the output function (policy implementation and coercion) yet low capacity in the input function (interest aggregation and elite recruitment), failed to contain the political expression of this urban distributional coalition.

As the distributional coalition was taking shape, the regime moved to cement its ties with the rural sector and to disengage from its alliance with big business. Following a poor harvest in 1969 and anticipating the end of the Public Law 480 aid,[7] the regime adopted a price support system to improve rural household income. The *saemaul* (new village) movement was then launched to overhaul the rural infrastructure, a campaign that had a hidden agenda—building a local political base for the ruling party. Rural industry also started to expand nonfarming employment. Apart from this new agricultural policy (NAP), an industrial decentralization program was introduced in 1970 to achieve more balanced growth and to revitalize small- and medium-sized industry. Meanwhile, the regime disciplined the leading business sector by unilaterally declaring several firms "insolvent" and accusing them of abusing bank loans, an arbitary measure strongly resisted by the powerful business association (the Federation of Korean Industries) and interpreted as an infringement of property rights.[8]

However, the rural, statist coalition was outpaced by the urban, societal one. Before the rural distributional coalition could deliver po-

[7] Public Law 480 subsidized the exports of overproduced American agricultural products to less developed countries. It took the form of American foreign aid.

[8] For the discord between the state and big business, see various issues of *Korea Times*, especially June 26, 27, and 29, 1969.

litical goods to the regime, the urban distributional coalition was already achieving a political breakthrough and threatening to seize political power through the democratic process. Facing political challenge, the South Korean military regime declared a national emergency in 1972 and imposed a *Yushin* (literally, revitalization) constitution. The *Yushin* vested the presidency with extraordinary administrative powers—a guaranteed winning share of seats in the legislature and lifetime tenure—and practically insulated political power from electoral constraints. The society, especially the urban political opposition, was being regimented and politics in any real sense ceased to exist. Following this political coup, the leadership announced the HCI plan for a thorough industrial transformation by which to achieve a goal of US$10 billion in export value and a per capita income of US$1,000 by the end of the decade (an ambitious South Korean version of the famous income doubling plan that Japanese Prime Minister Hayato Ikeda introduced in 1960 and that turned Japan into an industrially advanced country).

Political enclosure impelled as well as enabled the leadership to pursue a "big push" approach to EOI deepening. After the coup, the rural distributional coalition became politically redundant and was gradually dismantled. The rural coalition was costly and difficult to sustain. Grain subsidies were a heavy burden for a regime with constant deficits in domestic and international payments. To undo an already concentrated industry was difficult: a decentralization program merely added another industrial ring to the outer areas of two metropolitan cities (Renaud, 1971). Policies to promote small- and medium-sized industries, and to balance agricultural and industrial sectors, contradicted the "big push" approach to HCI (Hasan, 1976, chap. 4). The NAP was reversed in 1975. The reduction of grain price supports fell on producers (farmers) rather than consumers (including labor), and by 1980 the grain purchasing price dropped back to the 1970 level (Kim and Joo, 1982). Rural industries were not cultivated. Agricultural diversification into profitable livestock and dairy production was in many instances introduced by business firms. The *saemaul* movement—a self-help campaign with only symbolic financial input from the state—continued, but it was eventually ritualized (Moore, 1985).

If the rural distributional coalition was stillborn, the state-big business alliance was reactivated. A fiscal decree in August 1972 relieved the pressure of industry's private debt and punished the underground financiers (at the cost of switching off the flow of private capital to industry, however). The state then intensified its financial mobilization and earmarked 80 percent of industrial investment funds to big business, which joined the huge HCI ventures.

Three critical measures transformed the structure of South Korean business. First, exhorting the cause of nationalism, the military leadership solicited big business to assume the task of HCI. Apart from the steel industry, which was too costly for any firm to undertake, heavy industries—such as the shipbuilding, machinery, and petrochemical industries—were assigned to leading business groups. Since foreign technology and loans rather than capital were secured, Peter Evans's "triple alliance" for industrial deepening did not prevail in South Korea (Evans, 1979). Second, the leading business groups were given privileges to form general trading companies (GTCs), which had immense credit facilities. The GTCs were an instant success in terms of reducing South Korean dependency on foreign traders for export (but not for import) and achieving the export goal that Park had earlier set (Yamazawa and Kohama, 1985; Rhee, Ross-Larson, and Pursell, 1984, p. 69). But they also proved to be instrumental to vertical and horizontal integration in the business sector. The degree of financial interdependence increased within industrial groups. Many small- and medium-sized firms were absorbed into business groups via the GTCs. Additionally the insolvent firms were also auctioned off to big business, leading to further concentration in business. Third, overseas construction under the aegis of the state was again undertaken by leading business groups. Creating a prosperous and foreign exchange–earning industry in the Middle East, the leading business firms became national flag carriers. With these three profitable advances, the leading business groups were transformed into *chaebols* (octopus-like business conglomerates).

Political dynamics in Taiwan were a mirror image of those in South Korea. The KMT regime successfully preempted political opposition by sponsoring a broad yet low cost distributional coalition. Meanwhile the KMT liberalized politics and attempted to drain the pool of the counterelite. The necessity for maintaining such a coalition in an opening political arena precluded the KMT from following a "big push" approach to EOI deepening.

The distributional coalition that the KMT organized encompassed farmers, state employees, labor, and broadly defined consumer and household savers. Farmers in Taiwan had been systematically exploited. Decentralized industrialization alleviated but did not prevent the rural economy from deterioriating. State employees tended to lose ground since the labor market in the state sector is by definition imperfect and there was no union in Taiwan's public sector. Moreover, the huge size of the state sector—constituting 20 percent of total nonfarm employment—often inhibited an inflation-averse KMT regime from making basic remunerative adjustments for the civil service (Heller and Tait, 1984). Labor was not a major loser as were farmers and state employees. While unions were politically controlled, wages were not suppressed but rather reflected market-clearing rates. Wage gains were real and gradually increasing, and they even occasionally exceeded productivity rates after 1973 (Sun, 1983, pp. 86–87). Labor, however, was too important to be left out of the coalition. Policy initiatives that delivered concrete economic gains to these three sectors began with the 1972 NAP that turned agriculture from an economic surplus base into a subsidized sector. Since 1974 the compensation schemes for state employees were greatly overhauled and new tax shelters introduced. The KMT leadership also moved to revise labor legislation to expand the scope of workers' welfare (from medical care to retirement and severance payments, but not unemployment relief), much to the displeasure of economic bureaucrats and the business sector.

The sponsorship and maintenance of a distributional coalition from above went hand in hand with political liberalization. As in any rapidly developing economy, the early demands for political participation issued first from the intelligentsia (Huang, 1976). Since labor was dispersed and less volatile in Taiwan than in South Korea, and since farmers were exploited rather than simply neglected as in South Korea, the intellectuals seized the issue of rural deprivation rather than poor labor conditions to preach for political and social reform. Under NAP, the KMT effectively consolidated its rural power base and co-opted many social activists. This initial success of political inclusion led the regime to commit itself to liberalization. Opening up political space was not just a timely response to societal demands for participation, but a necessary step to rejuvenate the aging representative bodies, until then monopolized by the first-generation mainlander KMT elite. It also coincided with the leadership succession.

The KMT's ability to sustain a broad distributional coalition prevented any effective mobilization by the political opposition. Political liberalization led to the emergence of a political opposition that pushed for democratic transition. This, in turn, impelled the regime to enlarge and sustain its distributional coalition in order to constrict the opposition's social base. Although competitive politics were quite limited (only 25 percent of the legislative seats were subject to periodic elections), they were regarded as a real test of political legitimacy. The opposition was politically astute: it exploited the emotional issue of subethnic cleavage between the Taiwanese and Mainlanders, discredited the overused issue of national security, often finessed the rules of the game (for example, using literary associations as a proxy for party organization), and even forced the KMT regime to draw a line between the state and the party, hence restricting the political use of state fiscal and administrative resources. Yet the opposition had never broke through the 30 percent barrier at the polls (garnering only 15 percent of the elected delegates).

Maintaining a distributional coalition within a framework of competitive politics induced and enabled the KMT regime to follow a gradualist approach to EOI deepening. First, the magnitude of income transfers under this coalition was limited and its welfare effects can only be ensured and magnified by a macroeconomic policy for price stability. Farm subsidies in Taiwan were not as high as those in Japan; and there was no income policy based on any principle of indexation for state employees and labor. But as savers and consumers, their income gains are dependent upon stable economic growth. Farmers are producers too, but their investable funds were subsidized and not influenced by an anti-inflationary policy. Second, labor in Taiwan represented a "landed" class, hence the policy effects of NAP tended to spill over into the industrial sector. During recessions, a significant labor force flowed back to rural areas. Such mobility was not possible in South Korea. Like the self-employed, small industrial sector, a resurrected rural sector under NAP was a cushion for unemployment. Third, growth figures are not the only yardstick for political legitimacy; elections and distributional outcome are now in the equation.

If the KMT has had both the will and capacity to sustain a low-cost distributional coalition, neither was available to reorganize a developmental coalition with business, which further made the gradualist approach to EOI irresistible. The HCI projects in Taiwan were launched against the backdrop of an uneasy relationship between the KMT and the nouveaux riches. As mentioned above, the principal method for the prevention of big capital was through the dispersion of investment more than the limitation of private capital. By the early 1970s, the state sector was overwhelmed by the private sector, and "big" capital (the top one hundred firms) was readily identifiable. Private capital was big only in the eyes of the KMT (and not by international standards), and most "big" firms were in the downstream chemical or textile industries, lacking both horizontal and vertical integration.

After reassessing the development of private capital, the KMT leadership allowed the state sector to rebound after a decade-long moratorium, and to lead EOI deepening. The reentry of state capital was economically justifiable in the steel and shipbuilding industries: high capital intensity and a long gestation of investment might deter private entrepreneurship, even though domestic market demand could be ensured. In the petrochemical industry, however, the SOEs purposely crowded out private firms. Petrochemicals were a link between upstream petroleum refining, which had been a local market-oriented state monopoly, and the downstream plastics, synthetic rubber and fiber processing activities of export-oriented private businesses. Industrial deepening here took the form of private-public conflict over industrial linkages. The private sector lost the battle for backward linkage.

While blocking private initiatives for establishing petrochemical complexes, the regime attempted to incorporate local and foreign capital into the HCI, a "triple alliance" design under state leadership. This proved to be a failure. In the steel industry, it was not an alliance at all, as foreign capital never arrived and local capital did not join the venture. In ship-building, it was an abortive alliance as both local and foreign capital retreated soon after the first oil crisis occurred. In petrochemicals, a triple alliance was formed, but disintegrated after the second oil crisis intensified the confrontation between the state and private capital over import controls and the pricing of basic petrochemical materials. Most foreign firms withdrew while major local firms went multinational to secure alternative sources of supply. By design and by default, EOI deepening turned the state into the principal producer in HCI (*Bank of Taiwan Quarterly*, 1978).

The results of EOI deepening in Taiwan were threefold. First, by singularly assuming basic industrial production, the state became a party in, rather than an umpire mediating, the conflict between the upstream ISI firms and downstream exporters. Second, while the oil shock was responsible for the retrenchment of HCI projects, financial difficulties were also a contributing factor. Short of subscriptions from a capital-rich private sector, all HCI projects were more debt than equity-financed. Since the private sector did not participate in major IICI projects, it was unwilling to support ISI protection for the long-term interest of improving the national industrial structure. Third, the private sector became more independent of the state. Business firms in Taiwan were already less leveraged by the state-controlled financial system than in South Korea (Ito, 1982). Without diversifying into basic industry, and continuing to upgrade its production in existing industry, the private sector drastically improved its financial structure. Many leading firms also ventured into the liquidity-generating service sector (e.g., insurance, retail, and distribution). The private sector remained fragmented and unconcentrated, but "uncaptured" by the state.

CONCLUSION

The point of this chapter is not to repeat the well-told story of economic accomplishments in South Korea and Taiwan, but rather to identify and explain their different avenues to success through a political analysis. While both ways lead to success, there are debates on which approach makes better sense economically: South Korea's growth-first policy, its promotion of large industrial combines, and its heavy use of sector-specific, discretionary industrial policy; or Taiwan's policy of growth only with stability, its reliance on small and medium enterprises, and its more general industrial policy. Most economists deplored the South Korean approach to development (Scitovsky, 1985), while most corporate strategists and industrial policy advocates foresaw South Korea as a new Japan. Policymakers and technocrats in South Korea and Taiwan, for their parts, are now emulating each other, with South Korea experimenting with economic stabilization, revitalizing small enterprises, and trimming policy loans to *chaebols* while Taiwan is inducing business mergers, favoring existing rather than new enterprises, designating strategic industries and, for the first time in the postwar period, tolerating deficit financing to stem its sagging investment (Cheng and Haggard, 1987).

The two NICs appear to be breaking their respective orthodoxies. This deviation from long espoused approaches to development has yet to endure a political test, however. Stabilization in South Korea has been an economic success, yet with severe political repercussions: threatening the state-capital alliance without establishing any distributional coalition with other sectors to ease the political power of the military regime. Nurturing big capital in Taiwan will endanger the fragile distributional coalition that the ideologues within the state endeavor to maintain. The intensified, often violence-prone demand for democracy and the accelerated process of political liberalization since the mid-1980s compounded the process of the state's effort to reorganize a developmental coalition for further economic growth. Political constraints will define the limit of new policy departures.

Meanwhile, these two East Asian NICs are moving to a new phase of development, one that is equally export-oriented but more technology-intensive (see Schive, chap. 10, this volume). The shift to a new "stage" of development is in part a flexible response to the rampant protectionism in western markets, in part a realization that capital-intensive industries are not the forte of the East Asian NICs. This ongoing process of transition is not only beset with the internal problems of democratization, but it has to endure external pressure for economic liberalization as well (Cheng, 1988). Development strategies for further economic growth remain undefined, suggesting that the politics of development transition has just begun.

REFERENCES

Alavi, Hamza. 1974. "The State in Post-Colonial Societies." *New Left Review*, July–August.
Amsden, Alice H. 1985. "The State and Taiwan's Economic Development." In *Bringing the State Back In*, edited by Peter B. Evans, Dietrich Reuschemeyer, and Theda Skocpol. Cambridge: Cambridge University Press.
Bairoch, Paul. 1975. *The Economic Development of the Third World since 1900*. Translated by Cynthia Postan. Berkeley: University of California Press.

Ban, Sung Hwan, Pal Yong Moon, and Dwight H. Perkins. 1980. *Rural Development*. Cambridge: Council on East Asian Studies, Harvard University.

Bank of Taiwan Quarterly 1978. Special issue on the ten major industrial construction projects, in Chinese.

Bradford, Colin T. 1982. "The Rise of the NICs as Exporters on a Global Scale." In *The Newly Industrializing Countries: Trade and Adjustment*, edited by Louis Turner and Neil McMullen. London: George Allen and Unwin.

Buchanan, James. 1980. "Rent Seeking and Profit Seeking." In *Toward a Theory of the Rent-Seeking Society*, edited by James M. Buchanan, Robert D. Tollison, and Gordon Tullock. College Station: Texas A&M University Press.

Caiden, Gerald, and Young-Duk Jung. 1981. "Political Economy of Korean Development." In *Modernization of Korea and the Impact of the West*, edited by Changsoo Lee. Los Angeles: East Asian Studies Center, University of Southern California.

Chen, Chieh-hsien. 1977. "The Seventh National Congress of the Kuomintang of China." *China Forum* 4, no. 1.

Cheng, Heng-seng. 1978. "Alternative Balance of Payments Adjustment Experience: Korea and Taiwan 1973–1977." *Economic Review*. Federal Reserve Bank of San Francisco (Summer), pp. 57–62.

Cheng, Tun-jen. 1988. "The Interplay of Economic Liberalization and Political Democratization." Paper prepared for a conference on "NICs and Future NICs," University of California, San Diego, La Jolla, June 3–4.

Cheng, Tun-jen, and Stephan Haggard. 1987. *The Politics of Adjustment in the East Asian NICs*. Berkeley: Institute of International Studies.

Choi, Jang Jip. 1983. "Interest Conflict and Political Control in South Korea: A Study of the Labor Unions in Manufacturing Industries, 1961–1980." Ph.D. diss., University of Chicago.

Chou, Hsien Song. 1979. "Yin Chong Jong He Chong Hsin Ju Tong Jing Ban Si Tsu" [K.Y. Yin and the Tokyo Office of the Central Trust Bureau]. In his *Dang Zang Si Min Ying* [Private Enterprise Is the Right Way]. Taipei: Economic Daily.

Chou, T. C. 1985. "The Pattern and Strategy of Industrialization in Taiwan: Specialization and Offsetting Policy." *The Developing Economies* 23, no. 2, pp. 137–57.

Choy, Bong-youn. 1971. *Korea: A History*. Rutland, Vt.: Charles E. Turtle.

Clark, Donald N. 1986. *Christianity In Modern Korea*. Lanham, Md.: University Press of America.

Coble, Park. 1980. *The Shanghai Capitalists and the Nationalist Government, 1927–1937*. Cambridge: Council on East Asian Studies, Harvard University.

Cole, David. 1980. "Foreign Assistance and Korean Development." In David C. Cole, Youngil Lim, and Paul W. Kuznets, *The Korean Economy—Issues of Development*. Berkeley, Calif.: Institute of East Asian Studies.

Cole, David C., and Princeton N. Lyman. 1971. *Korean Development: The Interplay of Politics and Economics*. Cambridge: Harvard University Press.

Cole, David C., and Young Woo Nam. 1969, "The Pattern and Significance of Economic Planning in Korea." In *Practical Approaches to Development Plan-*

ning: Korea's Second Five Year Plan, edited by Irma Adelman. Baltimore: Johns Hopkins Univesity Press.

Cole, David C., and Yung Chul Park. 1983. *Financial Development in Korea, 1945–1978.* Cambridge: Harvard University Press.

Cumings, Bruce. 1984. "The Legacy of Japanese Colonialism in Korea." In *The Japanese Colonial Empire, 1895-1945*, edited by Ramon H. Myers and Mark R. Peattie. Princeton: Princeton University Press.

Deyo, Frederic C., ed. 1987. *The Political Economy of the New Asian Industrialism.* Ithaca: Cornell University Press.

Earl, David M. 1960. "Korea: The Meaning of the Second Republic." *Far Eastern Survey*, no. 29 (November), pp. 169–75.

ECLA (Economic Commission for Latin America). 1950. *The Economic Development of Latin America and Its Principal Problem.* Lake Success, N.Y.: United Nations.

Evans, Peter. 1979. *Dependent Development: The Alliance of Multinational, State, and Local Capital in Brazil.* Princeton: Princeton University Press.

Fei, John C. H., Kazushi Ohkawa, and Gustav Ranis. 1985, "Economic Development in Historical Perspective: Japan, Korea, and Taiwan." In *Japan and the Developing Countries*, edited by Kazushi Ohkawa and Gustav Ranis, with Larry Meissner. Oxford, N.Y.: Basil Blackwell.

FKI (Federation of Korean Industry). 1983. *Chon Kyong Lyon I Sip Nian Sa* [A Twenty-Year History of FKI]. Seoul: FKI.

Galenson, Walter, ed. 1979. *Economic Growth and Structural Change in Taiwan.* Ithaca: Cornell University Press.

Gates, Hill. 1979. "Dependency and the Part-Time Proletariat in Taiwan." *Modern Taiwan 5*, no. 3, pp. 381–408.

Gold, Thomas. 1986. *State and Society in the Taiwan Miracle.* Armok, N.Y.: M. E. Sharp.

Hahn, Ki-Shik. 1975. "Underlying Factors in Political Party Organization and Elections." In *Korean Politics in Transition*, edited by Edward R. Wright. Seattle: University of Washington Press.

Hamilton, Clive. 1984. "Class, State and Industrialization in South Korea." *Institute of Development Studies Bulletin* 15, no. 2, pp. 38–43.

Han, Sungjoo. 1985. "The Politics of Democratization in Korea: Problems and Opportunities." Paper presented at International Political Science Association, Paris, July.

———. 1980. "Student Activism: A Comparison between the 1960 Uprising and the 1971 Protest Movement." In *Political Participation in Korea: Democracy, Mobilization and Stability*, edited by Lim Chong Kim. Santa Barbara, Calif.: Clio.

———. 1974. *The Failure of Democracy in South Korea.* Berkeley: University of California Press.

Hasan, Parvez. 1976. *Korea: Problems and Issues in a Rapidly Growing Economy.* Baltimore: Johns Hopkins University Press.

Heller, Peter, and Allen Tait. 1984. "Government Expenditure and Pay: Some

International Comparison." International Monetary Fund staff paper no. 21, March.

Hirschman, Albert. 1971. *A Bias for Hope*. New Haven: Yale University Press.

Ho, Samuel P. S. 1988. "Economics, Economic Bureaucracy, and Taiwan's Economic Development." *Pacific Affairs* 60, no. 2, pp. 226–47.

———. 1982. "Economic Development and Rural Industry in South Korea and Taiwan," *World Development* 10, no. 11, pp. 982–90.

———. 1978. *Economic Development of Taiwan, 1860–1970*. New Haven: Yale University Press.

Hong, Wontack. 1977. "Growth and Trade Pattern." In *Planning Model and Macroeconomic Policy Issues*, edited by Chuk Kyo Kim. Seoul: Korea Development Institute.

Hong, Wontack, and Yung Chul Park. 1986. "The Financing of Export-Oriented Growth in Korea." In *Pacific Growth and Financial Interdependence*, edited by Augustine H. H. Tan and Basant Kapur. Sydney: Allen and Unwin.

Hsing, Mo-han. 1971. "Taiwan." In *Taiwan and the Philippines: Industrialization and Trade Policies*, edited by John H. Power, Geraldo P. Sicat and Hsing Mo-han. London: Oxford University Press.

Huang, Mab. 1976. *Intellectual Ferment and Political Reform in Taiwan, 1971–73*. Ann Arbor: Center for Chinese Studies, University of Michigan.

Ito, Ichiku. 1982. "Kai Fa Jing Jong, Jing Ji Chen Jang, Yu Jing Ji Wen Ding: Taiwan Yu Han Kuo" [Development Financing, Economic Growth and Economic Stability: Taiwan and Korea]. *Industry of Free China* 57, no. 5, pp. 1–16.

Jacobsson, Staffan. 1984. "Industrial Policy for the Machine Tool Industries of South Korea and Taiwan." *Institute of Development Studies Bulletin* 15, no. 2, pp. 44–49.

Jacoby, Neil H. 1966. *U.S. Aid to Taiwan*. New York: Preager.

Jones, Leroy P., and Il Sakong. 1980. *Government, Business and Entrepreneurship in Economic Development: The Korean Case*. Cambridge: Harvard University Press.

Keran, Michael W. 1983. "Comment." *Proceedings for the Conference on Inflation in East Asian Countries*. Taipei: Chung Hwa Institute of Economic Research.

Kim, Dae Jung. 1985. *Mass-Participatory Economy: A Democratic Alternative for Korea*. Washington D.C.: University Press of America.

Kim, Dong-hi, and Young-Jae Joo. 1982. *The Food Situation and Policies in the Republic of Korea*. Paris: OECD.

Kim, Jae Wong. 1986. "Import Liberalization in Korea." *Monthly Review* 20, no. 3, pp. 3–15.

Kim, Joungwon A. 1975. *Divided Korea: The Politics of Development*. Cambridge: Harvard University Press.

Kim, Kihwan. 1984. *The Korean Economy*. Seoul: Korea Development Institute.

Kim, Kwang Suk, and Michael Roemer. 1979. *Growth and Structural Transformation*. Cambridge: Harvard University Press.

Kim, Kyung-dong. 1976. "Political Factors in the Formation of the Entrepreneurial Elite in South Korea." *Asian Survey* 16, no. 5, pp. 465–77.

Kindleberger, Charles P. 1967. *Europe's Postwar Growth: The Role of Labor Supply*. Cambridge: Harvard University Press.

KMT (Kuomintang). 1957. *Di Ba Tse Chuan Huei Dan Wu Pau Kau* [Report on Party Affairs to the Eighth Party Congress]. Taipei: Central Committee.

Krueger, Ann. 1974. "The Political Economy of the Rent-Seeking Society." *American Economic Review* 64, no. 3, pp. 291–303.

Kuo, Shirley W. Y. 1981. *The Taiwan Economy in Transition*. Boulder, Colo.: Westview.

Kuznets, Paul W. 1980. "The Korean Economy." In Cole et al. (1980).

———. 1977. *Economic Growth and Structure in the Republic of Korea*. New Haven: Yale University Press.

Lee, Changsoo. 1981. "Civil-Military Relations and the Emergence of 'Civiltary' Bureaucrats in Korea." In *Modernization of Korea and the Impact of the West*, edited by Changsoo Lee, Los Angeles: Center for East Asian Studies, University of Southern California.

Lerman, Arthur J. 1978. *Taiwan's Politics: The Provincial Assemblyman's World*. Washington, D.C.: University Press of America.

Li, Kwoh-ting. 1976. *The Experience of Dynamic Economic Growth on Taiwan*. Taipei: Meiya.

Lim, Jong-chul. 1967. "Economic Development in Korea and U.S. Economic Mission's Report and Advice." *Koreana Quarterly* 9, no. 4, pp. 41–54.

Lim, Youngil. 1981. *Government Policy and Private Enterprises: The Korean Experience in Industrialization*. Berkeley, Calif.: Center for Korean Studies.

Lin, Ching-yuan. 1973. *Industrialization in Taiwan*. New York: Praeger.

Linz, Juan J. 1973. "The Future of an Authoritarian Situation." In *Authoritarian Brazil: Origins, Policies and the Future*, edited by Alfred Stepan. New Haven: Yale University Press.

Moore, Mick. 1985. "Mobilization and Disillusion in Rural Korea: The Saemaul Movement in Retrospect." *Pacific Affairs* 57, no. 4, pp. 577–98.

Myers, Ramon, and Mark Peattie, eds. 1984. *The Japanese Colonial Empire, 1895–1945*. Princeton: Princeton University Press.

Nam, Duck Woo. 1965. "Korea's Experience with Economic Planning." Paper presented at the International Conference on the Problems of Modernization in Asia, Korea University, Seoul, June 28–July 7.

North, Douglas C., and Robert Thomas. 1973. *The Rise of the Western World: A New Economic History*. New York: Cambridge University Press.

Oh, Byung-hun. 1975. "Students and Politics." In *Korean Politics in Transition*, edited by Edward R. Wright. Seattle: University of Washington Press.

Oh, John Kie-Chiang. 1968. *Korea: Democracy on Trial*. Ithaca: Cornell University Press.

Palais, James B. 1973. " 'Democracy' in South Korea, 1948–72." In *Without Parallel: the American-Korean Relationship Since 1945*, edited by Frank Baldwin. New York: Pantheon.

Ranis, Gustav. 1979. "Industrial Development." In Galenson (1979).

———. 1977. "Economic Development and Financial Institutions." In *Economic Progress, Private Values and Public Policy*, edited by Bela Balassa and Richard Nelson. Amsterdam: North-Holland.

Renaud, Bertrand M. 1971. "Regional Policy and Industrial Location in Korea." *International Liaison Committee of Research in Korea Conference Papers*. Seoul, August 22–29.

Rhee, Yung Whee, Bruce Ross-Larson, and Garry Pursell. 1984. *Korea's Competitive Edge*. Baltimore: Johns Hopkins University Press.

Sakong, Il. 1981. "Development Strategy and Finance in Korea." Conferences on Economic Development and Financial Markets, Seoul, June 24–25.

Saul, Johns. 1974. "The State in Post-Colonial Societies: Tanzania." *The Socialist Register*, pp. 349–72.

Schreiber, Jordan C. 1970. *U.S. Corporate Investment in Taiwan*. New York: Dunellen.

Scitovsky, Tibor. 1985. "Economic Development in Taiwan and Korea: 1965–81." *Food Research Institute Studies* 19, no. 3, pp. 215–64.

Scott, Maurice. 1979. "Foreign Trade." In Galenson (1979).

Smith, Thomas C. 1955. *Political Change and Industrial Development in Japan: Government Enterprises, 1868–1880*. Stanford, Calif.: Stanford University Press.

Steinberg, David. 1984. "On Foreign Aid and the Development of the Republic of Korea: The Effectiveness of Foreign Assistance." Mimeo, Agency of International Development, September.

Suh, Sang-chul. 1978. *Growth and Structural Changes in the Korean Economy, 1910–1940*. Cambridge: Harvard University Press.

Sun, Chen. 1983. "Tai Wan Shi Tze Min Di Jing Ji Ma?" [Is Taiwan a Colonial Economy?] In his *Toward a Wealthy and Courteous Society*. Taipei: Tienshia.

Tang, Anthony M., and Kuo-shu Liang. 1973. "Agricultural Trade in the Economic Development of Taiwan." In *Trade, Agriculture and Development*, edited by George S. Tolley and Peter A. Zadrozny. Cambridge, Mass.: Ballinger.

Tien, Hung-amo. 1975. "Taiwan in Transition: Prospects for Socio-Political Change." *China Quarterly*, no. 64 (December), pp. 615–44.

Triffin, R. (1960). "The Size of the Nation and its Vulnerability to Economic Nationalism." In *Economic Consequences of the Size of Nations*, edited by Edward A. G. Robinson. Conference proceeding, International Economic Association. London: Macmillan.

Tsiang, Sho-chieh. 1980. "Exchange Rate, Interest Rate, and Economic Development." In *Quantitative Economics and Development*, edited by Lawrence R. Klein, Marc Nerlove, and Sho-chieh Tsiang. New York: Academic Press.

Tucker, Robert C. 1961. "A Comparative Politics of Movement-Regimes." *American Political Science Review* 55, no. 2, pp. 281–89.

Wang, Tso-jong. 1981. "Tai Wan Jing Ji Fa Zang Zi Lou" [The Path of Economic Development in Taiwan]. In his *Tai Wan Jing Ji Fa Zang Lun Wen Zhi*. [Essays on Taiwan's Economic Development]. Taipei: Lienjing.

———. 1978. *Wo Men Ju He Chuang Tsao Ching Chi Chi Chi* [How We Created the Economic Miracle]. Taipei: China Times.

Westphal, Larry E. 1979. "Manufacturing." In *Korea: Policy Issues For Long-Term Development*, edited by Parvez Hasan and Dabeeru C. Rao. Baltimore: Johns Hopkins University Press.

———. 1978. "Industrial Incentives in the Republic of China (Taiwan)." Mimeo. World Bank.

Yamazawa, Ippe, and Hirohisa Kohama. 1985. "Trading Companies and the Expansion of Foreign Trade: Japan, Korea and Thailand." In *Japan and the Developing Countries*, edited by Kazushi Ohkawa and Gustav Ranis, with Larry Meissner. Oxford and New York: Basil Blackwell.

Yi, Dai-Gun. 1983. "Mi Gun Jong Ha Kwi Sog Jae San Cahe Li Wa Gu Hyo Gwa" [The Effects of the Disposal of Confiscated Properties under the American Military Government]. In *San Up Kyong Je Oe Yi Ron Kwa Bun Sug* [Theory and Analysis of Industrial Economics]. Seoul: Bi Bong.

Zysman, John. 1983. *Governments, Markets and Growth*. Ithaca: Cornell University Press.

CHAPTER 7

Economic Policy and the Popular Sector

Frederic C. Deyo

> Each sector of (Argentine) society forms a strong cluster of in-
> terests and is firmly anchored in a set of institutions. . . . The
> middle classes used the educational institutions and the profes-
> sions to lodge themselves . . . high . . . in the apparatus of the
> public administration. Workers defended their wages and their
> rights through the formation of strong unions. . . . State power
> does not seem to grow in Argentina at the expense of the com-
> peting institutions. . . . Argentina . . . easily falls prey to political
> decay. The state tends to lose whatever autonomy it may have
> attained vis-à-vis civil society and to become instrumentalized,
> not by a ruling class . . . but by a large plurality of narrow
> groups.
> —Corradi (1985, pp. 112–13)

> What effect did Taiwan's social structure have on development?
> . . . Why were workers, peasants, landlords, intellectuals, and
> the middle class so quiescent and cooperative?
> —Gold (1986, p. 9)

IT IS generally assumed that workers, peasants, middle classes, and other
popular sector groups play little direct role in the formulation of national
development strategies, even under democratic regimes (see Remmer and
Merkx, 1982; Canak, 1984). The constraints and possibilities presented
by the interests and capacities of developmental states, dominant social
classes, foreign capital, and the military have tended to dominate discussion of strategy-making and the political economy of growth.

While elite policies are rooted in more general developmental strategies
or doctrines, the determination of strategies has rarely engaged nonelite
groups. On the other hand, to the extent policy measures define the in-
strumentalities of broader strategic goals, the anticipated or actual public
response to policy delimits the political space within which strategic decisions must be made. Reflective of this important constraint is broad rec-

I am grateful to James Dinsmoor, Chris Ellison, Gary Gereffi, and Stephan Haggard for
helpful comments on an earlier draft of this chapter.

ognition of the *indirect* political role of the popular sector in opposing or encouraging particular policies that flow from more general strategies, and in seeking open political regimes through which their policy demands may be brought to bear in economic decision-making.

In broad terms, popular sector political action is seen here as imposing, with greater or lesser efficacy, distributional criteria in developmental strategies (see Kaufman, chap. 5, this volume). Historically specific economic circumstances and possibilities determine the extent to which trade-offs between distribution and accumulation become politically unmanageable within given political regimes. The relative influence of popular sector demand-making on state strategy depends in the first instance on the nature of political regimes through which demands articulate with policy. But more fundamentally, popular influence flows from autonomous class control over institutions that foster class or group interest articulation, political socialization, leadership, and communication, and which in turn provide an independent social foundation for economic demands or for an opening of political regimes through which such demands may be brought to bear in policy-making. Given the vulnerability of some such institutions (e.g., trade unions, professional associations, and political parties) to state repression, informal community-based institutions and networks are especially important in this regard.

This study contrasts the political role of popular sectors in four newly industrializing countries (NICs): Argentina, Brazil, South Korea, and Taiwan. Given the historical reality of continuing state and bourgeois domination throughout the post–World War II period of development, attention is largely confined to the varying capacity of popular-sector groups to support or to oppose specific state policies that are seen as affecting their material welfare, or alternately, to press for more liberal democratic regimes. Following a comparative overview of the political role of popular sector groups in these four countries, several explanations are offered for cross-national contrasts in the power of nonelite groups to influence policy. It is suggested that the most fundamental source of popular sector power lies in the social structural foundations for autonomous class politics.

THE POPULAR SECTOR AND ECONOMIC POLICY: CROSS-NATIONAL CONTRASTS

Comparisons among the East Asian and Latin American NICs suggest a stark contrast between Argentina, whose relatively weak state confronts strong societal forces, and Taiwan, where a strong developmentalist state faces a very weak popular sector. Arrayed between these extremes are Brazil and South Korea, whose strong states face civil groups of varying political efficacy.

Argentina

Argentina comprises the extreme case of a weak state and strong society. Indeed, labor support provided an indispensable political base for the ascendancy of Juan Perón, elected president in 1946 and the architect of the coalition of workers, industrialists, and middle class, which sought to contain the power of the conservative agrarian elite in the postwar years (Bergquist, 1986). Consolidation of this coalition was associated with heightened developmental commitment to social welfare, full employment, and real wage growth.

Such a cross-class coalition was undermined by a growing economic crisis during the 1950s, which forced curtailment of welfare and distributionist policies and which fostered a shift away from protection of domestic light consumer goods industry and toward greater reliance on foreign investment in heavy and consumer-durables industries. The growing political opposition to retrenchment of established welfare and consumptionist policies during the 1950s along with opposition from landowners, the Church, and major industrialists eventuated in collapse of Peronist rule.

The subsequent period (1955–1966) saw reversion to middle-class governance under military surveillance, along with efforts at dismantling Peronism, in part through exclusion of Peronists from electoral politics (Corradi, 1985). But even in this very restrictive political context, Peronist influence remained strong (Bergquist, 1986). Throughout the period, it was apparent that Peronist support or at least political acquiescence was a prerequisite for rule. For this reason, General Pedro Aramburu (1955–1958) continued to support wage increases and public welfare subsidies, refusing to comply with the terms of an IMF stabilization program. His successor, Arturo Frondizi, elected in 1958 in a nominal return to civilian rule, continued Aramburu's policies up until the economic crisis of 1958–1959, at which point he capitulated to IMF terms under which wages were frozen and state expenditures cut. These and other policies of orthodox stabilization, taken to ensure continued access to foreign loans, were met by increased labor militancy (Pion-Berlin, 1983). In part to regain Peronist support, Frondizi permitted Peronist participation in congressional elections in 1962. An unexpected Peronist victory in these elections led to military intervention and installation of Arturo Illia as the new president. Illia, like his predecessors, found it necessary to continue to court Peronist support through wage increases and economic reform. But renewed economic crisis subsequently led Illia to seek Peronist support for wage constraint. Labor intransigence and continued political-economic crisis, along with ever more forceful external demands for imposition of an orthodox stabilization program as a condition for foreign credit, eventuated in a military coup in 1966 (see Bergquist, 1986). Coup leaders sought to exclude popular sector groups from politics; to repress the courts, universities, and political parties, which had given popular groups an institutional base; and to give heightened emphasis to stabilization policies, on the one hand, and direct foreign investment in industry on the other (Buchanan, 1985). The stabilization measures, including wage containment and curtailment of public expenditures, drew growing opposition from lower-middle- and working-class groups, culminating in mass urban insurrections in 1969 and ultimately a return to Peronist power in 1973, an effective veto of exclusionary development policies (Pion-Berlin, 1983).

This cycle was repeated when military rule was reimposed in 1976: popular sector institutions were suppressed, and new economic stabilization policies were instituted. As in the earlier case, declining real wages, reduced public welfare expenditures and other assaults on the livelihood of salaried and wage-earning classes resulted in growing opposition and protest. As in 1966, loss of state control over unions, political parties, the media, and other institutions of political representation and socialization precipitated moves to destroy those institutions altogether (Foxley, 1983; Buchanan, 1985).

By 1984, strikes and public protest could no longer be contained under the Bignone government, and military rule gave way to new elections and the return to power of the middle-class Radical Civic Union (RCU) party, with significant working-class support.

Taiwan

Taiwan defines precisely the opposite pole: that of a strong state and weak society. As noted by Cheng (chap. 6, this volume), throughout the developmental periods of ISI, early EOI, and more recent economic restructuring into heavy and high technology industry, state planners have confronted weak, divided, and politically acquiescent civil groups and classes.

One of the very striking features of Taiwanese postwar development has been its unabated political exclusion of popular sector groups. Under continuing martial rule, political challenge to key principles of KMT rule was proscribed, oppositional political parties banned, publications and news media censored, unions controlled, and strikes prohibited.

During the early phase of export-led industrialization through the 1960s and early 1970s, economic policy was economically exclusionary.

The shift to EOI was predicated in part on maintenance of low industrial labor costs. Wages during this period remained very low by international standards, far lower than those in Argentina and Brazil (*Asia Research Bulletin*, 1982). This is especially true of workers in export processing zones, where wages were not sufficient to support a family at subsistence levels (Gates, 1979). More generally, the official minimum wage remained at approximately US$15 per day into the mid-1970s (Chen, 1981), and wages advanced far less rapidly than productivity. Farm product prices were depressed through government tax and marketing policies in order to subsidize industrial growth. And during recessionary periods (e.g., 1974 and 1980–1982), the inflation-averse state has failed to apply countercyclical public expenditures to alleviate problems of unemployment and economic hardship (Cheng, chap. 6, this volume).

Similarly, strategic emphasis on industrial growth and investment has been associated with very low levels of social welfare expenditure, well below those among the Latin American NICs. Taiwan has lacked a comprehensive national system of social security or worker compensation and has resisted periodic pleas to provide more fully for unemployment assistance. Table 7.1 shows a continuation of this cross-national difference even into more recent years, when public welfare expenditures have expanded rapidly in Taiwan.

While the longer-term economic welfare *consequences* of Taiwanese development have indeed been relatively favorable (see Gereffi, chap. 1, this volume; also discussion below), it is nonetheless clear that politically exclusionary regimes and restrictive economic policies marked a long period of rapid industrialization until the late 1970s. But such exclusion has remained virtually unchallenged during the entire period. In cases where workers sought greater state commitment to wage gains, social security, or public welfare, or to compensatory intervention to counteract periods of recessionary hardship, collective and political action was poorly orga-

TABLE 7.1
Percentage of Total Government Expenditure for Health, Social Security, and Welfare

Argentina (early 1980s)	40.1
Brazil (1985)	40.3
Mexico (1985)	13.4
South Korea (1985)	8.1
Taiwan (1984)	15.2

Sources: For Taiwan, Asian Development Bank (1985); for others, World Bank (1987).

nized and easily contained (usually with no violence) by police, employers, and controlled trade unions (see Deyo, 1984).

More important than direct opposition to state economic policy has been a continuing middle-class demand for political democratization. Such demands—centering especially among Taiwanese politicians, professionals, intellectuals (especially students), and others linked to culturally outward-facing institutions such as the press and universities—have been increasingly evident since the 1977 Chung-li antigovernment riots and the 1979 Kaohsiung human rights demonstrations (Gold, 1986). Lack of coalitional linkage to workers by the middle class political opposition has reduced the impact of political dissent.

All in all, the political insulation of strategy-making elites in Taiwan marks a sharp contrast to Argentina, as indeed to most other Third World capitalist countries.

Brazil

Brazil and South Korea fall between the polar cases of Argentina and Taiwan. The effective centers of civil sector power in Brazil lie not among popular sector classes but among state elites and a dynamic industrial and financial bourgeoisie. Throughout most of the period of Brazilian industrialization, middle and working classes have participated in politics largely at the fickle invitation of elites. But while these classes have had less of an impact on economic policy than their Argentine counterparts, this impact has been greater than that of popular sectors in the East Asian NICs, at least until very recent years in South Korea.

Following the 1930 revolution, and especially after the attempted 1932 conservative counterrevolution, state elites sought political support through a state-dominated populist alliance with the national bourgeoisie, workers, and salaried middle classes. Under the Estado Novo, instituted by President Getúlio Vargas in 1937, trade unions were tightly incorporated into the state apparatus. This authoritarian populist alliance (Dix, 1984), which was cemented through the early 1950s by expanded state welfare expenditures along with subsidies and protection for national industry, permitted continued domination by the Vargas government even under a regime of open electoral politics instituted after World War II under U.S. pressure. Between 1947 and 1960, populist politics were associated with an increased share of national income (from 56 percent to 65 percent) accruing to salaried and wage-earning classes (Pereira, 1984).

The growing exhaustion of domestic market-oriented import-substituting industrialization, economic crisis, and an increasing state inability to maintain high levels of public subsidies and welfare vitiated the economic basis for this "populist pact," as did growing income concentration and a shift to greater reliance on direct foreign investment. Politically, this coalitional crisis was manifest in an inability on the part of the Goulart government (elected in 1962) either to appease or to contain popular sector groups and trade unions as they sought continuation of populist policies under economic circumstances that made this impossible.

It is important to note a crucial difference between Brazil and Argentina at this point. Whereas in Argentina, the political left, an independent trade union movement, and a credible middle class opposition maintained an autonomous political presence, Brazilian popular sector groups were effectively harnessed first to the state, which provided substantial employment opportunities and public benefits through a system of political clientelism (Hagopian, 1986), and second to a bourgeois ideology of nationalism, industrialism, and state intervention. Bresser Pereira argues in this regard that popular sector political participation served ultimately as an "auxiliary political force to the industrial bourgeoisie" (1984, p. 75), as seen, for example, in popular electoral support for Juscelino Kubitschek, a representative of nationalist bourgeois interests, in the 1955 presidential elections.

Conversely, the collapse of the populist pact, which is to say withdrawal of coalitional support on the part of the bourgeoisie, rendered popular sector groups impotent in confronting their political exclusion following the 1964 coup, which replaced an elected President João Goulart with military rule. Under authoritarian rule, extension of an emergent pattern of dependent development, characterized by high levels of foreign capital penetration, income concentration, and a deepened shift into heavy industry and nontraditional (manufactured) exports was associated with economic policies of popular sector exclusion (Evans, 1979). Especially prominent were reduced state welfare expenditures, wage compression, minidevaluations, and increased public service rates, which marked the 1964–1967 period of economic stabilization (Aguiar et al., 1984), continuing with restrictive wage indexing into the 1970s (Kaufman, 1979; Keck, 1985). Regressive incomes policies were relaxed somewhat in the late 1970s, in part in response to recognition on the part of the industrial bourgeoisie that continued economic growth would require expanded purchasing power on the part of workers and salaried classes. The Democratic Social Pact of 1977, which symbolized this realliance around a project of both political and economic liberalization, was again to be ruptured after a series of strikes in 1979 and 1980 forced a frightened bourgeoisie to press for political closure (during 1980–1982) in order to contain public disorder. In 1983, an IMF stabilization program was adopted as a condition for continued foreign credit and loans. The negative consequences of this program for public welfare expenditures and wages were contested but not reversed.

Unlike the Argentine case, in which labor and middle class opposition to ruling policy brought down successive military governments, the Brazilian military takeover proved stable and effective over a period of nearly two decades (Remmer and Merkx, 1982). Peasant movements did not recover from the 1964 repression until the mid-1970s' rise in militancy among sugar estate and other rural workers (Keck, 1985). And during the decade following the suppression of large scale strikes in 1968, industrial trade unions did not mount a single major strike (Mainwaring, 1986).

Similarly lacking was an independent popular sector role in the gradual political liberalization from the mid-1970s. This liberalization and "political normalization" was in fact initiated by the military and supported by the bourgeoisie, not so much in response to public pressure as in recognition of the effectiveness of elite political domination (Mainwaring, 1986). It was only during the intense intraelite conflict over presidential succession in 1983 and 1984 that populist groups were able to play an effective role in pressing for political reform.

It should also be noted, however, that there are increasing indications of a maturation of an autonomous labor presence in Brazilian politics. Increasingly, workers have begun to challenge government-co-opted trade union leaders and to create more autonomous unions. The "new unionism" centering especially among automobile workers emerged most prominently during the surge of worker militancy during 1978–1980 which eventuated in major wage gains for low-paid workers (Keck, 1985). More important has been growing coalitional unity among middle classes and factory workers. Formation of the Workers' Party (PT) around labor rights issues in the late 1970s effectively linked proletarian economic demands with middle-class opposition to nondemocratic rule. In addition, continuing economic crisis and unemployment thrust upon organized workers the public welfare issues voiced by neighborhood associations among the very poor (Sandoval, 1985; Mainwaring, 1986).

South Korea

South Korea's strong, militarized state confronts a socially mobilized and politicized but organizationally weak civil society. South Korean development has thus been marked by relatively high levels of civil conflict and political opposition to ruling policy, on the one hand, but by exclusionary regimes that have proven even more enduring and effective than those in Brazil, on the other.

In the face of high levels of popular agitation during the final years of the Rhee regime and into 1960, when the middle class achieved temporary control over the state under the Chang Myon administration, populist demands threatened political stability and economic growth. Imposition of martial rule in 1961 forcefully excluded these sectors from national politics, while asserting renewed controls over trade unions, universities, mass media, and other institutional channels of dissent. Despite a partial restoration of labor and political rights from 1963, continued wage controls, reduced public welfare expenditures, and single-minded pursuit of export production from the mid-1960s generated rapid industrial expansion but the continued economic marginalization of a significant portion of the workforce (Koo, 1984). And the tight political controls imposed to support such economic policy, especially during the heightened repression of the 1970s (Cheng, chap. 6, this volume), wedded political with economic exclusion. Especially important for workers was the shift toward greater emphasis on foreign investment during the late 1960s and a corresponding need for heightened labor discipline. Following strikes at two foreign firms in 1968 and 1969, new legislation extended special protection against labor disruption to foreign investors and firms in export processing zones. These varied new restraints on workers are seen in very slow real wage gains for workers during the early 1970s (see below; also see Fields, 1984). Finally, in response to escalating inflation and growing foreign debt, stabilization measures were instituted under the Chun government in 1979–1980 and again in 1982, with a corresponding depressive effect on earnings and welfare (Kuznets, 1985).

Popular sector opposition to these policies and controls, especially during economic recession (i.e., in the mid- and late 1970s) was vocal and sometimes violent. As elsewhere, students, intellectuals and nationalist politicians led the fight against political repression, while workers (especially in the textile industry) sought improved wages and social welfare. In addition, there were efforts on the part of middle class groups to link their human rights demands to labor movements. Of particular importance was student involvement in worker demonstrations and work stoppages on the one hand, and organizational and educational efforts on the part of Christian church groups on behalf of workers on the other. In part in response to this emergent cross-class oppositional mobilization, new labor legislation enacted in 1981 proscribed "third party" involvement in labor disputes.

Over the 1970s and early 1980s, popular agitation resulted mainly in a tightening of political repression, paralleled by a continuance of low wages and extremely long working hours in labor-intensive export industries, and continuance of very low public expenditures on social welfare (see table 7.1), lack of enforcement of fair labor practices and industrial safety legislation, and other indications of inattention to worker demands. The contrast to the greater state vulnerability to popular sector political and economic demands in Argentina is clear.

POPULAR PRESSURES IN THE DEMOCRATIC OPENING OF THE 1980S

During the mid-1980s, all four countries have made a transition to more open, democratic regimes. Differences in the nature and extent of this transition confirm much of what has already been said regarding the political role of popular sector groups.

The collapse of Argentina's military regime in 1982–1983 can in part be attributed to military defeat in the Falkland Islands conflict with Britain. But subsequent events were to suggest the importance, too, of popular opposition. The rise to power of the middle-class Radical Civic Union (RCU) was based strongly on grass-roots political mobilization. Under RCU rule, the military was effectively subordinated to civilian control and former officers were prosecuted in civilian courts for earlier civil rights abuses. As important, the role of working class groups has been significant. Peronist influence rebounded after defeat in the 1984 elections, and President Raúl Alfonsín found it increasingly necessary to accommodate labor demands relating to wages, public works, housing, and welfare (*Latin American Weekly Review*, 1987). The Confederacion General de Trabajadores (CGT) remained powerful, organizing a number of relatively successful general strikes in opposition to announced anti-inflationary measures, including wage freezes. Despite Alfonsín's continued efforts to court labor support for his new "social pact" through wage concessions, proposal of a national health program, and repeal of existing restrictive labor legislation, the RCU proved no more successful than its predecessors in balancing strong popular demands for economic expansion and welfare gains against international pressures by foreign agencies and creditors for economic stabilization and austerity. In 1989, the Peronist party, under President Carlos Saul Menem, resumed power, only to try, once again, to gain popular support for wage restraint and restrictive economic measures in response to severe inflation and an enormous external debt.

Unlike the Argentine case, the 1985 shift to democratic rule in Brazil was a controlled, preemptory, and partial elite accommodation to changing elite perceptions and interests. Growing business opposition to clumsy state economic controls, along with a desire on the part of the military to extricate itself from direct involvement in governance, led to a partial regime opening. However, the Brazilian military has remained a powerful force in national politics, retaining cabinet-level positions in the government of newly elected President Jose Sarney, who routinely consulted the military in policy deliberations. The military retains the power to intervene in domestic politics on its own authority and indeed has intervened directly in several labor strikes. Indicative of continuing military power, there have been no reprisals against officers suspected of earlier civil rights abuses, and military salaries have increased dramatically while other wages and salaries have been tightly restrained.

The Brazilian middle class has remained politically more marginal than that in Argentina, and it has assumed a primarily oppositional rather than dominant role in national politics. Popular sector mobilization and opposition has been more vocal than effective. New land reform measures enacted in 1987 have met powerful resistance by large land owners. In response to IMF and domestic business pressure, Sarney imposed restrictive stabilization policies, including wage controls. And despite increased economic pressure on wage earners and other popular sector groups, Coller de Mello—a conservative committed to reduced government subsidies, privatization, and harsh austerity measures—defeated populist and labor-oriented candidates to replace Sarney in national presidential elections. His victory owed much both to oppositional disunity and to strong backing from business and conservative groups.

The South Korean democratic reforms beginning in 1986, like those in Brazil, were a controlled and partial accommodation on the part of a military-backed government to growing middle class—and, in this case, student—demands for open presidential elections. The political risk in this accommodation was greatly eased by political divisions among the opposition, which ensured the victory of Roh Tae Woo, the candidate of the ruling Democratic Justice Party. In addition, it was recognized that the military would retain a powerful role in any future government. Indeed, the special weakness of workers and peasants is reflected in recent economic policy under the new regime. Despite lip service to the need for expanded welfare programs and improvements in minimum wage and working conditions, economic policy has changed little from its long-established priority on growth, investment, and exports. Given that strong organized pressure for further democratization is largely confined to professionals, intellectuals, and students, military intervention is as likely as further democratic reform in response to continuing protest. On the other hand, while welfare and distributionalist demands have generally lacked a strong political base among workers or peasants, whose unions and other organizations have remained corporatively or repressively controlled by administrative agencies (e.g., the Security Branch, Ministry of Labor, and Ministry of Agriculture and Fisheries) (Park, 1987), there is indication of the emergence of a stronger, more autonomous labor movement. Strikes during the mid- and late 1980s among auto and shipyard workers have displayed greater solidarity and have been far more effective than earlier strikes on the part of light industry workers. We return to the possible implications of this departure later in the discussion.

Taiwan provides the extreme case of of top-down, guided, preemptory democratization. Under Chiang Ching-Kuo, political opposition groups were permitted for the first time to field candidates for the national legislature, and martial law has been replaced by a less restrictive national security law (Myers, 1987). But to an even greater extent than in Brazil and South Korea, a tiny military/administrative elite has controlled these political reforms with very little pressure from nongovernmental groups. All new political groups must endorse the KMT-imposed constitution, support KMT commitment to restore rule over the mainland in a reunified China, and promote "social peace." And despite the presence of multiparty competition during the 1989 national legislative elections, political commitment to continued democratic reforms appears to be confined to a rather narrow group of politicians and intellectuals (Myers, 1987).

Having noted marked contrasts in the policy influence of popular sector groups, how may one *explain* these contrasts? The following discussion explores the consequences of differences in the political, economic, and social dimensions of development for nonelite political groups in these countries.

SOURCES OF CROSS-REGIONAL CONTRASTS: ECONOMIC WELFARE

The lesser political impact of populist politics in Taiwan than in Argentina and elsewhere in Latin America has often been attributed to cross-regional differences in economic performance, employment, equity, and wages (Little, 1979). Indeed, while differences in welfare and distributional *policy*, noted above, would not support such an explanation, other indicators of actual living standards might.

Starting from high levels of unemployment in the early 1960s, both Taiwan and South Korea achieved stable full employment by the mid-1970s and indeed thereafter encountered growing labor shortages in many sectors. Conversely, unemployment has remained a chronic problem in most of Latin America, at roughly double East Asian levels, while underemployment has been greater still.

Wage trends, on the other hand, do not show such clear cross-national differences. Table 7.2 shows real wage change over recent years.

These data do suggest somewhat more rapid and continuing gains in East Asia than in Latin America. On the other hand, the differences are not great, especially over the late 1960s and mid-1970s, and certainly cannot support a strong argument for the power of an economic explanation of cross-national differences in popular sector oppositional politics. Taiwanese real wage gains are not markedly greater than those in South Korea or Brazil. And while Argentine wages did stagnate during the 1960s and 1970s, dropping sharply following the military coup of

TABLE 7.2
Index of Real Earnings in Manufacturing by Country and Year

	Argentina (1980)	Brazil (1980)	Mexico (1980)	South Korea (1980)	Taiwan (1971)	Taiwan (1981)
1967		44				
1968		46		36	88	
1969		50		41		
1970		67	93	43	89	
1971	53	75	93	45	100	
1972	81	86	95	46	104	
1973	142	88	96	55		
1974	102	94	96	57	96	
1975	118	89	98	60		
1976	82	98	105	67	123	74
1977	80	100	106	78		
1978	79	104	103	94		88
1979	90	109	102	105		
1980	100	100	100	100		97
1981	91	100	103	98		100
1982	80	92	101	103		105
1983	103	84	75	109		
1984	126	91	73	119		129
1985	104	93	86	119		

Note: Base year for construction of index noted in parentheses (e.g., 1980 means the index is based on 1980 = 100).

Sources: Argentina, Brazil, Mexico and South Korea: World Bank (1989). Taiwan: calculated from Republic of China (1988).

1976, they outpaced wage gains in both Taiwan and South Korea from 1978 up until the 1985 currency reforms.

Income equality (see Gereffi, table 1.5, this volume) provides an additional and often cited indicator of the more favorable economic outcomes of Asian industrialization. While income inequality data favor the East Asian countries, it may be suggested that part of this difference stems from the greater predominance of multiple wage earners among low-income East Asian households (Deyo, 1987). To the extent this is true, it suggests that cross-regional equality differences may in part be rooted in greater labor outlays among some East Asian families. More important, comparable data for Argentina (not shown) are again problematic. In 1970, the lowest income quintile of Argentine households earned 4.4 percent of total household income, a figure significantly higher than those for the other Latin American NICs (2.9 percent for Mexico in 1977, and 2.0

percent for Brazil in 1972) and not appreciably lower than that in South Korea (5.7 percent in 1976), where inequality in fact increased during the 1970s (Fields, 1984). Correspondingly, the ratio of income earned by the lower 40 percent of households to that of the top 10 percent was 0.4, again substantially better than in the other Latin American NICs (0.24 for Mexico and 0.10 for Brazil).

Income inequality comparisons are usefully supplemented by the Physical Quality of Life Index (PQLI) (see table 7.3). This index, based on life expectancy, infant mortality rates, and literacy, provides a direct indicator of changing material standards of living of the populations of these countries.

Again, it may be seen that Argentine PQLI scores are not low by East Asian standards. One may conclude that comparative economic welfare measures (real wage trends, income inequality, and PQLI) do not lend support to the argument that levels of economic deprivation explain corresponding differences in levels of populist political mobilization.

If cross-national economic differences do not provide support for a material welfare-centered explanation for political differences, neither do cross-sectional differences within countries. The strongest trade unions in both regions tend to be found not among low-paid insecure or casual workers so much as among better-off workers. It is clear, for example, that while levels of militancy among female workers in South Korean textile and electronics factories have been high, the major recent *successes* of South Korean worker protest are to be found in automobile, shipyard, and other heavy industries, which provide relatively higher wages and greater job security.

Nor do cultural differences provide a convincing explanation. It has been argued that East Asian Confucianism encourages conformity, avoidance of conflict, and deference to authority, while European-derived

TABLE 7.3
Physical Quality of Life Index Scores, Selected Years

	1976	1986
Argentina	84	89
Brazil	68	74
Mexico	75	80
South Korea	80	86
Taiwan	87	94

Source: Sewell (1988).

Note: High scores indicate relatively favorable general welfare levels as measured by a weighted, composite index of life expectancy, infant mortality, and literacy.

traditions of democracy, anarchism, and syndicalism have energized populist protest in Latin America, especially during earlier periods in Argentina (Bergquist, 1986). Such assertions fail to explain earlier periods of revolutionary turmoil and change in East Asia, the multiplicity of non-Confucianist traditions, or even the right of rebellion embedded in Confucianist thought itself. They also ignore the strong authoritarian corporatist thread of Iberian culture in Latin America.

It may finally be noted that economic and cultural explanations more usefully address the problem of political *activation* than that of the organizational *capacity* to translate action into power. Class power depends crucially on the emergence of autonomous class institutions. Argentina's Anarchistic and later Peronist trade unions, strong middle class political parties, and proletarian community institutions draw a striking contrast to Taiwan's controlled unions and community organizations and far weaker political parties. To understand this more fundamental institutional difference, it is necessary to examine the interaction between socioeconomic and political changes over recent decades of rapid industrialization. While political regimes provide the political opportunity for an insertion of popular class agendas in national policy-making, socioeconomic structural factors generate the capacity to create autonomous class organizations and thus to effectively seize such opportunities (Bergquist, 1985).

CLASS POLITICS: THE ROLE OF SOCIOECONOMIC STRUCTURE

Argentine development, to a far greater extent than that in Taiwan, favored concentrated urban industrial employment, especially following the influx of foreign capital into heavy and consumer-durables industry in the 1950s and 1960s. Taiwanese policy fostered dispersed, smaller scale, indigenous industry producing light consumer goods for world markets. Organizational and ecological concentration favored the emergence of stronger labor movements in Argentina. Conversely, dispersed industry encourages employer paternalism and patriarchal domination in Taiwan's small firms (discussed in Deyo, 1989), as well as efforts on the part of factory workers to set up small firms of their own, an effective safety valve for thwarted ambitions (Gold, 1986). Such differences characterize agriculture as well. Argentina's concentrations of rural wage workers on large estates contrasts with Taiwan's small-farm structure.

Second, Argentine capital-intensive and heavy industry has attracted semiskilled and skilled workers into generally secure, male-intensive urban employment. Portes (1985) estimates that Argentina's "formal sector" of contractually protected, generally unionized workers comprises roughly half of the economically active population. Conversely, Taiwan's predominantly light consumer-goods industries, especially during the 1960s and early 1970s, employed large numbers of low-skill female workers on a fairly short-term basis prior to their marriages. This pattern of female employment is especially evident in export processing zones, where young unmarried women comprise a very large proportion of the workforce (Galenson, 1979). But it applies more generally as well. The dispersal of industry to rural areas encouraged seasonal and short-term factory employment of rural youth, both male and female, as a supplement to farm income (Cheng, chap. 6, this volume). This difference in employment patterns is related to a deeper long-term commitment among Argentine workers to urban factory employment, and a correspondingly greater tendency to fight to protect their economic status rather than to move to other types of work or to leave the workforce altogether (see Gates, 1979). This cross-national difference is illustrated by contrasting worker responses to recession and unemployment. Whereas economic recession has tended to precipitate protracted industrial conflict in Argentina, it has more often resulted in withdrawal from formal sector employment in Taiwan.

Greater employment stability, welfare security based in earlier populist coalitions, and urban industrial concentration have fostered stable proletarian communities in the major industrial centers of Argentina. These communities form dense networks of religious, social, political, and ethnic organizations and associations that provide a social base for autonomous class action, even under the repressive regimes that imposed stringent controls over trade unions and other more vulnerable formal political structures during the 1960s and 1970s (DiTella, 1981). Such proletarian communities have been less in evidence either in Taiwan's urban industrial centers, with their floating workforce (Myers, 1984, p. 519), or in rural towns, whose social life and culture are dominated by leading commercial and business families. Greenhalgh's description of the Taiwanese urban industrial workforce is instructive in this regard:

> In 1980 only one-quarter of the residents of Taiwan's cities were natives of those cities. . . . Taiwan's population is extraordinarily mobile. . . . Contemporary migration represents not a permanent move of an individual, but a short-term strategy of a family, in which migrant family members—or sojourners—remain tied to their local systems through flows of information, money, and a myriad of other things. (1984, p. 531)

Greenhalgh goes on to show that many urban industrial workers form "secondary households," which are temporary in nature and tied firmly by bonds of loyalty and financial interdependence to primary households in rural areas. Such households, which have a short lifespan of only five or six years, severely undercut working-class community formation of the sort described for Argentina.

In Brazil, the need for hard authoritarian repression as well as more recent indications of the growing strength of populist groups is reflective of other economic structural factors that parallel those of Argentina. First, continuing rapid growth of heavy industry, led by the dynamic auto industry, has been associated with the emergence of a formal sector proletariat strongly committed to the creation of trade unions independent of traditional clientelist and state ties (Alves, 1984; Keck, 1984). Second, working-class urban communities have themselves achieved a degree of political autonomy sufficient to permit them to play a supportive role in oppositional social movements. Of special importance has been the Catholic Church, which has helped to raise strike funds, educate the public in political rights, assist the poor and unemployed in demands for increased public expenditures, provide safe meeting places for neighborhood groups, and challenge the legitimacy of state policy (Mainwaring, 1986). And given the far more effective state controls over trade unions here than in Argentina, and the much larger informal sector of self-employed and family workers, it is clear that the "unregulated" areas of Brazilian community social life have played a more essential role in fostering oppositional populist mobilization, especially in matters of collective consumption and community welfare (Portes, 1985; Sandoval, 1985).

South Korea presents a similarly intermediate case from the standpoint of structural empowerment. Relatively greater stress on heavy industry has fostered a more stable, intermediate- to high-skilled industrial proletariat. A more permanent migration flow from rural areas has been fostered by organizationally and spatially more concentrated industrialization, along with a relatively more stagnant agricultural sector unable to absorb return migrants from urban areas. It has been among these workers, particularly in heavy urban industry, that a politically strong and independent workers' movement has begun to emerge.

On the other hand, South Korean industrialization, like that in Taiwan, has fostered the development of a substantial floating workforce in light export industry (e.g., textiles, wearing apparel, and footwear), a workforce among whom effective organization remains elusive. For these workers, movement out of modern factory employment typically involves a shift into the informal urban sector rather than a return to the farm (Koo, 1976).

It may finally be noted that structural factors also help account for cross-national differences in political demands for democratic reforms, especially among middle class groups. Fuller, more egalitarian development in Argentina than in Brazil or Mexico has eventuated in a substantially larger urban middle class there. By the 1950s, the Argentine middle class comprised roughly 36 percent of the economically active population (EAP), thereafter expanding slightly to 38 percent in 1970. By contrast, in 1970, the middle class comprised only 19 percent of the EAP in Brazil and 24 percent in Mexico (Wilkie and Perkal, 1986). The early growth of an Argentine middle class paralleled the early growth of an urban proletariat in providing a structural base for populist politics. But in order more fully to comprehend the consequences of this difference among the Latin American NICs, as well as its very different outcome in East Asia, it is necessary to understand its relationship to changing political regimes in these countries.

POLITICAL REGIMES AND CLASS POLITICS

Structural factors suggest differences in the capacity for autonomous class politics among the four countries. These differences have in turn been reinforced by variation in the political opportunities for autonomous class organization.

The continuity of Taiwan's state-imposed exclusionary political regime, extending historically backward several decades, marks the strongest possible contrast to Argentina's sporadically open, competitive political system during most of the twentieth century. Argentine political regimes have generally presented ample opportunity for the building of autonomous political organizations through which to channel political dissent even under subsequent repression.

Closely related to regime differences is variation in coalitional and elite structure. Elite competition presents both negative and positive oppositional possibilities. Negatively, such competition creates politically exploitable fissures in the ruling apparatus. Positively, it offers the possibility of cross-class coalitions as weak elite factions seek support from subordinate groups against dominant elites. Argentina's political history is marked by shifting coalitions among elite groups, including landed classes (especially the cattle barons), industrialists, the military, and the state. Beginning in the postwar era, coalitional ruptures and conflict accompanying the "exhaustion" of light ISI encouraged cross-class coalitions that mobilized and energized popular sector organizations.

It is important to note the structural mobilization of Argentine popular sector groups and class institutions *prior* to state efforts to contain and repress populist politics. This was in part a consequence of the predominant role of foreign capital in urban industry and a corresponding lack of concern on the part of the domestic agrarian elite about labor organization and militancy. Thus, it was noted, Perón was forced to appease and co-opt an already established, strong labor movement in his attempt to cement a political support base for his presidency (Erickson, Peppe, and Spalding, 1974, p. 125). During later periods of economic crisis, labor unions, no longer able to be controlled, had to be repressed and destroyed (Frank, 1981, p. 239).

This sequencing, which permitted the development of autonomous and politically sustainable class organizations and ideology under subsequent state controls (Remmer and Merkx, 1982), reverses the Taiwanese pattern of an early imposition of exclusionary regimes prior to the socioeconomic mobilization of the popular sector. Even under the Japanese, authoritarian rule sank deep roots in community associations, farmers' groups, and other social organizations, thus ensuring an early preemptive filling of organizational space prior to social mobilization (see Cumings, 1987). Such preemptive organization was deepened and extended under the leadership of the Kuomintang (KMT) party after the departure of the Japanese. Following a ruthless liquidation of intellectuals and dissident groups during 1947–1949, virtually all remaining social groups (youth, women, community organizations, workgroups, unions, schools, professional, business associations, etc.) were harnessed to and sometimes financially subsidized by the KMT apparatus. The success of this preemptive organization of civil society, which began with a virtually clean slate in the late 1940s, is evident not only in the near absence of populist dissent during recessionary periods, but more dramatically in the "softness" of the authoritarian regime needed to maintain stringent economic and political control well into the democratic reforms of the 1980s (Winckler, 1984; Johnson, 1987).

In Brazil, initial populist inclusion in national politics came at the invitation and sponsorship of Vargas, who, like Perón, sought a populist political base during an early period of political consolidation. But Vargas, unlike Perón, created rather than inherited a strong labor movement. For this reason, Vargas was better able to assert preemptory political control over an emergent labor movement. The political dependency of organized labor on elite factions was to become clear when—in response to labor agitation against industrial denationalization, income concentration, and wage controls during the 1960s—a quick and virtually unchallenged military coup sufficed to silence populist and leftist opposition. This reactionary regime was strongly supported by the bourgeoisie and upper middle income groups, united by a shared fear of revolution.

South Korean political regimes have displayed greater continuity than those of Argentina or Brazil, though less than that in Taiwan. Here, a long history of authoritarian rule, extending to well before the Japanese annexation, was only briefly interrupted by social disruption and populist mobilization such as that of nationalist opposition to Japanese rule in the 1920s, leftist agitation immediately following World War II, opposition to the corrupt Rhee regime in the late 1950s, and popular protest during the political crisis beginning in the late 1970s. In each instance, elite disunity along with economic recession combined to trigger protest. But in each of the earlier periods of political crisis, protest was quickly suppressed following reestablishment of elite unity.

The effectiveness of such repression was rooted in a longer-term pattern of elite unity, albeit one punctuated by short-term crises. The destruction of the landlord class, the political discrediting of the "corrupt" bourgeoisie at the end of the Rhee regime, and a subsequent economic subordination of the industrial bourgeoisie under state-led development (Wade; Cheng; chaps. 9 and 6, respectively; this volume) have largely precluded the elite factionalism that has played an important role in politically mobilizing Latin American popular sector groups. Despite the democratic interlude of the immediate postwar period, liberal democratic culture has not sunk deep roots in South Korean society, and most committed radicals, who might have encouraged a leftward turn in South Korea's development strategy, have long since fled north.

The relative continuity of authoritarian rule and the post-1953 confrontation with North Korea have ensured tight preemptive state controls over unions and other formal organizations of political relevance to the popular sector. But these controls, lacking the organizational framework of a mass party, have failed to incorporate the full range of associational life encompassed by Taiwan's KMT party (Park, 1987). By consequence, social protest has had to be contained through primarily repressive regimes. This difference is especially clear with respect to the politically active Christian churches in South Korea that, along with university student organizations, have played a significant role in raising issues of economic equity and political reform. The radicalizing role of churches is especially apparent in the church-based industrial missions that have encouraged factory workers to challenge unfair labor practices and to demand rights to organize and act collectively. On the other hand, the relatively weak social foundation for effective popular sector political organization has ensured that recent democratic reforms were marked by substantial regime continuity, as evidenced in uninterrupted rule by the Democratic Justice Party (DJP) and consolidation of a ruling political coalition between the DJP and key opposition parties in early 1990.

MEXICO: A NOTE

While this chapter has not dealt with Mexico, it is clear that this third Latin American NIC highlights the importance of structural factors and preemptive regime sequencing for popular sector political influence in public policy. Populist politics and opposition have played a minimal role in Mexico since the Cárdenas era in the late 1930s (Kaufman, chap. 5, this volume). This is seen most dramatically during recent years, when urban workers and salaried groups have mounted very weak opposition to economic stabilization policies that have been associated with severe retrenchment in real wages and living standards. Indeed, the combination here of a politically quiescent population and a relatively unfavorable economic record from the standpoint of real wages (table 7.2), income inequality (Gereffi, chap. 1, this volume, table 1.4) and PQLI (table 7.3) further undercuts a welfare explanation for cross-national differences in the political mobilization of popular sector groups.

In part, the explanation for the minimal political role of Mexican popular sectors is to be found in economic structural factors: a large agrarian population, a relatively small middle class, and weaker development of an urban, heavy-industry proletariat alongside the rapid growth of transitory industrial employment in light, female-intensive export manufacturing under the Border Industrialization Program (see Bustamente, 1983; Fernandez-Kelly, 1983). But equally important is an early and highly successful preemptive incorporation of popular sector groups into the PRI/state apparatus (Evans, 1979, p. 300; Kaufman, 1979). This party-based corporatist political system, which penetrates the labor movement, communities, and a wide range of social groups, is paralleled by a cultural preemption by the PRI of an ideology of nationalism and social reform deriving from the Mexican Revolution. Mexico's structural demobilization of workers and preemptive regime sequencing suggest striking parallels with Taiwan.

CONCLUSION

The literature on Third World development suggests a number of roles popular sectors may play in development strategy formulation. These include: (1) the definition of developmental "needs" to which strategy is at least in part addressed; (2) the determination of the array of human resources (education, skills, market power) and of sociocultural and organizational resources or constraints, which impinge on the success of particular strategies; (3) the generation, with lesser or greater force, of distributionist and welfare demands on elites; and (4) the mobilization of demands for political reforms, often relating to the creation of democratic regimes. Such political demands impinge on strategy through their consequences for the influence of nonelite groups on national decision-making. The present discussion has been addressed largely to the latter two demand-making roles.

Cross-national comparisons point to substantial variation in the impact of popular sector demands on economic policies and political regimes. Insofar as such policies implement broader development strategies, and insofar as regimes serve to politically insulate or legitimate strategy decision-makers, popular demands may impinge strongly on national strategy. Popular-sector demands *have* played this role in Argentina to a far greater extent than in the other countries included in this study. This difference is in part explained by corresponding differences in the nature and sequencing of social change.

Socioeconomic changes that encourage popular sector mobilization include employment concentration, the emergence of class-homogeneous communities, and the growth of a large middle class. But whether such changes in fact empower popular sectors depends additionally on the temporal relationship between these structural changes on the one hand, and political changes on the other. Where preemptive political organization precedes social mobilization under stable and cohesive ruling coalitions, the emergence of autonomous class institutions and political action is aborted. Where the reverse sequencing occurs, popular sectors acquire an independent base for the mounting of distributionist and class politics under even subsequently repressive regimes.

REFERENCES

Aguiar, Marco, Marcos Arruda, and Parsifal Flores. 1984. "Economic Dictatorship Versus Democracy in Brazil." *Latin American Perspectives* 11, no. 1, pp. 13–25.

Alves, Maria Helena Moreiga. 1984. "Grassroots Organizations, Trade Unions, and the Church: A Challenge to the Controlled Abertura in Brazil." *Latin American Perspectives* 11, no. 1, pp. 73–102.

Asian Development Bank. 1985. *Key Indicators of Developing Member Countries*. Vol 16, supplement. October.

Asia Research Bulletin. 1982. June 30.

Athey, Lois. 1984. "Democracy and Populism: Some Recent Studies." *Latin American Research Review* 19, no. 3, pp. 172–83.

Bergquist, Charles. 1986. *Labor in Latin America*. Stanford, Calif.: Stanford University Press.

———. 1985. "Export Production Structures and the Latin American Labor Movements." In *Technology Change and Workers' Movements*, edited by Melvyn Dubofsky. Beverly Hills, Calif.: Sage Publications.

Bresser Pereira, Luiz Carlos. 1984. *Development and Crisis in Brazil, 1930–1983*. Boulder, Colo.: Westview.

Buchanan, Paul. 1985. "State Corporatism in Argentina: Labor Administration under Perón and Onganía." *Latin American Research Review* 20, no. 1, pp. 61–95.

Bustamante, Jorge A. 1983. "Maquiladoras: A New Force of International Capitalism on Mexico's Northern Frontier." In *Women, Men, and the International*

Division of Labor, edited by June Nash and Patricia Fernandez-Kelly, Albany, N.Y.: SUNY Press.

Canak, William L. 1984. "The Peripheral State Debate: State Capitalist and B-A Regimes in Latin America." *Latin American Research Review* 19, no. 1, pp. 3–36.

Chen, Yu-hsi. "Dependent Development and Its Socio-Political Consequences: A Case Study of Taiwan." Ph.D. diss., University of Hawaii.

Cleaves, Peter. 1980. "Implementation Amidst Scarcity and Apathy: Political Power and Policy Design." In *Politics and Political Implementation in the Third World*, edited by Merilee S. Grindle. Princeton: Princeton University Press.

Corradi, Juan E. 1985. *The Fitful Republic: Economics, Society, and Politics in Argentina*. Boulder, Colo.: Westview Press.

Cumings, Bruce. 1987. "The Origins and Development of the Northeast Asian Political Economy." In Deyo (1987).

Deyo, Frederic. 1989. *Beneath the Miracle: Labor Subordination in the New Asian Industrialism*. Berkeley: University of California Press.

———. 1987. "State and Labor: Modes of Political Exclusion in East Asian Development." In his *The Political Economy of the New Asian Industrialism*. Ithaca: Cornell University Press.

———. 1984. "Export Manufacturing and Labor: the Asian Case." In *Labor in the Capitalist World-Economy*, edited by Charles Bergquist. Beverly Hills: Sage.

DiTella, Torcuato. 1981. "Working-Class Organization and Politics in Argentina." *Latin American Research Review* 16, no. 2, pp. 33–56.

Dix, Robert. "Populism: Authoritarian and Democratic." *Latin American Research Review* 20, no. 2, pp. 29–52.

Ehrenthal, David, and Joseph Newman. 1988. "Explaining Mexico's Maquila Boom." *SAIS Review* 8, no. 1.

Eisenstadt, S. N. 1966. *Modernization: Protest and Change*. Englewood Cliffs, N.J.: Prentice-Hall.

Erickson, Kenneth, Patrick Peppe, and Hobart Spalding. 1974. "Research on the Urban Working Class and Organized Labor in Argentina, Brazil, and Chile." *Latin American Research Review* 9, no. 2, pp. 115–42.

Evans, Peter. 1985. "After Dependency: Recent Studies of Class, State, and Industrialization." *Latin American Research Review* 20, no. 2, pp. 149–60.

———. 1979. *Dependent Development: The Alliance of Multinational, State, and Local Capital in Brazil*. Princeton: Princeton University Press.

Felix, David. 1983. "Income Distribution and the Quality of Life in Latin America: Patterns, Trends, and Policy Implications." *Latin American Research Review* 18, no. 2, pp. 3–33.

Fernandez-Kelly, Patricia. 1983. *For We Are Sold: I and My People*. Albany: SUNY Press.

Fields, Gary. 1984. "Employment, Income Distribution, and Economic Growth in Seven Small Open Economies." *Economic Journal* 94, March, pp. 74–83.

Foxley, Alejandro. 1983. *Latin American Experiments in Neo-Conservative Economics*. Berkeley: University of California Press.

Frank, Andre Gunder. 1981. *Crisis in the Third World*. New York: Holmes and Meier.

Galenson, Walter. 1979. "The Labor Force, Wages, and Living Conditions." In his *Economic Growth and Structural Change in Taiwan*. Ithaca: Cornell University Press.

Gates, Hill. 1979. "Dependency and the Part-Time Proletariat in Taiwan." *Modern China 5*, no. 3, pp. 381–408.

Gereffi, Gary. 1983. *The Pharmaceutical Industry and Dependency in the Third World*. Princeton: Princeton University Press.

Gold, Thomas B. 1986. *State and Society in the Taiwan Miracle*. Armonk, N.Y.: M.E. Sharpe.

Greenhalgh, Susan. 1984. "Networks and Their Nodes: Urban Society on Taiwan." *The China Quarterly* 99, September, pp. 529–52.

Hagopian, Frances. 1986. "State Capitalism and Politics in Brazil." Working Paper no. 63, Helen Kellogg Institute for International Studies, Notre Dame University.

International Labor Organization. Various years. *Bulletin of Labor Statistics*.

Johnson, Chalmers. 1987. "Political Institutions and Economic Performance: The Government-Business Relationship in Japan, South Korea, and Taiwan." In Deyo (1987).

Johnson, Dale. 1982. "Toward a Historical and Dialectical Social Science." In *Class and Social Development: A New Theory of the Middle Class*, edited by Dale Johnson. Beverly Hills, Calif.: Sage.

Kaufman, Robert. "Industrial Change and Authoritarian Rule in Latin America: A Concrete Review of the Bureaucratic-Authoritarian Model." In *The New Authoritarianism in Latin America*, edited by David Collier. Princeton: Princeton University Press, 1979.

Keck, Marjorie. 1985. "Labor and Politics in the Brazilian Transition." Paper presented at the annual meetings of the Latin American Studies Association, Albuquerque, N.M., April.

———. 1984. "Update on the Brazilian Labor Movement." *Latin American Perspectives* 11, no. 1, pp. 27–34.

Koo, Hagen. 1984. "The Political Economy of Income Distribution in South Korea: The Impact of the State's Industrialization Policies." *World Development* 12, pp. 1029–37.

———. 1976. "Small Entrepreneurship in a Developing Society." *Social Forces* 54, no. 4, pp. 775–87.

Kuznets, Paul. 1985. "Government and Economic Strategy in South Korea." *Pacific Affairs* 58, no. 1, pp. 44–67.

Lee, Man-Gap. 1982. *Sociology and Social Change in Korea*. Seoul: Seoul National University Press.

Little, Ian. "An Economic Reconnaissance." In *Economic Growth and Structural Change in Taiwan*, edited by Walter Galenson. Ithaca: Cornell University Press, 1979.

Mainwaring, Scott. 1986. "The Transition to Democracy in Brazil." Working Paper no. 66, Helen Kellogg Institute for International Studies, Notre Dame University.

Moore, Wilbert. 1979. *World Modernization: The Limits of Convergence*. New York: Elsevier.

Myers, Ramon H. 1987. "Political Theory and Recent Political Developments in the Republic of China." *Asian Survey* 27, no. 9, pp. 1003–22.

———. 1984. "The Economic Transformation of the Republic of China on Taiwan." *The China Quarterly* 99, September, pp. 500–28.

Pak, Chi-Young. 1982. *Political Opposition in Korea: 1945–1960*. Seoul: Seoul National University Press.

Park, Moon Kyu. 1987. "Interest Representation in South Korea: The Limits of Corporatist Control." *Asian Survey* 27, no. 8, pp. 903–17.

Paul, Samuel. 1983. *Strategic Management of Development Programmes*. Geneva: International Labour Office.

Perlman, Janice. 1980. "The Failure of Influence: Squatter Eradication in Brazil." In *Politics and Policy Implementation in the Third World*, edited by Merilee Grindle. Princeton: Princeton University Press.

Petras, James. "The Peripheral State: Continuity and Change in the International Division of Labor." In *Capitalist and Socialist Crises in the Late Twentieth Century*, edited by James Petras. Totowa, N.J.: Rowman and Allanheld Press, 1983.

Pion-Berlin, David. 1983. "Political Repression and Economic Doctrines: The Case of Argentina." *Comparative Political Studies* 16, no. 1, pp. 37–66.

Portes, Alejandro. 1985. "Latin American Class Structures: Their Composition and Change During the Last Decades." *Latin American Research Review* 20, no. 3, pp. 7–39.

Remmer, Karen, and Gilbert Merkx. 1982. "Bureaucratic-Authoritarianism Revisited." *Latin American Research Review* 17, no. 2, pp. 3–40.

Republic of China, Directorate General of Budget, Accounting, and Statistics. Various years. *Statistical Yearbook of the Republic of China*.

Sandoval, Salvador. 1985. "Strikes and Working-class Organization in Brazil: 1960-1980." Paper presented at the annual meetings of the Latin American Studies Association, Albuquerque, N.M., April.

Seers, Dudley. 1982. "The New Role of Development Planning." In *Problems and Politics in Small Economies*, edited by B. Jalan. London: Croom Helm.

Sewell, John. 1988. *Agenda 1988: Growth, Jobs, and Exports in a Changing World Economy*. Washington, D.C.: Overseas Development Council.

United Nations. Economic Commission for Asia and the Pacific. 1982. *Yearbook for Asia and the Pacific*.

United Nations Statistical Office. Various dates. *Monthly Bulletin of Statistics*.

United States, Bureau of Labor Statistics. 1972. "Labor Law and Practices in the Republic of China (Taiwan)." Report no. 404. Washington D.C.: GPO.

Wilkie, James, and Adam Perkal, eds. 1986. *Statistical Abstract of Latin America*. Los Angeles: UCLA Latin American Center Publications.

Winckler, Edwin. 1984. "Institutionalization and Participation on Taiwan: From

Hard to Soft Authoritarianism." *The China Quarterly* 99, September, pp. 481–99.

World Bank. 1989. *World Tables*. 1988–1989 ed. Baltimore: Johns Hopkins University Press.

———. 1987. *World Development Report*. New York: Oxford University Press.

Zuzik, Michael. 1964. "Labor Law and Practice in Taiwan." U.S. Department of Labor, Bureau of Labor Statistics, Report no. 268. Washington D.C.: GPO.

PART THREE

Development Strategies: Do They Make a Difference?

CHAPTER 8

Contrasts in the Political Economy of Development Policy Change

Gustav Ranis

MUCH RECENT LITERATURE has focused on an assessment of the development effort in the developing countries attempting a transition from agrarianism to modern growth as described by Simon Kuznets (1966). Most of this work has focused on a variety of sectoral and aggregative dimensions of performance, including "bottom line" indices implying success or failure in reaching basic development objectives. While Kuznets was himself more concerned with describing the attributes of "modern growth" than with the transition effort, others have tried to examine deviations from the "normal" structure in terms of initial conditions and subsequent man-made organizational or policy choices. Kuznets envisioned government policies as either obstructing or accommodating some sort of natural evolution of a system over time, but he essentially excluded policy formation from his descriptive canvas. Other researchers, such as Chenery, built policy choices into the very typology they constructed, for example, by dividing countries into outer-oriented and inner-oriented systems (Chenery and Syrquin, 1975). While organizational and policy choices are clearly basic to any explanation of developmental success and failure, what has largely eluded analysts and observers to date and constitutes an important field for further investigation is just how to endogenize such policy change over time.

The current interest in comparing East Asia and Latin America, which was not fashionable as little as half a dozen years ago, is based on the acceptance of the notion that different policy choices can, in fact, make a good deal of difference. But the difficulty with most of that literature is that it is largely descriptive in presenting the success of some of the East Asian countries in contrast to the lack of success of some of the Latin American countries. What was accomplished is fully treated, but the basic question of "why" is hardly addressed. Some of the explanation surely resides in differences in such initial conditions as man/land ratios, natural resource endowments, and size. It is much too facile to attribute significant differences in national performance to cultural differences that are not subject to modification by acts of man over time. Confucianism, for example, can hardly be "the" simple answer when we recall the long centuries of stagnation in China.

It is by now well recognized that both the East Asian and Latin American economies did pass through specific subphases of transition growth. First, we encounter the familiar "easy" import substitution subphase focused on nondurable consumer goods. In Latin America this initially occurred in the 1930s as the by-product response to the Great Depression and was continued in the early postwar period as part of a more deliberate, conscious effort to industrialize. The same emphasis on the home production of previously imported nondurable consumer goods can be dated from the early postwar period in the newly independent countries of East Asia.

This so-called easy import substitution in both Latin America and East Asia thus represents the "natural" outgrowth of a prior colonial, agricultural export-focused pattern of resource flows. Once exchange controls are imposed and government intervenes to direct foreign exchange earnings from reinvestment in the traditional export enclaves to these new domestically oriented industrial activities, the pattern in Latin America and East Asia are indeed quite similar. What mainly differentiates the typical East Asian from the typical Latin American economy is the nature of the societal choice made at the inevitable end of this easy import substitution subphase, as domestic markets for nondurables run out. More on this below.

The policies to be focused on can be indexed by such macroeconomic parameters as the rate of protection, the exchange rate, the interest rate, the tax rate, and the rate of monetary expansion, but they also include sectoral policies such as actions affecting manpower and labor markets, the role of public sector enterprises, the allocation of government expenditures, as well as the role accorded to science and technology. The explicit (on the table) or implicit (under the table) nature of any particular set of policies, of course, makes a substantial difference as well. For example, a certain rate of protection can be provided by quantitative controls or by equivalent tariffs, and a certain volume of resource transfers from agriculture to industry can be effected by overvalued exchange rates as well as by land taxes.

Major policy instruments such as the interest rate, the rate of protection, and the tax rate must, of course, be interpreted as political tools to achieve certain societal objectives, usually benefiting some groups at the expense of others. The key question is whether such polices are explicit, debated, and negotiated—or implicit, clandestine, and imposed. An essentially political process effecting "under the table" income transfers is usually symptomatic of governments' myopic need to solve short-run problems while putting off the social conflict consequences to a later point in time. In contrast, explicit tax and expenditure policies, whether examples of public goods or favoring specific private parties, serve to accommodate the transition growth process, in the sense that they are an inevitable part of the landscape in even the most laissez-faire advanced economies. In other words, initial politicization is common to virtually all developing countries; but some systems tend to shift from "under the table" to "on the table" interventions after a time, a shift that can be identified as a move toward market liberalization. Such a shift is unlikely to be linear but to oscillate around a trend; nor is it likely to signify a diminished but rather a changed role for the government as its explicit fiscal and monetary functions may well increase more than its implicit functions diminish. But it does mean an organizational shift in the direction of the behavior pattern of the mature mixed economies.

Finally, one might ask what gives us the right to make comparisons across regions as different as East Asia and Latin America. It is clearly a challenge to focus on the elements of transferability in terms of man-made problems (which can be overcome by man) as opposed to nature-made differences (which can only be ameliorated but not overcome by policy change).

While countries are admittedly imperfect laboratories at best, this problem is hardly unique in social science. It is well to remember, moreover, that development seems to have focused on two currently convergent approaches to this problem: (1) the cross section analysis of the early postwar period associated with the names of Kuznets and Chenery; and (2) historical approaches associated with the names of Lewis (1954), Fei and Ranis (1975), and Kelley, Williamson, and Cheetham (1972), among others, pursuing what might be called comparative historical analysis. While late Chenery certainly moved away from the notion that every country was "the same"—that is, a point of observation in his cross sectional regressions—those working in the historical/analytical mode equivalently rejected the proposition that every country is *sui generis* and that its transition growth experience would thus defy any effort at generalization and transferability. We can be skeptical about the effort to extract general conclusions for development from the photo exposure of country data points; but we should not be driven to the other extreme, which is that every country is different at every point in its history.

The recognition of the validity of typologies permits convergence between these two schools of thought. Whatever the intellectual point of departure, a typological approach assumes that there exist meaningful family affinities among subsets of developing countries, giving them a certain uniqueness not necessarily shared by other LDCs. The most obvious example is the role of trade and other open economy dimensions in small versus large countries. A less obvious example is the difference between a

Japanese and a Spanish colonial heritage. Acceptance of such a typological approach, of course, does not connote a lack of awareness of the fact that even within any one subfamily there may, and usually do, exist important and instructive differences among countries. Nevertheless, differences along one typological dimension—for example, size, man/land ratio, or natural resource endowment—are likely to be less pronounced than differences across typologies. A really helpful typological approach, no matter what its intellectual origins, should help bring us closer to focusing on the important elements of interfamily differences while not suppressing meaningful intrafamily variation.

The differential policy responses recorded, which we are trying to render as endogenous as possible here, are, of course, also likely to "cross over" or overlap, perhaps even more than the initial conditions. Thus, South Korea at certain points in the postwar period clearly behaved not very differently from Brazil, both countries being viewed as policy outliers with respect to each of their families. But that does not change the centrality of "on the average" differentiable policy packages.

Kuznets indeed insisted that discussions of policy be kept out of the examination of transition growth, which he based more on the twin phenomena of differing initial conditions and different points of observed (if unexplained) structure over time. He was content, for example, to observe a relatively shrinking agricultural sector, a relatively expanding manufacturing sector, and a fairly stable services sector. Deviations from such an expected pattern of structural change would then be largely and casually attributed to differences in nature, that is, in the objective initial environment. However, in the real world, deviations from "normal" behavior in either direction may be, in fact, related to whether government policies accommodate or obstruct the underlying economic forces at work, an issue that lies at the heart of the matter, the political economy of development policy change. Even Kuznets, averse as he was to the premature introduction of policy, knew full well that the normal metamorphosis of a society is subject to breakdowns and conflict among socioeconomic groups. As he expressed it, "If established groups attached to large economic sectors suffer or foresee contraction of their share or base in economic society . . . they are likely to resist by using political pressure to slow down the process" (1980, p. 419).

It is thus our basic contention that typological subclassifications among LDCs represent useful constructs on the way to a general theory of development. Secondly, we believe that the distinction between policies that accommodate rather than obstruct the transition to modern growth can be defined for each typology and that initial conditions that do play an important role in establishing the typology in the first place also may have an important but not necessarily dominant impact on the choice of policies along the way.

In our view, therefore, there clearly exists no unique metamorphic transition growth path for any one type of LDC, just as there exists no meaningfully "average" behavior pattern for the typical LDC. In other words, there is no implication of any sense of inevitability of movement along a fixed historical pattern. Instead, we see the need to make empirical observations about what, in fact, has happened in some of the major typological cases around the world; moreover, to see if major divergences in patterns of behavior can be clearly identified; and thirdly, also most importantly, to see if such divergences in behavior can be better understood in terms of both differences in initial conditions and in the political economy of policy change over time. Especially if the latter is more fully understood, it is a legitimate hope that the scope for policy to be more flexibly responsive to differences in the initial conditions can be increased and the power of the initial constraints gradually overcome through man-made responses to the environment. But clearly the first step must be a better understanding of the meaning of accommodating versus obstructing policy packages en route to modern growth for different types of developing countries.

In this chapter, I have selected two of the medium-sized East Asian countries, Taiwan and South Korea, to avoid the extreme city/state cases of Hong Kong and Singapore, along with two medium-sized Latin American countries, Mexico and Colombia, where "medium-sized" is, of course, relative to the rest of that subfamily. For each of these pairs of representatives I hope to demonstrate, in the next section, the differences in the policy package and growth pattern chosen at the end of the inevitable easy import substitution subphase and, in the last section, to try to better understand it within the political economy context of this chapter.

DIFFERENTIAL POLICY CHOICE AND PERFORMANCE

Taiwan and South Korea, at the time of the beginning of their transition growth effort in the early 1950s, typified the case of the relatively small-to medium-sized, heavily labor-surplus economy, relatively poor in natural and relatively rich in human resources. In both South Korea and Taiwan, the system's colonial antecedents, moreover, featured heavy attention on infrastructural and organizational investments in the rural sector and on the food crops required by Japan, the mother country. Additional dimensions of these initial conditions included a fairly equal distribution of assets, especially land, thanks to both colonial and post-independence land reforms. The land ownership Gini for Taiwan, for example, was in the neighborhood of 0.6 in 1949 and fell to 0.4 by 1953, which stands in marked contrast to land ownership Ginis of around 0.8 typical of Latin America (see table 8.1).

Our very notion of transition growth presumes an evolutionary view of economic development. This metamorphic stance envisions the existence of subphases, with each subphase characterized by a distinct set of structural characteristics and a distinct mode of operation helpful for the analysis of post-independence performance. During the colonial or pre-transition period, both East Asian systems routinely consumed imported factory-produced nondurable consumer goods, while exporting traditional agricultural products—for example, rice and sugar in the case of Taiwan. While Taiwan possessed somewhat more favorable natural/ geographic features in terms of climate, soil, the potential for multiple cropping, and related land-saving technology change, both South Korea and Taiwan benefited from the Japanese colonial emphasis on such infrastructural investments as irrigation and on such institutional investments as farmers' organizations.

Turning to the two Latin American cases, the most striking characteristic encountered (see table 8.1), is their more favorable initial man/land ratios, their more concentrated rural assets structure, their somewhat larger size, and their substantially higher initial levels of wealth and per capita income. Nevertheless, the initial colonial resources flow pattern bears a substantial resemblance to the East Asian case—that is, the exportation of mainly land-based raw materials (mostly minerals and tropical cash crops) in exchange for mainly industrial consumer goods. Import substitution started here in the Depression years of the 1930s, but focused equally on reallocating the proceeds from traditional natural resource based exports to finance new nondurable consumer goods types of import substituting industries.

Thus both East Asia and Latin America initiated their modern transi-

TABLE 8.1
Initial Conditions, Approximately 1950

	Agricultural Population/ Arable Land (hectares)	Adult Literacy (percent)	Land Distribution (Gini)
Taiwan	2.04	50.1	0.4
South Korea	8.11	76.8	0.5
Colombia	1.65	62.3	0.8
Mexico	0.32	56.8	0.8

Sources: United Nations (1953); UNESCO (1963); World Bank (1976; 1980).

tion growth effort via the well-known easy import substitution pattern of development. Such import substitution, financed by traditional exports, entails two observable phenomena—that is, increased substitution in the sense that foreign exchange resources are now increasingly used for producer goods importation and substitution in the sense that the domestic market for nondurables is now increasingly satisfied by domestic production.

Foreign trade as a percentage of national income can be expected to gradually decline during this subphase, given the fact that the policy syndrome that accompanies it strongly favors domestic markets and protective devices in support of a new industrial class. During this period modern factory production for domestic markets expands rapidly, often with the help of foreign capital; traditional populations are converted into modern factory workers; land-based or commercial entrepreneurs are converted into industrial entrepreneurs capable of absorbing modern science and technology; and law-and-order-oriented civil servants tend to become developmental change agents.

It is well known that during this subphase all the policies of government are indeed directed to supporting the new industrial class. With profits taking on a windfall character less directly linked to productive efficiency, we usually encounter increasingly inefficient, capital-intensive technology and output mixes, a neglect of rural industry and an even more serious neglect of the food-producing agricultural sector. The policies normally deployed to achieve that objective include the following: substantial protection via a combination of tariffs and quantitative controls, especially for the nondurables; exchange controls, import licensing, and an overvalued exchange rate usually becoming more overvalued with time as a consequence of an increasing exposure to inflationary pressures; a low official interest rate in repressed and heavily rationed money markets; a tax system which is anemic and largely indirect (i.e., import and export duty based); a government expenditure pattern favoring urban industrial interests; government interventions in the staple food markets to maintain low prices of wage goods to urban consumers; minimum wage legislation; and government support of unions to maintain organized sector wages at levels substantially in excess of agricultural wages.

This policy syndrome is essentially shared by the East Asian and Latin American cases. But it is noteworthy that the East Asian countries chose a relatively mild and more flexible version of the package. For example, they neglected their agricultural sectors less, raised their real interest rates earlier, and maintained lower levels of effective protection of their industries than the Latin Americans.

This process of easy import substitution growth, lasting approximately ten to fifteen years in most LDCs, must inevitably come to an end. The inevitability of its termination rests on the fact that, once all nondurable manufactured goods imports have been substituted for by domestic output, any further industrialization has to slow to the pace of population and per capita income change.

Difficult societal decisions now have to be made—that is, whether to maintain the import substitution strategy but shift to the domestic production of previously imported producers' and durable consumer goods or move toward the exportation of the same nondurable consumer goods previously produced for domestic markets. The East Asian countries, after some hesitation, chose the latter path, that is, to enter what may be called primary export substitution based on the fact that the basis for comparative advantage in foreign trade now gradually shifts from land to unskilled labor-intensive products. By the end of the 1960s, the relative importance of these two kinds of exports had, in fact, been dramatically reversed, from 90 percent land-based to 80 percent labor-based (as seen in tables 8.2c–8.2e), while the level of overall trade orientation, E/GDP, increased markedly as a consequence of prodigious increases in these labor-intensive industrial exports (see table 8.2f).

Moreover, the rate of labor reallocation, the shift of the labor force from agricultural to nonagricultural pursuits over time, accelerated substantially during this subphase due to a combination of rapid agricultural productivity increase and the expansion of labor intensive industrial output now destined for relatively unlimited international markets. Once industrial entrepreneurial maturation, combined with the restoration of a fair game for food producing agriculture, had laid the foundation, labor intensive export industries offered a full opportunity, really for the first time, to absorb the system's underemployed on a massive scale. This labor-based "vent for surplus" led to a pronounced increase in the rate of domestic intersectoral labor reallocation, culminating in not only a relative but an absolute decrease in the agricultural labor force, and, in the course of little more than a decade, the exhaustion of the labor surplus condition, as indexed by nearly constant unskilled wages giving way to rapidly rising wages in both South Korea and Taiwan.

This export substitution mode, it should be noted, implies both vigorous domestic intersectoral growth and a substantial integration of the East Asian economies into the world economy. It meant a spurt in domestic agricultural/nonagricultural exchanges as well as a spectacular expansion of international trade. At the same time, capital inflows more than replaced the earlier infusion of concessional foreign capital—in spite of the considerable political and strategic uncertainties, especially in the case of Taiwan.

Such a shift into export substitution must, of course, be accommodated by a difficult-to-achieve shift in public policy. Any enhanced orientation toward international markets on a competitive basis requires, first of all, a shift from an inflationary (under the table) method of taxing the landed interests on behalf of the new industrial classes to one of more explicit (on the table) taxation. It requires, moreover, a reduction in protection, the adoption and maintenance of more realistic exchange rates, interest rates closer to their shadow levels, the continued avoidance of the temptation to artificially depress domestic agriculture's terms of trade, and a willingness to avoid raising the real wages of unskilled workers as long as a labor surplus persists. The transition to export substitution in East Asia was, moreover, facilitated by such direct government actions as the allocation of infrastructure to the rural sector, and the establishment of export processing zones and the rebating of import duties on raw materials destined for exports as transitional devices.

This primary export substitution subphase, of course, also has its limits. Once the unskilled labor surplus has been exhausted, as it was by the early seventies in East Asia, unskilled real wages began to rise in a sustained fashion. Competitive industrial output and exports tended to become more skilled labor, technology and capital intensive, that is, the subphase of secondary import and export substitution was gradually reached. In other words, as their skill, entrepreneurial, and technological capacity increased further, Taiwan and South Korea have, since the mid–1970s, moved into the production, for the domestic market and almost simultaneously for export, of capital goods, consumer durables, and the processing of raw materials—with the degree of simultaneity related to the importance of economies of scale in the context of the size of the domestic market. At the same time, the slack in the system's agricultural sector in the form of sustained productivity increases of the "Green Revolution" type had by now been substantially mopped up; as that sector became less of a leading sector and more of an appendage to the rest of the economy, the basic need for food imports in an essentially long-term, natural-resources-poor system increasingly asserted itself. As is well recognized, East Asia now supplies both domestic and foreign markets with producers' goods while importing an increasing volume of food.

The per capita income growth rates in South Korea and Taiwan during their more than a quarter century of transition growth have been remarkably high (see table 8.2a). At least as interesting is an examination of their employment, labor share, and income distribution performance, which have also been outstandingly favorable by any standard. We should not, of course, be too surprised by an improvement in income distribution equity once the labor surplus is absorbed, wages rise, and industrial output shifts in continuing response to changes in the endowment; this is in accordance with both cross-sectional evidence and the crude theorizing surrounding the inverse-U-shaped or Kuznets curve hypothesis (Kuznets,

TABLE 8.2a
Annual Real per Capita GDP Growth Rates (percent)

	1950–59	1960–69	1970–79	1980–84
Taiwan	4.7 (1952–1959)	5.9	8.1	3.9 (1980–1983)
South Korea	1.3 (1953–1959)	4.9	7.5	3.1
Colombia	1.7 (1951–1959)	1.9	3.9	0.4 (1980–1982)
Mexico	9.3 (1952–1959)	4.1	1.9	0.1

Sources: United Nations (various years); Summers and Heston (1984, pp. 207–62); Republic of China (various years).

TABLE 8.2b
Income Distribution (Gini coefficients)

	1953	1960	1970	1980
Taiwan	0.56	0.44 (1959)	0.29	0.29 (1978)
South Korea	—	—	0.37	0.38 (1976)
Colombia	—	0.53	0.56	0.52 (1982)
Mexico	—	0.54	0.58	0.50 (1977)

Sources: Jain (1975); Fei, Ranig, and Kuo (1979).

1955). What is of special interest, however, is that the distribution of income seems not to have worsened, even to have improved substantially (see table 8.2b, especially for the Taiwan case), during the period of most rapid early transition growth, the 1960s, a feature which runs counter to general LDC experience and the inverse-U-shaped hypothesis.

The East Asian countries under discussion thus provide a striking case of systems choosing a change in policy regime at the end of easy import substitution and being rewarded by a remarkably strong growth performance combined with low and falling levels of income inequality, largely because of the initially high and rising relative share of labor and the rapid absorption of unskilled labor hours in new rural and urban activities. The distribution of rural families' merged "agricultural incomes" also showed an improvement during the fifties and sixties not only due to the initially favorable effects of land reform but also because technologies were developed and promoted that rendered small farm holdings more productive over time. This was a function both of the more intensive use of land via double cropping and of the shift to such new, more labor intensive, higher valued crops as vegetables and fruit for the domestic market and mushrooms and asparagus for the foreign market, in contrast to the more land intensive traditional crops. Such shifts in cropping pattern were of particular benefit to the poorer (smaller) farmers who were able to participate more than proportionately in these activities.

Turning to our Latin American cases, it should be noted (see table 8.2a) that growth rates during the early post–World War II easy import substitution period were, on the average, as high in Mexico and Colombia as in East Asia, undoubtedly related to their higher levels of initial endowments and per capita incomes. On the other hand, the Latin American version of the easy import substitution policy package may be judged to have been more severe, partly as a consequence of its substantially longer duration, that is, from the thirties to the early sixties. One important consequence of this was a relatively much greater neglect of the food producing agricultural subsector, reinforcing colonial policy antecedents that concentrated attention on the lucrative export-oriented enclaves.

In short, both types of LDCs shared an infant industry rationale that called for the creation of a new industrial class out of the landlord or commercial elite with the help of reasonable levels of protection and profit transfers. The most striking difference then occurred in terms of the societal choice made at the end of the easy import substitution subphase. Faced, as in the East Asian case, with a decline in the rate of industrial growth and the threat of price wars in protected domestic markets for consumer nondurables, the Latin Americans decided to continue with the import substitution mode, but now focused on the manufacture of producers' and durable consumer goods, first for the domestic market and, somewhat later, for export as well.

This Latin American metamorphosis may, at first blush, seem to parallel the secondary import and export substitution subphase recently reached by the East Asian countries. But only at first blush. The most crucial difference is that the Latin Americans tried to move *directly* from primary import substitution into the production of the more skilled labor, capital, and technology intensive products instead of *by way of* the unskilled labor intensive primary export substitution subphase. Thus, in a secular sense, we observe not only the maintenance of the prior protection and controls oriented policy structure, but indeed its frequent deepening and strengthening over time.

Liberalization episodes do occur, but they are usually followed by a return to import substitution, with the long-term trend at best unclear. During the 1960s, for example, after the end of easy import substitution, while the rates of effective protection declined somewhat in East Asia, they rose in most of Latin America—with the exception of Brazil and Colombia. Interest rates generally remained at low, if not negative, real levels everywhere; the agricultural sector's terms of trade continued to be depressed, and even traditionally food self-sufficient or food exporting countries became net importers. In the mid–1970s we see some efforts toward liberalization in various key markets but also a return to import substitution policy regimes under the impact of external shocks.

We should note that, especially in the seventies, given their still narrow domestic markets for the products of secondary import substitution, the Latin American NICs in fact pushed for, and achieved, some sizable increases in their nontraditional, industrial exports (see table 8.2e). While some of this expansion has admittedly been in the consumer nondurable goods area, particularly shoes and textiles, as a consequence of liberalization episodes in countries like Brazil and Colombia, most of it has taken place in such high technology, high capital intensity areas as automobiles, electrical machinery, chemicals, even aircraft. In many cases it has been related less to the march of dynamic comparative advantage or the product cycle and more to the government's willingness to subsidize industrial exports that are generally viewed as synonymous with successful development.

This Latin American industrial export phenomenon has thus, over time, differed markedly from the primary export substitution subphase encountered in East Asia in that it entails a goodly component of the promotion of exports "on top of" a continued import substitution policy regime. It is distinguished both by a difference in the composition of industrial output, by the fact that it is not preceded by a change in the overall policy package, and by the prevalence of substantial subsidies. Under this regime particular industries or firms are selected for direct encouragement via public sector tax rebates, differential interest rate and export subsidies, or via enforced private sector cross-subsidization—that is, by assuring companies of continued high windfall profits in protected domestic markets in exchange for compliance with rising export targets.

The secular prolongation of import substitution in this fashion, with export promotion eventually added, is evidently likely to be socially costly even if privately profitable. But the key fact is that it can be "paid for" by a favorable natural resources base, as exports and tax proceeds can continue to "pay the piper" and help maintain very respectable growth rates (see table 8.2a). What is less clear, however, is whether the consequences of this "skipping" of export substitution are acceptable from the employment and distributional points of view.

Both the composition of exports, as between traditional and nontraditional (see tables 8.2c–8.2e), and the change in the overall export orientation present a startling contrast, with Latin America remaining much more domestic market oriented (see table 8.2f). Secondly, the relative early neglect of food producing agriculture is exacerbated as protectionism deepens secularly; as a consequence, with more and more traditional

TABLE 8.2c
Agricultural Exports as Share of Total Exports (percent)

	1950	1960	1970	1980
Taiwan	—	51.7	22.5	10.2
South Korea	82.3	51.4	16.7	8.9
Colombia	83.1	78.9	81.2	76.7
Mexico	53.5	64.1	48.8	14.2

Sources: UNCTAD (various years); Republic of China (1982).

TABLE 8.2d
Mineral Exports as Share of Total Exports (percent)

	1950	1960	1970	1980
Taiwan	—	2.1	0.7	3.6
South Korea	11.2	8.3	8.3	10.5
Colombia	16.3	18.9	10.8	2.9
Mexico	38.6	24.0	21.2	71.6

Sources: UNCTAD (various years); Republic of China (1982).

TABLE 8.2e
Manufactured Exports as Share of Total Exports (percent)

	1950	1960	1970	1980
Taiwan	—	46.2	76.8	86.2
South Korea	6.4	40.3	74.9	80.2
Colombia	0.5	1.4	8.0	19.7
Mexico	7.9	11.9	30.0	10.9

Sources: UNCTAD (various years); Republic of China (1982).

granaries empty, more of the cash crop exports proceeds, supplemented by foreign capital, typically have to be devoted to food imports.

The differences in the "bottom line" on employment and income distribution outcomes can be traced to the same policy divergence. In the rural sector, the combination of a worse distribution of land with the relative shift toward, rather than away from, traditional primary export cash crops, tended to make for lower labor intensity and a higher (less

TABLE 8.2f
Export Orientation Ratios (exports/GDP: percent)

	1950	1960	1970	1980
Taiwan	10.1	11.1	29.6	52.2
South Korea	2.1	3.3	14.3	37.7
Colombia	10.9	15.7	14.6	16.3
Mexico	17.0	10.6	8.2	22.4

Sources: IMF (various years); World Bank (1980); *National Income of the Republic of China* (various years).

favorable) agricultural income Gini in Latin America. With respect to rural nonagricultural incomes, which in Taiwan were more equally distributed than agricultural incomes, these constituted 30 percent of farm family incomes initially, rising to 60 percent; in contrast, in Colombia, they fell from a low level of 15 percent to 10 percent over time. Moreover, such rural industry and services as did exist, given the maintenance of the import substitution regime, were much more capital intensive and contributed much less to favorable employment and distributional outcomes in Latin America. Rural industry's labor share in Colombia, for example, was much lower and falling (as compared with Taiwan's) over virtually the entire period under discussion here. The same sources indicate a sizable gap in the urban labor share as between the two countries. The much less favorable and worsening distributional outcome associated with the Latin American choice of a growth path should therefore come as no surprise.

As we have already pointed out, both the Latin American and East Asian NICs adopted an internally oriented policy during the easy import substitution subphase, deploying macro-policies to provide protection for their new industrial entrepreneurs and insulating them from exogenous disturbances. During this period, monetary, fiscal, and exchange rate policies were used to accommodate deficit finance, permit money creation, and provide windfalls, all to assist private entrepreneurs by manufacturing profits on their behalf. Policy was based on the conviction that interest rates can be artificially repressed to generate profits for this class, and government can acquire all the goods and services it needs by direct action, that is, covert taxation without consent. Price inflation can be depended upon to lighten the repayment burden of entrepreneurs and thus force the public to save. Such direct growth promotion can be undertaken without difficulty as long as the LDC government has the power to monopolize the expansion of the money supply. All it takes is the political will to use its power persistently.

At the end of easy import substitution, when, as we have observed, the policies diverge, we observe a consistent, more or less monotonic, "liberalization process" setting in in the East Asian cases, but one beset with oscillation and retrenchment episodes in the Latin American cases. In the realm of monetary policy, this means that the East Asians gradually came to recognize that money should serve principally as a medium of exchange rather than providing the power for government to acquire resources; that the foreign exchange rate should be more realistic; and that the interest rates should approach the cost of capital. This represents a movement toward a relatively greater role for the market and away from the notion that an all-powerful, newly independent government can take care of everything. It also means a shift from "under the table" taxation through inflation to "on the table" taxation with consent, with private entrepreneurs gradually learning to earn more of their profits through competitive productive performance rather than through rent-seeking activities.

This movement, while still more pronounced in East Asia, seems to be gaining ascendancy elsewhere. Viewed in longer run historical perspective, it constitutes an organizational evolution companion to the transition toward the epoch of modern growth—that is, as an economy becomes increasingly complex, sooner or later the notion that economic decisions must be decentralized seems to surface, even in the so-called socialist economies. It should also be recalled that during easy import substitution governments will typically penetrate the market system to determine not only the overall volume of aggregate demand but even individual investment decisions. Such "directional controls" also tend to atrophy as the economy becomes more complex, calling increasingly for market solutions to replace civil servant discretion in determining specific resource allocations.

In contrast with East Asia, this gradual long-term liberalization process has been much less smooth and linear in Latin America, where the existence and persistence of large rents seems to invite the continuation of rent-seeking policies and the return to them at intermittent intervals. It is, moreover, true that the liberalization process may be more disturbed by exogenous shocks in the natural-resource-rich Latin American countries—that is, through price changes in primary products in world markets as well as the business cycle in the industrially advanced countries.

Another specific example is the role of minimum wage legislation, government supported unionism, and other interventions in labor markets, conspicuous by their presence in Latin America and their absence in East Asia. One might, in fact, assert that union unrest and strikes may be an indicator of social unrest traceable (via inflation and income redistribution) to the unevenness for different social groups of the impact of macroeconomic policies. But clearly a differential wage rate structure—that is, much higher real wages for the small urban organized labor force in Latin America—can be extremely damaging to the possibilities of export substitution as the competitive export of labor-intensive manufactured goods can be effectively blocked, contributing to the persistence of unemployment and underemployment.

The major macroeconomic policy instruments—the interest rate, the exchange rate, the change in the money supply, the rate of protection, the rate of taxes, and government expenditures—must all be viewed as tools of the growth-oriented activists in government providing support to certain private sector participants in the mixed economy. The basic principle that underlies such growth promotion is an income transfer strategy, so that the purchasing power generated in the production process, usually by the exploration of raw materials in rural areas, can be transferred, either covertly or overtly, to favored private entrepreneurs or to the government itself. Once notions of liberalization are entertained at the end of easy import substitution, their consideration often begins rather hesitantly because anything smacking of laissez-faire usually runs counter to the lingering political ideology that holds that growth is a public concern that must be managed directly by the exercise of political power. Thus both the East Asian and Latin American economies have to contend with the legacy of a prior import substitution phase, which constitutes a more or less control-oriented institutional/organizational package even though it may be less severe in the East Asian case.

All the evidence indicates that East Asia more or less pursued a linear path of policy liberalization and registered far and away the best development performance. On the other hand, in Latin America we have witnessed a different, less clear-cut and more oscillatory pattern of policy or organizational choices, with market-oriented episodes replaced by a return to import substitution types of intervention in a more or less continuously oscillating pattern and accompanied by much less successful outcomes in terms of any assessment of economic performance.

It is indeed a challenge for social scientists to try to move toward a better understanding of the fundamental causes of this divergent pattern. In that sense it is necessary to proceed beyond the above description of divergent growth performance, that is, the attempted "skipping" of a particular subphase in the case of Latin America, and toward a comparative development perspective that includes the evolution of different policy choices as part of the explanatory framework. We need to have a better understanding, in other words, as to why in East Asia a more or less conformable evolution of policy resulted in the linearity of policy change, while in Latin America we have been witness to oscillation around inconsistent trends in spite of the profusion of "good advice" offered by the profession and the donor community. It is this political economy explanation of the divergence of performance to which we now turn.

Toward Endogenous Policy Change

It is hypothesized that the explanation for the observed divergence of performance must be found in a combination of marked differences in initial conditions when the curtain rises and in various political and economic forces that shape the adoption or rejection of organizational and policy changes over time. The former appear as given obstacles or advantages; but even the latter are relatable to differences in initial conditions, most particularly the differences in natural resource endowments as between the Latin American and East Asian cases.

All LDCs seem to initiate their transition growth efforts with political forces penetrating their mixed economies during their so-called early or easy import substitution subphase. When they subsequently move into some sort of export orientation, either of the export substitution variety (that is, East Asia) or of the export promotion cum secondary import substitution variety (that is, Latin America), the difference in the monotonicity or oscillation of performance can be explained by the way in which the political economy of policy change plays itself out over time.

Given the record of almost four decades of postwar transition growth efforts now before us, we are indeed in a position to examine the evolution of LDC policies in a fashion that is complementary to the empirically focused, policy neutral, description of growth paths presented above. While we would like to avoid any sort of economic determinism relating policy sequences and economic events, an effort to probe the endogeneity of the observed LDC policy evolution over time clearly involves reasoning about both economic and political phenomena in order to understand the logical necessity of a differential ordering of policy events as between East Asia and Latin America.

At this stage we are by no means in a position to present a deterministic model of such a complex set of relations but can only hope to demonstrate a methodology to be followed with the help of some country cases. The methodology we have in mind consists of (1) the recognition of differences in initial conditions and their impact; (2) an evolutionary tracing of policy events over time; (3) an evolutionary tracing of the economic performance with respect to growth, income distribution, and employment over the same historical period; and (4) the precise quantification of the above in the context of an effort to trace causal relations among them.

Our fundamental hypothesis is that major policy instruments such as the interest rate, the foreign exchange rate, the rate of protection, the rate of taxation, and the rate of money supply increase must be interpreted as political instruments used by governments to promote growth through the transfer of income among social groups—that is, to manufacture profits for one group at the expense of others. One of the ways to understand the difference between export substitution in East Asia and export promotion plus secondary import substitution in Latin America is to note that the former systems are gradually but consistently shifting away from "under the table," or implicit, income transfers among groups and toward "on the table," or explicit, revenue and expenditure related policies of government. Increasingly, the focus is on taxation, the provision of overheads, and organizational and institutional construction—that is, constituting a more indirect, though by no means less important, role for the government.

The persistence of the import substitution mode (the Latin American path), is related in part to the ability to pay for it—that is, the ample availability of traditional natural resources and, in part, the governments' felt need to try to be viewed as solving all problems, with the possibility of social conflict arising later (e.g., inflation with a time lag) put to one side. The best example of this is, of course, the policy of monetary expansion, which may solve a problem of sectoral clashes today but leads to inflation of the typical Latin American type after one or two years. It is in this context that the familiar macro policy tools, including the foreign exchange rate and the interest rate, are interpreted as growth promoting instruments to effect income transfers in the Latin American context. On the other hand, in the East Asian case a continued trend toward liberalization in various markets at the end of primary import substitution is tantamount to the gradual withdrawal of political forces from the economic arena. This can be observed from the comparison of overall tax rates, the relative importance of internal taxes, and the trend of real effective exchange rates (see tables 8.3a–8.3c).

Let me now schematically contrast the political economy of policy change in the natural-resources-poor East Asian case with the natural-resources-rich Latin American case. First of all, Taiwan's primary import substitution subphase could be relatively mild partly because of its initially strong domestic cohesion, which meant that the government could concentrate on a few basic economic problems and did not have to overpromise and involve itself directly in too many areas simultaneously. Such "mildness" exhibited itself in a relatively high interest rate and anti-inflation policy and an emphasis on closing budgetary deficits in Taiwan as early as the 1950s—a policy that was, moreover, maintained linearly throughout the next three decades. An effort at maintaining realistic exchange rates was adopted by the late 1950s, with quantitative controls

TABLE 8.3a
Tax Rates (percent of GDP)

	1950	1960	1970	1980
Taiwan	11 (1952)	11	14	17 (1979)
South Korea	6 (1953)	10	16	18
Colombia	3	4	9 (1972)	10
Mexico	8	7	9	13 (1975)

Sources: IMF (various years); World Bank (1980).

TABLE 8.3b
Composition of Taxes (custom duties/total taxes)

	1950	1960	1970	1980
Taiwan	26 (1952)	23	28	24
South Korea	17 (1953)	21	13	12
Colombia	18	27	19 (1972)	18
Mexico	34	31	20	11

Sources: IMF (various years); World Bank (1980).

TABLE 8.3c
Real Effective Exchange Rates (1975 = 100)

	1965	1970	1980
Taiwan	—	96.17	95.50
South Korea	98.18	73.00	94.84
Colombia	79.71	81.20	81.73
Mexico	112.42	106.33	107.02

Sources: IMF (various years); World Bank (1980).

and multiple exchange rates abolished by the early sixties. Tariffs, on the other hand, have been maintained at relatively moderate levels until the present day; major tariff reform is currently under way.

In this context it should be recognized that such devices as export processing zones and the rebating of tariffs for exports represented useful transition devices permitting exports to become competitive while the domestic consumer could continue to be "squeezed" through the maintenance of modest tariffs. The political economy significance of these policy devices, also maintained more or less monotonically, is that in the absence of strong vested interests in traditional agricultural exports and its large rents, it became necessary early on to begin to shift toward the export of nontraditional commodities, which encompasses not only the well-known shift from rice and sugar to textiles and electronics but also the prior shift toward such higher valued, labor-intensive agricultural commodities as mushrooms and asparagus. It is also true that the fact that landless farmers were incorporated into new nonagricultural activity more than proportionately—while medium-sized farmers who lost out during the 1949–1951 land reforms became owners of industrial assets through the rent compensation method—diminished the conflict between the two classes early on.

Since liberalization or depoliticization is always difficult, when there is an absence of large rents accruing from agriculture to be allocated to non-agriculture this also means that the struggle for rents in the sectors which have benefited (among the new industrialists) is toned down, that is, the rent-seeking society characteristics are substantially diminished. It should be noted that while there was some pulling and hauling in the late fifties about which path Taiwan should take, necessity sooner or later became the mother of consistent policy change in the direction of depoliticization. When primary import substitution is mild and relatively short-lived, it also means that less fear of foreign competition is built up; hot-house conditions certainly carry the seeds of their own continuation in the political economy sense.

Thus, the role of government quickly shifted from that of implicit intervention through the five major policy instruments—the interest rate, the tariff rate, the exchange rate, the budget deficit, and monetary expansion—to one of a direct role for government in institutional/organizational change. Specifically, this resided increasingly, especially as labor surplus came to an end, in such areas as (1) education, science and technology infrastructure, and patent laws; (2) a second land reform permitting the reconsolidation of small holdings and the transfer of land as well as the appearance of the so-called cultivating firm selling services to farmers; (3) the expansion and reorganization of financial institutions, still under way today, to permit a shift from the public sector's role in directly productive activities, occasioned mainly by the inability to marshal enough private funds for large projects; (4) an early shift from planning for resources to planning for policy coordination; (5) the privatization of public sector activity, which had been postponed to much later in the transition process.

What is interesting about the East Asian case thus is not only the policy changes that were adopted and more or less linearly adhered to but also the sequence in which they were adopted. Developing countries cannot digest all the requisite liberalization moves at the same time—nor does it make sense to do so even if one could. Depoliticization clearly meant, first, a shift from indirect taxation via inflation to taxes—that is, shifting from "under the table" taxes on agriculture to "on the table" taxes. Second, it meant a shift to greater central bank autonomy and an early decline in reliance on the expansion of the money supply accompanied by a higher interest rate policy. Third, a postponement of tariff reductions was forced by the need for revenue, plus the fact that, while foreign consumers could no longer be taken for granted, it was still possible, and necessary, to squeeze domestic consumers for some time to come; meanwhile, export processing zones and tariff rebates for exports were deployed as transitional devices.

Fourth, we might also note that social welfare legislation, including the support of minimum wages and unionism, which really represent acts of government in the sense of helping to share out unearned rents between industrial entrepreneurs and industrial workers, has not been a feature of the East Asian landscape until this day. This phenomenon is often put at the doorstep of a repressive government. However, unless one is unduly mesmerized by the political trappings or legislative protections of an urban working elite it is highly doubtful that the economic participation and welfare of the East Asian populations was adversely affected by such delays in social legislation and unionization. It is indeed also important to better understand the relationship between economic participation and political pluralism.

Let us look at the Latin American natural-resources-rich country type in contrast. Not only does the existence of plentiful natural resources provide the wherewithal for maintaining import substitution longer than would otherwise be desirable, but it also provides the vulnerability to inevitable terms of trade fluctuations. It thus has two effects on the transition growth path. One, it postpones the opening toward competitive exports, in rendering export orientation something that is superimposed "on top of" a continued import substitution structure; second, it means that even when episodes of liberalization are recorded, it makes the system much more vulnerable to backsliding in response to inevitable oscillations in the terms of trade. Thus, what we find in the Latin American case is liberalization/interventionist cycles, as external shocks are felt, around a secular trend of export promotion coupled with continued secondary import substitution as described above.

To be more precise, during a period of terms of trade recovery one might well encounter some liberalization with a devaluation, an increase in the foreign exchange reserves, an increase in the money supply, in tax revenue, and spending. But once the terms of trade deteriorate, one is then likely to encounter a tendency to substitute domestic spending for the decline in foreign exchange reserves. There follow large budget deficits and an increase in the money supply, in combination with an effort to "fix" the exchange rate. The system then gradually drifts back to import substitution type policies, with the exchange rate becoming increasingly overvalued, in order to fight so-called externally caused inflation. Ultimately, a large devaluation does become necessary and the cycle can once again repeat itself.

Thus, what we observe is cycles of retreats to import substitution cum export promotion and shifts back toward liberalization and export substitution in many of the developing countries of Latin America. As a consequence, the shifting of profits from agricultural sources to favored parties in the nonagricultural sector is both maintained for a longer period secularly; and there is always a tendency to drift back toward the import substitution policy syndrome. Both the money supply and the level of exchange reserves are viewed more as instruments for governments' capturing resources rather than as mediums of exchange as they are in the typical developed country.

Thus the seemingly inevitable by-product of a plentiful supply of land-based rents available to a society is a reduced willingness or capacity to withdraw the "goodies" from the major vested interest groups, the urban industrialists and organized labor, and the civil servants who parcel out the specific benefits of import substitution. As a consequence, not only is there much greater hesitation in dismantling quantitative restrictions and tariffs in a secular sense but also unions and minimum wage legislation as a way of sharing out these rents among the privileged groups clearly assume greater importance. Once such legislation does exist and such habits are formed it may well be true that only relatively strong governments can rescind them. In lieu of more taxation with consent, we instead are likely to get more protection, lower real interest rates, more monetary expansion, and more overvalued exchange rates as a way of continuing to manufacture profits for governments and favored interest groups in the nonagricultural sector. It is this broader version of the "Dutch Disease," rather than the narrower impact of natural resource bonanzas on the exchange rate, which has made a large difference in determining the observed differential growth performance as between East Asia and Latin America.

Needless to add, foreign capital inflows "for the asking" can have a similar impact on the political economy of policy change. It is no accident that the current debt crisis, fueled by liberal commercial bank lending in the seventies, has been more pronounced in Latin America than in East Asia. While foreign capital, like natural resources, should theoretically constitute a potential advantage for a system trying to restructure its policies (by enhancing its ability to "bind the wounds" of affected interest groups) the political economy effects are otherwise. The absence of natural resources and the withdrawal of aid are more likely to jolt the system into the realization that it has to rely increasingly heavily on its human resources if it is to navigate successfully in the direction of modern growth.

In sum, when economic rents in the form of returns to nonaugmentable natural resources are predictably scarce and running out, there exists a necessity to depoliticize and liberalize the economy, provide less incentive for various interest groups to do battle for the spoils and thus strengthen the accommodative nature of policy change in the transition growth process. Such countries are then forced by circumstance to shift their attention earlier to the deployment of their human resources, both unskilled and skilled. In Latin America, with less necessity to make such politically difficult decisions, they could more easily be delayed. As a consequence, a good natural resources base and good foreign friends willing to provide foreign capital—both potentially of benefit to a society in soothing the inevitable pains of policy change—are likely to become political economy obstacles to effecting those very changes.

References

Chenery, Hollis B., and Moshe Syrquin. 1975. *Patterns of Development, 1950–1970*. New York: Oxford University Press.

Fei, John, and Gustav Ranis. 1975. "A Model of Growth and Employment in the Open Dualistic Economy: The Cases of Korea and Taiwan." *Journal of Development Studies* 11, no. 2, pp. 32–63.

Fei, John, Gustav Ranis, and Shirley Kuo. 1979. *Growth with Equity: The Taiwan Case*. New York: Oxford University Press.

IMF (International Monetary Fund). Various years. *International Financial Statistics Yearbook*. Washington, D.C.: IMF.

Jain, Shail. 1975. *Size Distribution of Income*. Washington, D.C.: World Bank.

Kelley, Allen C., Jeffrey G. Williamson, and Russell J. Cheetham. 1972. *Dualistic Economic Development: Theory and History*. Chicago: University of Chicago Press.

Kuznets, Simon. 1980. "Driving Forces of Economic Growth: What Can We Learn from History?" *Weltwirtschaftliches Archiv*, band 116, pp. 409–31.

———. 1966. *Modern Economic Growth: Rate, Structure and Spread*. New Haven: Yale University Press.

———. 1955. "Economic Growth and Income Inequality." *American Economic Review* 45, no.1, pp. 1–28.

Lewis, Arthur W. 1954. "Economic Development with Unlimited Supplies of Labour." *Manchester School of Economic and Social Studies* 22, no. 2, pp. 139–81.

National Income of the Republic of China. Various years. Taipei: Directorate General of Budget, Accounting, and Statistics.

Republic of China. Various years. *National Income of the Republic of China*. Taipei: Directorate General of Budget, Accounting, and Statistics.

Republic of China. Various years. *Statistical Yearbook of the Republic of China*. Taipei: Directorate General of Budget, Accounting, and Statistics.

Republic of China. 1982. *The Trade of China*. Taipei: Inspectorate General of Customs.

Summers, Robert, and Alan Heston. 1984. "Improved International Comparison of Real Product and its Composition." *Review of Income and Wealth* 30, pp. 207–62.

United Nations. 1953. *Production Yearbook* 4, part 1. Rome: Food and Agriculture Organization.

United Nations. Various years. *Statistical Yearbook*. New York: United Nations.

UNCTAD (United Nations Conference on Trade and Development). Various years. *Yearbook of Trade and Development Statistics*. Geneva: UNCTAD.

UNESCO (United Nations Education, Scientific and Cultural Organization). 1963. *Statistical Yearbook*. Paris: UNESCO.

World Bank. 1976, 1980. *World Debt Tables*. Baltimore: Johns Hopkins University Press.

CHAPTER 9

Industrial Policy in East Asia: Does It Lead or Follow the Market?

Robert Wade

WITHIN THE SPACE of less than thirty years, Taiwan and South Korea have jumped so far up the economic hierarchy of nations as to become competitive in a range of capital-intensive and high-technology industries. Taiwan moved from the world's sixty-fourth biggest exporter in 1962 to eleventh in 1986, South Korea from 101st in 1962 to fourteenth in 1986.[1] This export performance occurred at the same time that they were undergoing the most "compressed" transformation from light to heavy industries that the noncommunist world has ever seen. Their ratio of value added in light industries over heavy industries fell from 4 to 1 in fifteen years, compared to twenty-five years in Japan and fifty years in the United Kingdom (Watanabe, 1985).

Increasingly, their governments and firms do not take the international market as a given, because their actions affect the responses of other governments and multinational companies. Multinationals seek them out not only to gain access to their growing domestic market but also to integrate them in regional or global supply networks. South Korea may become the first new producer in two decades to break into the oligopolized world car industry, and it is one of the world's three main fabricators of large capacity (VLSI) memory chips.[2] Taiwan is a leading source of computers, computer peripherals, and add-ons; it is up with the world leaders in semiconductor design; it is acquiring mastery over state-of-the-art semiconductor production; and it has become one of the biggest sources of

---

This chapter is based on a theme in Wade (1990). More ample footnotes and citations are given in the book. Related published papers are listed in the bibliography. The views expressed are my own and are not to be mistaken for those of the institutions with which I am affiliated. My thanks to Gary Gereffi and Dorothy Robyn for comments on an earlier draft.

[1] The ranking includes Eastern European countries and Hong Kong, and is for all exports. Sources: *World Bank Atlas* data, based on IMF, *International Financial Statistics Yearbook*; UN, *Monthly Bulletin of Statistics*; UNCTAD, *Handbook of International Trade and Development Statistics*.

[2] VLSI stands for very large scale integrated circuits—chips with 100,000 transistors or more, roughly the number needed for a 64K dynamic random access memory chip, or bigger.

car replacement parts. Several other industries in both countries are very competitive internationally, including steel and machine tools.

The great question is how this happened in countries that looked very unpromising in 1955.

One popular interpretation of East Asian economic success holds that it is due to the vigor of private entrepreneurs operating in relatively open economies. Openness and governmental restraint have allowed prices to reflect real, as distinct from policy-induced, scarcities, and these prices have led entrepreneurs to overcome the limitations of small markets by exporting manufactures at competitive prices. The resulting growth dynamic has been far greater than would have otherwise occurred. By contrast, countries that adopted more inward-looking strategies based on the domestic market have stagnated because of limited economies of scale and because the regulations needed to support the inward-looking strategy choked the initiative of private business people, depriving them of the stimulus of rivalry and misdirecting their remaining energies into rent-seeking. This could be called the "self-adjusting market" theory of capitalist East Asian success.

This theory recognizes that strong government action was necessary to eliminate earlier import-substitution policies. But once the dials were correctly set in favor of a more neutral set of incentives, the role of government has been limited largely to improving the infrastructure of the market system and preventing a shift in the dials due to "politics." The very openness of the economy and the smallness of the public sector kept the state firmly in its place.

The literature supporting one or another variant of this interpretation of East Asian success is vast. For example, Ian Little (1979) and Gustav Ranis (1979) wrote twenty-thousand-word essays on Taiwan's development, which both make only casual reference to the government's industrial promotion policies. The World Bank's *World Development Report 1987* classifies South Korea as a "strongly outward oriented" economy, meaning that it has had a relatively neutral set of policy incentives (neutral as between export sale and domestic market sale, and neutral as between different industries). Kreuger (1983), Lal and Rajapatirana (1986), and Galenson (1982) provide other examples of the genre.[3]

Another interpretation holds that the role of the state has gone well beyond the limits of the self-adjusting market theory. Those who hold this view do not deny the importance of markets and private property and do not imply that the government's role comes close to Soviet or Cuban-style central planning. The argument is, rather, that East Asian governments

---

[3] Wade (1990) cites more examples, and distinguishes two variants of this theory, the "nearly free market" version and the "simulated free market" version.

(minus Hong Kong) have been active players in the market, able to influence the use of public and private resources in line with a vision of how the industrial structure of the country should be evolving. They can be seen as both the rule maker and the first player in a multistage game, whose moves influence the credible options of the other players. It is further argued, explicitly or implicitly, that government interventions of this type have in fact been able to improve upon the results of self-adjusting markets. So, not only have the macropolicies of East Asian governments been important, but so has intervention at the sectoral, product, and even firm level. This could be called the "governed market" or the "developmental state" theory of East Asian success.

The clash between these two views of the role of government in East Asia is of far-reaching importance for development strategy. For we have here, in Taiwan, South Korea, and pre-1970 Japan, three of the most successful cases of economic development on record. We know that all three governments had an intense and nearly unequivocal commitment to building up the competitiveness of the domestic economy. The question is what the governments did to pursue this objective—what policies they used, what institutional arrangements they fostered in both public and private sectors. If we find that the policies and institutions were in line with the "self-adjusting market" theory, this provides support for arguing that other countries are best advised to follow a more or less free market strategy. If we find that the role of government in all three cases went far beyond the limits of the self-adjusting market theory, this urges caution in recommending other countries to pursue a strategy of comprehensive liberalization. What then was the role of government in the economic development of the most successful cases of all?

LEADING OR FOLLOWING THE MARKET?

The debate about the appropriate role of government is often discussed in terms of "more or less intervention in the market," intervention being treated as a single dimension and without being weighted for the amount of power or influence behind it. The very bluntness of the term has the not inconsiderable advantage of permitting the proponents to talk endlessly past each other. In the interests of narrowing the grounds of disagreement, however, I want to distinguish, first, between macroeconomic policies and industrial policies. Macroeconomic policies affect overall demand, and while they affect different industries differently, they are not aimed at producing such differential effects. Industrial policies aim to aid industries, either to grow faster or to decline less disruptively, by affecting production and investment decisions of decentralized producers (and hence are more limited than the total of all government policies that affect industry). I distinguish, second, between functional and industry-specific industrial policies. Functional industrial policies aim to affect a function across all or many industries (so they might also be called generic or horizontal industrial policies). Examples are subsidies for manpower training or for research and development. Industry-specific (or selective, sectoral, or vertical) industrial policies target particular industries. Examples are promotion plans for steel, petrochemicals, or semiconductors. Within the category of industry-specific industrial policies, I want to distinguish two roles of government: leading the market, and following the market. This is not a distinction between types of policies, for the same policy (e.g., credit subsidies) may be used in a leadership or a followership role. It is a distinction between, on the one hand, intervention that helps decentralized producers to do what they would do whether assisted or not and therefore that does not make much difference in production and investment, and on the other, intervention that leads decentralized producers to do something other than what they would otherwise have done or even creates new producers to undertake initiatives.

Hence a selective industrial policy that follows the market simply assists private firms in a given industry to do what they would in any case do in response to price signals. It confers the government's "seal of approval" on some (not necessarily all) of the industry's intentions. A selective industrial policy that leads the market involves (1) government initiatives about what products or technologies should be encouraged; (2) public resources or influence over private resources to carry through these initiatives, and (3) a larger before-the-fact plan or strategy.

Those proponents of the self-adjusting market theory of East Asian success who recognize the *fact* of East Asian selective industrial policy tend to say or imply that it made little or no difference to what would have happened anyway as the result of market forces. In my terms, they are embracing the government followership theory of East Asian industrial policy. A possible rationale for this theory might run as follows: East Asian governments need to *appear* to be responsible for industrial success because of the shakiness of other grounds on which they might claim legitimacy for the exclusionary features of their authoritarianism (in the case of Japan, the reference is to the 1950s and 1960s). They can appear to be responsible, *without actually being*, if they can buy into an association with private sector industrial projects that will be successful. They consult with business for the purpose of informing themselves about what the private sector thinks are good bets. They then put some of their own resources behind some of those bets, in the form of fiscal incentives, concessionary credit, mild tariffs, and so on. But the amount of resources is typically very small, for the purpose is less to modify private sector decisions than to obtain an association with decisions that the private sector would have made anyway. The fact that the private sector would do the projects whether assisted or not is more assurance that the projects will be successful; and if they are not, both the private sector and the government have a joint interest in blaming failure on external events beyond anyone's control. So the government can distance itself from failures while associating itself with successes.[4]

This theory is consistent with an economics view of bureaucratic motivation. Being highly risk-averse, bureaucrats do not want to expose themselves by being connected with failures. If no private firms could be persuaded to enter an activity without government help, the officials who went ahead and gave them help would be in an exposed position. They are unlikely to do so.

The argument also provides a way of accommodating Hong Kong. Hong Kong's industrial success is an important fact for those who say that government is unimportant in the explanation of East Asian success. If Hong Kong did as well as the other apparently more *dirigiste* countries, this shows that government industrial policies must have been insignificant because Hong Kong, it is said, has come as near as possible to a free market economy.

To determine whether a given intervention constitutes leadership or followership, we need to examine what happens in government-business consultations and business-government lobbying. We need to know about the objectives of the parties and about who influences whom. In the clearest case of followership, business representatives would give government officials a list of projects for which they wish stipulated kinds of assistance, and the officials would accept the list in toto. In the clearest case of leadership, the government would twist the arm of private firms to undertake a project, or it would by-pass reluctant private firms by means of a public enterprise.

But leadership and followership can also be considered at another level, in terms of the causes of the investment pattern. We can examine (perhaps econometrically) to what extent government investment priorities must be brought in to explain the investment pattern observed in a particular industry or across industries, or to what extent the pattern is satisfactorily explained in terms of standard self-adjusting market models. For example, we can distinguish leadership from followership at this level by examining trends in production from heavy and chemical industries before and after the end of "labor surplus." If production grew at high speed while labor was still in structural surplus, and if government was the initiator of many heavy and chemical industry projects, we can say that the

---

[4] I am grateful to Brian Hindley for suggesting this line of interpretation; see also Hindley (1984).

government led the market. Decentralized profit-maximizing entrepreneurs would have instead invested in more labor-intensive projects.

I deal with Taiwan, South Korea, and Hong Kong, in that order. The section on Taiwan aims to show that, the vast bulk of the literature notwithstanding, the Taiwan government has indeed exercised a substantial amount of leadership in some industries at some points of time over the course of the past forty years. The section on South Korea deals more selectively with only two industries, automobiles and information, to show the differences between Taiwan and South Korea in *methods* of leadership. The section on Hong Kong addresses the argument that if Hong Kong has done as well as the other two (or better), this shows that selective industrial policies in the other two—specifically government's industrial leadership—must have been unimportant enough to ignore.

TAIWAN

One of the most striking features of Taiwan's development is the rate of industrial deepening or "roundaboutness" in production (see Schive, chap. 10, this volume). This can be measured by the change in the ratio of intermediate to final demand. In a sample of nine middle- and high-income countries for the period from the mid-1950s to the early 1970s, Taiwan had by far the highest rate of change—10.0 percent per decade compared to second-place South Korea's 6.1 percent, fourth-place Japan's 4.2 percent, and last-place Norway's 1.4 percent (Kubo et al., 1986, table 7.1). Another indicator is Taiwan's share of chemicals and machinery (ISIC 35 and 38) in total manufacturing. This went up from 24 percent of manufacturing value-added in 1961 to 50 percent by 1974. The rate of increase was much greater than South Korea's: the corresponding share in South Korea went from 23 percent in 1961 to 39 percent in 1974 (Bank of Korea; Galli, 1980). If initially Taiwan began its export drive as an "export platform," sucking in huge amounts of raw materials and intermediates and applying cheap labor to them before re-exporting, it soon became a much deeper economy—in a way that dependency theory critics of East Asian export-led growth used to claim could not happen.[5]

How much was this deepening due to the operation of self-adjusting markets? Taiwan's era of labor surplus came to an end around 1968–1970 (Fei et al., 1979). In neoclassical accounts of Taiwan, it is usually suggested that the drive into heavy and chemical industries began in the early or mid-1970s in response to, rather than in anticipation of, changes in comparative advantage, and especially in response to the onset of labor

[5] See references in Gold (1986), Wade (1982).

shortage. If so, the trend was market-led, even though the state was deeply involved in the move through its public enterprises.

Samuel Ho elaborates the argument:

> With protectionist sentiments rising in the developed countries, continued rapid expansion of the light manufactured exports on which Korea's and Taiwan's industrial growth had been based appeared problematic. Rising wages in Korea and Taiwan also suggested that their comparative advantage was shifting away from the semiskilled, labor-intensive industries that grew so rapidly in the 1960's. *To policy makers in both countries, these changes in external conditions suggested a need to restructure the industrial sector.* [Accordingly,] in both Korea and Taiwan, the economic plans that emerged in the mid-1970s (Taiwan's Seventh Plan for 1976–1981 . . .) reflected these concerns. Planners advocated a move away from the labor-intensive industries. . . . The new direction of industrialization (towards heavy and chemical as well as skill-intensive industries) was mapped in the *mid-1970s*, shortly *after the first oil crisis*. (Ho, 1981, pp. 1197, 1181, emphasis added)

The foregoing figures on production trends question this interpretation. They suggest that the sort of shift Ho refers to began in a significant way much earlier than the mid-1970s in Taiwan. The point can be made more sharply by testing the following assertion by Walter Galenson, which is consistent with Ho's argument: "Beginning around 1976 in Taiwan . . . the production of more capital-intensive goods began to *accelerate*—synthetic textiles, paper, chemicals . . . tires, glass, steel products, machine tools, and heavy machinery. The supply of cheap labor was drying up, and *Marshall's principle of substitution was operating*" (Galenson 1982, p. 781, emphasis added).

Table 9.1 shows the average compound growth rate in the sectors Galenson identifies for two periods to 1976 and two periods after 1976. With the single exception of basic metals, growth rates in both periods prior to 1976 were *higher* than growth rates subsequently. Galenson's claim that growth rates accelerated around 1976 is correct only if 1974 and 1975 are taken as starting points, because these were years of slight decline in industrial production. Hence the evidence on production trends provides more support for the governed market theory than for the self-adjusting market theory.

Sectoral Histories

Any overall characterization of a government as interventionist or noninterventionist has to be rooted in accounts of what the government was doing in important industries. Although it is conceptually possible to have an interventionist government that uses only *functional* industrial

TABLE 9.1
Production in Selected Manufacturing Sectors in Taiwan: Average Compound
Growth Rates, Pre-1976 and Post-1976

Sector	1965–1969	1969–1973	1976–1980	1980–1984
Textiles	31.1	26.4	8.3	4.4
Paper	17.8	20.2	13.6	4.0
Chemicals	25.1	26.8	18.4	12.2
Rubber products	35.6	26.2	7.6	11.6
Nonmetallic mineral products	15.1	13.4	7.8	4.3
Basic metals	12.1	18.0	16.3	15.7
Metal products	23.0	20.8	6.6	7.6
Machinery	17.6	16.2	9.0	6.3
Electrical machinery	52.6	43.5	17.6	21.5

Sources: DGBAS (1981, 1985).

Notes: The production indices are based on 1976 = 100. Growth rates are calculated using a standard least-squares regression. 1974 and 1975 are dropped because in these years production untypically declined in the wake of the oil price rise. I thank Rao Katikineni for help with the computations.

policies, we are not likely to want to call a government "interventionist" without evidence of industry-specific industrial policies targeted on important industries. Once we find evidence of industry-specific industrial policies, the question remains to what extent these policies led or followed the market and when. Let us examine several important industries in Taiwan from this perspective. My aim is simply to show that in all the industries to be described, the government exercised a substantial amount of leadership at one time or another. The interest in doing so, to repeat, stems from the inattention paid in the economics literature about Taiwan to the evidence of leadership.

In the 1950s the state commonly established new industries—often single factories—itself. Then it either handed the factories over to selected businessmen—as in the case of glass, plastics, and cement—or ran them as public enterprises. Public enterprises dominated the fuel, chemical, mining, metal processing, textile, fertilizer, and food processing industries in the early 1950s. Throughout the 1950s public enterprises accounted for over half of industrial production.

In textiles a whole battery of market-distorting and even market-replacing methods were used to establish the industry quickly. Profitability was boosted by tariffs and quantitative restrictions on imports of yarn and finished products, also by controls on entry of new producers to prevent "excessive" competition. From 1951 to 1953, a government agency substituted for market allocation altogether, supplying raw cotton directly to the spinning mills, advancing all working capital requirements, and buying up all the production. It did much the same at the weaving stage (Gold, 1981). The business response was dramatic; between 1951 and 1954, production of cotton yarn and woolen yarn went up by over 200 percent and 400 percent, respectively (Lin, 1973, table A-16). In 1953, with the industry well established, the government stopped the market-replacing method of nurturing, but continued with tariffs and quantitative import restrictions.

In consumer electronics and electrical appliances, the government initially promoted the industry in the 1950s by the familiar techniques of protection, public procurement, and credit. In keeping with the first Four Year Plan (1953–1956), protection and other incentives were given for production of radios, fans, meters, fluorescent lights, low voltage transmitters, and cables. The government also helped to negotiate the few technology agreements and joint ventures between local firms and foreign (mostly Japanese) firms established during the 1950s and early 1960s.

The plastics industry was also established under state tutelage. As early as 1953 an American consulting firm recommended that plastics be targeted. The government, with the help of U.S. advisers, built a plant to make polyvinyl chloride (PVC) and transferred it to a private businessman in working order. (That businessman, Y. C. Wang, went on to become the owner/manager of the country's biggest conglomerate, Formosa Plastics.) Similarly for artificial fibers, the government decided in 1954 to establish a rayon-making plant as part of a strategy to diversify textiles away from cotton fibers. It brought together an American artificial fiber company with several local textilers, both public and private, and oversaw negotiations on the terms of the joint venture. The plant came on stream in 1957. This case set the pattern for future developments through the 1960s, with government identifying gaps in the production structure and taking the lead in bringing together foreign companies with local firms (Gold 1981; 1986).

In 1962 this same publicly owned rayon company together with a state financing agency formed another company to make nylon, which began production in 1964. The original rayon company diversified into polyesters in 1967. Private firms soon followed. The point to emphasize is not just that government was deeply involved in the early history of artificial fibers, but the initial push came through publicly owned companies.

As early as the late 1950s and early 1960s, the government began to push resources into heavy industry. In the words of the 1961–1964 Plan (written in 1960), "Heavy industry holds the key to industrialization as it produces capital goods. We must develop heavy industry so as to support the long-term steady growth of the economy" (Ministry of Economic Affairs, 1961, p. 34). The 1965–1968 Plan continued:

> For further development, stress must be laid on basic heavy industries (such as chemicals, wood pulp, petrochemical intermediates, and large-scale integrated steel production) instead of end-product manufacturing or processing. Industrial development in the long run must be centered on export products that have high income elasticity and low transportation cost. And around these products there should be development of both forward and backward industries, so that both specialization and complementarity may be achieved in the interest of Taiwan's economy. (CIECD, 1965, p. 122)

Not only heavy and chemical industries were targeted. Planning documents from the early 1960s pick quite specific products in electrical appliances and electronics for promotion, including transistor radios, electronic components, watches, and clocks. These were thought to be of particular interest to foreign investors. By moving in these directions, the 1965–1968 Plan went on, "We shall then be able to meet the changing situation in the world market brought about by the rapid industrial progress of the emerging nations and the growing sophistication of the industries of the developed countries" (CIECD, 1965, p. 124).

These guidelines were approved by the political leadership in the early 1960s, at least five years before the end of labor surplus, still longer before protectionist barriers began to go up (except in textiles), and well over a decade before the Plan to which Ho attributes the first expression of restructuring concerns.

Through the 1960s and 1970s, the government withdrew from some industries, wholly or partly, but took up new ones in their place. Much of the expansion in artificial fibers was carried out at the initiative of private firms (in contrast to the case before then), with the government concentrating on steering the structural evolution of the industry. It steered especially by identifying gaps, then helping to find foreign companies willing to share the needed technology, and negotiating with them on the terms. In plastics and many other petrochemicals, on the other hand, the government's direct role has continued to be large, in the form of joint ventures between public enterprises, private domestic firms, and foreign companies, and in the form of controls on entry. In the late 1960s it *forced* a merger of four private PVC firms with two public enterprises to form a new producer using a more effective technology. By the end of the 1960s Taiwan's petrochemical industry was producing ethylene, polyethylene, polystyrene, PVC, PVAC, synthetic rubber, artificial fibers, and many other products.

In basic metals the government acquired a substantial presence in steel production from 1962 onwards, when it took over a large, loss-making private plant. Although the decision to build a large-scale integrated steel mill was not finally taken until 1970, the project was under active consideration from the mid-1950s onwards. A public enterprise (China Steel) runs the mill efficiently enough to make Taiwan the second biggest steel exporter to Japan after South Korea. Aluminum and copper smelting have also been carried out by public enterprises. In shipbuilding a public enterprise undertook a large increase in capacity in 1962. At about the same time, two public enterprises in metal manufacturing made big expansions. A small pilot nuclear reactor began in 1961. Construction of a full-scale commercial reactor, by a public enterprise, began in 1968 and finished in 1977. Now let us look at automobiles and electronics in more detail, with an eye to subsequently comparing the government's role with what the South Korean government did in the same industries.

Automobiles

In automobiles, Taiwan has relied on private firms.[6] The government has been notably unsuccessful, until recently, in putting pressure on them to become internationally competitive, and its recent modest success has been achieved partly by threatening to use a *public* enterprise to bypass them.

The first assembly plant was established in 1958 to assemble semi–knocked-down kits under license from a Japanese company (Nissan). In 1961 the government announced Measures for the Development of the Automobile Industry. The measures prohibited further investment in simple assembly and empowered the Ministry of Economic Affairs to impose whatever import restrictions it deemed necessary to promote the domestic industry. In 1965 the government imposed a 60 percent local content requirement—unrealistically high but intended to give officials bargaining leverage with future producers. From 1967 to 1969 four new firms were allowed to enter the assembly industry with diluted local content requirements, each with Japanese participation. Here, in the early period, we see the government attempting to promote an industry without using public enterprises or subsidized finance, instead relying on entry regulation, import controls and tariffs, and local content requirements. But the overall market was tiny in relation to what was needed for economies of scale—less than 20,000 vehicles a year at the end of the 1960s.

Over the 1970s, as the Korean government embarked on a concerted

---

[6] Much of my account of the automobile industry in Taiwan comes from the excellent studies by Yun-han Chu (1987), and Arnold (1989). Further details in Wade (1990).

strategy to develop automobiles into a major export, Taiwan's automobile policy wobbled and drifted. The government was preoccupied elsewhere—with ten major infrastructure projects then under construction, and with the development of petrochemicals, chemicals, plastics, steel, and electronics. The 1974 oil crisis made matters worse, by dampening expectations of rapid growth of demand for cars. In addition, the government was split on the automobile strategy. Some officials saw the industry as a major exporter, others accorded it a central role in Taiwan's defense strategy, still others thought the emphasis should be on developing an advanced parts and components industry on the basis of which an internationally competitive assembling industry might be built at a later time. The latter reasoned that even domestic car prices remaining far above international levels would not harm the economy's international competitiveness much in the way that high prices of intermediates would have. Besides, Taiwan's roads were already congested, and some officials opposed the diversion of investible resources into cars and associated consumption (a reflection of a generally austere style of development, compared to Latin America). Taiwan continued to produce the world's most deservedly obscure automobiles.[7]

In 1978, spurred by news of South Korea's big push into autos, the government announced a general proposal to establish a large-scale plant with an annual capacity of two hundred thousand units or more, producing compact cars mostly for export. The strategy was to induce a foreign carmaker of world standing to enter a joint venture with a domestic enterprise, and through the joint venture obtain technology not only for assembling but also for upgrading the capability of the component suppliers. The foreign partner could not hold more than 45 percent of the equity and would have to export 50 percent of production. Later the government announced that the principle local partner would be a public enterprise, China Steel. China Steel's chairman was made director of the "Big Auto Plant preparatory committee." With this announcement the government demonstrated that it intended to keep tight control of the project.

Several international car makers expressed interest, with the final

[7] Taiwan's economists tend to take the auto industry as the stock example of the evils of protection. But plenty of other industries in Taiwan have received protection, with different results. Two reasons can be mentioned, among others: One, the Taiwan government decided, like the Korean government, to limit the size of the domestic market for cars, but because of very high entry barriers to internationally competitive car assembly, a large domestic market is important for attaining international competitiveness. Two, the Taiwan government was unable or unwilling to reduce the number of existing assemblers, as the Korean government did, so as to bring the remaining ones nearer to economies of scale. With exceptions, the Taiwan government has been less willing than the Korean government to bang private industrialists' heads together and force industrial restructuring.

choice coming down to Nissan and Toyota. In 1982 Toyota's bid was chosen. Seven domestic private firms (none in autos) were persuaded, some reluctantly, to split a 30 percent equity share in the new venture between them.

Faced with this real threat, the domestic assemblers began to show signs of life. They lobbied against the Big Auto Plant, which would have passed them by; and the assemblers were unusually influential within government, particularly because the first assembler was unusually closely connected to the inner circle around the president's family (this being one important reason why the government had been so timid in pressuring the industry to become more competitive). But more than this, they established export-oriented expansion plans, established a joint design center to develop the island's first domestically designed car, and in the case of the Ford joint venture, announced that the Taiwan subsidiary would henceforth be integrated into its global supply network. Meanwhile the Toyota negotiations ran into difficulty. The government insisted on the 50 percent export ratio and on a "substantial" transfer of technology, despite Toyota's protestations that these should be goals rather than fixed targets; and the government added a further "request" of 90 percent domestic content. It planned to hold Toyota to a strict timetable for achieving these conditions by refusing to allow it to take profits from the venture if it failed to meet the timetable. Toyota feared that the conditions would be impossible to meet. On top of this, Taiwan's cabinet was reshuffled in 1984, bringing to the fore officials who had been more wary of the Big Auto Plant than their predecessors. The Toyota–China Steel joint venture was canceled shortly afterwards.

Meanwhile other Japanese automakers were showing much interest in joint ventures in Taiwan. Spurred on by this outside interest, the Taiwan government finally acted decisively to restructure the industry. The new Automobile Industry Development Plan of early 1985 reversed several basic policies of the previous twenty-five years: it proposed to lower greatly both tariffs and domestic content requirements on finished cars (over six and three years, respectively), with import bans limited to small Japanese cars; it removed the earlier ceiling of 50 percent foreign ownership, allowing 100 percent foreign ownership in export-only car or components production; and it imposed export ratios and technology-transfer requirements case-by-case. The Ministry of Economic Affairs has encouraged the existing producers either to merge or form joint ventures with Japanese companies, but has not (unlike South Korea) forced them. For one thing, the firms have unusually low debt/equity ratios and are therefore less subject to leverage through the state-owned banking system. The existing producers have chosen to align themselves with Japanese companies rather than merge. Nissan has bought 25 percent of Yue-

Loong, Mitsubishi has bought 25 percent of China Motors, and Toyota has been allowed to reenter with few strings. The preexisting Ford-Lio-Ho joint venture continues. All are planning to make Taiwan an active offshore site for parts and components in the 1990s, and Toyota and Nissan are thinking of it for finished small car production as well. They may hope that Taiwan will give them a fast track into the China market, ahead of South Korea.

Electronics

The government's role has been quite different as between electrical appliances and consumer electronics, on the one hand, and computer and industrial electronics on the other. In the former the government has adopted a followership role since the mid 1950s, supporting private initiatives. However, local content requirements were an important device to nudge these private initiatives in the direction of buying inputs from domestic components makers, thus deepening the industrial structure, especially in refrigerators, televisions, air conditioners, and other consumer durables. In 1965 the first export processing zone opened, where foreign and domestic firms could enjoy unfettered conditions in return for exporting all of their production; many of the export items were in consumer electronics and appliances. In 1966 the government published a plan to turn Taiwan into an "Electronics Industry Center." The planning agency formed a working group to assist in marketing, coordinating production with the demands of foreign buyers, procuring raw materials, training personnel, improving quality, and speeding up bureaucratic approval processes. It also arranged two major exhibitions in 1967 to bring foreign investors together with local producers. In short, the government assisted the growth of consumer/low-end electronics primarily in a followership mode.

By contrast, in sophisticated electronics, especially semiconductors and computers, the government exercised more leadership from the early 1970s onwards. Before then, most domestic production was by subsidiaries of multinational companies, who valued Taiwan as a site for the more labor-intensive phases of production. While this helped to integrate Taiwan into global or regional networks, the multinationals did not have much interest in shifting high value-added activities to Taiwan (or other developing countries). The role of the state was therefore crucial for the initial acquisition and mastery of advanced semiconductor and computer technology.

State officials made plans for Taiwan to acquire semiconductor design and production capability as early as 1972. In 1973–1974 they formed the *publicly owned* Electronics Research and Service Organization

(ERSO), with responsibility to recruit a foreign partner to help develop and commercialize the technology. In 1976 ERSO opened the country's first model shop for wafer fabrication, and a year later signed a technology transfer agreement with a U.S. firm (RCA) in integrated circuit design. By 1987 ERSO had grown to a staff of 1,700.

By the late 1970s, government officials had begun to envisage an integrated information industry for Taiwan, linking telecommunications, semiconductors, computer systems, and computer software.[8] The resulting "information industry" received very high priority. Two senior cabinet ministers were put in charge of a newly formed information industry task force, reporting directly to the premier. An industrial park for science-based firms was opened in 1980, modeled after the Stanford Industrial Park in California. Foreign high-tech firms have been aggressively sought, especially semiconductor firms in California's Silicon Valley. They are lured by low start-up costs, access to eight public research labs and two major universities, a computer facility, cheap long-term financing, and state equity participation of up to 49 percent. A publicly owned Information Industry Institute started in 1979 especially for software development. This comprehensive approach to the information industry was spelled out in the Information Industry Development Plan of 1980–1989.

Commercialization of the advanced microelectronics technology developed in the public research labs has been undertaken primarily by United Microelectronics, initially an ERSO subsidiary with a 45 percent equity share held by five private firms (by 1988 privates had a majority share). United Microelectronics in turn formed agreements with three Silicon Valley Chinese-American firms relocated in the science-based industry park. These agreements emphasized design rather than production, and by 1986 were producing a number of design innovations yielding a handsome flow of royalties. Already by early 1985, a 256K CMOS DRAM[9] had been designed, and by 1986 a one megabit chip. These projects were already not far short of the world design frontier. But as of 1986, no Taiwan firm had the capacity to make such large-capacity (VLSI) chips in commercial quantities. Fearing that the time for collecting technological rent would run out before a commercial-sized fabrication facility was built, ERSO and its partners sold the production licenses to a South Korean and two Japanese firms—to the dismay of senior government officials. This spurred the government to redouble the effort to find a multinational firm to make VLSI chips in Taiwan (an attempt that had gone on

[8] On Taiwan's information industry, see especially Chu (1987).
[9] CMOS stands for complementary-metal-oxide-semiconductor; DRAM stands for dynamic random access memory.

intermittently since the early 1980s). Finally, Philips agreed in 1986 to start a wafer fabrication facility for large-capacity chips, with the government orchestrating the collaboration between Philips and several domestic public and private firms and contributing almost half the capital. Characteristically, the project is concentrating on application-specific chips rather than confront the Japanese multinationals in high-volume memory chips as the Koreans are attempting to do. As well as making chips to order for multinationals (such as Texas Instruments and Intel), it is also making them for Taiwan's many semiconductor design houses. Many of these design houses are staffed by ex-ERSO engineers.

Even in personal computers, where entry costs are much lower than in semiconductors, ERSO has had a big role. Most of Taiwan's more than one hundred makers of computers, peripherals, and add-ons are private. But ERSO has provided them with key technologies to allow them to compete and upgrade. For example, it developed an IBM compatible basic input-output system for the makers of IBM "clones," to ward off legal action by IBM. Over the first half of the 1980s it has dedicated major research projects to some twenty information products, including a microprocessor local area network system, a twenty-four-dot-matrix printer, and even a thirty-two-bit microprocessor. Together with the government's Industrial Development Bureau, it identifies firms willing to commercialize the products once it has mastered the technology. Many of ERSO's products are being commercialized by spin-off companies rather than by existing private firms. Similarly in software—the Information Industry Institute has evolved into a public enterprise, itself taking most major software projects in the public sector instead of channeling demand to the private sector, and it too has created its own subsidiary to commercialize some of its results. The same pattern is seen in biotechnology.

Has the Taiwan Government Led the Market?

To decide whether the sectoral histories provide evidence of government leadership of the market, we need first to make some more distinctions. We need to distinguish government leadership from government control, for the government may have a large measure of control in an industry without taking initiatives. For instance, it may have a public enterprise that is large in relation to private firms in the industry but that does little by way of innovation. Indeed, since initiatives by definition come to an end we expect that in any one industry, even one where the government has a major presence, leadership interventions will be episodic rather than continuous. Leadership interventions can also occur, of course, where government control is weak. This may be the case with respect to the familiar devices of fiscal investment incentives and concessional credit targeted at the production of specified products, where the subsidies are simply made available to firms that wish to meet the conditions but where the items do not get made if firms do not want to make them, however much the government wishes them to be made. Here the dichotomous distinction between leadership and followership begins to look more like a spectrum. Much depends on the amount of resources dedicated to the programs, and on how the products are identified. The larger the amount of subsidy in relation to total cost, and the more that the items are chosen in a process dominated by officials rather than by industry representatives, the more leadership is involved. So leadership intervention in an industry may be "big" either because a public enterprise undertakes initiatives that affect the whole configuration of the industry or because the government makes available sizable resources to private firms in return for them moving in government-specified directions. (The government need not provide the resources itself. Where it has much influence over the lending pattern of the commercial banks, a small amount of government resources to priority sectors may trigger a large flow of "private" lending to those sectors because of the signaling effect.)

For Taiwan, my sectoral histories in cotton textiles, artificial fibers, plastics, metals, autos, and information concentrated on public enterprise initiatives as an indicator of leadership. The conclusion is straightforward. Even using just this one indicator, we have to say that the Taiwan government has been rather active in leading the market in some industries some of the time. And this, for my purposes, is enough, because it undermines the implicit or explicit argument of the bulk of the literature on Taiwan's economic development that the role of the government in promoting the development of targeted industries has been unimportant.[10] We could also—though not here—consider the importance of various subsidy and trade policies as they impact on different industries, and of how decisions are made to grant subsidies and import protection. These considerations would reinforce the central conclusion, by showing, for example, that industry representatives have little input into such decisions. Figure 9.1 shows the approximate periods of control and "big" leadership episodes in the industries we have considered.

Broadly speaking, government intervention of a leadership kind has focused on industries or projects that are capital intensive (e.g., steel, petrochemicals), or which use technology that must be imported from a small number of potential suppliers (e.g., semiconductors), and also (though this is not an aspect we have discussed) industries with an intimate relationship to national security (e.g., shipping). It has concentrated

[10] For an exception see Amsden (1979)

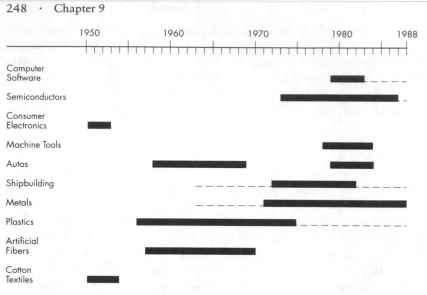

FIGURE 9.1
State Control and Leadership Episodes in Taiwan's Industrialization (selected industries).

(The solid lines refer to big leadership, the dotted lines to control. The dates should be taken as rough approximations. The diagram does not show all industries that have experienced big leadership, nor is it necessarily complete for all industries shown.)

on industries that are expected to become internationally competitive but have not yet become so, and on industries that, though losing competitiveness, the government considers important for the economy's future growth. It is absent in industries or projects without these characteristics (e.g., wigs, wallets, and nondurable consumer goods). Within "high intervention" industries, leadership episodes are concentrated at the stage of creating distinctly new capacities (whether in new or existing industries), especially when such creation faces large indivisibilities or other entry barriers. So in any one industry, and in the industrial sector as a whole, we can distinguish episodes of leadership and followership or laissez-faire, sometimes beginning with leadership and then moving to followership (as in some of the heavy and chemical industries), or conversely beginning with laissez-faire or followership and then moving to more of a leadership role (as in machine tools, where the government saw that without much more assistance most of Taiwan's machine tool makers would not succeed in making the jump to computer-controlled machine tools).

Over time, from the 1950s until today, there has been a secular decline in the relative amount of government leadership in industry. Once a base of heavy and chemical industries had been established, fewer big initiatives were needed across many industries at about the same time. Also, the growing size and financial strength of private firms and the relatively declining importance of public enterprise reduced the amount of leadership. But to say there has been a long-term decline is not to say that government leadership today is unimportant. The government still intervenes in a leadership role to push the international competitiveness of industries it identifies as important, as in autos and semiconductors. Leadership is applied to a shifting band of industries.

But much of the economy, especially Taiwan's large segment of small-scale firms, has been little affected in any direct way by government intervention of a leadership or followership kind, except when transactions involve the external economy (via import controls and foreign exchange controls). To oversimplify, the government's role in the small-scale segment is akin to the "Hong Kong" paradigm, while its role in the large-scale segment is closer to the "Korean or Japanese" paradigm. Those who say or assume that Taiwan's success is due to (nearly) free markets and a government limited to providing public goods assume that the small-scale segment constitutes the whole economy. Even according to the census data, which biases firm size downward, firms with less than twenty employees have produced only 10 percent of industrial value-added since the early 1970s, while firms with more than five hundred employees have produced nearly half (Census of Commerce and Industry, Fourth, Fifth, and Sixth). Small firms produce a disproportionately high share of Taiwan's exports (firms with less than 300 employees produced about 65 percent of manufactured exports in 1985), but these same firms are linked to—and often get assistance from—upstream suppliers, so their performance cannot be isolated from that of the large-scale segment.

And just for this reason, much of the small-scale segment of the economy works rather differently from the Hong Kong paradigm. Even though government does not intervene directly, the behavior of small-size firms is affected by the distribution of opportunities in the surrounding large-scale segment and by help from large-scale firms. The configuration of opportunities and risks in the large-scale segment *is* much affected by government intervention, both of the leadership and followership type. Indirectly, then, the government can influence investment within the small-scale segment as well.

SOUTH KOREA

An examination of the same ground for South Korea would show that there too the government has led the production and investment pattern of some important industries some of the time. Rather than make a comprehensive comparison with Taiwan, we take only the automobile and information industries. These will serve to illustrate the different ways of industrial leadership.

Automobiles

From the start South Korea's government exerted a stronger hand in shaping the automobile industry than Taiwan's.[11] In 1962, four years after Taiwan, a public enterprise established the first assembly plant (also in cooperation with Nissan). At the time the plant went into production, the government instituted tight import controls on finished vehicles, duty-free import of components, and tax exemptions for the producer. In 1965 the government transferred the hitherto publicly owned assembler to a private firm and approved a new technology agreement with Toyota. A domestic content requirement of 50 percent in five years was also instituted and, unlike in Taiwan, enforced (firms that failed to meet the schedule suffered loss of preferential allocation of foreign exchange). With heavy protection plus domestic content requirements in place and with domestic components production growing fast, three more private firms were allowed to enter between 1965 and 1969 to fight for a market of less than twenty-thousand units a year. So by 1970 the structure of the automobile industry in South Korea resembled Taiwan's.

Subsequently Korea's industry forged ahead with government leadership of private firms, while Taiwan's languished. Autos were identified as one of the priority industries in the Heavy and Chemical Industry Plan of 1973. In 1974 an industry-specific plan for automobiles was published covering the next ten years. The objectives were to achieve a 90 percent domestic content for small passenger cars by the end of the 1970s and to turn the industry into a major exporter by the early 1980s. The government stipulated the three primary producers, [12] the minimum size of each producer, and the maximum size of the car engine; it also required to approve their plans and precluded them from changing their model within a set time. The three primary producers were parts of South Korea's large-scale private conglomerates (*chaebols*), whose emergence the government was promoting in imitation of Japan's. Also in 1974 the government launched a complementary promotion plan for the parts and components industry. The plan required the three primary producers to meet a domestic contents schedule; it required them to cooperate in the production of standardized parts and components (something that the

[11] On Korea's auto industry, see especially Chu (1987) and other references in Wade (1990).

[12] Hyundai, Kia, and GM Korea. The latter was renamed Saehan in 1976, and renamed Daewoo in 1978 when the Daewoo group bought a 50 percent stake from the Korea Development Bank, with the other 50 percent held by GM (Chu, 1987, p. 212)

Taiwan government tried but failed to get its producers to do); and it empowered the Ministry of Trade and Industry serially to select certain items and their assigned producers for special promotion, with a complete import ban once the item met the government's price and quality standards. Later the three producers were required to set export targets (first in peripheral markets of Southeast Asia, Latin America, the Middle East, and then Canada, in order to prepare for an assault on the U.S. market). They were encouraged to set their export price well below the cost of production and allowed to set the domestic price well above cost of production so as to cross-subsidize exports; they received heavy direct and indirect export subsidies (especially credit); and they were allowed to import a limited number of top-of-the-range models in kit form for lucrative domestic elite sale, the number tied to their *export* performance. In these circumstances the South Korean producers invested heavily in anticipation of the export drive (unlike their Taiwan counterparts).

In 1980, following the second oil crisis and the rapid deterioration of domestic and world economic conditions, the government undertook a comprehensive rationalization of heavy and chemical sectors, including autos. It forced the auto producers to make a clear-cut division of labor between them, granting each producer a monopoly in some segment (small cars, light trucks, heavy trucks, buses) in return for getting out of others. It also reduced the excise tax on cars to stimulate domestic demand, halved the export targets and greatly increased the volume of concessional credit. The investment drive resumed in late 1981 as the economy recovered. By 1986 the Hyundai Excel became by far the best-selling new car import in U.S. history, following its earlier success in Canada. (But note that the Excel is a near-clone of the Mitsubishi Mirage, including Mitsubishi-made engine and transmission. Mitsubishi has owned 10 percent of Hyundai since 1982.)

In response to this ample evidence of South Korea's automobile manufacturing capability, Ford and Chrysler rushed to establish joint ventures with South Korean partners to catch up with GM's already existing joint venture with Daewoo. (Ford tried to line up with Hyundai, which declined, then reached agreement with the second biggest, Kia, with the help of its Japanese equity partner, Mazda, which had a small equity stake in Kia. Chrysler lined up with Samsung, but Samsung failed to get government permission to start an export-oriented joint production plant.)

Meanwhile, the government works to keep control in South Korean hands and to reconcile the objective of international competitiveness with the objective of high domestic content. (The Taiwan government, by contrast, has given up on national control and high domestic content, in the interests of doing everything possible to enhance international competitiveness.) South Korea's domestic market continues to be highly protected and the government prevents new domestic entrants. In response to intense U.S. pressure for trade liberalization, the government announced an automobile liberalization schedule that permits small car imports for the first time in over twenty-five years, but with a duty of 200 percent to be lowered to 100 percent. It is still not clear whether one or more South Korean companies will succeed in becoming technologically fully independent (for which they would have greatly to improve their design capability and their production of engines and transmissions); or whether they will remain semi-independent technological subsidiaries of the big Japanese and U.S. companies. But even to have reached the present point after one and a half decades is a very remarkable achievement.

Electronics

From the mid 1970s onwards, the South Korean government helped to excite a consensus that electronics should become one of South Korea's main manufacturing sectors. For example, the Ministry of Science and Technology study "The Year 2000" (1986) shows a high percentage of industrial output coming from electronics. The industry has benefited from targeted concessional credit, as well as from general research and development subsidies, which benefit electronics disproportionately because of its high research and development intensity. Protection has been another favored promotional device; as of 1984 over a third of the 450 electrical and electronic products listed in the tariff schedule were subject to quantitative import controls. Public procurement policies have also been used to steer domestic demand toward Korean-made products. Finally, the government has helped South Korean companies to negotiate technology transfer deals with multinationals, with the aim of obtaining as much as possible through licensing agreements rather than joint ventures. We now look at semiconductors, and then briefly at computers.[13]

In semiconductors, three stages of South Korean government policy can be distinguished, roughly corresponding to decades (Park, 1987). In the 1960s government policy encouraged foreign direct investment in semiconductors and other electronics, at the same time as the government adopted a very restrictive posture to foreign direct investment in general. In the 1970s government policy established an infrastructural base for South Korea to acquire its own capability in semiconductors, in terms of research and development facilities and in terms of expertise. In the 1980s the emphasis shifted toward government support for firms' initiatives. The three stages show a sequence from policy followership, to leadership,

[13] On Korea's information industry, see Chu (1987), Park (1987), Mody (forthcoming), World Bank, (1987), and Wade (1990). For my general interpretation of the Korean government's role in development, see Wade, (1982, chaps. 1, 8).

to followership. But this is followership of a "big" kind, much more important in facilitating private firms' initiatives than would be consistent with the "government followership" theory of East Asian industrial policy sketched at the beginning.

In the 1960s government encouragement of foreign direct investment in semiconductors (mostly from U.S. companies such as Komi, Fairchild, and Motorola) aimed primarily at increasing South Korea's exports, rather than obtaining technology for South Korean firms. And in fact little technology diffusion occurred, because U.S. companies located only the labor-intensive and peripheral stages of production in South Korea (as also in Taiwan).

By the early 1970s the government decided to undertake a big push to develop South Korea's own technological capacity in semiconductors. The Eight Year Electronics Industry Development Plan, published in 1974, identified three main thrusts. The first was to create mission-oriented research institutes, both public and private. The second was to expand advanced training capacity in electronics. The third was to encourage technology imports via licensing and consultants (rather than by foreign direct investment).

For all three thrusts, a new public research institution, the Korea Institute of Electronics Technology (KIET), was to be the vanguard (Park, 1987). Established in 1976, its charter gave it responsibility for planning and coordinating semiconductor research and development; importing, assimilating, and disseminating foreign technologies; providing technical assistance to South Korean firms; and undertaking market research. It was to operate in close consultation with private firms, and this consultation was built into its governance arrangements. The board of directors included four from government ministries, one from KIET, one from the Electronics Industry Association, one from universities, and five from firms. Responsible to the board of directors were three working groups, one for equipment, one for the work program, one for the training program, each of which included representatives from industry as well as from government and KIET.

Internally, KIET was divided into three functional divisions (semiconductor design, processes, and systems), each headed by a South Korean with both academic training and industry experience in the United States. In addition, a project development division processed information on marketing opportunities and kept abreast of foreign technologies. The function of keeping abreast of foreign technologies was also central to the work of another important component, KIET's liaison office in Silicon Valley, center of the U.S. semiconductor industry. Established in 1978, the liaison office helped KIET obtain equipment and technology licenses, build contacts with U.S. semiconductor firms, and, crucially, to create a network among South Korean researchers working in U.S. semiconductor companies. Through the network, KIET was able to help South Korean firms identify particular individuals with skills or access that they needed, and either enlist their help while remaining in situ or repatriate them to work in South Korea. KIET also mounted training programs for South Korean firms and administered a program to send South Korean engineers and scientists abroad for experience in research institutes or firms. KIET also took an active part in all technology transfer negotiations between South Korean firms and foreign firms, and here its Silicon Valley output and its project development division were especially important. KIET opened South Korea's first pilot wafer fabrication facility in 1978, two years after Taiwan's, in a joint venture with a leading U.S. semiconductor firm (VLSI Technology). A year later it began to build South Korea's first full-scale commercial wafer fabrication facility. As of 1987 KIET (or ETRI, as it is now called, for Electronics and Telecommunications Research Institute) had 1,300 staff.

By the late 1970s most of the semiconductor industry in South Korea was still concentrated at the assembly, packaging and testing stages, with little spillover into core processes. Only a few local firms had established fabrication facilities, which were dedicated to semiconductors at the bottom end of the market. The existing local firms were clearly much too small to undertake the huge investments needed to make large-capacity chips, or to establish their own research and development capability. On the other hand, some of South Korea's already huge *chaebols*, those which had a major presence in consumer electronics, were keen to invest in advanced semiconductor production, especially because of their big in-house demand for semiconductors and their sense of vulnerability to manipulation by the major foreign semiconductor suppliers. The question for the firms and for the government was how to overcome the colossal entry barriers.

Two of the *chaebol* took over existing local semiconductor firms in the late 1970s to provide their starting point for entry into semiconductor fabrication. A third entered with completely new investments. Then the government began to restructure the information industry so as to facilitate their success, as laid out in the Basic Plan for Promotion of the Electronics Industry, published in 1981. The aim was to integrate upstream and downstream segments (maximizing economics of scale and technological spillovers), in conscious imitation of Japan's structure of semiconductor companies that are divisions of larger electronics companies, themselves part of giant conglomerates.

One of the key steps was to use the government's tight control of the telecommunications industry to aid the big South Korean firms' entry into advanced semiconductors. The telecommunications industry was overhauled, with some private firms being forced out and others assigned government-selected monopoly segments, and with all foreign technology agreements with foreign telecommunications firms being subject to renegotiation. This was partly to align the champions in semiconductors (Samsung, Goldstar, Daewoo) with profitable segments of the protected telecommunications industry, target of a *multibillion*-dollar modernization program. The champions were then able to enter joint ventures with multinational firms (ITT, AT&T, Northern Telecom) by offering lucrative and risk-free business in telecommunications in return for transferring various kinds of nearly state-of-the-art semiconductor technology. They were also able to cross-subsidize their own efforts in semiconductors from the profits of telecommunications.

In 1982 the government published the Long-Term Semiconductor Industry Promotion Plan for 1982–1986, which targeted large amounts (US$346 million) of cheap credit on the four semiconductor firms—by this time Hyundai had been allowed to enter the race—at the same time that the government was cutting back on targeted credit in general. With much government facilitation, two of the firms succeeded in going from green-field sites to operating plants for 64K DRAM chips in only eight months in 1984, half the time it took in the United States and two-thirds of the time in Japan (*Forbes* 1985, p. 44). The scale of the South Korean investment is huge; the combined semiconductor investment of the four firms in 1983–1986 period ($1.2 billion) was ten times greater than the combined investment of Taiwan's three state-sponsored semiconductor projects over the 1984–1988 period (excluding the new Philips VSLI foundry).

Meanwhile, with the entry of the *chaebols* into advanced semiconductors, the government planning mechanism changed to give a still bigger role to the firms than in the past in setting the content of government policy. The government realized that in a field changing as rapidly as semiconductors it alone could not keep abreast of markets and technologies, and could not even be confident of the effect of its policies on firms. Firms had to be more integrally involved in policy decision-making. Hence an even more elaborate consultative system was established than in the past, drawing in experts from firms, universities, national research and development laboratories, as well as government officials. "The answers to the questions of where the government should intervene, and how it should do so, were to a significant extent sought from the appropriate sections of local industry," according to Yong-chan Park (1987, p. 102).

KIET, having pioneered the mastering of medium-scale semiconductor technology, found that by about 1984, the *chaebols* had much superior fabrication facilities and were rapidly expanding their in-house research and development capacity. So its mandate was changed. It sold most of its fabrication facilities to one of the *chaebols*, changed its name to the Electronics and Telecommunications Research Institute (the new name signaling the bridge between semiconductors and telecommunications), and initiated parallel basic research efforts focused on technology frontiers further from commercialization than KIET's work had been; for research close to commercialization could now be left to the *chaebols* on their own. Much of its research is in the form of research consortia with private firms, following the Japanese model. For example, ETRI has mobilized the leading firms to collaborate in research and development for the four megabit chip, with the government offering $175 million in grants and low-interest loans. In addition, the government has made concessional credit and tax credits available for research and development institutes, for importing research and development equipment, and for importing semiconductor fabrication equipment.

As for computers, the government at first relied primarily on obligatory public procurement of Korean-made machines. It then issued the Computer Industry Promotion Master Plan in 1984, which intensified the role of the national research labs (especially the Electronics and Telecommunications Research Institute) in the initial acquisition of computer technology and imposed a complete ban on imports of microcomputers to assist the domestic industry. (This ban was removed in 1987.) The public sector greatly expanded its use of microcomputers and targeted its demand on domestic suppliers *according to their levels of domestic content*. In 1986 the government announced domestic content guidelines for all microcomputers and peripherals whether they are sold to the state or not.

TAIWAN AND KOREA

Now let us compare the two cases. When the Taiwan government has wanted to give a big push to some sector it has often relied on direct state involvement, either through existing public enterprises, in the case of capital-intensive and standardized production, or through state research organizations, in the case of new high-technology sectors. It attempts to pressure the private firms more indirectly than its Korean counterpart, via import controls, domestic content requirements, entry restrictions, and tax incentives, and it is more hesitant to force mergers or divisions of labor. The Korean government has used direct and indirect pressure on the big conglomerates (which it helped to create) by means not only of import controls, entry restrictions, domestic content requirements and foreign equity restrictions, but also through large amounts of concessional credit and other subsidies and direct instruction backed by the ability to cut off credit and foreign exchange (Chu, 1987). In a sense, Taiwan's public enterprises have been the equivalent of Korea's *chaebols*, with the very important qualification that they are much smaller in size and less multisectoral.

The difference in overall style is seen in the differences between Taiwan's ERSO and Korea's KIET (or ETRI). Both have played leadership roles in their country's mastery of semiconductor and computer technologies, and both have been publicly owned. But ERSO is bigger, gets more of its revenue from government grants and less from industry contracts, and lacks KIET's elaborate consultative arrangements with industry. And whereas ETRI (as KIET is now called) has moved to what could be described as a "big followership" role, ERSO remains in a "big leadership" role.

The reasons for the difference in the instruments of leadership are beyond the scope of this paper, but they relate on the Taiwan side to (1) the absence of very large Korean- and Japanese-style firms and business groups, (2) a tenacious suspicion of big Chinese capitalists among Taiwan's industrial policymakers for most of the postwar period, and (3) the ethnic tension between the Mainlander-dominated government and the native Taiwanese business sector. As a result, Taiwan's policymakers have seen a greater conflict of interests between the state and the private sector, while Korea's and Japan's have seen more of a fusion—to the point where the western concept of "private" is misleading when applied to South Korea's and Japan's conglomerates.

Moreover, the various parts of the Taiwan government are probably less centralized than South Korea's, and in particular the ministry responsible for industrial success (Ministry of Economic Affairs) is less preeminent in relation to the other ministries than in South Korea. This makes government leadership of private firms somewhat more difficult than in South Korea, and supports a lower amount of leadership overall.

Take the telecommunications industry, for example. The Taiwan government attempted, like its South Korean counterpart, to make a close integration between telecommunications and semiconductors, but with less success. Taiwan's telecommunications industry was largely in the hands of joint ventures that linked two major U.S. multinationals (ITT and GTE) with some local firms connected to high level people in the KMT party.[14] For reasons relating to Taiwan's more dependent relations with the United States and to the local firms' political connections, the Ministry of Economic Affairs was anxious not to offend these companies by renegotiating the agreements. It decided to bypass them and make a new agreement with AT&T for advanced telecommunications and related integrated circuit technology, using the lure of public sector procurement.

[14] Taiwan has been run as a KMT party-state since 1945. It had been a Japanese colony for the previous fifty years.

But given the existing agreements not so much business could be assured for AT&T, and in any case, the Ministry of Communications was lukewarm about the AT&T deal, having closer relations with ITT and GTE. Consequently, the Ministry of Economic Affairs was able to negotiate a less beneficial deal from Taiwan's point of view than the South Koreans did in terms of equity participation and technology transfer. This reflects the fact that Taiwan's Ministry of Economic Affairs is less influential in relation to other parts of the nondefense bureaucracy than its South Korean counterpart, the Ministry of Trade and Industry (Chu, 1987). These differences in governmental organization—South Korea's greater hierarchical consolidation, Taiwan's more dispersed control (except at the very top of government)—are congruent with differences in the organization of business groups. South Korea's are much larger, more central in the economy, and are managed by a single person in a single position operating through a unified management hierarchy spanning the whole group. Taiwan's are smaller, less important, less integrated, and are managed by a set of relatives holding the senior most positions in most of the firms of the group (Hamilton et al., 1987).

HONG KONG

Hong Kong has long been much wealthier than Taiwan and Korea, with a per capita income two and a half times Taiwan's in the early 1960s and twice as high today. If Hong Kong has done as well as (or better than) the other apparently more *dirigiste* East Asian countries, does not this suggest that public management of industrial restructuring and external transactions is a minor element in the superior economic performance of all the East Asian capitalist economies? Has not Hong Kong been as close to a free market economy as it is possible to get?

There are several arguments against this view. One is that Hong Kong is too special to be put alongside the others as an equivalent unit (e.g., Ranis 1979). Hong Kong's population is small (5 million in 1980, against Taiwan's 18 million). It has no significant productivity depressing agricultural sector. It did not face the same temptation to establish heavy and chemical industries. It benefited from an organizational and marketing capacity that was already in place prior to industrialization, built up over decades by British-linked trading companies, in a way that Taiwan and Korea did not. And its economic growth is a function of its service role in a wider regional economy—as entrepôt trader, regional headquarters for multinational companies, and refuge for nervous money. Finally, its size means that even with industrial and financial capital operating from a strictly *international* perspective, full employment and wide diffusion of the benefits of growth within the small population can occur.

A second argument presents Hong Kong as a variant of a guided market economy. It is true that the formal institutions of government perform mainly custodial functions and that Hong Kong has no controls over imports, foreign exchange, foreign investment, wages, and prices. Tax revenues to GNP are very low, at 13.7 percent in 1977, compared to Taiwan's 24.2 percent (Hofheinz and Calder, 1982, p. 34). But to conclude from this that Hong Kong is close to a free market economy is misleading. Hong Kong's peak private economic organizations, notably the major banks and trading companies, are closely linked to the lifetime expatriates who largely run the government. (Just one bank, the Hong Kong and Shanghai Banking Corporation, holds assets worth well over twice the colony's annual GNP). This coalition, and in particular the association of large banks, provides a point of concentration of power at which negotiations in line with an implicit and encompassing development strategy can be conducted. Both the generation and implementation of policy are insulated from the demands of small business, organized labor, and other nonestablishment groups by the exclusionary and authoritarian colonial state (Deyo 1987). Ironically the Chinese government has helped to check the disruptiveness of left-wing unions over the 1970s and 1980s, as its direct interest in the colony's prosperity grew. The Hong Kong government also has available some unusual instruments for influencing industrial activity. It owns all the land, which it sells on leasehold to raise revenue instead of relying on taxes. It controls rents in part of the private housing market and supplies subsidized public housing to roughly half the population, thereby helping to keep down the cost of labor. And its ability to increase or decrease the flow of immigrants from China also gives it a way of affecting labor costs. All told, the Hong Kong economy works very differently from the textbook picture of a free market economy or from economies of the Anglo-American kind (as does Singapore's [Lim, 1983]).

A third argument questions whether Hong Kong has done as well as the other more *dirigiste* countries. Its rate of industrial restructuring over the 1970s and 1980s has been much slower than the others', and its export composition has remained stuck at the relatively low end, with labor-intensive and low-technology goods continuing to make up by far the largest share. Most exports are still textiles, toys, consumer electronics, or watches and clocks. From the mid-1970s to the mid-1980s, its rate of growth of export value added has been slower than in South Korea, Taiwan, or Singapore (*Far Eastern Economic Review*, 1985). Indeed, concern about industrial slippage pushed the Hong Kong authorities in 1987 into what officials call a "radical" departure. The government is entering the business of what it calls "development support." To help companies with training and technology transfer in three areas where it believes the

Hong Kong electronics industry should be focusing, it is setting up a digital communications laboratory, a surface mount technology laboratory, and a customized integrated circuit design center. The government also plans to employ consultants to study promising new technologies with industrial applications and to see whether support services should be provided for them. These departures have echoes of a late conversion to a "help to make the winners" policy such as has long been practiced in Taiwan, South Korea and Japan (*Financial Times*, 1988, p. 5).

Where Hong Kong has been notably successful in restructuring is in finance rather than in industry, with the major banks leading the way. This difference in performance is consistent with the developmental state argument for institutional centralization, which has been stronger for financial capital than for industrial capital in Hong Kong (Deyo, 1987; Haggard, 1986).

So whether we take Hong Kong as a special case or as a (less successful) variant of the guided market, we can at least reject the argument that—since Hong Kong is a free market economy, and since the causes of successful performance must be something Taiwan, Korea, and Japan share with Hong Kong—industrial policy must have been unimportant.

CONCLUSION

We began with the mainstream interpretation of East Asian success within economics, which I called the self-adjusting market theory. It gives government an important but background role as regulator and provider of public goods. Whatever else we conclude from the present evidence, we can surely say that the governments of Taiwan and South Korea have gone well beyond this theory—beyond the role described for them in neoclassical accounts, and beyond both the practice of Anglo-American governments and the neoclassical principles of good economic management.

The second conclusion is that much of this intervention has been of a leadership rather than just a followership type. It has done more than assist private producers to go where they have gone anyway. This second conclusion does not imply that leadership has helped rather than hindered development. But it does undermine the popular view that these countries' selective industrial policies amounted to little more than window-dressing, or a seal of approval on private sector plans.

The third conclusion is that the mode of leadership is substantially different between Taiwan and South Korea. The Taiwan government has relied more on public enterprises or public research and service organizations to undertake big pushes in new fields and to exercise control in important industries. The South Korean government has relied more on pushing and prodding very large "private" firms, which are backed by much direct or indirect state assistance. That this difference between the two countries is seen in industries with rather different technological characteristics (e.g., automobiles, semiconductors, computers) suggests there may be country-specific differences in styles of intervention (Chu, 1987).

Fourth, the amounts of leadership and followership do not seem to be closely connected to phases in the standard economic chronology of these countries' development. The standard chronology shows both countries beginning with a period of "bad" primary import substitution (lasting to about 1960 in Taiwan and to about 1963–1965 in South Korea), followed by a phase of "good" export promotion or outward orientation (lasting to the early to mid-1970s), followed by a period of "bad" secondary import substitution, especially bad in South Korea (lasting to the late 1970s and early 1980s), followed by a period of "good" course correction, or liberalization. Each "bad" period is associated with "excessive" government intervention. It is remarkable how much this chronology is repeated, with so little concern for its analytical underpinnings. My suggestion is that if one thinks of intervention in terms of leadership and followership, one will *not* find leadership being greater in periods of import substitution and followership being greater at times of export promotion. In Taiwan's case, for example, there is no sharp fall off in government leadership at the time of the first economic liberalization episode around 1960.

Fifth, Hong Kong does not serve to reject the argument that selective industrial policies, operating to lead the market in some important industries some of the time, have been important in accelerating the development of Taiwan and South Korea. I would argue further, though not here, that the role of government in pre-1970 Japan fits closely those features that are common to both Taiwan and South Korea, and that it fits South Korea closer than Taiwan where the two differ. The common features of all three countries constitute a plausible answer to the question of what is the most economically effective way for a late industrializing country to organize the institutions of capitalism.

Nothing I have said justifies the conclusion that other well-meaning governments should try to emulate the East Asian three. Some governments have a greater capacity for industrial leadership than others (cf. Wolf 1979, Lal 1983). However, even in conditions where leadership is unlikely to work, an industrial policy in more of a *followership* mode can still be worth pursuing. Here the government does not do anything by itself, and does not force anything on the private economy. It does, however, establish a consultation process in which government, management, and labor can enter into strategic agreements about consumption, investment, incomes, and work practices to which the government brings its own ideas about the long run evolution of the economy and in which government help is given only in return for stipulated performance by the other parties. For some countries this may be a more politically feasible route than leadership. But economies whose governments can intervene effectively in a leadership mode have more *potential* for welfare-enhancing transformation than those whose governments cannot.

That, at least, is a reasonable inference from East Asian experience. But a well-worked out economic rationale for such actions is lacking. The absence of a theoretical rationale permits economists to exercise a selective inattention to the data that would upset a "self-adjusting market" interpretation of East Asian success. They can simply assume that anything outside this framework is unimportant enough to ignore and press the evidence only to the point of confirming the assumption. Hence the Japanese, South Korean, and Taiwanese experiences are held up to vindicate the truth of nearly free market economics. "The real explanation for the Japanese economic miracle," says David Henderson, "is the country's laissez faire policies on taxes, antitrust, banking and labor" (1983, p. 114).

Yet an economic rationale for what East Asian governments actually did could be constructed from familiar economic concepts. Some of their industrial policies make sense as an attempt to lower entry barriers and thereby allow quick capture of economics of scale and learning-by-doing—in other words, as an attempt to use public resources and influence to offset the effects of both deficient capital markets and limited internal firm capacity to generate the capital necessary to finance new ventures. Some make sense as an attempt to capture externalities (or spillover effects) within the national boundaries. In the absence of intervention these externalities would result in slower productivity gains due to underinvestment in research and development, human capital, and learning-by-doing. Externalities may also cause inadequate investment in relatively capital-intensive activities with significant scale economies, when profitable entry to a new upstream (downstream) activity is precluded by the nonexistence of downstream (upstream) buyers or suppliers (assuming that the transactions costs of participation in foreign trade are not trivial). Again, linked to but separate from the above, some government actions can be understood as an attempt to substitute for weak and difficult-to-develop capital and insurance markets, which are more prone to information asymmetries and other sources of failure than commodity markets, especially in developing countries. And where entrepreneurs with experience of large-scale organization are scarce, the decentralized preferences of entrepreneurs and capital market suppliers can lock the country into specialization in industries that have inferior longer-term prospects.

These are some of the avenues that might be pursued in an attempt to provide a theoretical rationale for what East Asian governments actually did to promote industry. The aim is to identify the conditions in which total domestic benefit might be expected to exceed the cost of the promotion measures. Given the strong presumption in neoclassical theory that many of the policies that these governments actually used could not help growth, it is wise to begin by erring in the opposite direction: by assuming that, in view of their outstanding economic success, their principal policy instruments must have had effects whose overall benefits exceeded the cost. Take protection, for example. Practically all neoclassical economists would agree that protection is always a second-best means of promoting domestic industry, or worse than second-best, and that quantitative restrictions (QRs) are always inferior to tariffs. Yet these countries used substantial amounts of protection, much of it through QRs (Wade 1988c). The standard and easy reply is that had they used less protection and replaced QRs with tariffs their performance would have been still more outstanding. A more demanding response would be to examine carefully the implementation of protection in East Asia. We would find that much of the protection was made conditional upon performance, and that QRs have advantages over tariffs in terms of administrative flexibility in response to new conditions. Again, take "government" as another example. Economists' characteristic suspicion of government's ability to devise and implement policies that improve upon market outcomes owes much to the American and British philosophical repugnance to government involvement in promoting the fortunes of specific industries, a repugnance that is translated into organizational incompetence at doing the same. But not all governments are designed to be incompetent at carrying out deliberately concerted industrial policies. By calibrating the theoretical assumptions about government (or about protection, or about other policies discussed here) to East Asia, and by abandoning the assumption that only those things consistent with the neoclassical prescription for economic success could have contributed, we open the way to important advances in the theory of economic growth.

REFERENCES

Amsden, Alice. 1979. "Taiwan's Economic History: A Case of Etatisme and a Challenge to Dependency Theory." *Modern China* 5, no. 3, pp. 341–80.

———. 1977. "The Division of Labor Is Limited by the Type of Market: The Case of the Taiwanese Machine Tool Industry." *World Development* 5, no. 3, pp. 217–34.

Arnold, Walter. 1989. "Bureaucratic Politics, State Capacity, and Taiwan's Automobile Industrial Policy." *Modern China* 15, no. 2, pp. 178–214.

Bank of Korea. Various years. *National Income Accounts*.

Chen, Wen-lang, C. Tu, and W. Wang. 1987. "The Principle of Trade Liberalization in Taiwan R.O.C. and Its Impact on Industry." Mimeo, Chung-hua Institution for Economic Research, Taipei (Chinese).

Chu, Yun-han. 1987. *Authoritarian Regimes under Stress: The Political Economy of Adjustment in the East Asian NICs*. Ph.D. diss., University of Minnesota.

CIECD (Council for International Economic Cooperation and Development). 1965. *Fourth Four-Year Plan for Economic Development 1965–68*. Taipei.

Deyo, Frederic C. 1987. "Coalitions, Institutions, and Linkage Sequencing." In his *The Political Economy of the New Asian Industrialization*. Ithaca: Cornell University Press.

DGBAS (Directorate-General of Budget, Accounts and Statistics). 1981. 1985. *Statistical Yearbook*. Taipei.

Far Eastern Economic Review. 1985. "Hong Kong's problems are masked by prosperity." September 26, pp. 102–3.

Fei, John, Gustav Ranis, and Shirley Kuo. 1979. *Growth with Equity: The Taiwan Case*. New York: Oxford University Press.

Financial Times. 1988. "FT Report—Asia's Pacific Rim." June 30.

Forbes. 1985. "The Koreans Are Coming." February 25, p. 44.

Galenson, Walter. 1982. "How to Develop Successfully—The Taiwan Model." In proceedings of a conference on *Experiences and Lessons of Economic Development in Taiwan*. Taipei: Institute of Economics, Academic Sinica.

Galenson, Walter, ed. 1979. *Economic Growth and Structural Change in Taiwan: The Postwar Experience of the Republic of China*. Ithaca: Cornell University Press.

Galli, Anton. 1980. *Taiwan: Economic Facts and Trends*. IFO Development Research Studies. Munchen: Weltforum Verlag.

Gold, Thomas. 1986. *State and Society in the Taiwan Miracle*. New York: M. E. Sharpe.

———. 1981. *Dependent Development in Taiwan*. Ph.D. thesis, Harvard University.

Haggard, S. 1986. "The Newly Industrializing Countries in the International System." *World Politics* 38, pp. 343–70.

Hamilton, Gary, Marco Orrú, and Nicole Biggart, 1987. "Enterprise Groups in East Asia: An Organizational Analysis." *Financial Economic Review* (Tokyo) 161, pp. 78–106.

Henderson, David. 1983. "The Myth of MITI." *Fortune*, August 8, pp. 113–16.

Hindley, Brian. 1984. "Empty Economics in the Case for Industrial Policy." *The World Economy* 7, no. 3, pp. 277–94.

Ho, Samuel. 1981. "South Korea and Taiwan: Development Prospects and Problems in the 1980s." *Asian Survey* 21, no. 12.

Hofheinz, R., and K. Calder. 1982. *The Eastasia Edge*. New York. Basic Books.

Inkster, Ian. 1983. "Modeling Japan for the Third World." In *East Asia: International Review of Economic, Political, and Social Development*, Frankfurt: Campus Verlag, part 1.

Jacobsson, Steffan. 1984. "Industrial Policy for the Machine Tool Industries of South Korea and Taiwan." *IDS Bulletin* 15, no. 2.

Johnson, Chalmers. 1988. "Political Institutions and Economic Performance: A Comparative Analysis of the Government-Business Relationship in Japan, South Korea, and Taiwan." In *The Political Economy of the New Asian Industrialism,* edited by Frederic C. Deyo. Ithaca: Cornell University Press.

———. 1986. "The Nonsocialist NICs: East Asia." In *Power, Purpose, and Collective Choice: Economic Strategies in Socialist States,* edited by Ellen Comisso and Laura D'Andrea Tyson. Ithaca: Cornell University Press.

Krueger, Anne. 1983. *Synthesis and Conclusions.* Vol. 3 of *Trade and Employment in Developing Countries.* Chicago: University of Chicago Press.

Kubo, Yuji, Jaime de Melo, Sherman Robinson, and Moshe Syrquin. 1986. "Interdependence and Industrial Structure." In *Industrialization and Growth: A Comparative Analysis,* edited by Hollis Chenery, Sherman Robinson, and Moshe Syrquin. New York: Oxford University Press.

Lal, Deepak. 1983. *The Poverty of Development Economics.* London: The Institute of Economic Affairs.

Lal, Deepak, and Sarath Rajapatirana. 1986. "Foreign Trade Regimes and Economic Growth in Developing Countries." Paper for conference on Free Trade in the World Economy: Towards an Opening of Markets. Institute for World Economics, Kiel, West Germany, June 24–26.

Lim, L. 1983. "Singapore's Success: The Myth of the Free Market Economy." *Asian Survey* 23, pp. 752–65.

Lin, Ching-yuan. 1973. *Industrialization in Taiwan, 1946–1972: Trade and Import Substitution Policies for Developing Countries.* New York: Praeger.

Little, Ian. 1979. "An Economic Renaissance." In Galenson (1979).

Ministry of Economic Affairs. 1961. *Taiwan's Third Four-Year Economic Development Plan.* Taipei.

Ministry of Science and Technology (Korea). 1986. "Long-term Technology Forecast for the Year 2000." Seoul.

Mody, Ashok. Forthcoming. "Recent Evolution of Microelectronics in Korea and Taiwan: An Institutional Approach to Comparative Advantage." *Cambridge Journal of Economics.*

Park, Yong-chan. 1987. *The National System of Innovation in Korea with an Introduction to the Semiconductor Industry.* MSc thesis, Science Policy Research Unit. University of Sussex, Great Britain.

Ranis, Gustav. 1979. "Industrial Development." In Galenson (1979).

Trezise, Philip. 1983. "Industrial Policy Is Not the Major Reason for Japan's Success." *Brookings Review* 1 (Spring): 13–18.

Ueno, Hiroya. 1980. "The Conception and Evaluation of Japanese Industrial Policy." In *Industry and Business in Japan,* edited by Kazuo Sato. New York: M. E. Sharpe.

Wade, Robert H. 1990. *Governing the Market: Economic Theory and the Role of Government in East Asian Industrialization.* Princeton: Princeton University Press.

Wade, Robert. 1982. *Irrigation and Politics in South Korea*. Boulder, Colorado: Westview Press.

———. 1984. "Dirigisme Taiwan-Style." In *Developmental States in East Asia*, edited by Robert Wade and Gordon White. *IDS Bulletin* 15, no. 2, pp. 65–70.

———. 1985a. "East Asian Financial Systems as a Challenge to Economics: Lessons from Taiwan." *California Management Review* 27, no. 4, pp. 106–27.

———. 1985b. "Taiwan." In "Some Pacific Economics." *Economic and Social Research Council Newsletter*, no. 54, pp. 12–15. Economic and Social Research Council, United Kingdom.

———. 1988a. "State Intervention in Outward-Looking Development: Neoclassical Theory and Taiwanese Practice." In *Developmental States in East Asia*, edited by Gordon White. London: Macmillan.

———. 1988b. "The Role of Government in Overcoming Market Failure: Taiwan, South Korea, and Japan." In *Achieving Industrialization in Asia*, edited by Helen Hughes. Cambridge: Cambridge University Press.

———. 1988c. "The Rise of East Asian Trading States—How They Managed Their Trade." Mimeo, Trade Policy Division, World Bank.

Watanabe, T. 1985. "Economic Development in Korea: Lessons and Challenges." In *Economic Policy and Development: New Perspectives*, edited by T. Shishido and R. Sato. Dover: Auburn House.

Wolf, Charles. 1979. "A Theory of Nonmarket Failure: Framework for Implementation Analysis." *Journal of Law and Economics*. 22, no. 1, pp. 107–39.

World Bank. 1987. *Korea: Managing the Industrial Transition*. 2 vols. Washington, D.C.

Zysman, John. 1983. *Governments, Markets, and Growth: Financial Systems and the Politics of Industrial Change*. Ithaca: Cornell University Press.

Zysman, John, and Stephen Cohen, 1983. "Double or Nothing: Open Trade and Competitive Industry." *Foreign Affairs* 61, no. 5, pp. 1113–39.

CHAPTER 10

The Next Stage of Industrialization in Taiwan and South Korea

Chi Schive

THE EXPORT-LED growth of four Asian newly industrializing countries (NICS), Taiwan, South Korea, Singapore, and Hong Kong, is well documented (Galenson, 1985; Lau, 1986; Bradford and Branson, 1987). Of these four, Taiwan and South Korea have received the most attention because of their rapid, large-scale industrializations. Export-led economic growth raises two problems. First, what changes occur in the domestic sector of a NIC to produce and replace the materials and equipment originally imported to facilitate exports? Second, when conventional exports (such as textiles, footwear, and steel) begin to face increasing difficulties in the world market—low-cost competition from less developed countries on the one hand, and trade protectionism by developed countries on the other—is it possible for NICs to develop high-tech industries as substitutes to conventional exports to penetrate the fenced markets, a strategy for continued export-oriented industrialization (EOI) (Gereffi, chap. 1, this volume)? The first question has not been adequately treated in the existing literature, while the second presents a real challenge to the economies of NICs. In point of fact, some materials and equipment are themselves the products of high-tech industries. Thus, exploration of these two questions (with reference here to Taiwan and South Korea) will not only be of intellectual interest, but will serve a wide range of policymakers as well.

This chapter will begin with a bird's-eye view of the general development of these two economies, and of changes in their manufacturing structures. The second section will focus on the two countries' development of their domestic materials and equipment industries to replace imports, a process called secondary import substitution (SIS) (Ranis, 1979). The third section examines the issue of high-tech industry by focusing on a narrowly defined product, VLSI (very-large-scale integrated circuits). The fourth section focuses on the policy issues. Some conclusions on the

The author wishes to thank Professor Gary Gereffi for his detailed and valuable comments and suggestions when revising this chapter. Thanks are also due to other conference participants, particularly Professors Gustav Ranis, Robert Wade, and Wontack Hong for their stimulating comments and C. L. Chou for his painstaking work in compiling data.

next stage of industrialization of NICs, Taiwan and South Korea in particular, are given at the end.

INDUSTRIALIZATION IN TAIWAN AND SOUTH KOREA, 1965–1986

Taiwan and South Korea have many common features in their geology, modern history, and culture; both countries' marvelous achievements in economic development mark another obvious similarity. Between 1965 and 1986, Taiwan's and South Korea's economies grew at annual rates of 9.3 percent and 8.5 percent, respectively, by quickly expanding their manufacturing sectors. During that period, the manufactured output in real terms increased about 14.8 times in Taiwan, and about 36.8 times in South Korea. Both economies changed in a relatively short time from predominantly agricultural to highly industrialized.[1]

Exports of manufactured products have played a vital role in their growths. In the twenty-two years ending in 1986, Taiwan raised its ratio of exports to GNP from 18.7 percent to 59.1 percent; South Korea did equally well, increasing that ratio from 6.8 percent to 34.8 percent. After this rapid expansion in trade, both economies have become heavily dependent upon the trading sector. This is why these economies are frequently referred to as models of export-led growth.

Industrialization in the two countries accelerated not only by rapidly expanding the manufacturing sector, but also by changing the manufacturing structure at no less speed. In the mid-1960s, the food, beverage, and tobacco industries took the lion's share of manufacturing in both economies; those shares have declined sharply and stably since that time. The nonmetallic mineral products industry also declined over these years. On the other hand, production of metal, metal products, and machinery (including equipment and fabricated metal products, such as electronics) have taken the lead and now dominate those manufacturing sectors. Other major industries, such as textiles; clothing and footwear; and chemicals, petroleum and coal showed first increasing, then declining, trends in both economies, though the degree of trend variation seemed to be larger in South Korea than that in Taiwan. Generally speaking, the industrial structure of both economies has changed from light to heavy industry.[2] The metal and machinery industries including electricals and

---

[1] Taiwan's GDP share from manufacturing outpaced that from agriculture in 1968 (24.1 percent vs. 22.0 percent), whereas South Korea reached that same turning point in 1978, when the two sectors contributed 24.6 percent and 22.6 percent to GDP, respectively (CEPD, 1988; EPB, 1988).

[2] The difficulty of classifying production into light and heavy industry is well known. For a consistent comparison, Scitovsky's format and data of Taiwan and South Korea for 1965, 1971, and 1975 were adopted (Scitovsky, 1986, p. 177).

electronics were the key to this change. If we look into the machinery industry, several products of a short life cycle and requiring heavy research and development investments fit the characteristics of the high-tech industry. Taiwan and South Korea might have also entered the production of certain high-tech products (industries) in the 1980s.

A few remarks based on the data comparison of these two countries will enhance our understanding of their current development situations. First, the manufacturing sector in South Korea has been developed toward more heavy industry oriented in the relative sense than that in Taiwan during the period observed. Second, among the heavy industry group, South Korea's machinery industry clearly outperformed the Taiwanese counterpart, especially in the 1980s. Third, in the 1980s Taiwan was ahead of South Korea in the chemicals, petroleum, and coal industry, mainly petrochemicals.

SECONDARY IMPORT SUBSTITUTION DEVELOPMENT IN TAIWAN AND SOUTH KOREA

The Issues

In the stage analysis of its economic development, Taiwan was characterized in the 1950s by import substitution, and in the 1960s by export promotion (substitution) (Paauw and Fei, 1973). South Korea followed a similar pattern, but entered the second stage a few years later (Balassa, 1985, pp. 148–50). The great success of the export-substitution strategy has colored the first stage, import substitution, as inefficient, unnecessary, and even sinful. However, the rapid export expansion of those economies created a significant market for imported intermediates and capital goods, which might have been gradually replaced by domestic supply—that is, secondary import substitution.

The secondary import-substitution industry differs from the usual import-substitution industry in two ways: (1) The former refers to the intermediates (materials) and capital goods industry, while the latter covers mainly the consumer durables and nondurables industry[3] and (2) many materials industries enjoy economies of scale, and tend to be capital-intensive and "technology-intensive" compared to many consumer goods industries. It is because of the industrial characteristics linked to technology, factor endowments and market size, that many developing countries run into difficulty by setting up materials or capital goods industries (Myint, 1981). Realizing these difficulties, Taiwan and South Korea, rather than extending the first, easy stage of import substitution beyond

[3] There have been studies that add automobiles to the SIS category. See Gereffi, chap. 1, this volume.

1960, have created a favorable environment for exports.[4] Crucial changes paved the way for their rapid export-led development since that time.

Is the strategy of developing secondary import substitution, however, a fatal one? Or is Hirschman's argument for backward linkages—"every nonprimary activity will induce attempts to supply through domestic production the inputs needed in that activity" (1958, p. 100)—irrelevant and useless? Consider the following situations: (1) exports have greatly expanded the domestic market for intermediates and capital goods; that is, exports have created strong backward linkages; (2) the relative scarcity of capital to labor has gradually been leveled out by the accumulation of capital, on one hand, and the exhaustion of surplus labor, on the other; and (3) technological capabilities and experience have been sufficiently upgraded over time. Is there a right time for an economy to move into its secondary import-substitution stage?

To begin with, how do we know that an economy or industry is at the stage of secondary import substitution? Used loosely, import substitution refers to the augmentation of domestic production to replace imports. To define it more strictly, import substitution occurs in an industry during a certain period only when the import share of that industry (imports over total supply) decreases; this, in turn, contributes to the industry's growth. As regards measurement of secondary import substitution, calculation with positive sign will indicate the proportion of an industry's growth attributable to the decreasing share of imports limited to intermediate use, or to final use for capital goods alone. On the contrary, a negative value of the measure will imply an industry becoming more dependent on imported intermediates in the process of expansion.

The process of secondary import substitution can be explored further by considering the sequence of its development. For example, imported metal materials are used mainly by the metal processing industry, but also by other industries. Assuming that the main user of an intermediate is likely to start producing the intermediate for its own use (defined as the intra-industry SIS) before that of other users (defined as inter-industry SIS), then secondary import substitution in a given industry will begin first within that industry, followed later by other industries. It is thus hypothesized that intra-industry/sector secondary import substitution proceeds ahead of inter-industry/sector SIS.

Import Substitution in Taiwan and South Korea

During the two subperiods of 1966–1971 and 1971–1976, Taiwan's economy failed to enter the import-substitution (IS) phase. A close look

[4] The outward-looking policies in Taiwan in 1958–1960 and in South Korea in 1960–1965 are well documented. See Balassa (1985, pp. 148–51) and Kuo and Fei (1985, pp. 48–55).

reveals that the negative value of total IS was due mainly to the much larger negative value (in absolute terms) of IS for intermediates—that is, secondary import substitution. Taiwan's economy, therefore, had become more dependent upon imported materials during that time. Given the fact that Taiwan's exports in real terms grew at 26.9 percent annually from 1966 to 1971, and at 20.7 percent from 1971 to 1976, it is understandable that the domestic supply of intermediates was not able to catch up with the expansion in exports. The situation changed only during the second half of the 1970s, when SIS measurements turned positive. Since the late 1970s, Taiwan has reversed its trend of reliance on imported materials to facilitate export expansion.

Regarding the sequence of SIS, table 10.1 shows that intrasector SIS changed from negative (minus 5.54 percent) to positive (4.44 percent) during the first two subperiods, while intersector SIS remained negative (minus 4.63 percent and minus 8.45 percent) during both. The positive intrasector and negative intersector SIS measurements during the second subperiod suggest a general picture of production in Taiwan at that time: more materials were produced and used by the same industries, but that production failed to meet the needs of other industries. Comparison of these measurements indicates the possibility that intrasector SIS is easier and may progress faster than intersector SIS when secondary import substitution begins; this phenomenon ought to be observable at the industry level. In the third subperiod, 1976–1981, measures of both intra- and intersector SIS were positive. It may thus be claimed that Taiwan moved into the secondary import-substitution stage on all fronts during the second half of the 1970s, while simultaneously expanding exports (by 17.18 percent per year during that subperiod).

South Korea's case is similar to Taiwan's with minor differences. During the first subperiod, 1963–1970, all measures of import substitution in South Korea were negative, with the difference that Taiwan had, by that point, succeeded to some extent in replacing imports for final use. During its second subperiod, 1970–1975, however, South Korea, according to all measures, also entered the stage of import substitution, including SIS measurements. This, again, is similar to what Taiwan experienced, except that Taiwan's negative intersector SIS was so dominant that it changed the sign of the overall measure of SIS. South Korea's basic performance during its third subperiod repeats that of its second.

There are other similarities between the findings for these two countries. For example, the development of import substitution for final goods generally precedes IS for intermediates. For those intermediates, intra-sectoral SIS is usually ahead of inter-sectoral. It seems that the sequence of import substitution followed a stable pattern in both countries.

Focusing on the differences between these two countries during the second half of the 1970s, we find that South Korea apparently performed

TABLE 10.1
Secondary Import Substitution in Taiwan and South Korea (unit percent)

Measure	Taiwan			South Korea		
	1966–1971	1971–1976	1976–1981	1963–1970	1970–1975	1975–1980
Total measure of import substitution	−8.73	−1.71	2.30	−10.75	4.29	5.79
Import substitution for final goods	1.44	2.31	0.77	−4.38	2.76	5.56
Import substitution intermediates (secondary import substitution)	−10.17	−4.01	1.53	−6.83	1.53	0.23
Intrasector SIS	−5.54	4.44	0.68	−3.94	2.27	1.76
Intersector SIS	−4.63	−8.45	0.85	−2.44	−0.73	−1.54

Sources: CEPD (1966, 1971, 1976, 1981); Bank of Korea (1963, 1970, 1975, 1980).

Notes: Calculations were performed as follows: (1) Input-output tables in different industry classifications were homogenized; (2) total transaction tables were used to compile import gross measures; (3) for the South Korea data, all values for production and imports were deflated by wholesale price index or GNP deflators. For measure fomulas, see Schive (1987).

better in overall import substitution, especially in imports for final use, than did Taiwan. This finding can be attributed to the fact that Taiwan had by that time liberalized its import policy and had begun to allow greater imports of consumer goods. As a result, import substitution for final use in Taiwan was reduced by the end of the 1970s (Schive, 1987). South Korea, on the other hand, did much better in bringing down imports for final use; some of this decline was due to the decreasing import share of capital goods.[5]

Taiwan's Secondary Import-Substitution Industries

A summary of Taiwan's major secondary import-substitution industries is presented in table 10.2. During the subperiod 1966–1971, three industries—rubber and rubber products, artificial fibers, and miscellaneous manufactures—achieved a significant (defined as greater than 10 percent) import substitution for intermediate use. During the second subperiod, the artificial fibers industry continued to replace imports for intermediate use; the rubber and products, and miscellaneous manufactures

TABLE 10.2
Secondary Import Substitution Industries in Taiwan, 1966–1981

Measure	1966–1971	1971–1976	1976–1981
IS for intermediates			
Rubber and products	35.63	−10.32	2.57
Artificial fabrics	−16.18	12.42	1.17
Artificial fibers	38.11	34.67	5.86
Miscellaneous chemical			
manufactures	−50.94	15.42	−1.46
Iron and steel	−15.58	23.17	5.21
Miscellaneous manufactures	18.67	−5.13	1.03
IS for final goods			
Machinery	20.02	−12.15	12.70
Electrical apparatus			
and equipment	12.19	7.82	1.34
Transportation equipment	10.17	19.77	2.53

Source: CEPD (1966, 1971, 1976, 1981).
Notes: These industries were selected by the criterion that the figures for each industry were greater than 10 percent in at least one of the subperiods.

[5] Import shares of capital goods in South Korea in 1970, 1975, and 1980 were 29.7 percent, 26.2 percent and 23.0 percent, respectively (Bank of Korea, 1970, 1975 and 1980).

industries, however, showed a negative trend—that is, greater imports were made by these industries for further processing. The three remaining industries—artificial fabrics, miscellaneous chemical manufactures, and steel and iron—started the process of import substitution for intermediate use.

Two conclusions can be drawn from the above findings. First, development of secondary import substitution is much more discernible for individual industries than at the aggregate level (as represented by the measures in table 10.1). It should not, therefore, be concluded from negligible changes in macro measures of IS/SIS that all materials industries have failed to develop quickly, or to enter the secondary import substitution stage. Second, there seems to be no clear pattern of change in these measures over time. For example, with the exception of the artificial fibers industry, which showed significant positive values in two consecutive subperiods, the measures for all six of the industries presented in table 10.2 changed erratically. The first finding is obvious; the second is more interesting and requires explanation.

One explanation is that, following significant achievement in developing domestic raw materials industries to replace imports, there is a limit to further improvement of the measure. That could have been the case with the artificial fibers industry, which has already acquired 95 percent of its total materials locally in 1976 and with the rubber and rubber products industry around 75 percent in 1971.[6] As a result, further expansions of the domestic material production for these two industries became unlikely to continue from SIS. Another explanation, equally likely, is that industry classifications are not homogeneous. The products grouped into a given category may have different scale, technology, and capital requirements. Therefore, in the absence of strong policy intervention, such as the local content requirement applied to automobiles and certain electrical products, the development of the intermediate products within an industry will be very much determined by the comparative advantages associated with each product. If these comparative advantages differ significantly, there is no reason to expect a uniform pattern of change among the measures over time.

So far, discussion of the secondary import substitution industry has been limited strictly to the materials industries. For full coverage, the case of capital goods industries should also be included. It should be noted that the correct measure in this case covers import substitution for both final and intermediate use. Table 10.2 indicates that the machinery industry did well in replacing imports for final use during 1966–1971 and 1976–1981. The electrical equipment and apparatus and the transportation equipment industries, which cover both consumer durables and cap-

---

[6] Both figures were available from CEPD (1971, 1976).

ital goods, also did well in 1966–1976, but not in 1976–1981. The slow-down in these industries' replacement of imports could, among other explanations, be attributed to the previously mentioned liberalized trade policy adopted in the late 1970s.

South Korea's Secondary Import-Substitution Industries

South Korea's successes in replacing imports with intermediates indus-tries were all concentrated in the metal- and machinery-related industries (iron and steel, steel products, finished metal products, electrical machin-ery, and transportation equipment), and occurred mostly in 1970–1975. As regards secondary import substitution for capital goods, the machin-ery industry showed a significant improvement in reducing imports in the 1970s and the electrical machinery industry in the first half of that de-cade, and the transportation equipment industry in the second half did even better.

The data presented in table 10.3 will support several inferences. First, when the South Korean economy started picking up in the 1960s, the SIS phenomenon was totally nonobservable, which is not the case in Taiwan. However, a group of metals and capital goods industries did respond ef-fectively to the expanding domestic market in the first half of the 1970s, which is consistent to the assertion that South Korea's SIS started from 1973 (see Gereffi, chap. 1, this volume). The second possible inference is that South Korea's transportation equipment industry performed ex-

TABLE 10.3
Secondary Import Substitution Industries in South Korea, 1963–1980

Measure	1963–1970	1970–1975	1975–1980
IS for intermediates			
Iron and steel	− 16.73	45.30	5.07
Steel products	− 4.70	10.84	11.90
Finished metal products	− 15.68	24.62	0.57
Electrical machinery	− 4.64	23.66	− 0.02
Transportation equipment	− 5.68	28.33	− 38.97
IS for final goods			
Machinery, except			
electrical machinery	− 256.59	28.26	18.08
Electrical machinery	− 2.20	45.20	2.92
Transportation equipment	− 3.80	0.10	48.81

Source: Bank of Korea (1963, 1970, 1975, 1980).

Note: These industries were selected by the criterion that the figures for each industry were greater than 10 percent in at least one of the subperiods.

tremely well, far better than that in Taiwan, in import substitution in the late 1970s, although its reliance on imported parts had increased, as indicated by the large negative measurement of SIS for intermediates of that industry (−38.97 percent). Both findings lead to the strong belief that secondary import substitution occurs sooner or later on both the macro and micro scales in both countries. It is noteworthy, finally, that, unlike Taiwan's, South Korea's light industry, textiles and fibers in particular, proceeds much slower in developing the materials industries, mainly the petrochemicals, as of 1980.[7]

THE DEVELOPMENT OF VLSI IN TAIWAN AND SOUTH KOREA

As has been pointed out before, many SIS industries are capital- and technology-intensive, which are not in line with the comparative advantage of a capital-poor and technology-lagging developing economy. However, when Taiwan's and South Korea's economies were developed NICs, the original disadvantageous and constrained factors would have become less influential. As a result, certain high-tech and capital-intensive SIS industries were established. This section deals with the experience of Taiwan and South Korea in developing such a truly high-tech product, very-large-scale integrated circuit (VLSI), which marks the beginning of a new era in both countries' modern stage of development (see also Gereffi, chap. 1, this volume).

Since the development of the integrated circuit (IC) in 1959, a series of new developments have been achieved. When metal-oxide surface (MOS) technology became available in the late 1970s, the size of ICs, as measured in kilobytes of memory, began to expand with great speed. For the purposes of this paper, VLSI refers to ICs with dynamic random-access memories (DRAM) of 64K or more (Preston, 1983).

VLSI has two important characteristics. First, its design and manufacturing technology change very rapidly; new designs with successively larger capacities are regularly announced. Second, the price of VLSI continually declines, due in part to the first characteristic, mentioned above, and to the significant learning effect in the industry. For instance, the price of 64K DRAM dropped in late 1985 to one tenth its cost a year earlier (Yoon, 1988).

Taiwan and South Korea were both eager to become producers of such a dynamic product, which has become a cornerstone of modern technology. Each country approached the enterprise in a way that epitomizes its

[7] Korea's textile fabrics and fiber spinning industries did show small positive values of SIS measure in 1970s.

industrial policies and organization and, very likely, the efficiency of its industrial development.

The VLSI Industry in Taiwan

Taiwan's IC design industry began in 1977 when the government-financed research body, the Industrial Technology Research Institution (ITRI), on behalf of its electronics research branch, the Electronics Research and Service Organization (ERSO), signed a technology transfer contract with RCA (Simon and Schive, 1986, p. 159). More than $3 million was spent for training engineers and for consultation. After the technology had been established, a private company, United Microelectronics Company (UMC), was formed in 1979 to commercialize some innovations. Two years later, UMC began operation with a total capital of $20 million, some of which was controlled by ERSO in exchange for technical know-how. UMC has worked closely with ERSO and is run by ERSO staff. The new profit-seeking company turns out a variety of ICs for consumer applications, such as watches, calculators, musical equipment, digital televisions, and four-, eight-, and sixteen-bit microprocessors.

In 1983, ERSO was asked to draw up a five-year VLSI plan with a total budget of $74 million. This time ERSO did not turn to a large foreign semiconductor firm for technology, but signed an agreement for a joint research project with a Silicon Valley–based research company, Vitelic, which had been formed by overseas Chinese that same year. Another major feature of the project was an experimental VLSI factory and a common-design center accessible to outsiders.

At this point, the project looks promising. In April 1985, the line width of a 256K complementary metal-oxide surface (CMOS) DRAM chip was pushed from 1.5 microns to 1.25 microns (a micron is one-millionth of a meter). Theoretically speaking, the narrower the linewidth of the circuit, the greater the capacity of the VLSI chip. In June 1986, the technology for a one-megabyte (= 1024K) CMOS DRAM chip became available.

UMC followed its parent company and did equally well in developing VLSI technology. First, UMC set up a subsidiary, Unicorn Microelectronics Corporation, in California's Silicon Valley for easy access to the technology, and it signed joint research agreements with two firms there, Mosel and Quasel. This is not to say, however, that UMC relies upon foreign technology. UMC has 150 engineers and technicians, and half of them are involved in research and development. New products from these joint research programs include 64K CMOS static random-access memory (SRAM). By the middle of 1985, the 1.5-micron technology had become manageable.

The VLSI design industry in Taiwan has spiraled since 1983. All three of EROS and UMC's foreign partners established local companies in 1984, and these companies have been strikingly active in turning out new designs. For example, when Mosel announced a breakthrough in developing a 256K CMOS DRAM in April 1985, it became only the third company in the world, after Intel and Hitachi, to achieve that ability. A year later, when Mosel was able to produce a 256K CMOS SRAM, a chip equivalent to a 1M DRA, only Toshiba and Texas Instruments were ahead. Quasel has specialized in more specific VLSIs such as HP RAM (high-performance RAM). Vitelic's major achivement, among others, was its joint production with ERSO of a 1M CMOS DRAM (*Dataquest*, 1986).

While Taiwan's design capability has been beyond doubt since 1985, manufacturing those designs has been a problem. None of the five research organizations mentioned above has a VLSI factory; UMC has one, but it is not suitable for manufacturing VLSI in large amounts. Two consequences are expected: (1) those innovations will be licensed to foreign companies in the short run and (2) the Taiwanese companies will be interested in setting up their own VLSI manufacturing in the long run. There is abundant evidence of the first move. For example, Mosel sold its 16K CMOS SRAM technology to Fuji, its 64K CMOS SRAM to Hyundai, and its 256K SRAM to Sharp, although Mosel did turn out a small number of its own 16K and 64K SRAM chips from UMC's plant. Vitelic's licensees include Sony and NMBS in Japan, and Hyundai in South Korea. Vitelic also has a research agreement with Philips New Zealand. It has been reported that half of Vitelic's estimated $30 million revenue for fiscal 1987 will come from royalties (Wan, 1986, p. 50). Some of these licensing contracts involve repurchasing agreements to allow the companies to sell the products they have designed in Taiwan (*Dataquest*, 1986).

The second expectation has manifested itself in a more roundabout manner. First, after achieving a number of major breakthroughs in 1985 and after, the three local firms came out with manufacturing proposals totaling $275 million. This marks the change since 1984, when, because of the uncertainty and size of investment, the government took no action on ERSO's VLSI manufacturing proposals. Since then, talks on setting up a foundry-type VLSI plant to manufacture custom orders for all designers have seemed promising to the firms involved. In September 1985, a $250 million proposal along those lines was approved by the government, with the proviso that government funds would be less than 50 percent of the capital.

Because it required an initial capital commitment of around $20 million from each of the three VLSI companies involved, the government plan was not as appealing to them as it was to foreign companies. Philips expressed a great interest in the project, as did Mitsushita and Texas Instruments. To demonstrate its commitment to that investment, Philips established an IC design center and, along with two subsidiaries, a semiconductor plant and a television tube factory in Taiwan; the tube factory is, in fact, the world's largest, with some 3,500 employees.

In June 1985, Philips was awarded the contract, which included the following provisions:

1. The new company, Taiwan Semiconductor Manufacturing Corporation (TSMC), would be founded with a total investment of $207 million, $145 million of it in capital stock.
2. The government would contribute 48.3 percent of the capital, Philips 27.5 percent, and private investors the rest. After three years, however, Philips would be allowed to increase its share to 51%.
3. The VLSI plant would be the foundry with a monthly capacity of 40,000 six-inch wafers by 1990. Until that time, TSMC was to rent the VLSI plant from ERSO.

The formation of TSMC is not the end of this complicated process. UMC, at this point the only VLSI company with manufacturing capability, has announced a $150 million expansion project, largely self-financed, over the next years from 1985. UMC has good reason to do so, given that (1) it was the most profitable publicly traded company in Taiwan in 1985; (2) the initial capital requirement would be only $10.5 million; and (3) its debt-equity ratio is close to 1, far less than the average 2-to-1 ratio in Taiwan (Scitovsky, 1986, p. 177).

The VLSI Industry in South Korea

South Korea's semiconductor industry dates back to 1975, but it did not begin VLSI production until 1983, when it immediately began manufacturing on a large scale. Between 1983 and 1984, Samsung Semiconductor & Telecommunications Corporation (Samsung), Goldstar Semiconductor Corporation (Goldstar), Hyundai Electronics (Hyundai) and seven others invested approximately $1 billion; that total could climb to over $1.9 billion by the end of 1987.[8] Total VLSI exports were expected to exceed $2 billion by 1987, making South Korea the world's third-largest VLSI producer, surpassed only by the United States and Japan. Obviously, these are impressive achivements.

The development of South Korea's VLSI industry in a scant four years can be attributed not only to the enormous capital invested, but also to heavy reliance on foreign technology. For instance, Hyundai received its

[8] Data were adjusted and provided by the Market Information Center, the Institute for Information Industry, R.O.C. and originally from the Korean Institute for Economics and Technology.

256K CMOS DRAM manufacturing technology from General Instruments and Vitelic. Other sources of technology include Mosel, Inmos, ICT, and Sharp. Hyundai also set up a product-development subsidiary, Hyundai Electronics America, in the Silicon Valley, but with less success (more on this later). Samsung has sought VLSI technology from Micron Technology, Mostek, and Exel. In 1983, Samsung, too, set up a Silicon Valley subsidiary, Tristar. Goldstar is a licensee of Fairchild, AMD, and AT&T (*Dataquest*, 1986).

As regards their manufacturing capabilities, Samsung and Hyundai were able to turn out large numbers of 256K CMOS DRAM chips by mid-1986, Goldstar exports 64K SRAM to Japan. Samsung pioneered the production of 1M DRAM in 1987. All these companies were involved in producing certain application-specific VLSI, such as erasable programmable ROM (EPROM) and gate array ICs. As for development of new technology, a joint research program (Samsung, Goldstar and Hyundai) to foster the technology to manufacture 4M CMOS DRAM by 1989 has been announced. There is no doubt that the South Korean VLSI industry will continue to announce new products.

The deficit incurred by the South Korean VLSI industry in 1985 will pose a real challenge to that industry in the uncertain future market. For example, Hyundai revealed a $9 million loss in 1985 and wrote off another $20 million for its Silicon Valley subsidiary (Schiffman, 1986). These losses were caused by several factors, some uncontrollable, others the result of the company's lack of high-tech experience. Among the factors beyond Hyundai's control was the unexpected slowdown in the world economy in 1985, which reduced the demand for and the price of ICs. However, these price changes were not entirely due to weak demand, but also to the short life-cycle of ICs, a result of their rapidly changing technology. Under these circumstances, "new" product prices can fall below expectations for the second or third producer. While it can be argued that much of this price drop is due to the learning effect throughout the VLSI industry (and subsequent higher total production), this hardly compensates the quick follower of the innovator. The case becomes even worse when existing producers adopt aggressive pricing to fend off newcomers. Though the price situation of VLSI improved significantly due to the strong worldwide demand in 1987, no profit has been reported. In short, the great uncertainty of VLSI prices and the technology gap after the original innovator present the highest hurdles for South Korea companies.

A Comparison

Taiwan and South Korea built up their VLSI industries in very different ways, but a few similarities remain. First, both countries had huge electronics industries, which produced, among other things, computers and peripherals before they moved into the VLSI industry. Realizing the importance of VLSI in the information industry and its impact on the automotive, shipbuilding, home appliance, and other industries, both countries targeted VLSI as the leading product in this leading industry. Since 1983, however, the two countries have diverged from each other in their pursuit of that goal.

Taiwan began by first developing the technology, then moving into manufacturing as evidenced by its licensing of several indigenous VLSI innovations to foreigners and by its having forty IC design houses by 1977. South Korea did the reverse. The immediate result is that Taiwan seemed to be ahead of South Korea in technological capability; on the other hand, Taiwan may not catch up with South Korea's manufacturing capability in any foreseeable future. A few figures will fully substantiate the latter assertion. For example, TSMC has established a plant with an annual capacity of 120,000 six-inch wafers in 1987 and 480,000 wafers by 1990. Hyundai, on the other hand, already (1986) has a plant that turns out two hundred thousand five-inch and three hundred thousand six-inch wafers annually. The other two South Korean giants also have large current capacities, as well as vigorous expansion plans.

The sharp differences between these two countries stem from the very different industrial organizations they have built over the past two decades. All three South Korean VLSI firms are members of top conglomerates that are very large even by international standards. In contrast, the largest company in Taiwan's electrical and electronics industry, Tatung, had a total capital of only $115 million in 1985, which is about one tenth the capital available to Goldstar, the smallest of South Korea's top three VLSI conglomerates. The smaller size of Taiwanese firms obviously has a great bearing on their capability to invest in such huge projects. It should not be thought, however, that Taiwan's VLSI technology development has been limited by the same factor. On the contrary, ERSO acquired IC design technology in the late 1970s with direct government support, and had a research and development force of between three hundred and four hundred people. ERSO, moreover, is the parent company of UMC, which in turn created three major private companies specializing in IC design. The design people trained by ERSO and UMC, plus those working in local VLSI firms and their overseas affiliates, make up the backbone of Taiwan's research force. This research potential (especially the link to overseas Chinese), however, is not duly reflected by the common measure of research and development spending.

The strategy of separating research from manufacturing has some merit. Because research involves a great deal of labor training and development of laboratory facilities, its main product is knowledge and expertise, not simply patents, which benefit the innovators alone. The considerable externalities associated with research and development make it worthwhile for government to support and subsidize it. On the other hand, manufacturing and the commercialization of innovations hinge upon competitiveness and should be judged by the market. It was only at the point that manufacturing capability hindered further development (as evidenced by local firms licensing their technical know-how abroad) that manufacturing received government support.

The establishment of TSMC in Taiwan was motivated largely by profit-seeking. TSMC will begin as a small company, concentrating on application-specific ICs and operating as a foundry, taking production orders and designs from customers with the commitment of never entering the IC market directly. The new company's name will not even appear on its products. Run in this unique fashion, TSMC is expected to become profitable a year after it begins operation. This is why Philips expressed such interest in the project and retains the option of increasing its share to 51 percent after 1989.

Both Taiwan and South Korea should know that VLSI manufacturing will not be to their countries' static comparative advantages, given the huge capital involved, though it will be more so for South Korea than for Taiwan, because of the differences in their foreign debts and foreign exchange reserves.[9] Both countries, therefore, must look out for some kind of dynamic comparative advantage, and for the externalities embedded in the industry. Taiwan's policy has seemed to emphasize the latter feature, while South Korea has favored the former. By the time Taiwan's government took an active part and finally pushed the project through, however, large South Korean conglomerates had already made substantial investments. This, obviously, resulted from the sharp differences in these two countries' industrial organizations.

As to the likely outcomes of these two different approaches, Taiwan's success will depend upon the quick response to changes in market demand and higher prices for ASICs due to the scale constraint in operating facilities, all else being equal. South Korea's success will be decided by its ability to cut costs sufficiently to remain competitive in the current world market. In regard to the market destination, Taiwan's VLSI industry could have served both the domestic and foreign customers by adopting the foundry type operation in manufacturing and by emphasizing ASICs. On the other hand, the South Korean VLSI industry would rely heavily on export because of the mass production of a single product. Therefore, both countries try to develop the VLSI industry to continue the export-

---

[9] South Korea's foreign debt was $35.6 billion by 1987, and its foreign exchange reserves were $7.0 billion in March 1986. The figures for Taiwan were $4.2 billion of foreign debt in 1986 and $74.8 billion in foreign exchange reserves in March of that year.

oriented industrialization, although South Korea's VLSI industry is even more export-oriented than that of Taiwan. Finally, should both countries' industries survive, any choice between their two systems should take into account the huge opportunity cost involved in the South Korean case.

INTERPRETATIONS AND POLICY ISSUES

Interpretations of SIS Measures

The development experiences of Taiwan and South Korea over the past two decades show that when their economies moved into the export expansion stage with great success, their domestic materials industries were likely to lag behind the market created by exports. That is to say, earlier exports relied heavily upon imported materials, a phenomenon referred to as a "shallow economy" or "trade enclave" (Myint, 1981, p. 125). Unless this phenomenon is taken explicitly into account, the contribution of exports to domestic output growth will be exaggerated.[10] After some time, however, a "trade enclave" may start melting into the domestic economy, and a "shallow economy" may improve. In either case, the relevant means is secondary import substitution.

When an export commodity begins with the assembly of imported parts, the export contribution to GNP will be minimal, and measurements of SIS may be negative. Taiwan and South Korea in the 1960s and the first half of the 1970s did reveal moderate-to-small negative values for these measures. There are several possibilities. First and likely the most important, some domestic materials industries might have caught up quickly and expanded at the same rate as exports, so that import ratios remained unchanged and the values of SIS measurement were small. At the industrial level, this was indeed the case for Taiwan's plastics and plastics products industry, which has, since its beginning, depended minimally upon imported materials. Thus, the measurements for secondary import substitution were constantly small.

Second, when exports remained an enclave, domestic materials industries might have been set up, aimed at processing for domestic use. That is, secondary import substitution may have taken place in the domestic, not the exporting, sector. Third, different industries may have moved into the secondary export substitution stage at different times, with their opposite results effectively canceling out each other and leading to small aggregate figures. In all these cases, secondary import substitution would have taken place, but it would have been difficult to identify.

---

[10] For example, assuming equal local content between exports and domestic final demand, exports contributed 80.6 percent of manufacturing output growth in Taiwan during 1971–1976 (Kuo and Fei, 1985, p. 69).

The two countries reveal consistent patterns of sis development: from products for final demand, to intermediates mainly to supply users in the same industry, and finally to production for other users. The dynamics of this development are in direct alignment with Hirschman's backward linkage argument (1958). It may also be noted that the original linkage concept refers to an induced "attempt"—*ex ante*, not *ex post*. Therefore, the linkage effect must take time to materialize, or sis development follows a stable sequence.

Market-Led Development of SIS and High-Tech Industries

When the backward linkage concept is applied to explain the development of sis industries, the key point is that, after a market for intermediates has been created by setting up certain industries, backward linkage will tend to reduce market uncertainty and to facilitate investment in that market. Many sis industries, however, benefit from economies of scale, and are capital- and technology-intensive. Obviously, these conditions do not exist in most LDCs. Nonetheless, export-led industrialization may quickly dry up surplus labor in a smaller economy, particularly if the economy consults its comparative advantages in expanding its trade. This is precisely what Taiwan and South Korea experienced in the 1960s. Numerous studies show that the exporting industries in both countries in the 1960s were labor-intensive (Balassa, 1985, pp. 155–57; Kuo and Fei, 1985, p. 86; Schive, 1987). As both countries' real wage rates have risen since the late 1960s, the comparative disadvantages to their entering the sis industries have declined.

As a rule, capital-intensive industries are large-scale and involve more complicated technologies. The scale problem, which is also linked to market size, can be alleviated by the growth of downstream industries. Moreover, if local materials industries enjoy a certain degree of protection (Balassa, 1982), then it is feasible for export prices to be lower than domestic prices. In several cases, if comparative disadvantage and technology pose no problem, then materials industries can become export-oriented—which is exactly what happened with several materials industries in Taiwan and South Korea.[11] In this case, the sis is mixed with secondary EOI (see Gereffi, chap. 1, this volume).

Another constraint on development of sis industries is lack of technology. Although the technologies used in different industries may differ significantly, certain relationships among them may still exist. For example, while process patents in the chemical and related industries may be

[11] To name a few, the petrochemical industry in Taiwan and the iron and steel industries in both countries.

unique, the operation, setup, and equipment of plants may be alike. It is possible, therefore, for a chemical manufacturer to diversify its product line either vertically or horizontally. In certain cases, the technology for manufacturing a part can be developed by constant use; this often occurs in the machinery and electronics industries. For example, a TV manufacturer may progress from assembly parts to picture tubes to tube guns by learning the technology step by step. This is not to say that the technology used in producing related products can be acquired by learning or by trial and error. On the contrary, technology for new products is often acquired from outside. What is important is the investment confidence built up by technological competence and knowledge of the market before taking action. This is especially true in the Asian NICs, where many firms of related products—such as plastic materials and its products, machinery parts and machinery, belong to the same conglomerate or the same person. It is vital, therefore, to possess the technology of one industry before starting the next. This is where experience counts most, especially in high-tech industries.

There seems to be a trend in international trade that may facilitate SIS development—the surge in international protectionism, on the one hand, and low-cost competition by LDCs for NICs' exports on the other. One way to overcome this difficulty is to upgrade products and improve labor productivity. Another approach is either to develop new products beyond LDC followers' short-term capabilities, or to turn inward by developing products not subject to trade embargo. The development of high-tech industries fits both requirements.

Finally, imperfections in the world market also provide incentives for local production of materials. The first incentive comes from the opportunity to minimize transportation costs, as well as transit time and risk. In addition, a premium may be paid for local supplies of imported goods. These incentives provide natural protection to domestic producers. Moreover, if imports come from monopolistic suppliers, then import prices charged may vary with local supply conditions. Local production of certain products very often brings down import prices,[12] which benefits all domestic users.

State-Led Development of SIS and High-Tech Industries

There are three types of government intervention to help set up SIS industries: local content requirements (meaning that certain local products must contain minimum quantities of local commodities); import con-

---

[12] This situtation occurred mainly for Japanese exports. Examples range from petrochemical materials to gears and from steels to machinery (Schive, 1987).

trols; and targeted-industry policies, which include preferential tax credits or loans for specific industries, government funding to establish industries, and other, nonpecuniary, government support.

The local content requirement policy was adopted in Taiwan in 1962. In the late 1950s, a few Japanese firms had moved their market to Taiwan. This investment, obviously motivated by import control on the products assembled and by the much lower tariff rate for parts, was considered speculative and wasteful of foreign exchange. In response, nine electrical and machinery products were made subject to a minimum local content rate of 40 percent, first for foreign firms, then for all producers.[13]

While this policy did help certain parts industries domestically, particularly the automobile industry, the overall effect is in serious doubt because calculations of local content are questionable and exports are exempt from the regulation. In the first case, official figures for local content may deviate from reality because of the difficulty of defining "locally made" parts; as a result, the regulation cannot be properly implemented. The second case is more important and has more far-reaching implications. If materials or parts are allowed to flow in for eventual re-export with full tariff rebate, then domestic producers must compete head-to-head with imports at the international price, which means no tariff protection at all. Therefore, since most items subject to the regulation are produced in small quantities (like tractors), produced in large numbers (like cars and motorcycles), but with many loopholes, or are major export items (like televisions), this policy cannot be expected to have a significant overall effect in promoting sis industries.

Because tariffs are not levied on materials used in exports, imports controls provide solid protection. Several materials were made subject to this control under various conditions. First, shortly before the second oil crisis, exports of all major plastic materials were banned because of strong demand abroad and short supply at home. With the onset of the world recession, import prices dropped so low that no local firm could survive. Because export of these products had been banned and import prices were resented as dumping prices, local plastic materials makers had good reason to ask for protection. That request was granted, but the policy created tremendous difficulties for downstream processors. The mess was finally straightened out, and control was continued under two provisions: (1) products for re-export would be priced at the international level, subject to government approval; and (2) feedstocks (ethylene and others) for plastics would also be charged at the international price. Because ethylene

[13] The products originally were refrigerators, air conditioners, transformers, television receivers, transistor radios, automobiles, motorcycles, tractors, and diesel engines; the items change over time. Local content is calculated as one minus the ratio between imported parts and finished product (both measured in FOB prices).

was produced solely by the Chinese Petroleum Company, a state enterprise, the second provision was met without difficulty (Schive and Yeh, 1981). This policy was gradually abolished as world plastics prices returned to normal and was done away with entirely at the beginning of 1986.

Two other products, steels and stainless steels, used to have similar restriction—that is, buy first from local suppliers at the international price. The provision seems redundant. If the domestic price is right, what purpose does an agreement serve? It may, however, greatly help marketing. Judging by the prosperity of the plastic- and metal-products industries in the 1980s, it may be concluded that the policy has not seriously distorted the market mechanism.

South Korea does not seem to have implemented any local content requirement of the same degree and scope of Taiwan's. South Korea's only similar action was establishing a local content requirement for government loans for plant exports (CEPD, 1982).

The target industry policy can be pursued in three ways: public enterprises, special loans, and tax incentives, the most effective of which is public enterprises. In Taiwan, the Chinese Petroleum Company built its first naphtha cracker in 1968 and has added three more since then. In 1977, the Chinese Steel Corporation went smoothly into operation. Both companies are government-owned and reduce imports by downstream industries (see table 10.1). However, two other public enterprises, one in copper refining and the other in aluminum reduction, were dissolved because of bad management, high energy prices, and strong competition from abroad. The VLSI venture, TSMC, can also be considered a government-founded company, but one which will eventually become private and predominantly foreign-owned. TSMC obviously receives nonpecuniary support from the government.

On the South Korean side, in 1973 the government announced its intention of promoting the chemical and heavy industries. Six target industries were selected: steel, petrochemicals, nonferrous metals, machinery, shipbuilding, and electronics (CEPD, 1985). All of these are typical secondary import substitution industries. Pohang Iron & Steel Company was founded in 1973 with an annual capacity of 1.03 million tons. The company has grown quickly since then, and it reached a total capacity of 9.10 million tons by 1983. With the production of other steelmakers, South Korea's combined capacity reached 13 million tons by 1983. In petrochemicals, South Korea's first naphtha cracker, with an annual capacity of one hundred thousand tons of ethylene, was set up in 1972. Both Pohang Steel and Korea Petroleum were set up as public ventures, but both were later transferred to private control.

In terms of tax credits and special loans, Taiwan targeted two industries, information and machinery, as strategic, and it selected 199 items (mostly parts, software and capital goods) for preferential treatment. The major incentive provided is special low-interest loans at two percentage points lower than the regular long-term rate. However, the total amount of fund committed was limited and amounted to $200 million by early 1987 (Schive and Hsueh, 1987). In 1986 a tax credit on up to 30 percent of the amount of personal or corporate income invested in government-approved, high-tech industries became available. Also in 1986, the South Korean government called for investment of around $500 million to develop the electrical and electronic parts industries; the government itself will provide 60 percent of the funding.

In short, considering those policies aiming at developing sis industries in Taiwan and South Korea, the local content requirement regulation in Taiwan was not considered as effective in stimulating the growth of the products selected. Indeed, the scope of the regulation was reduced to automobiles and motorcycles only in 1988. Many other parts and materials industries were developed in direct response to the booming local derived demand. The import control of certain materials products, as Taiwan's experience indicates, could be hazardous to the downstream industries. Finally, the government's direct investment in certain sis industries in both countries seemed to be successful.

Conclusion

While exports have, in the past, helped develop many industries in Taiwan and South Korea by providing large markets, they have also stimulated domestic materials and capital goods industries to supply the need for exports. This is what Taiwan's and South Korea's economies have experienced from the 1970s on. Looking toward the future, both countries—facing rising wages, expanding markets, more experienced entrepreneurs, and more highly skilled labor—will encourage the development of capital- and technology-intensive sis industries. Looking outward at surging protectionism and at mounting pressure from competition with LDCs, both countries see an urgent need to develop sis and high-tech industries. It is expected that this development trend in Taiwan and South Korea will continue through the 1980s.

Although prospects are promising, the past development of sis and high-tech industry in both countries has been a slow, trial-and-error process. While it has been easier for Taiwan, with more policy instruments, to begin the process, the country has paid a price and has had to close down two public enterprises. In South Korea, the strong desire to speed up the process has obviously contributed to the increase in foreign debt. Taiwan's movements in high-tech industry have been more cautious, evidenced by limited amount of investment, while South Korea's actions are much larger in size and still subject to a cruel market test. The former is a "gradualist" approach, while the latter is more like a "big push" approach (see Cheng, chap. 6, this volume). After all, this development strategy is not simply a response to a country's static comparative advantage but a process of continual search for dynamic advantage. This development, therefore, should not be thought of as a substitute for trade, as the term suggests but rather as a way to maximize trade benefit in a dynamic world.

The limited findings arrived at so far may have several implications for these two countries and for NICs and LDCs in general. First, as Taiwan and South Korea move successfully into the SIS stage and their balance of payments situations improve (which is obviously the case for Taiwan since the 1970s and South Korea since 1985), their trade on all fronts—consumer goods in particular—should be liberalized in earnest. This will leave ample room for imports from both developed countries and LDCs.

Second, because SIS development seems to have followed a stable pattern in Taiwan and South Korea (i.e., from final demand to intra-industry use and finally to inter-industry use), other NICs and even LDCs should have opportunities to do the same, assuming the domestic market is large enough (as in Latin America), and provided other conditions are reasonably suitable. These constraints—market size and technological experience in particular—do not favor duplication of this process by economies like Singapore and Hong Kong.

Last but not least, should a promotive policy be adopted, subsidies are better than protection, as suggested by classical wisdom and evidenced by Taiwan and South Korea (especially the issues involved in Taiwan's petrochemical industry). Survival in market competition is still the most conclusive proof of effectively used resources.

REFERENCES

Bank of Korea. 1963, 1970, 1975, and 1980. *Input-Output Tables of Korea.* Seoul: Bank of Korea.

Balassa, Bela. 1985. "The Role of Foreign Trade in the Economic Development of Korea." In *Foreign Trade and Investment*, edited by Walter Galenson. Madison: University of Wisconsin Press.

———. 1982. *Development Strategies in Semi-Industrial Economies.* Baltimore: Johns Hopkins Press.

Bradford, Colin I., and William J. Branson, eds. 1987. *Trade and Structural Change in Pacific Asia.* Chicago: University of Chicago Press.

CEPD (Council for Economic Planning and Development). 1988. *Taiwan Statistical Data Book.* Taipei: CEPD.

CEPD. 1985. *The Development of Heavy and Chemical Industries in Korea* (in Chinese). Taipei: CEPD.

——. 1982. *The Current Situation, Issues and Policy of Plant Exports in Korea*. (in Chinese). Taipei: CEPD

——. 1966, 1971, 1976, and 1981. *Input-Output Tables, Taiwan, ROC*. Taipei: CEPD.

Dataquest. July 1986. "MOS Memory Licensing Agreements and Joint Ventures, 1982 to 1986." *Dataquest Research Newsletter*. Menlo Park, Calif.

EPB (Economic Planning Board). 1988. *Major Statistics of Korean Economy*. Seoul: EPB.

Galenson, Walter, ed. 1985. *Foreign Trade and Investment: Development in the Newly Industrializing Asian Countries*. Madison: University of Wisconsin Press.

Hirschman, Albert O. 1958. *The Strategy of Economic Development*. New Haven: Yale University Press.

Kuo, Shirley W. Y., and John C. H. Fei. 1985. "Causes and Roles of Export Expansion in the Republic of China." In Galenson (1985).

Lau, Laurence J. ed. 1986. *Models of Development: A Comparative Study of Economic Growth in South Korea and Taiwan*. San Francisco: Institute for Contemporary Studies.

Lee, Eddy, ed. 1981. *Export-Led Industrialization and Development*. Singapore: International Labor Office.

Morley, Samuel A., and Gordon W. Smith. 1970. "On the Measurement of Import Substitution." *American Economic Review*, no. 60, pp. 728–35.

Hla Myint, U. 1981. "Comparative Analysis of Taiwan's Economic Development with Other Countries." *Experience and Lessons of Economic Development in Taiwan*. Academia Sinica.

Paauw, Douglas S., and J. C. Fei. 1973. *The Transition in Open Dualistic Economies*. New Haven: Yale University Press.

Preston, Glenn W. 1983. "The Very Large Scale Integrated Circuit." *American Scientist* 71, no. 5, pp. 466–72.

Ranis, Gustav. 1985. "The Industrial Development" In Galenson (1985).

——. 1979. "Industrial Development." In *Economic Growth and Structural Change in Taiwan*, edited by Walter Galenson. Ithaca: Cornell University Press.

Schiffman, J. R. 1986. "Hyundai Stumbles in High-Tech Venture." *Wall Street Journal*. April 17.

Schive, Chi. 1987. "Trade Patterns and Trend of Taiwan." In Bradford and Branson (1987).

Schive, Chi, and Kuang-tao Hsueh. 1987. "The Experiences and Prospects of the High-Tech Industrial Development in Taiwan, R.O.C.—The Case of the Information Industry." 1987 Joint Conference on the Industrial Policies of the Republic of China and the Republic of Korea, Taipei: Chung-Hwa Institute for Economic Research.

Schive, Chi, and Ryh-song Yeh. 1981. *The Price Structure of Petrochemicals*. Taipei: Council for Economic Planning and Development (in Chinese).

Scitovsky, Tibor. 1986. "Economic Development in Taiwan and South Korea." In Lau (1985).

Simmon, Denis F., and Chi Schive. 1986. "Taiwan's Informatics Industry: The Role of the State in the Development of High-Tech Industry." In *The National Policies for Developing High-Tech Industry*, edited by Francis W. Rushing and Carloe G. Brown. Boulder, Colo.: Westview.

Wan, W. K. 1986. "Why Can Vitelic Make a Profit when the Semiconductor Industry Is in Recession?" *Information and Computer*, pp. 50–51 (in Chinese).

Yoon, C. H. 1988. "International Competition and Market Penetration: A Model of the Growth of the Korean Semiconductor Industry." Mimeo, Korea University, Seoul, p. 5.

CHAPTER 11

The Latin American Strategy of Import Substitution: Failure or Paradigm for the Region?

René Villarreal

FROM THE 1950s until the beginning of the 1980s, Latin American countries maintained high rates of economic growth that provided the basis for making far-reaching economic and social changes. Nonetheless this process was accompanied by the recurrent problems of external disequilibrium (balance of payments difficulties) and internal disequilibrium (inflation and disparities in the distribution of income).

This pattern of economic growth in Latin America was perceived as quite acceptable by academics and institutions in the developed countries. In fact, during the 1970s diverse studies were carried out and projections made that tried to find alternative ways to accelerate such growth, with the objective of narrowing the divide between the Latin American nations and the developed countries belonging to the Organization for Economic Cooperation and Development (OECD).[1] One of the development goals was to reduce the per capita income gap between both groups of countries from 12 to 1 in 1970 to only 7 to 1 by the year 2000 (Sanchez-Arnau, 1986, p. 69). It is interesting to note that a supposedly indispensable condition for attaining more rapid growth rates than those registered during the 1950s and 1960s was to increase the rate of capital formation in Latin America to between 30 and 40 percent of the gross domestic product (GDP).

The perception of the Latin American countries themselves regarding their achievements as well as their needs and problems, on the other hand, led them to try to strengthen their international position by obtaining a larger amount of external resources, along with greater national and regional autonomy in using them. The behavior of foreign investment, for example, had been disappointing. It usually entailed big multinational oligopolies that took advantage of local protection and incentives intended to foster the development of national firms, without transferring

This chapter was translated from Spanish by Gary Gereffi. The assistance of Christopher G. Ellison of Duke University in editing the manuscript is gratefully acknowledged.

[1] One of the most influential studies was the Leontief Report, which was commissioned by the United Nations to examine the necessary conditions for achieving the objectives of the Second Decade of its International Development Strategy (see Leontief, 1977).

any technology from abroad and with a high cost in terms of the current account of the balance of payments. Latin American activism in international forums and the creation of diverse regional organisms clearly expressed these concerns.[2]

While the consensus regarding the need to establish more ambitious goals and to accelerate the progress of the Latin American region was being forged, however, changes during the 1970s already had begun to undermine the previous gains and even reverse them in the 1980s. Latin America has been forced in the 1980s to generate continual trade surpluses to satisfy its international debt obligations, and now the region is a net exporter of 4 to 5 percent of its GDP. This has set back the development process by ten years.

The years of sustained growth (previously unsatisfactory but today seen as an "economic boom"), like the efforts to chart optimistic projections for the region, have been left behind. It is now fashionable to carry out ex post facto studies contrasting the Latin American countries with the successful histories of East Asian nations. These result in simplistic and unimaginative lessons,[3] which tend to come from elementary economics textbooks and serve as the inspiration for the adjustment programs followed in Latin America.[4]

The objective of this chapter is to use the present to examine the future of Latin America, trying to piece together a viable development strategy in the context of the present difficulties. This comparative analysis primarily will look at Mexico and Brazil, countries that have maintained a long-term strategy of import-substituting industrialization (ISI). To place Mexico and Brazil in a broader regional context, we will briefly examine certain aspects of the neoliberal orthodoxy that has been tried by the Southern Cone countries (Argentina, Chile, and Uruguay). These latter nations have undergone extensive deindustrialization and severe financial upheavals due to the rising interest rates for international credit, not to mention the high social and political costs of these experiments, which were endorsed by cruel military regimes.

In an effort to chart a constructive development strategy for the region, we challenge two aspects of current conventional wisdom on develop-

[2] One example is the creation of the Andean Pact, which initially grouped together six countries: Bolivia, Colombia, Chile, Ecuador, Peru, and Venezuela. Another illustration is the Sistema Economico Latino Americano (SELA), which was created in October of 1975 and has twenty-six member countries in Latin America and the Caribbean.

[3] These lessons are simple to recommend but not easy to put into practice—that is, liberalization, privatization, productive efficiency, export growth.

[4] There are other detailed, less ideological studies that have recognized the basic similarities between the development policies of the East Asian and Latin American countries, such as the inadequacy of certain adjustment policies (see Sachs, 1987).

ment issues. First, while we acknowledge that one of the problems of the import substitution strategy in Latin America has been the creation of an anti-export bias in the productive sector of the economy, we argue that the way to eliminate this is *not* liberalization at all costs. This has not been implemented in the East Asian nations[5] (or anywhere else, for that matter). Instead, what is needed are mechanisms such as temporary import permits for inputs used to produce exports (these were widely used in South Korea), as well as incentives to nascent export industries.

Second, it is necessary to push beyond the false dilemma that is posed between "inward-oriented development" and "outward-oriented development." As many of the chapters in this volume indicate, both approaches are present and indeed complementary in the development experiences of the Latin American and East Asian nations (see Gereffi, 1989).

The remainder of the chapter is organized as follows. First, we adopt a comparative perspective by focusing briefly on the neoliberal experiments in the Southern Cone of Latin America and on the sustained ISI strategies of Brazil and Mexico, especially with regard to the manufacturing sector and foreign trade. Second, we present the case of Mexico by means of a detailed analysis of its ISI and export phases. Third, we advance a *three-dimensional industrial model*, based on a rational and selective opening to international competition, as a possible solution to Mexico's current development dilemmas. While this development strategy is both feasible and necessary for Mexico, it could perhaps be considered a paradigm for the region.

THE DEVELOPMENT STRATEGY DEBATE IN LATIN AMERICA

The nations of Latin America have pursued a range of strategies aimed at hastening structural change and increasing socioeconomic welfare. These variations in industrial strategies have given rise to sharp debates among academics and policymakers throughout the region. Before proceeding to a more detailed examination of the Mexican case, we will explore three competing models of industrialization in Latin America: the neoliberal strategy of the Southern Cone countries, the extended ISI strategy pursued in Brazil, and the oil-led growth model followed by Mexico in the mid-1970s and early 1980s.

The two international oil crises of the 1970s led Latin American countries to revise their previous ISI policies. The quadrupling of oil prices in 1973–1974 introduced significant advantages and disadvantages that af-

[5] Instead of going from indiscriminate protectionism to complete openness and liberalization, which is being advocated for Latin America, these nations have maintained selective protection and strict exchange controls.

fected Latin America in diverse ways and brought different reactions. Thus, while Brazil intensified its ISI strategy, Mexico opted for the development of its oil industry and the Southern Cone countries moved toward a neoliberal strategy. This latter approach, which favored the allocation of resources in terms of comparative advantage and the free play of market forces, resulted in a process of deindustrialization.

Some of the implications of these intraregional differences in development strategies are clarified by the figures in table 11.1. First, both Argentina and Chile increased their propensities to import consumer, intermediate, and capital goods in 1979–1981, as compared with the 1970–1978 period. These increases are most substantial in the Chilean case. Second, Mexico also shows a marked growth in its tendency to import intermediate goods; however, there is no significant change in average import propensities for consumer or capital goods. Third, these patterns contrast strikingly with the performance of Brazil: during the same period, Brazil considerably reduced its propensities to import both intermediate and capital goods, with no change in its import propensity for consumer goods.

In the 1980s, the anti-inflationary policies of the industrial countries,

TABLE 11.1
Average Propensities to Import Consumer, Intermediate, and Capital Goods, 1970–1984

Period	1970–1978	1979–1981	1982–1984
Argentina			
Consumer goods	0.3	2.1	0.5
Intermediate goods	11.2	13.6	11.3
Capital goods	5.6	9.9	6.8
Chile			
Consumer goods	3.0	8.2	5.0
Intermediate goods	25.2	30.5	22.4
Capital goods	21.7	26.6	17.0
Brazil			
Consumer goods	0.4	0.4	0.4
Intermediate goods	8.9	6.6	4.8
Capital goods	8.7	5.6	5.0
Mexico			
Consumer goods	1.5	1.5	0.6
Intermediate goods	7.5	14.9	10.1
Capital goods	10.9	11.1	7.3

Source: IDB (1985, p. 28).

especially the United States, the unprecedented rise in interest rates, and the sharp decline in the terms of trade for Latin America combined to create serious debt payment problems for Latin American countries, which led to a subsequent cutoff of international loans. This became known as "the international debt crisis." It is interesting that despite their diverse development strategies, most Latin American countries fell into the same problem of external debt. Due to the constraints imposed by the debt crisis, the average propensities to import declined sharply in Argentina, Chile, Brazil, and Mexico across all industrial sectors during the 1982–1984 period.

Toward EOI: The Experience of Latin America's Southern Cone

Currently, economic liberalization policies for the indebted countries are receiving top priority through invoking the successful cases of South Korea and Taiwan, while the recent experience of the countries in the Southern Cone of Latin America is forgotten. It is worth recounting how both the liberalizing nations and those with different economic orientations in the region fell into excessive indebtedness and subsequent debt repayment troubles in the 1980s (see Villarreal, 1983, for a more extended treatment of this topic).

If we focus on the monetarist experience in Chile under General Augusto Pinochet, which is considered to be the most successful case, the principal elements of the Chilean program are as follows:

1. Foreign trade was completely liberalized, since it was believed that the most effective way to attain sustained development was to eliminate all controls on external trade so the market can determine the most profitable activities for a country to specialize in (Fishlow, 1985; Muñoz Goma, 1986, 233–56).
2. The state reduced to a minimum its intervention in the economy, not only in terms of its regulations and traditional controls but also in areas such as the promotion of investment and social development.
3. The financial sector was shaped by two central characteristics: first, interest rates were set by market forces, rather than by the government; and second, parallel financial institutions were fostered that could enter into short-term capital markets in order to complete the opening toward the international economy.
4. A final element in this model was the elimination of any restrictions regarding the entry of foreign capital.

The model of ultraliberalism is irresponsible because it applies measures that tend to destroy many activities in the short run (especially in industry) without knowing what alternatives will emerge or which activities will be sparked by the new conditions. These measures underlie what I call the financial trap of liberalization.

The major group that benefits from this model is the financial sector. If the government abandons its role of regulating credit and fixing interest rates, financial liberalization leads to a sharp increase in the interest rate. On the other hand, when the state no longer guides the economy, either through direct or indirect action (e.g., public investments), this leadership role shifts to big financial groups like banks or parallel financial institutions (such as the stock exchange).

To the extent that investment resources and decisions remain in the hands of financial agents, however, the opportunities for investment contract. First of all, uncertainty is created with regard to the changes in economic policy. Secondly, the productive sector is less profitable due to greater competition with foreign imports. Third, since the rise in interest rates increases the cost of capital for new investments and reduces the range of profitable projects, the only justifiable investments are marginal adjustments to plants and equipment.

The previous conditions tend to create a financial boom vis-à-vis the stagnation of the productive sector. This is a kind of *financial trap*, because the financial sector is supposed to supply resources and the productive sector to use them. If the investment opportunities of the productive sector are delayed or canceled, then the financial groups that hold the resources are confronted with the enormous temptation to become their users. This has led to considerable speculation in financial bonds and securities as well as real estate (Muñoz Goma, 1986, 256–59).

In view of the high initial profitability of these speculative shifts, industrial firms divert their productive resources in order to participate in speculative investment, which raises the interest rates even more (which seem low when compared with speculative gains). This situation leads to the progressive deterioration of the productive sector, even when part of these resources are channeled toward production, because the profitability and maturation of productive investments cannot match those in the speculative sector.

Thus, in the 1970s the manufacturing sector's share of GDP fell in Argentina and Chile, while it increased in Brazil and Mexico. The opposite occurred with the share of financial services in the GDP. During the 1980s, however, the manufacturing sector has continued to decline in all four of these countries, while the trends in the financial sector are reversed: it has grown smaller in Argentina and Chile, and it has increased in size in Brazil and Mexico.

The neoliberal monetarist model in effect was replacing the manufacturing sector with a service economy:

In practice, the monetary approach in its Southern Cone application was equivalent to favoring services at the expense of tradables, and particularly, manufactured products. Industry was exposed to new competition from abroad, and unable to compete. Services were the answer. The trouble is that they are not an independent source of economic development. They respond passively to higher incomes emanating from other sources; they do not propel economies forward or provide the basis for continuing increases of productivity; nor do they guarantee a continuing stream of exports required in the future to service debt and pay for complementary imports. (Fishlow, 1985, p. 136)

These same policies, when applied to Argentina in 1976–1981, produced "the longest and most intense crisis that the country has experienced in the last half century of its history" (Tomasini, 1982, p. 129), affecting the manufacturing sector in particular. In 1980 the gross industrial product was less than in 1974. Within the general process of stagnation and instability, the manufacturing sector was the only one that suffered a permanent decline (Tomasini, 1982). A comparative study of the industrial dismantling carried out in Argentina and Chile argues that these policies have the severest effects on those economies that are the most industrially advanced (Ferrer, 1980).

Secondary ISI: The Experiences of Brazil and Mexico

In the Latin American context, Brazil and Mexico have been the countries with the highest levels of industrialization and the most effective development strategies. Import-substituting industrialization was the basic strategy of both countries until the 1970s. Brazil advanced further in its phase of secondary ISI, however, due in part to its larger internal market. Its more extensive industrial integration also was a product of two deliberate decisions by the government: (1) to give a high priority to establishing a local capital goods industry and (2) to foster a greater concentration of income in the upper and upper-middle classes in order to create a dynamic market for durable consumer goods, in contrast to the previous period of development of the nondurable consumer goods industries whose growth was compatible with a more egalitarian distribution of income (Bresser Pereira, 1987).

The external shocks of the 1970s affected the two countries in different ways and thus led them to adopt divergent strategies in 1974. For Brazil, the import bill for oil rose to $9 billion at the same time as the nation's terms of trade were deteriorating, which was a decisive determinant in its search for a new political-economic path. The objective was twofold: first, to finance a medium-term adjustment based on a new stage of ISI, focusing principally on intermediate and capital goods; and secondly, to expand and diversify Brazilian exports. To harmonize these goals, a policy package was established that included programs of selective credit, new import barriers, and financial and fiscal export incentives. At the same time, the price of fuel for domestic industry was subsidized and external debt was used to complement the financing needed to carry out this ambitious program.

The favorable results that were obtained in terms of economic growth rates, a lowering of imports, and the increase in exports encouraged the Brazilian government to respond in a similar way to the second oil price shock in 1979. International financial conditions took a turn, however, as loans were offered for shorter terms and at higher interest rates. This, combined with the recession in the industrialized countries and the resulting reduced demand for exports, meant that Brazil's new strategy could not be sustained. There was a severe economic crisis in 1982, precipitated by the freeze on voluntary lending in international financial markets.

For Mexico, the great liquidity in the world-economy at the beginning of the 1970s, together with sharp increases in the price of oil, led the country toward a new industrialization path with distinct challenges and opportunities. Mexico decided to further its strategy of secondary ISI by continuing to develop the consumer durable, intermediate, and capital goods industries,[6] but it also pushed for a diversification of nontraditional exports while simultaneously expanding its broad program of exploration for hydrocarbon reserves.

After the discovery of vast new oil fields in Mexico was made public, the government decided in 1977 to accelerate the rhythm of growth by means of an ambitious program of public investment to endow the country with the necessary infrastructure for an expanded export capacity, as well as to establish complementary industries to that of oil. This led to a rapid increase in imports and external debt. The speed and efficacy of Mexico's adaptation to these new opportunities is shown by the fact that at the time of the second oil price shock in 1979, Mexico was the biggest oil exporter in Latin America and the sixth largest in the world.

The oil boom and the high availability of foreign exchange generated a dynamic internal market and extensive investments in Mexico, which resulted in an annual GDP growth rate of around 8 percent. Giant industrial complexes, many of them with significant public-sector involvement, consolidated the national industrial structure in areas such as steel and petrochemicals. These industries were oriented not only to satisfy national

---

[6] Guillermo O'Donnell (1977) has elaborated an entire social, political, and economic paradigm to explain how this "difficult" phase of ISI requires authoritarian governments to force nations to overcome the multiple obstacles that this strategy presents.

demand by substituting for imports, as in petrochemicals, but also to attain a growing presence in world markets.

Evolution of the Productive Structures

As a result of their ISI strategies, both Brazil and Mexico significantly expanded their productive capacity in the period before the crisis of the 1980s. The manufacturing sector registered particularly high rates of growth, and around 1980 it was structurally more balanced and diversified than it was in 1972–1973, a period when there was a greater concentration in consumer goods of relatively low technological complexity. The manufacturing share of GDP was 24.8 percent in Mexico in 1980 (up from 22.3 percent in the early 1970s), while in Brazil the figure reached nearly 30 percent.

Agricultural production, in spite of showing a relative decline with regard to GDP between 1972–1973 and 1980 (from 10.9 to 9.5 percent in Brazil, and from 10.4 to 8.9 percent in Mexico), actually grew in important ways in both countries. Brazil had the best agricultural results in its export crops (like soybeans and citrus fruits) as well as in energy-related production (sugar cane for gasohol), while Mexico's most dynamic area of production was basic foodstuffs (such as rice and wheat). In relation to their main exports, Brazil, the world's leading producer of coffee, suffered a decline in its 1979–1980 output, but it recuperated rapidly the following year. Mexico, on the other hand, increased its production of oil by a factor of five between 1972–1973 and 1980–1981. By 1984, it grew by an additional 40 percent.

Brazil used two means to reduce its dependence on oil imports: the push for internal production of oil and the promotion of alternative sources of energy. By 1980 Brazil was able to compensate for the two oil shocks because its self-sufficiency in energy was around 66 percent, which was equivalent to its 1973 level. Since then, the internal production of energy has grown markedly to the point where in 1984 the level of self-sufficiency was 80 percent.

The productive structure of Brazil is comparatively more advanced than that of Mexico in the period ranging from 1972–1973 to 1980, as can be seen by looking at the sectors of greatest technological complexity: electrical and nonelectrical machinery, and transport equipment. These capital goods industries accounted for 19.4 percent of Brazil's total output in 1980 (down slightly from the early 1970s), while in Mexico capital goods production rose from 12.9 percent in 1972–1973 to 15.9 percent in 1980 (see table 11.2). By the beginning of the 1980s, the composition of manufacturing production in the two countries showed other notable changes. There was a decline in the share of nondurable consumer goods, especially in Brazil (10 percentage points), while there was an equally sharp increase, again in Brazil, in the share of industrial intermediate goods in the production structure (33.8 percent in Brazil in 1980, compared to 13.3 percent in Mexico). The production structure in Mexico is characterized by a high, although decreasing, share of food, beverages, and tobacco in overall production (from 33.5 percent in 1972–1973 to 28.6 percent in 1980) (table 11.2).

In terms of employment in the manufacturing sector, there are opposing trends in the two countries. While employment in the consumer nondurable goods sector has increased in Mexico (from 40.3 to 42 percent of the total), it has been reduced substantially in Brazil (from 40 to 32.1 percent). Similarly, while Brazil increased slightly the employment in its industrial intermediate goods sector, Mexico showed a similar sized decline. However, if we consider that Brazil's relative production of industrial intermediate goods was over two-and-a-half times that of Mexico in 1980 (33.8 percent and 13.3 percent, respectively), yet Brazil's employment in this sector was substantially *less* than Mexico's (16.1 percent compared to 19.9 percent) (table 11.2), then it becomes apparent that Brazil's pattern of industrial growth is much more capital-intensive than that of Mexico.

In synthesis, the energy crisis of the 1970s affected these two countries in opposite ways. Brazil, a major importer of oil, gave top priority to ISI, and as a result achieved a fuller integration of its productive structure. Mexico, on the other hand, became a prominent oil exporter and its top priority was economic growth and the creation of infrastructure; the structural integration of the economy, though, took several steps backward. These options were pursued in the context of an oversupply of international credit and negative real interest rates.[7] Both countries, as a result, utilized extensive external credit to support their respective strategies.

Foreign Trade of Brazil and Mexico in the 1970s

In 1972–1973 Brazil and Mexico, together with Argentina, were the most advanced countries in Latin America in terms of manufactured exports. In addition, their relatively balanced and diversified industrial structures gave these countries a rather low import propensity in the majority of their manufacturing branches. Nevertheless, both Brazil and Mexico were faced with recurrent trade deficits in the early 1970s. This situation worsened for Mexico by the early 1980s since it fell into the trap of petro-dependency (i.e., an excessive reliance on oil exports). Brazil, on the other hand, had greater success not only in export promotion but also in ISI

[7] The real interest rates for long-term credits to developing countries were: − 11.8 percent in 1977; − 7.4 percent in 1978; − 9.7 percent in 1979; − 6.0 percent in 1980; 14.5 percent in 1981; 16.7 percent in 1982; and 15.9 percent in 1983 (Reisen, 1985, p. 89).

TABLE 11.2
Brazil and Mexico: Structure of Production and Employment in the Manufacturing Sector

| | Production | | | | Employment | | | |
| | Brazil | | Mexico | | Brazil | | Mexico | |
Type of Good	1972–1973	1980	1972–1973	1980	1972–1973	1980	1972–1973	1980
1. CONSUMER NONDURABLES	39.2	29.0	56.4	48.8	40.0	32.1	40.3	42.0
2. Foodstuffs, beverages and tobacco	21.0	16.3	33.5	28.6	15.1	13.4	21.6	25.0
3. Textiles and apparel	12.4	10.6	11.6	9.5	18.5	16.9	15.1	10.0
4. Chemical products	3.3	2.1	8.5	8.1	2.3	1.8	3.6	7.0
5. INTERMEDIATE INDUSTRIAL GOODS	24.3	33.8	12.2	13.3	15.8	16.1	20.1	19.9
6. Oil and coal by-products	—	—	5.1	4.9	—	—	0.8	0.8
7. Steel and iron	12.3	16.7	5.0	5.9	11.3	12.7	11.6	11.0
8. Basic chemicals	12.0	17.1	1.0	1.1	4.5	3.4	5.3	5.2
9. INTERMEDIATE CONSTRUCTION GOODS	6.0	4.0	10.0	12.0	11.1	7.0	14.8	13.3
10. CAPITAL GOODS	20.9	19.4	12.9	15.9	20.7	22.1	16.2	17.7
11. Nonelectrical machinery	6.8	6.4	2.1	3.1	8.3	10.5	0.8	1.1
12. Electrical machinery	4.9	5.4	4.3	4.8	5.4	5.5	6.8	6.8
13. Transport equipment	9.2	7.6	6.5	8.0	7.0	6.1	8.6	9.8
14. OTHER MANUFACTURED GOODS	9.6	6.2	8.5	10.0	12.4	12.7	8.6	7.1
TOTAL	100	100	100	100	100	100	100	100

Source: IILA (1986, tables 7, 8, and 12). The data are from World Bank (1987).

ISIC Classification:

1. = 311 + 312 + 313 + 314 + 321 + 322 + 323 + 324 (Mexico only) + 332 + 352.
2. = 311 + 312 + 313 + 314.
3. = 321 + 322.
4. = 352.
5. = (Brazil) 351 + 371 + 372 + 381.
   (Mexico) 351 + 353 + 354 + 371 + 372.
6. = 353 + 354.
7. = 371
8. = 351
9. = 331 + 361 + 362 + 369 + 381 (this code included in Intermediate Industrial Goods for Brazil).
10. = 382 + 383 + 384
11. = 382
12. = 383
13. = 384
14. = 341 + 342 + 355 + 356 + 385

across a wide range of industries, and thus it converted its trade deficit in manufacturing into a trade surplus.

After 1981, in the period following the second oil crisis, Brazil and Mexico managed to increase even more the penetration of their manufactured exports in foreign markets. Between 1982 and 1984, Brazil's share of world exports grew from 1.14 to 1.26 percent, while Mexico also showed a substantial increase, from 0.44 to 1.01 percent. With respect to imports, Mexico's share of the world total expanded from 0.7 to 1.13 percent during this three-year period, while Brazil's imports remained virtually the same, 1.27 and 1.28 percent (ECLA, 1985).

Brazil's manufactured exports were growing rapidly as a share of its total exports between 1972–1973 and 1980, from 28.6 to 52.7 percent, respectively, while in Mexico manufactured exports fell from 51.6 percent of the total in the former period to 27.0 percent in 1979 (IILA, 1986, appendix tables A2 and A5). This reflects Mexico's takeoff as a major oil exporter in the 1970s and the sustained progress toward manufacturing development in Brazil.

The composition of the two countries' exports shows that Brazil has a larger agricultural base, in spite of its more advanced industry. The average share of the agricultural sector in total Brazilian exports declined from 62.5 percent in 1972–1973 to 36.4 percent in 1980–1981, while agricultural imports remained relatively stable as a percentage of total imports in the two periods (9.7 and 9.4 percent, respectively). For Mexico, the agricultural sector's export share declined from 43.2 to 26.2 percent between 1972–1973 and 1979, while agricultural imports rose slightly from 10.6 to 10.8 percent of the total. Throughout the 1970s, therefore, the agricultural sector in Brazil played a more positive economic role (i.e., it generated more exports and fewer imports) than it did in Mexico.

The situation is reversed with regard to the mining and energy sectors. Brazil's mineral and energy exports were 7.4 and 9.4 percent of total exports in 1972–1973 and 1980–1981, respectively, while imports in these sectors soared from 13.7 to 46.2 percent. In Mexico, on the other hand, mineral and energy exports went from 5.1 percent of the total in 1972–1973 to 46.8 percent in 1979, while imports dropped from 6.2 to 4.0 percent in the same period (IILA, 1986).

Table 11.3 provides comparative figures on exports and imports in Brazil and Mexico as a share of domestic production. These figures suggest that Brazil is more advanced in the capital goods sector, while Mexico shows greater strength in certain intermediate goods. During the 1970s, Brazil substantially improved its export performance in nonelectrical machinery and transport equipment, while Mexican exports of capital goods as a share of domestic production declined significantly during the decade. Brazil also showed a slight increase in its exports of consumer non-

TABLE 11.3
Brazil and Mexico: Exports and Imports as a Share of Domestic Production (percentage)

| | Exports/Production | | | | Imports/Production | | | |
| | Brazil | | Mexico | | Brazil | | Mexico | |
Type of Good	1972–1973	1980	1972–1973	1979	1972–1973	1980	1972–1973	1979
1. CONSUMER NONDURABLES	4.4	6.7	1.8	1.5	3.5	3.6	1.9	1.9
2. Foodstuffs, beverages & tobacco	4.9	8.3	0.8	1.2	1.3	1.2	1.1	1.0
3. Textiles and apparel	4.5	4.7	3.9	2.1	1.3	0.5	2.4	2.1
4. INTERMEDIATE INDUSTRIAL GOODS	1.7	2.9	8.4	6.5	11.1	6.7	13.2	22.2
5. Oil and coal by-products	—	—	1.4	1.4	—	—	6.0	5.5
6. Steel and iron	2.5	4.5	3.0	2.6	13.9	6.3	7.0	20.8
7. Basic chemicals	0.8	1.4	20.7	39.5	8.2	7.1	87.9	103.2
8. INTERMEDIATE CONSTRUCTION GOODS	4.8	6.4	2.8	3.1	6.5	5.1	3.6	4.4
9. CAPITAL GOODS								
10. Nonelectrical machinery	4.1	15.3	23.3	8.5	47.9	25.4	122.4	127.2
11. Electrical machinery	3.2	5.9	7.9	2.6	24.1	16.9	30.6	21.9
12. Transport equipment	2.1	11.2	4.9	5.9	7.4	7.1	22.3	35.0
13. OTHER MANUFACTURED GOODS	4.9	13.3	4.0	2.6	11.8	14.8	15.2	15.4
TOTAL	3.5	6.7	3.8	3.1	10.7	8.1	9.7	13.4

Source: IILA (1986, table 12). The data are from World Bank (1987).
ISIC Classification: see table 11.2.

durables, particularly foodstuffs, beverages, and tobacco, as well as an increased tendency to export other unspecified manufactured goods. On the other hand, the 1970s saw Mexico double its exports of basic chemical products (e.g., petrochemicals) as a share of domestic production, from 20.7 percent to 39.5 percent, while Brazilian exports of intermediate industrial goods remained relatively weak.

The figures in table 11.3 also reveal divergent importing trends in the two countries. While Brazil sharply reduced its imports of most intermediate and capital goods as a share of domestic production, Mexican imports of these goods skyrocketed. These patterns confirm two central points of our analysis. First, Brazil had advanced further down the path of secondary ISI than Mexico and therefore was able to substitute crucial domestically produced inputs for those previously imported. Second, Mexico's consistent expansion of imports throughout the decade may reflect the importance of oil revenues in accelerating the growth of the Mexican economy during the late 1970s, in part through a substantial increase in imports.

In summary, the productive structure of Brazil was more advanced than Mexico's at the beginnning of the 1970s, notwithstanding the fact that Brazil's exports were more intensive in natural resources.[8] For Mexico, this pattern was exhausted by the second half of the 1960s and Mexico began to emphasize manufactured exports. The radical changes in the price of oil in the 1970s, however, which were equivalent to a devaluation of agricultural goods versus energy resources, led Brazil and Mexico to reverse their exporting strategies. The oil shocks of the 1970s pushed Brazil to accelerate its manufactured exports in order to earn the foreign exchange needed for energy imports. Mexico, on the other hand, gave renewed importance to its natural resources, in particular to the creation of a vastly enlarged export capacity for oil. This strategy is discussed in more detail below.

In the 1980s, the debt crisis placed Brazil and Mexico on parallel tracks once again. This time the pressure to service the external debt, coupled with the fall in oil prices, led both countries to give top priority to manufactured exports.

DEVELOPMENT STRATEGIES IN MEXICO: IMPORT-SUBSTITUTING
  INDUSTRIALIZATION AND EXPORT EXPANSION

We turn now to a more detailed historical discussion of the Mexican case, focusing on two issues. First, we examine the emergence and development

---

[8] This pattern remains in effect due to the lesser density of Brazil's population, compared to Mexico's, and the former's position of world leadership in certain goods, such as coffee.

of three stages of import-substituting industrialization in Mexico over a period of sixty years. Second, we explore the transformation of Mexico's external sector, with particular emphasis on the post-1975 period.

The Stages of ISI in Mexico

The process of ISI began in Mexico around 1929 due to the need to supply itself during the Great Depression and the Second World War. Later this orientation was fortified by ad hoc governmental policies. Seen from an historical perspective, the ISI process had three distinct stages (see table 11.4): (1) the phase of *effective ISI* in which the strategy shows a sustained advance, measured by the ISI index (i.e., the ratio of imports to total supply); (2) the phase of *stagnating ISI* and *import desubstitution*, in which there was rapid economic growth and the beginning of oil mono-exports without deindustrialization; and (3) the phase of apparent or *recessive ISI* in which economic growth showed a "stop-go" pattern, and the decline in the ISI index reflects the fact that both the GDP and imports fell substantially.

EFFECTIVE IMPORT-SUBSTITUTION (1929–1970)

As can be seen in table 11.4, ISI began in the period from 1929 to 1939 in the consumer goods industries, called the "easy" stage of industrialization. This shift from imports to local production in the consumer-goods sector implied a simultaneous increase in the proportion of imports to

TABLE 11.4
Import Substitution Index, 1929–1986

Stage	Year	Consumer Goods	Intermediate Goods	Capital Goods	Total Manufactured Goods
I	1929–1939	35.2–22.2	55.5–55.9	56.0–90.3	56.7–48.6
	1939–1950	22.2– 6.9	55.9–41.6	90.3–73.6	48.6–31.1
	1950–1959	6.9– 6.6	41.6–34.4	73.6–63.8	31.1–27.8
	1959–1970	6.6– 7.0	34.4–18.1	63.8–46.7	27.8–21.2
II	1970–1976	7.0– 5.6	18.1–18.6	46.7–45.2	21.2–21.4
	1976–1981	5.6–12.3	18.6–22.6	45.2–50.7	21.4–28.0
III	1981–1986	12.3– 2.5	22.6–14.0	50.7–37.1	28.0–14.7

Source: SPP (1986).

Note: The import substitution index figure is defined as the participation of imports in total supply, classified by types of finished good: (Mx / Mx + Px), where M = Imports, P = production, x = type of finished good.

total supply in the intermediate and capital goods sectors. Nevertheless, there is a net positive effect for all manufactured goods in the period, as the ISI index drops from 56.7 percent to 48.6 percent. Between 1939 and 1950 the substitution of consumer, intermediate, and capital goods imports proceeds in parallel fashion, which further reduces the ISI index for all manufactured goods from 48.6 percent to 31.1 percent. This trend toward parallel ISI in all three types of manufactures remains uninterrupted until 1970, which marks the end of the stage of four decades of effective ISI.

For all manufactured goods in Mexico, the import share between 1929 and 1970 fell from 56 to 21 percent. In other words, while in 1929 imports represented more than one-half the total supply of manufactured products, by 1970 imports were only one-fifth of this supply.

This macroindustrial pattern reflects the steady and sustained growth of the Mexican economy and per capita income, in a context of exchange rate and price stability that favored savings and helped to establish a solid internal market. This market is the basis of industrial dynamism. Between 1960 and 1971 industrial output doubled while there was a pronounced change in the sectoral structure: farming, livestock, oil and mining experienced declines in their share of GDP (from 20.2 percent in 1960 to 14.7 percent in 1970), while the manufacturing sector grew in importance (from 20.3 percent to 23.7 percent). This is the phase of "inward-oriented development" induced by ISI.

STAGNATING ISI AND IMPORT DESUBSTITUTION (1970–1981)

Between 1970 and 1976, the import share in the total supply of manufactures in Mexico remained practically the same (21.2 percent in 1970 and 21.4 percent in 1976), which represents a stagnation of the ISI process. Subsequently, this turns into a phase of import *de*substitution as the ISI index rises to 28 percent in 1981. In other words, the share of imports in total supply grew from about one fifth in 1976 to more than one fourth five years later.

From 1979 to 1981, GDP grew at an average annual rate of 8 percent, but imports rose even more rapidly because of the pressure of aggregate demand and an overvalued exchange rate. Thus ISI was moving backward due to the accelerated growth of the Mexican economy at full capacity. Nevertheless, it is important to characterize Mexico as a case of import desubstitution *without* deindustrialization in order to distinguish it from the experiences of Argentina and Chile in the 1970s, which had import desubstitution *and* deindustrialization.

Mexico's rapid growth was still centered on the internal market, as industrial output doubled once again, with a more diverse and complex array of manufactured goods (the automobile industry was particularly dynamic). Two new elements were added: a higher level of direct industrial support from the public sector (big oil and steel) and growing exports. The latter factor contributed to an abundance of foreign exchange from oil exports and the greater availability of external credit, backed up by Mexico's oil wealth. Meanwhile, there were further changes in the industrial structure, as the manufacturing, oil, and mining sectors were increasing their shares of the GDP at the expense of the farming and livestock sector.

APPARENT OR RECESSIVE ISI (1982–1988)

From 1982 to 1988, plummeting oil prices, the halt in voluntary international lending, and the high interest rates caused by the enormous budgetary and trade deficits of the United States (which sharply raised the debt service payments of borrowers), had a combined impact on Mexico that forced a severe internal adjustment. Economic growth became a process of "stop-go" adjustment in which the recessionary trend predominated.

In this phase the ISI index dropped from 28 to 14.7 percent, which indicates an apparent advance in the ISI process of nearly 50 percent (see table 11.4). However, since there was a net reduction in GDP during the 1981–1987 period, imports fell proportionately more than the GDP and thus the ISI index necessarily declined. This phenomenon can be observed more clearly in the capital goods sector, where the ISI index fell from 50.7 percent to 37.1 percent (see table 11.4), which represents an apparent ISI gain of 13.6 percent as a result of the increased domestic production of these goods. Because of the prolonged recession and the stagnation in investments, though, imports declined more than local production. The National Chamber of Manufacturing Industries in Mexico reported the closing or bankruptcy of more than half of the Mexican enterprises that made capital goods.

In effect, there has been a trade surplus in the balance of payments since 1982. However, this is more the result of a decline in the import ratio and an increase in the export ratio due to a severe recessionary adjustment, rather than to effective ISI in an expanding economy. It was imperative to generate a trade surplus in order to finance the structural deficit caused by the country's foreign debt service payments. The adjustment process, then, was based on a contraction of domestic production instead of economic growth.

In summary, the ISI index has declined by 35.5 percentage points from 1929 to 1970 (from 56.7 to 21.2 percent), while there were significant gains in the industrialization process (output doubled during the 1960s). By contrast, in the 1970s manufacturing output also doubled, but was accompanied by import desubstitution as the ISI index rose 6.6 percentage points (from 21.2 percent in 1970 to 28 percent in 1981). Finally, during the 1981–1986 period, the ISI index was nearly halved (to 14.7 percent in 1986), but domestic industrial facilities had substantial idle capacity and GDP in the manufacturing sector fell by 5.7 percent. Thus, the productive sector in Mexico faced outright stagnation and recession, which led to the paradox of ISI gains that were only apparent or recessive.

The Evolution of Mexican Exports: From Oil Mono-Exports to Export Substitution

In addition to this focus on the ISI process, a fuller understanding of contemporary Mexican industrial strategies requires an examination of the shifting composition of Mexico's exports. The overall performance of Mexican exports from 1960 to 1987 has been quite dynamic. The national economy has become more outward-oriented, with the external sector (exports plus imports) increasing from 17.8 percent of GDP in 1960 to 23 percent in 1987. Exports have grown especially fast, climbing from 7.1 to 14.6 percent of GDP in the twelve years following 1975. Non-oil exports became much more prominent during the 1980s, which represents a significant change in the composition of Mexico's total exports.

Between 1940 and 1985, the structure of Mexican exports was sharply transformed: they went from being natural-resource intensive (agriculture and extractive industries) to being intensive in skilled and unskilled labor.[9] The dynamic performance of non-oil (and especially manufactured) exports in recent years, however, is due in part to the redirection of the country's installed capacity toward the external market as a result of the recession affecting the domestic market, rather than because of new and growing industrial capacity stemming from fresh investments. The index measuring the economy's openness (the sum of exports plus imports divided by GDP), on the other hand, has risen steadily from 17.3 percent in 1970 to 23 percent in 1987.

There have been three main stages in Mexico's export performance since 1975: (1) the takeoff and growth of oil mono-exports (1976–1981), (2) the transition from oil mono-exports to export substitution (1982–1986), and (3) effective export substitution (1987–1988). "Petroleum mono-exports" and "external petrodependence" mean that the external sector of the national economy, foreign exchange income, and fiscal revenues depend heavily on oil exports. The entire Mexican economy is not

[9] Manufactured exports in 1985, in their order of importance, were: (1) automobile motors, (2) passenger autos, (3) automobile parts, (4) silver bars, (5) frozen shrimp, (6) diverse iron and steel manufactures, (7) artificial textile fibers, (8) beer, (9) glass and crystal, (10) plastics and resins, (11) polycarboxilic acid, (12) fuel oil, (13) prepared fruits and vegetables, (14) gasoline, and (15) butane and propane gas.

petrolized however, since the oil sector in its most dynamic phases only accounts for 7 percent of the GDP, unlike some oil-exporting countries in which oil represents around 50 percent of total national production. "Export substitution" occurs when manufactured exports replace primary product exports, and in Mexico's case oil exports, as a leading share of total national exports.

THE TAKE-OFF AND GROWTH OF OIL MONO-EXPORTS (1976–1981)

From 1976 to 1981, Mexican exports registered a high rate of growth, going from $3.7 billion to $20.1 billion. This represents a 550 percent increase for the entire period and an annual growth rate of nearly 90 percent. The main factor explaining this export boom was the surge in oil exports, which expanded from just $563 million in 1976 to $14.6 billion in 1981 (see table 11.5). In the latter year, nearly 75 percent of Mexico's total export sales were accounted for by oil. This is characterized, therefore, as the oil mono-export phase of Mexican development.

The evolution of this phase is the flip side of what has been referred to here as "import desubstitution." Given the limits imposed by external constraints on the ISI model, oil provided the means to resolve the disequilibria that accelerated economic growth (8 percent per year) generated in the trade and current account balances. The income derived from oil exports ($32.5 billion in the 1976–1981 period) not only allowed these disequilibria to continue and sharpen, but it undermined and eventually postponed the reforms needed in the productive structure of the economy to deal with the shortcomings of the ISI model. This tendency was accentuated because in addition to generating foreign exchange, Mexico's oil resources became a form of collateral that enabled the country to obtain around $60 billion in external credit during this same period. Thus oil mono-exports and import desubstitution were interrelated processes.

Mexico's macroeconomic, industrial, and trade policies were subordinated to the oil-export model. Aggregate demand grew rapidly, the exchange rate was overvalued, and finally the manufacturing sector accumulated a trade deficit of $48.7 billion, with total exports of just $58.8 billion between 1976 and 1981 (see table 11.5). Coupled with high protectionism, this situation reinforced the anti-export bias toward non-oil (and especially manufactured) exports. The continued reliance on oil led to an obvious case of oil dependence by the end of the 1976–1981 period, with oil jumping from 15 to 73 percent of Mexico's total exports and oil revenues generating nearly 50 percent of the government's fiscal income.

Between 1976 and 1979, Mexico's oil exports rose from $563 million to $4 billion, while non-oil exports went from $3.1 billion to $4.8 billion. During this period, new discoveries in the oil-producing zones of Tabasco

TABLE 11.5
Mexican Exports during the Export Boom and the Adjustment Period, 1976–1987

Year	Total Exports	Oil Exports	Non-Oil Exports	Manufactured Exports
1976	3,655 (100%)	563 (15.4%)	3,093 (84.6%)	1,730 (47.3%)
1977	4,649 (100%)	1,037 (22.3%)	3,612 (77.7%)	2,125 (45.7%)
1978	6,063 (100%)	1,863 (30.7%)	4,200 (69.3%)	2,574 (42.5%)
1979	8,817 (100%)	3,974 (45.0%)	4,824 (55.0%)	2,936 (33.3%)
1980	15,511 (100%)	10,441 (67.0%)	4,692 (33.0%)	3,383 (21.8%)
1981	20,102 (100%)	14,574 (72.5%)	4,846 (27.5%)	3,427 (17.0%)
1982	21,229 (100%)	16,447 (77.6%)	4,753 (22.4%)	3,386 (15.9%)
1983	22,312 (100%)	16,017 (71.8%)	6,295 (28.2%)	5,448 (24.4%)
1984	24,196 (100%)	16,601 (68.6%)	7,453 (31.4%)	6,843 (28.2%)
1985	21,663 (100%)	14,767 (68.2%)	6,896 (31.8%)	6,428 (29.7%)
1986	16,031 (100%)	6,307 (39.3%)	9,724 (60.7%)	7,782 (48.5%)
1987	20,746 (100%)	8,746 (42.2%)	12,000 (57.8%)	10,577 (51.0%)

Source: Banco de México (1977–1988).

and Chiapas put Mexico's oil reserves at more than 60 billion barrels, which acquired considerable importance after the international oil price shock provoked by the revolution in Iran in 1979. The Iranian Revolution not only pushed the price of oil to $30 a barrel, but it raised expectations that by the 1980s oil prices could soar to $60 to $90 per barrel. Mexican economic policies, especially in the area of foreign trade, began to be formulated on the basis of these delusory expectations regarding oil prices, which collapsed soon thereafter. Mexico decided to become a major exporter of crude oil after 1979. Oil exports skyrocketed from $4 billion to $14.6 billion in just two years (1979 to 1981), while non-oil exports stagnated at $4.8 billion (table 11.5).

Beginning in 1981, international oil prices began to turn downward because of the glut in world markets caused by national energy policies in both the consuming as well as in the oil-producing countries. The optimistic predictions regarding the oil market were shattered in May of 1981 when oil prices plummeted to $4 a barrel. The oil mono-export phase in Mexico thus confronted a new international reality, in which the price of oil became extremely sensitive to changing patterns of world production.

THE TRANSITION FROM OIL MONO-EXPORTS TO EXPORT SUBSTITUTION (1982–1986)

Mexico's annual oil exports remained very stable between 1982 and 1984, fluctuating in a narrow range from $16 billion to $16.6 billion during each of these three years (table 11.5). Nor was there much variation in Mexico's volume of oil exports, which averaged about 1.5 million barrels per day. However, the internal macroeconomic disequilibria that affected the national economy at the end of 1982, along with the disequilibria in Mexico's external accounts, motivated the new De la Madrid government to implement a set of political economic measures oriented toward the growth of non-oil exports.

A variety of factors, including conflicts among the oil-exporting nations and especially Saudi Arabia's decision at the end of 1985 to abandon its stabilizing or cushioning role in the oil market, led finally to a fall in oil prices. The decline that began in 1985 accelerated the following year when the OPEC producers, who could not reach a mutual accord, all tried to assure their share of the world market by offering discounts and price reductions. These policies led to a genuine price shock. For Mexico, this meant a loss of more than $8.5 billion in foreign exchange in 1986, since oil exports that year totaled only $6.3 billion compared to $14.8 billion in 1985.

EXPORT SUBSTITUTION (1987–1988)

These events resulted in a process of export substitution in which oil exports were displaced as the principal source of Mexico's foreign exchange. In 1987 oil exports were $8.7 billion, while non-oil exports reached a level of around $12 billion and manufactured exports set a record at $10.6 billion (see table 11.5). This shift was due to domestic changes in the level of economic activity and wage costs as well as to the fall in international oil prices.

Export substitution was a real phenomenon, even if we control for the effect of the oil market. Suppose that world demand in 1987 would have permitted Mexico's oil exports to reach the same level as in 1982—that is, $16.5 billion—while non-oil exports maintained their 1987 values. Total exports thus would have been $28.5 billion, with manufactured exports representing a 37 percent (instead of 51 percent) share of this hypothetical total. In either case, there was an export-substitution take-off.

Whereas in 1982 non-oil goods were 22 percent of total exports and manufactured goods just 16 percent, five years later these figures had climbed to 58 and 51 percent, respectively. Non-oil exports, therefore, had grown more than two-and-a-half times, while manufactured exports more than tripled. In 1987, the overseas sale of manufactured items exceeded that of oil by over 20 percent, and manufactured exports accounted for 60 percent more foreign exchange than was obtained by tourism; Mexico's border (*maquiladora*) industries; and agricultural, livestock, and mineral exports combined.

The competitiveness of the manufacturing sector deserves to be analyzed more carefully, since it is related to the economic policies and macroeconomic situation of the country. First and foremost, this export growth has been stimulated by the undervaluation of the Mexican exchange rate and by a steady decline in Mexico's real wage rates in dollar terms. Second, one must take into account the prevailing macroeconomic conditions that include a recession that has sharply curtailed internal demand and a decrease in the utilization of installed capacity in the industrial sector, both of which contribute to a reorientation of production toward the external market. Third, a variety of new export promotion measures have been put in place to stimulate national exports, including the relaxing of import restrictions,[10] preferential credit in all phases of the export process, trade agreements, and trade fairs. Finally, we cannot forget another factor of great importance to Mexico's exports, which is the economic growth of its major external market, the U.S. economy, at steady rates of 2.5 percent or more in the mid-1980s.

Mexico's industrial competitiveness requires new export-oriented investments, increases in productivity, and an appropriate linkage to the global manufacturing system that is now emerging. It also is necessary to diversify the contribution of the manufacturing sector. Currently just ten products account for 49 percent of the country's manufactured exports. The contribution of Mexican firms needs to be strengthened as well, since

[10] This refers to a program in which an exporter can freely import goods that will be transformed and used in the production of exports.

almost 50 percent of manufactured exports are carried out by the subsidiaries of multinational corporations.

Mexico's manufactured exports actually have been countercyclical in nature, growing when the GDP contracts and diminishing when GDP increases, thus underlining the weakness of the country's current export capability. The proof of fire that will determine whether export substitution in manufactures is apparent or real will come once the Mexican economy regains its traditional rate of economic growth, and the real wages and other benefits of workers are increased.

In 1986, Mexico entered into a phase of export promotion that diminished the country's petro-dependency and diversified its insertion into the world economy. With the relative rise in oil prices in 1987, however, oil exports grew to $8.7 billion and slightly increased their share of total exports to 42 percent (from 39 percent the preceding year).

The growth of manufactured exports should help Mexico to earn foreign exchange that is not subject to the cyclical fluctuations that characterize the international sale of raw materials. Furthermore, manufactured exports create a higher level of value added in the national economy, which highlights the importance of Mexico's productive integration into what has been called "the global factory" (see Gereffi, 1989). In this phase of export substitution, the main challenge is to consolidate the long-term capability of the non-oil and manufacturing export sectors to generate a net surplus of foreign exchange. To accomplish this, industrial restructuring and structural change are required.

A THREE-DIMENSIONAL INDUSTRIAL MODEL FOR MEXICO: ENDOGENOUS GROWTH, INDUSTRIAL EXPORTS, AND SELECTIVE ISI

Historical evidence shows that the size of a country's economy is fundamental in explaining the degree of its external openness and its dynamic pattern of export-led growth. Thus, the size of Mexico's GDP in 1985 was $177.3 billion, with exports accounting for 16 percent of the GDP. Countries that are similar in size to Mexico, such as Brazil (with a GDP of $188.2 billion), Spain ($164.2 billion), and Australia ($162.5 billion), show comparable ratios of exports to GDP: Brazil, 14 percent; Spain, 23 percent; and Australia, 16 percent (World Bank, 1987, pp. 207, 220). Japan, which is the most dynamic of the exporting nations, had a 1985 GDP of $1,328 billion, with an export/GDP ratio of around 15 percent. The United States, with a GDP of $3,947 billion, has an export/GDP ratio of just 7 percent.

In smaller countries, such as South Korea, the size of its economy is half that of Mexico ($86.2 billion), while its exports as a share of GDP are 36 percent. The same is true of Singapore, with a GDP of $17.5 billion (one-tenth Mexico's) and an export-GDP ratio of 150 percent. Nevertheless, Mexico's exports in 1985 were $21.7 billion, which is greater than the GDP of Singapore and Israel ($20.3 billion) and more than two-thirds of Hong Kong's GDP ($30.7 billion).[11]

Therefore, if we consider that Mexico is a country with a large internal market, it is not appropriate to think that the objective of its strategy of external growth is to reach export/GDP ratios that are similar to those of smaller nations such as South Korea and Hong Kong, which are oriented almost exclusively to the external market and therefore are more vulnerable to the cycles of international trade. Rather, Mexico's objectives, similar to those of countries like the United States and Japan, should be to base the economy primarily on a dynamic internal market, coupled with realistic export goals. The latter should take account of the population and territorial expanse of the country, the size of the internal market, Mexico's rates of consumption, savings, and investment, and the average rate of growth that is desired.

Given the foregoing considerations, we believe that the most viable Mexican industrialization strategy involves (1) an expansion of manufactured exports and (2) endogenous industrial growth centering on basic goods and inputs. In turn, this external orientation should be supported by (3) a process of selective ISI in which links in the productive chain are created that promote intraindustrial and intersectorial articulation, and competitive and efficient production. This three-dimensional industrial strategy, based on a model of export-oriented and endogenous industrialization, presupposes a rational opening to external markets whereby excessive and indiscriminate protection will be eliminated, along with the anti-exporting bias.

This strategy addresses the internal challenge of generating jobs and basic goods for the entire population. Concretely, the Mexican economy must increase the ratio of investment to GDP to at least the level of its internal savings. The fundamental problem is not one of generating more internal savings but rather the fact that a large percentage of these savings is being transferred abroad to service the foreign debt. Thus it is essential to look for a long-term solution to servicing the external debt. To confront this challenge implies effectively reactivating the Mexican economy and providing more jobs.

In addition, this option addresses the external challenge of financing

---

[11] Apparent exceptions would be countries like Belgium (with a GDP of $79.1 billion and an export/GDP ratio of 78 percent) and the Netherlands (a GDP of $125 billion and an export/GDP ratio of 64 percent). On the other hand, we should not forget that these nations are part of the European Economic Community, where countries are open to trade flows within the common market and relatively restrictive with regard to trade flows from outside the region.

Mexico's imports given the exhaustion of external indebtedness and the collapse of oil prices. Consolidating structural change in the external sector means implementing a selective ISI policy along with an increasing capacity to export. If the economy begins to grow again at around 4 or 5 percent annually, and the programs of selective ISI and export expansion are *not* effectively articulated, then once again there would be an external constraint on the growth process.

Further, the proposed strategy recognizes the need to maintain the high level of diversification of Mexico's industrial structure. Although industry in Mexico is not well integrated, it has generated a sector of basic goods (food, textiles, garments, furniture) and widely used inputs (cement, glass, metal rods) in which the import-substitution process is finished.

The strategy we propose will involve the following steps. First, the phase of export substitution must be guaranteed and strengthened, principally during the process of economic reactivation. Several policy components will be critically important:

The development of an integrated export policy;

The development of infrastructure in different fields: for example, transportation, telecommunications, and ports.

The implementation of macro-industrial policies that eliminate the anti-export bias; and

At the micro-industrial level of the firms, the restructuring of the economy's productive base.

Second, the three-dimensional model involves moving from a phase of apparent ISI to one of effective ISI, which also implies the need to improve intraindustrial and intersectoral linkages. The following policy directions will be necessary:

A policy of rational and selective protection for the national economy that eliminates excessive, permanent, and indiscriminate protection, but that also guarantees the minimal temporary protection that would allow for the take-off of new ISI projects. In this regard, Mexico has a particular need to advance in the capital goods sector since it is behind countries at a similar level of development like Brazil.

A unified policy to develop the capital goods sector will be required, with long-term financing and the purchasing power of the public sector playing a role.

The development of new industries with state-of-the-art technology (for example, electronics, biotechnology, and new materials) that could be the foci for technological diffusion throughout the industrial sector and the national economy.

Third, implementation of the three-dimensional model requires strengthening, developing, and linking the endogenous industrial sector in order to convert it into the motor of economic growth. This will assure the production of basic goods and widely used inputs; at the same time this sector could become pivotal for expanded exports. Production for the domestic market will permit the reduction of unit costs and allow the country to have a more solid base from which to enter export markets (as is the case with Japan, the United States, and Brazil). On the other hand, this also will permit a more efficient utilization of the broad base of small and medium-sized enterprises and allow for the creation of more jobs in the industrial sector. This buildup of endogenous industry will require the following, among other things:

> The recuperation of sustained economic growth rates through programs that increase internal demand and at the same time raise the standard of living of the population through the production of basic goods and housing, which would have a multiplier effect on the rest of the industrial and primary sectors; and

> Various programs of support for the small and medium-sized firms in the industrial sector, including initiatives to expand their subcontracting arrangements with large enterprises, public as well as private.

CONCLUSION: TOWARD A NEW REGIONAL PARADIGM?

After more than forty years of efforts to develop Mexico by means of ISI, the country is faced with the imperative of changing its strategy of industrial development and economic growth in order to meet the two fundamental challenges of development: to create jobs and basic goods for the domestic economy and to reduce the country's external economic vulnerability. Every year it is necessary to generate approximately 1 million new jobs that are permanent and fairly remunerated for the individuals that are entering the labor market. Similarly, basic goods and services need to be produced to satisfy nearly 2 million Mexicans who are born each year (i.e., a population of 80 million people with a 2 percent annual rate of growth).

In terms of Mexico's foreign economic relations, the challenge for the 1990s is to reduce the country's vulnerability to sharp fluctuations in the areas of trade, oil, and financial markets. For example, if the average price of oil goes down by $1 per barrel, Mexico loses $550 million in foreign exchange. If international interest rates increase by 1 percent, the country has to pay an additional $1 billion to service its external debt. And finally, if the economic growth rate of OECD countries is reduced by 1 percent, or if they adopt protectionist policies with a similar effect on their demand for imports, Mexico's current account income would diminish by $500 million per year.

Efforts to chart such a future strategy for Mexico and other Latin American nations must be guided by the lessons of regional economic history. The neoliberal experiments in the Southern Cone, based upon errant interpretations of East Asian developments, experienced enormous social and political costs, and they are being abandoned or redesigned. However, the strategies adopted by Brazil and Mexico have shown their viability and resilience despite the problems they have confronted. Both countries count on an ample and diversified industrial base, and they have advanced to different degrees of ISI, industrial integration, and manufactured exports. Thus, they are in a position to reestablish the integrity of the much-criticized Latin American model of development.

REFERENCES

Banco de México. 1977–1988. *Informe Anual*. México, D.F.: Banco de México.
Bresser Pereira, Luiz Carlos. 1987. "El Nuevo modelo de desarrollo brasileño." *Investigación económica*, no. 182, 307–31.
ECLA (Economic Commission for Latin America), United Nations. 1985. *Crisis and Development: The Present Situation and Future Prospects of Latin America and the Caribbean*. Santiago: ECLA.
Ferrer, Aldo. 1980. "El monetarismo en Argentina y Chile." *Ambito Financiero*, August 22.
Fishlow, Albert. 1985. "The State of Latin American Economics." In *Economic and Social Progress in Latin America 1985*. Washington, D.C.: Inter-American Development Bank.
Gereffi, Gary. 1989. "Development Strategies and the Global Factory." *Annals* of the American Academy of Political and Social Sciences, no. 505, pp. 92–104.
IDB (Inter-American Development Bank). 1985. *Economic and Social Progress in Latin America*. Washington, D.C.: IDB.
IILA (Istituto Italo-Latino Americano). 1986. *Report on the Medium-Term Prospects for Latin American Countries*. Rome: IILA.
Leontief, Wassily. 1977. *The Future of the World Economy*. Oxford: Oxford University Press.
Muñoz Goma, Oscar. 1986. *Chile y su industrialización pasada: Crisis y opciones*. Santiago: Corporación de Investigaciones Económicas para América Latina (CIEPLAN).
O'Donnell, Guillermo. 1977. "Corporatism and the Question of the State." In *Authoritarianism and Corporatism in Latin America*, edited by James Malloy. Pittsburgh, Pa.: University of Pittsburgh Press.
Reisen, Helmut. 1985. "Disequilibrium Prices and External Debt: An Empirical Analysis for 1978–1984." In *Europe and Latin America in the World Economy*, edited by Colin Bradford, Jr. New Haven: Yale Center for International and Area Studies.
Sachs, Jeffrey D. 1987. "Trade and Exchange Rate Policies in Growth-Oriented

Adjustment Programs." Working paper no. 2226. Chicago: National Bureau of Economic Research.

Sanchez-Arnau, Juan C. 1986. "Medium-Term Scenarios for the Future of Latin America." In *Latin America, the Caribbean and the OECD*, edited by Angus Maddison. Paris: Organization for Economic Cooperation and Development.

SPP (Secretaría de Programación y Presupuesto). 1986. *Cuentas Nacionales 1960–1985*. México, D.F.: SPP.

————. 1985. *50 años del Banco Mexicano de Comercio Exterior*. México, D.F.: SPP.

Tomasini, Roberto. 1982. "Reflexiones sobre un perfil de industrialización alternativo para la Argentina." In *Argentina, políticas económicas, alternativas*, Mexico, D.F.: Centro de Investigación y Docencia Económica.

Villarreal, René. 1983. *La Contrarevolución monetarista*. México, D.F.: Editorial Oceano.

World Bank. 1987. *World Development Report 1986*. Washington, D.C.: World Bank.

PART FOUR

Emerging Agendas for Comparative Development Research

CHAPTER 12

The United States and Japan as Models of Industrialization

Fernando Fajnzylber

THE MAIN PURPOSE of this chapter is to engage in critical reflection on regional development experiences and on current debates regarding industrialization options and development strategies. As a modest contribution toward this end, the chapter analyzes the development experiences of three Latin American countries—Argentina, Brazil, and Mexico[1]—and one East Asian case, South Korea. The primary objective here is to identify sets of structural features that comprise distinctive regional *patterns* of development.

It is important at the outset to clarify the notion of "patterns of development" and to distinguish it from that of "development strategies." The former concept assumes the existence in each country of complex processes that generate distinctive national structures of social organization and conditions of human and material resource allocation. These national conditions have the purpose of resolving issues related to the production and consumption of goods and services (Pinto, 1976; see also Graciarena, 1976; Sunkel, 1981). By contrast, the idea of "development strategies" denotes "coherent sets of state policies designed to promote particular economic outcomes" (see Gereffi, chap. 1, this volume).

While strategies often influence the emergence of development patterns, the analysis of strategies alone provides an insufficient explanation for the economic reality of a specific nation or region. The precise role of conscious strategies is an issue for empirical investigation because it varies from country to country. For instance, strategies may appear to be

The interpretations and views presented in this paper are those of the author and do not necessarily reflect the views of the Economic Commission on Latin America and the Caribbean (ECLAC) or the United Nations Industrial Development Organization (UNIDO). The assistance of Christopher G. Ellison of Duke University in editing this chapter is gratefully acknowledged.

[1] About 64 percent of the Latin American population is concentrated in Argentina, Brazil, and Mexico. These three countries together generate 72 percent of the regional gross domestic product and 77 percent of the industrial product. In addition, they account for 80 percent of the regional total in scientific and technology-related expenditures and 83 percent of the regional automotive industry.

more salient determinants of development patterns in Japan than in the United States, in South Korea than in Latin America, and in Brazil than in Argentina. Thus, the comparison of patterns of development offered here can supply only an introduction to the issue of development strategies.

Moreover, insights drawn from the field of economics may prove more useful in *characterizing* patterns of development than *explaining* them. When development experiences emerging from different "cultural universes" are contrasted, as they are here, and discussion focuses solely upon economic behavior and outcomes, the interpretive scope and normative potential of the analysis are necessarily limited. While the historical, political, and social determinants of development patterns are discussed elsewhere in the present volume, the primary task here will be to formulate a parsimonious framework for the cross-national and cross-regional comparison of development experiences.

Marked differences exist between the respective patterns prevailing in the newly industrializing countries (NICs) of Latin America and East Asia. However, a better understanding of these requires not only a consideration of the NICs themselves but also a discussion of those development experiences that continue to serve as their "models." While the principal source of inspiration for post-1960 South Korean development policy has been Japan, the main contemporary referent for Latin American elites has been the United States. Therefore, a brief comparison of patterns of development in the United States and Japan may shed considerable light on the experiences of the contemporary NICs.

The remainder of the chapter will be organized as follows. First, it is necessary to develop a schematic contrast between the patterns (and historical experiences) of the United States and Japan. This section centers upon a set of working hypotheses that form the basis of a broader ongoing research project. More importantly, however, it provides background information useful for a subsequent comparison of Latin American and East Asian development patterns. The chapter concludes with reflections upon the fundamental development challenges and policy options for industrialization that confront the elites of the Latin American NICs.

COMPARING PATTERNS OF DEVELOPMENT: JAPAN AND THE UNITED STATES

Key aspects of the development patterns of South Korea and the Latin American NICs may be understood as outgrowths of efforts to emulate the Japanese and American experiences, respectively. In brief, East Asian countries have generally emphasized strategic industrialization, international competitiveness, and the "conquest" of major markets—including that of the United States. Latin American countries, on the other hand, have sought primarily to reproduce, among elite strata, the "American way of life." Among other important features, the resulting pattern of development is characterized by (1) consumption trends that are heavily skewed in favor of urban elite groups at the expense of the rural and lower income majorities and (2) productive structures that are biased toward production for domestic rather than external markets.

Consequently, it is appropriate to identify several basic features of the American and Japanese patterns of development. The list in table 12.1—although neither specific nor exhaustive—provides the basis for a discussion of the respective development experiences of these "models."

Clear differences in development patterns appear at least partly rooted in the distinctive contemporary histories of the United States and Japan and in the international postures and self-perceptions that these experiences have engendered. Japan has emerged gradually from World War II with a renewed sense of national purpose. The internal legitimacy of Japanese political leadership is inextricably linked with the successful recovery of national dignity. As a small, insular nation with scarce natural resources, Japan has constructed its economic power via careful sectoral strategies and long-range planning. In turn, the resulting pattern of vig-

TABLE 12.1
Patterns of Development in Industrialized Nations

Japan	United States
One finds a strategic, long-term orientation toward economic affairs.	One finds a tactical, short-term orientation toward economic affairs.
There is a clear tendency toward high levels of saving.	There is a clear tendency toward high levels of consumption.
The lack of natural resources virtually requires industrial development.	The abundance of natural resources and the "continental economy" permit intersectoral neutrality.
Firms are oriented toward the "conquest" of international markets.	Firms are concentrated around large and secure domestic markets.
Given the dearth of natural resources, the educational system is considered a national priority.	The educational system is considered an investment in human resources, subject to a cost-benefit evaluation.
There is a relative predominance of careers related to technology (e.g., engineering).	There is a prevalence of careers related to legal and financial organization.
Social *integration* is essential for the political legitimacy of the ruling elites.	The social order is structured largely via the operation of market forces.

orous growth has legitimated the Japanese political leadership and existing institutional arrangements.

On the other hand, the United States has become accustomed to the role of the paramount global power in the post–World War II era. The United States has served as a model for other nations by virtue of its language, the strength of its currency, the attractiveness of its affluent lifestyle, and its productive, continental economy. Despite its seemingly enviable world position, however, the United States has experienced relatively slow growth, weak increases in industrial productivity, the subsequent erosion of international competitiveness, repeated shifts in political and economic policy, and consistent inattention to sectoral planning options (President's Commission on Industrial Competitiveness, 1985).

A number of factors account for the comparatively lower American rates of capital formation, and hence lower rates of economic growth: (1) low rates of family savings; (2) high fiscal deficits; (3) the relatively higher cost of capital required by the productive sector; and (4) the clear tendency of the tax system to favor consumption rather than investment.

In contrast to the pervasive Japanese pattern of austere consumption, the United States has experienced a much greater availability of certain basic consumer goods, such as automobiles. These goods have become important symbols of the "American way of life" at home and around the world. One especially revealing statistic seems to summarize the fundamental difference in American and Japanese orientations toward consumption and investment: In 1981, the relative density of automobiles in Japan was roughly one third that of the United States, while Japan's per capita income was more than three fourths of the comparable American figure (World Bank, 1985; President's Commission on Industrial Competitiveness, 1985). For comparative data on other social indicators, see table 12.2.

The Japanese manufacturing sector appears notably more important than that of the United States. Indeed, manufacturing industries contribute some 29 percent of the gross domestic product (GDP) in Japan in 1987, compared to only 20 percent in the United States (World Bank, 1989, p. 169). Table 12.3 indicates that in Japan the manufacturing sector generates sufficient foreign exchange to balance the deficits in all the natural resource sectors. For instance, in 1987 Japanese manufacturing industries accounted for a surplus of $167 billion. In the United States, however, the only sector producing a consistent surplus is the agricultural sector, as in many Latin American countries. Such differences between Japan and the United States do not reflect divergent developmental ideologies, but result instead from Japan's dearth of natural resources. The success of Japanese development depends heavily upon the intellectual

TABLE 12.2
Patterns of Consumption: Different Indicators

	United States	Japan
Consumption/GDP (1986)	85%	68%
Savings/GDP (1986)	15%	32%
Savings/disposable income (1984)	5.2%	22.5%
Fixed domestic capital formation/GDP (1986)	18%	28%
Automobile/1,000 persons (1983)	540	221
Person/rooms in dwelling (1980)	0.5	1.0
Dwellings with fixed bath or shower (1979)	5.2%	65.6%
Energy consumption/person (1986) (Kg. equivalent of oil)	7,193.0	3,186.0
Daily calories/needs (1983)	137%	113%

Sources: Joint ECLAC/UNIDO Industry and Technology Division based on data from President's Commission on Industrial Competitiveness (1985); World Bank, World Development Report 1988.

value-added, which its population can introduce via the manufacturing sector.

The contemporary erosion of the international competitiveness of the U.S. manufacturing sector has been nothing short of dramatic. Despite a surplus of $21 billion in 1975, the manufacturing sector declined to a $146 billion deficit by 1987. This loss of competitiveness involved not only the "low technology" sector (e.g., textiles, naval industry), but also the "medium technology" (e.g., automobiles, television sets) and "high technology" (e.g., computer equipment) sectors (U.S. Department of Commerce, 1986, chap. 36). For additional indicators of international competitiveness, see table 12.4.

Explanations for this decline have frequently focused on the sharp increases in oil prices in the 1970s. Given that the loss of $50 billion experienced by the manufacturing sector between 1975 and 1983 coincided with a rise of $28 billion in the U.S. energy bill, such accounts enjoy superficial plausibility. However, although the effect of the oil shocks may have contributed to the erosion of the manufacturing sector's competitiveness in the United States, it is important to note that Japan more than covered the $34 billion increase in its oil bill from 1975 to 1983 with a $71 billion surplus in the manufacturing sector. In 1987 the United States and Japan both had equivalent oil trade deficits of $39 billion, but Japan

TABLE 12.3
United States–Japan: Trade Balance by Sector of Economic Activity (US$ millions)

		1970	1975	1981	1983	1985	1986	1987	1988
Agriculture[a]	U.S.	+631	+12,069	+25,344	+16,518	+3,659	−320	+3,813	14,953
	Japan	−5,292	−13,931	−24,929	−23,301	−24,264	−27,892	−34,787	—
Manufacturing industry[b]	U.S.	+4,154	+21,196	+13,369	−28,925	−107,566	−138,626	−146,010	−139,723
	Japan	+13,180	+42,393	+119,152	+113,403	+137,550	+162,311	+167,254	—
Energy[c]	U.S.	−1,480	−21,922	−73,974	−50,349	−45,759	−31,652	−39,014	−35,896
	Japan	−3,858	−25,432	−72,091	−58,636	−55,319	−36,565	−38,779	—
Mining[d]	U.S.	−863	−1,295	−5,183	−5,298	+1,302	−6,087	−5,440	−5,915
	Japan	−3,698	−5,734	−11,223	−10,055	−9,662	−8,657	−10,962	—
Other sectors[e]	U.S.	+196	+640	+758	−1,268	−245	−3,961	+7,963	+14,749
	Japan	+105	+594	−2,168	−877	−1,992	−6,454	−3,020	—
Total	U.S.	+2,638	+10,688	−39,686	−69,322	−148,609	−180,646	−178,688	−151,832
	Japan	+437	−2,110	+8,741	+20,534	46,362	82,743	+79,706	—

Source: Joint ECLAC/UNIDO Industry and Technology Division based on United Nations, Commodity Trade Statistics, Statistical Papers, various years.

[a] Includes: SITC sections 0, 1, 2, and 4 less divisions 27 and 28.
[b] Includes: SITC section 5 to 8 less division 68 (nonferrous metals).
[c] Includes: SITC section 3.
[d] Includes: SITC divisions 27, 28, and 68.
[e] Includes: SITC section 9.

TABLE 12.4
International Competitiveness: Different Indicators (percent)

	United States	Japan
Civilian R + D/GNP (1985)	1.9	2.6[a]
Growth of manufactured exports (1965–1986)	11.1	16.9
Engineering exports/total manufactured exports (1986)	59.0	72.0
Engineering exports/world engineering exports (1963–1986)	61.0	515.0
Engineering exports/engineering imports		
1963	408.0	266.0
1986	64.0	1,317.0
Productivity growth in manufacturing[b]		
1965–1973	2.8	11.0
1975–1981	1.7	8.7
1980–1986	3.7	5.4
Manufacturing exports/manufacturing imports (1984–1986)	57.0	518.0

Sources: Joint ECLAC/UNIDO Industry and Technology Division based on data from President's Commission on Industrial Competitiveness (1985); World Bank, *World Development Report 1988*; U.N., *Bulletin of Statistics on World Trade in Engineering Products* (1986); OECD (1986); National Science Foundation, *International Science and Technology Data Update* (1986).

[a] 1984.

[b] OECD, DSTI/IND 88.14 (June 1988).

had an overall trade surplus of $80 billion based on the stellar performance of its manufacturing sector while the United States suffered an overall trade shortfall of nearly $180 billion because of its worst manufacturing deficit ever—$146 billion (Table 12.3). Thus, arguments that attribute the erosion of American competitiveness to the rise in oil prices may lack empirical credibility. Instead, one of the key factors responsible for the erosion in competitiveness appears to be a comparative decrease in U.S. civilian technology expenditures as a proportion of the gross national product (GNP).[2]

[2] The lack of emphasis placed on the international competitiveness of the manufacturing sector by American economists is striking. For instance, in one of the most prominent analyses of the American industrial structure to appear in recent years (see Feldstein, 1980), the subject of international competitiveness is omitted altogether. Evidence of similar neglect

In view of the latter explanation, the divergent orientations of the American and Japanese educational systems merit attention. During the post–World War II era, only two major events have produced calls for increased technical education in the United States: the 1957 launching of Sputnik by the Soviets and the invasion of world markets by Japanese manufactured goods during the 1970s. The relative deemphasis of engineering and technical fields in the United States contrasts with the obvious priority of engineering in Japan; in 1982, the density of engineering students in Japan was double that of the United States. While some 66 percent of the executives of leading Japanese enterprises are engineers, a similar proportion of executives in the United States are lawyers or commercial specialists. The overall density of lawyers in the two nations is revealing as well. While in the United States one person in four hundred is an attorney, the comparable figure in Japan is one in ten thousand. Thus, the density of attorneys in the United States is twenty-five times higher than in Japan.

Styles of social integration in the two countries differ strikingly. While Japanese society and enterprises are conceived and organized around quasi-familial patterns, American society ostensibly reflects "market forces." Despite the limitations of figures on income distribution, a comparison of American and Japanese data is instructive. Among all industrialized nations, Japan and the Scandanavian countries exhibit the highest levels of distributive equity, while the United States and France are characterized by the greatest inequality (World Bank, 1989, p. 223).

To facilitate a concise comparison of the experiences of the United States and Japan, this chapter calls attention to four structural features of their respective patterns of development:

1. consumption (measured via automobile density);
2. income distribution (measured in terms of the relationship between the lower 40 percent of incomes and the highest 10 percent);[3]
3. international competitiveness (measured by the ratio of imports to exports within the engineering industry);[4] and
4. long-term dynamism (measured as per capita GNP, 1960–1979).

An analysis of these dimensions helps us to identify crucial differences in patterns of development (see figure 12.1 and table 12.5). The contrasts

---

may be found in the classical texts used in the instruction of American industrial economists (e.g., Scherer, 1970).

[3] For a thorough analysis of the methodological problems associated with the measurement of income distribution in the United States, see Blinder et al. (1980).

[4] The "technological density" of the engineering sector is considerably higher than that of the remainder of the industrial sector. Thus, the relative competitiveness of the engineering sector provides an indication of comparative levels of "intellectual value added."

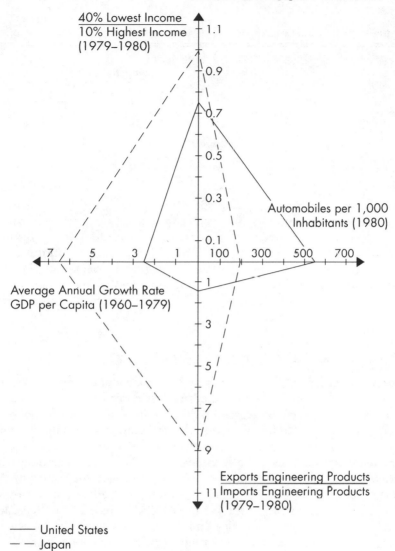

FIGURE 12.1
Strategic Profiles: United States–Japan.

(*Source*: Table 12.5.)

between the United States and Japan highlighted here parallel those between the major Latin American countries and South Korea, respectively. As might be anticipated, the United States exhibits higher levels of consumption than Japan. However, Japan surpasses the United States in the areas of dynamism, international competitiveness, and distributive eq-

TABLE 12.5
United States–Japan: Synthetic Comparison Indicators—"Patterns of Development"

	GNP per Capita Average Annual Growth Rate 1960–1979	Equity of Income Distribution 40% Lowest/ 10% Highest	No. of Automobiles per 1,000 Inhabitants	Engineering Products Exported/Engineering Products Imported 1979–1980 Coefficient
United States	2.5	0.75 (1980)	548	1.41
Japan	6.6	0.98 (1979)	196	9.00

Sources: United Nations (1980); World Bank (1985); UNCTC (1983a); CEPAL (1984).

uity. Despite the conventional wisdom that growth and equity involve tradeoffs, the dimensions of relative Japanese success appear to be reciprocally reinforcing. In short, the two figures in figure 12.1 denote distinctive patterns of development: (1) a pattern that embodies a strategic, industrial-centered, competitive, socially integrated orientation (Japan); and (2) a pattern that reflects a preoccupation with short-term planning, consumption, domestic markets, and relatively low levels of social integration (the United States).

"REINDUSTRIALIZATION" DEBATES IN JAPAN AND THE UNITED STATES

The economic ascendancy of Japan and the concomitant relative decline of the United States have stimulated extensive debate within U.S. academic and political circles regarding the need for—and the potential contours of—a national industrialization policy. While these debates warrant close attention for a number of reasons, they are particularly significant for the major countries of Latin America and East Asia. The industrial policies of the major economic powers help to shape the course of the world economy, presenting new opportunities and constraints for other nations. Thus, shifts in U.S. or Japanese policies may determine which development strategies and policy "mixes" are most useful for the NICs.

Debates over national industrial policy in the United States have taken on important political and ideological colorings. In particular, "conservative" and "progressive" positions offer markedly divergent interpretations of Japanese economic success. Proponents of each perspective stress the salience of certain features of the Japanese experience over others, and they suggest the potential implications of these key features for future U.S. economic development.

In brief, conservative commentators have called attention to at least four characteristics of contemporary Japanese development that they consider salutary: (1) the economic leadership and hegemony of the en-

trepreneurial sector; (2) the relative social harmony within Japanese enterprises; (3) the scarcity of public participation in the articulation of social programs; and (4) the open and intense competition in the domestic
market.

In contrast to this understanding of the Japanese experience, progressive analysts emphasize a much different set of features. First, these observers highlight the capacity of the Japanese state to define strategic national options and long-term sectoral priorities on the basis of perceived
trends in the international market. Second, they also note the leadership
of the industrial sector and the subordinate role of financial interests in
shaping industrial policy. Finally, progressive interpretations stress three
aspects of the public sector role in supporting the interests of domestic
enterprises over foreign interests: (1) the restrictive nature of state policies
regarding direct foreign investment; (2) the priority assigned to Japanese
firms in the domestic market; and (3) the high degree of governmental
support for domestic enterprises attempting to enter into the world market.

Given such diverse understandings of the Japanese economic experience, it is not surprising that one finds an array of opinions regarding the
desirability, feasibility, and shape of a U.S. reindustrialization policy.
Nevertheless, it is possible to classify the range of views in terms of two
major issues: (1) the perceived degree of erosion of international competitiveness of the U.S. industrial sector; and (2) the importance accorded to
the industrial sector relative to the service sector.

Table 12.6 depicts the broad contours of the recent debates. Like all
typologies, the table simplifies a complex reality and therefore should be
interpreted with caution. In particular, authors within each quadrant of

TABLE 12.6
U.S. "Reindustrialization" Debates: A Typology of Views

	The Industrial Sector Must Recover Its Leadership Role	Transition to a Service-Oriented Economy Is Feasible and Desirable
The international competitiveness of U.S. industry has been sharply eroded	A	C
The erosion of the relative international competitiveness of U.S. industry is not a structural problem	B	D

the table may harbor important differences of opinion on issues not captured by these twin axes.

The primary advocates of an industrial policy are located in quadrant A of the table. These authors contend that a deindustrialization process is under way in the United States and endorse a national strategy to reverse the prevailing trend toward industrial decline (Reich, 1983; Thurow, 1986; Scott, 1984). By contrast, quadrant D houses the main supporters of the policies of the Reagan administration. They contend that no real process of deindustrialization is taking place and see no need for a countervailing state policy (U.S. Government, 1984).

The remaining two sectors of the table represent intermediate positions in the debate. Authors located in quadrant C acknowledge internal and external erosion in U.S. industrial leadership. However, they interpret this trend as evidence of a desirable transition toward a "post-industrial" society (Bell, 1979; Birch, 1981). In their view, while the traditional leadership of the manufacturing sector must be supplanted by the service sector, an industrial policy is unnecessary.

Those authors in quadrant B acknowledge the internal erosion of the industrial sector, but they argue that its internal recovery can be accomplished via the available macroeconomic policy instruments. These analysts remain skeptical of both the necessity and institutional viability of a national industrial policy in the United States (Badaracco and Yoffie, 1983).

The future of these debates remains uncertain. However, it is clear that their outcome may shape the development strategies most useful for other nations. Therefore, while a fuller account of these debates lies beyond the scope of the present chapter, they represent a promising area for further investigation and discussion.

LATIN AMERICA AND EAST ASIA: SHOWCASE VS. ENDOGENOUS MODERNITY

In the area of economic development, the United States has served as the primary inspiration for both industrialized and Third World nations during the post–World War II period. It is a cardinal contention of this chapter that the respective patterns of development that characterize the major Latin American countries and South Korea derive from differences in the interpretation and internalization of the United States experience.

Like Japan, South Korea has adapted to the American example in ways that both maximize domestic economic potentialities and fulfill internally defined societal objectives. South Korea has implemented a self-conscious strategy of garnering impressive shares of international markets—particularly within the world's leading economy, that of the United States.

While in some respects reproducing a "way of life" identified with the United States, South Korea has harnessed the forces of economic development to generate *endogenous modernity*.

The Latin American pattern of development contrasts starkly with this experience. Latin American elites have pursued a less ambitious project than their East Asian counterparts, content to reproduce the United States model of consumption to the extent that available resources have allowed. In the absence of clearly articulated national strategies, the development process in Latin America has frequently failed to protect the interests of politically and economically excluded segments of the population. Such a pattern of development may be termed *showcase modernity*.

While this phenomenon of showcase modernity appears throughout the major countries of the region, the distinctive character of each nation's development experience results from a number of historically conditioned factors. A partial listing of these would include the following: (1) specific social structural features, (2) differing degrees of intranational social and cultural integration; (3) variations in factor endowments; (4) geographical conditions; (5) variations in population dynamics and migratory patterns; and (6) internal political structures and their dynamics.

Despite this caveat, it remains possible to identify several features common to the development experiences of the Latin American NICs. These similarities reflect an uncritical attempt on the part of Latin American elites to reproduce aspects of the U.S. model of development.

This chapter focuses on eight quantifiable dimensions along which the Latin American and South Korean development experiences can be evaluated: (1) dynamism, (2) social articulation, (3) consumption patterns, (4) international competitiveness and technological development, (5) structure of production and international trade, (6) external borrowing, (7) capital flight, and (8) entrepreneurial leadership. Discussion of these developmental dimensions permits a "synthetic comparison" of the patterns that prevail in Argentina, Brazil, Mexico, and South Korea.

Dynamism

The economic dynamism of a developing nation entails an array of significant consequences. An ongoing pattern of rapid economic growth legitimates the political system under which it occurs and with which it comes to be associated. The experience of growth—and the prospect of further economic expansion—can mitigate conflicts of interest that polarize various social groups. In addition, an environment of economic dynamism can also ameliorate popular discontent over oppressive political structures (the so-called democratic nostalgia). Moreover, the fact of an ever-expanding economic pie frequently renders burgeoning economic disparities more acceptable (see Hirschman, 1973).

In short, the experience of economic dynamism fosters the widespread conviction that the social conflicts emerging from the development process may be resolved not through the reallocation of economic resources (i.e., redistribution), but through continued expansion. Within such a context, economic growth itself becomes both the paramount objective and the primary focus of reflection and discussion.

Nevertheless, an examination of the Latin American development experience demonstrates that conflicts of interest were only temporarily postponed, and subsequently intensified, via the pursuit of unbridled economic growth based upon social, cultural, and economic disarticulation, and upon the exclusion of entire social sectors. This "spasmodic" growth—accomplished through income generated by valuable natural resources or from the permissive character of the international financial system—has been sufficient to enable the physical transfer of showcase modernity to Latin America. However, such a growth pattern does not contribute to (1) the improvement of domestic economic and social organization or (2) the solid insertion of Latin American countries into the international economic order.

With these considerations in mind, an examination of "rhythms of growth" in the NICs proves instructive. The economies of these nations appear comparable. Indeed, the per capita GDP in each of the four countries under discussion is similar—approximately $2,000. However, the levels of economic dynamism experienced by these countries vary considerably. Of the Latin American NICs, Brazil appears the most dynamic, while Argentina is experiencing virtual stagnation. However, while the total GDP of South Korea is relatively small (roughly two fifths that of Brazil, one half that of Mexico, and until recently only slightly higher than that of Argentina), South Korea continues to grow far more rapidly than *any* Latin American economy (see Gereffi, chap. 1, tables 1.1 and 1.2, this volume).

Social Integration

The concept of integration and its converse, disintegration, refer to both (1) the structure of domestic production systems and (2) social, spatial, and even cultural aspects of development. These concepts are crucial in distinguishing between the productive structures of developed countries, East Asian nations, and Latin American NICs.

While developed countries benefited from gradual processes of integration, Latin American NICs experienced fundamentally different developmental dynamics. In brief, the mining centers and agrarian structures (both estate and plantation) were often superimposed upon peasant communities of varying structures and origins. This historical fact resulted in demand patterns for specific consumer goods and equipment that differed from those that emerged in developed countries. The structure of demand in Latin America proved incapable of stimulating mass production of basic and standardized goods. As a result, the self-sustaining linkages between rural-agrarian and urban-industrial demand that fueled the balanced and integrated growth of developed countries never materialized in the Latin American cases. The technological options adopted during the course of modernization originated within the social and economic contexts of developed nations. The selection of technologies by Latin American elites had the effect of reinforcing the dualistic character of their productive structures (see Fajnzylber, 1986, for further discussion).

What were the results of this distinctive development experience? First, instead of self-sustaining development, Latin American industrialization aimed at satisfying a set of elite consumption patterns appropriate for developed countries. However, this industrial growth held few benefits for the majority of Latin American populations. Hence, the multiplier effects of demand were turned abroad.

Second, the articulated growth of various components of the industrial complex—achieved in developed countries by the market mechanism (e.g., the United States) or via state intervention and planning (e.g., Japan)—did not occur in Latin America. Only a fragmentary "transplant" of such an industrial structure emerged, while crucial functions were allocated to external forces such as transnational corporations (TNCs).

Four indicators reflect aspects of social (dis)integration: (1) income distribution, (2) the percentage of the workforce employed in agriculture, (3) the level of "poverty," and (4) participation in secondary and higher education. Of the Latin American NICs, Argentina has the most equal pattern of income distribution, while Brazil exhibits the greatest inequality. Thus, an intraregional comparison suggests that dynamism and equity may be *inversely* related. Such an observation lends superficial support to the widespread perception in Latin America that distributive inequality is a transitory (and necessary) price to be paid for high levels of economic growth.

However, consideration of the South Korean case confounds this interpretation. South Korea surpasses both Argentina in the attainment of social equity and Brazil in the achievement of economic dynamism.[5] Thus,

---

[5] South Korea's performance appears all the more impressive given the fact that its peasant population is actually greater than the peasant population of Brazil. The property structure in these countries differs strikingly: In 1960, properties of under five hectares accounted for 100 percent of the arable land in Korea. The comparable figure was 84 percent in Japan.

South Korean "superiority" to the performance of the Latin American NICs parallels Japanese ascendancy vis-à-vis the United States. Both East Asian nations have experienced higher levels of growth and equity than their Western counterparts.

With regard to the other social indicators mentioned above, Argentina and South Korea have performed far more impressively than Brazil and Mexico. For instance, rates of educational participation in the former countries appear comparable to those in developed nations. South Korean achievements in the area of secondary education are particularly noteworthy, while Argentina has excelled in providing higher education. Brazil and Mexico notoriously lag behind the other two NICs in all indicators of social equity.

Consumption Patterns

This comparison continues by focusing on three indicators of consumption in the NICs: (1) automobile density, (2) availability of staple foods for domestic consumption, and (3) patterns of overall food intake. Automobile density appears a particularly useful indicator of the national consumption pattern for several reasons. First, the automobile symbolizes "modernity" and the "American way of life" as they have frequently been depicted around the globe. In addition, the automobile sector may influence the broader pattern of national development. For instance, the prominence of automobiles affects the allocation of family savings. Moreover, the prevalence of this sector influences public policies concerning the provision of physical infrastructure and shapes the national pattern of energy usage. Finally, the automobile sector is an important user and disseminator of technical progress, and it enjoys key linkages with various service sectors, such as marketing, finance, and mass media. (For comparative data on other social indicators, see Table 12.2.)

The available information reveals a remarkable contrast between levels of automotive density in Latin America and South Korea (UNCTC, 1983a). Specifically, while South Korea has become a leading exporter of automotive products, its domestic automobile density equals only one tenth to one fifteenth that of the Latin American NICs that have overall economies of similar size.

Examination of other indicators also reveals interesting comparative patterns. In Brazil and Mexico one finds clear neglect of staple food output for the domestic market. During the last decade, both countries have significantly increased agricultural production for export at the expense

---

In Brazil, only 1 percent of the arable land was owned in parcels of fewer than five hectares, while 44 percent of the land was owned in properties of 1,000 hectares or more.

of domestic consumption. For instance, Brazil has boosted sugar cane production to compensate for a declining oil situation, while per capita production of cereals has actually decreased during the same period. In both Brazil and Mexico, the cereal import coefficient has been rising steadily, approaching 20 percent in the early 1980s.

By contrast, Argentina and South Korea have both largely solved the problem of staple food output for domestic consumption. The per capita caloric intake among Argentinians is similar to that of Americans and higher than that of Japanese and most Western Europeans. This statistic primarily reflects the abundant natural resource base enjoyed by Argentina. On the other hand, South Korea's successful resolution of this dilemma owes much to the high priority that state planners have accorded to national self-sufficiency in food.

Although *total* caloric and protein intake in all NICs are comparable, the *composition* of the average diet appears vastly different. Data provided by the Economic Commission on Latin America and the Caribbean (ECLAC) and the Food and Agriculture Organization (FAO) clarify the divergent contents of the average food diets in Latin America and South Korea, respectively. In contrast to the predominance of grain and fish in South Korea, one finds relatively greater consumption of animal foods in Latin America. Further, while South Korea has compensated for its deficiencies in food production by maximizing the potential for self-sufficiency and distributive equity, the higher income groups within the major Latin American nations have emulated the food consumption pattern of the United States. Therefore, within Latin America the food consumption pattern of upper- and middle-class urban sectors parallels that of the United States middle-class, while peasant and lower-class urban sectors consume considerably lower levels of protein (i.e., dairy products and meat).

Regional patterns of food consumption also vary according to their energy efficiency.[6] For example, analyses of the United States food consumption system, which is the pattern imitated by Latin American NICs, have highlighted the inefficiency resulting from the transformation of cereal protein into meat protein. Specifically, some nine calories of "fossil" energy are required for each calorie actually supplied to the consumer (Schejtman, 1985, p. 53).

In comparison, Japanese and South Korean patterns of food consumption appear far more efficient. Only the highly uneven distribution of food consumption patterns prevailing in Latin America permits such inefficient use of resources among elite strata (Sunkel, 1981; Schejtman, 1985). Al-

[6] This refers to the biological energy (or commercial energy) required per one-calorie unit consumed by an average consumer.

though there are tendencies in both Japan and South Korea to imitate U.S. consumption tendencies in automobiles, food, and energy, the pursuit of consumption receives lower priority in East Asian countries than dynamism and social integration.

International Competitiveness

An examination of the international competitiveness of the Latin American countries and South Korea reveals important differences as well. In South Korea, the relative importance of exports and the proportion of exports comprised of manufactured goods are substantially higher than in the Latin American NICs (see Gereffi, chap. 1, tables 1.3 and 1.4, this volume). Moreover, although the South Korean GDP equals only 15 percent of the composite Latin American figure, South Korean manufactured exports exceed the entire Latin American total.

While a number of factors contribute to this disparity in international competitiveness, the present discussion calls attention to the salience of research and development in scientific and technological areas. Of particular importance is the application of such research to leading engineering fields, including chemistry and electronics. A cross-national comparison underscores the significance of research and development differentials in areas embodying high levels of technological progress. In the engineering industry, South Korea boasts an export/import coefficient considerably higher than that of any Latin American country (see table 12.10).

Despite its low export coefficient, Brazil enjoys the greatest relative competitiveness in Latin America. Brazilian exports of manufactured goods comprise one half of the regional total. At the same time, the absolute level of scientific and technical resources devoted to productive sectors by Brazil is twice that of the other two Latin American NICs combined. Further, the ability of Brazil to offset the crisis of the domestic market encountered in the early 1980s by expanding exports demonstrates an exceptional productive capacity and a strong potential to compete internationally. While U.S. imports grew by 26 percent in 1984, Brazilian exports to the United States increased by a whopping 54 percent. This performance compares favorably even with that of East Asian exporters during the same period.

Structure of Production and International Trade

Comparative analysis of the contribution of specific productive sectors to the balance of trade helps to distinguish further a set of national development patterns (see table 12.7; Bradford, chap. 2, this volume). First, natural resources form the cornerstone of international trading for the

Latin American countries. However, while agriculture appears crucial for Argentina and agriculture and mining remain central for Brazil, oil has provided essential foreign exchange for Mexico since the mid-1970s. Second, South Korea has compensated for deficits in virtually all sectors related to natural resources with high levels of manufactured exports. Thus, the case of South Korea parallels that of Japan: soaring oil costs are offset by increases in manufacturing exports, in turn providing an impetus for future growth.

Third, when Latin American nations confronted severe downturns in their domestic markets in the early 1980s, only Brazil generated a trading surplus in the manufacturing sector. Due to the Brazilian effort at import substitution during the late 1970s (see Hirschman, 1987), the manufacturing sector appears unlikely to burden the external sector in the forseeable future.

Fourth, while Brazil has improved the trade balances of both its agricultural and industrial sectors simultaneously, thus compensating for a deteriorating energy profile, Argentina has experienced relative self-sufficiency in energy and mining, and an agricultural surplus adequate to cover deficits incurred by the industrial sector. Fifth, in contrast to the largely beneficial performances of other regional NICs, Mexico has suffered declines in the agricultural and mining sectors along with a stagnating industrial structure. High levels of Mexican borrowing during the 1970s—totaling approximately $30 billion—were channeled primarily toward oil production, rather than toward technical or industrial upgrading.

External Borrowing

The four countries under consideration exhibit both similarities and differences with regard to external borrowing. In each country, the ratio of debt to GDP approached 30 percent in 1981. However, the nations diverge substantially on three key dimensions: (1) the relative weight of the external debt, (2) the impact of the external shock (i.e., via higher interest rates and the deterioration of terms of trade), and (3) the use of externally derived financing (i.e., the proportion devoted to investment and consumption, and the sectoral distribution of investment).

Perhaps the major difference between the experiences of Latin America and South Korea in this area has to do with the relative burden of the external debt with regard to exports: whereas in the Latin American NICs the external debt/export ratio is approximately 3 to 1, in South Korea it is less than 1 to 1. Despite the absence of precise figures regarding the use of borrowed funds, it is clear that certain sectors in each country received the lion's share of externally derived capital. In the case of Mexico, for

TABLE 12.7
Productive Structure: Trade Balance (US$ millions)

	Total Sectors	Agriculture	Manufacturing Industries[a]	Energy	Mining	Others
Argentina						
1970	78	1,257	−988	−73	−119	−1
1975	−985	1,777	−1,938	−504	−316	−4
1981	−280	5,771	−5,566	−402	−86	3
1983	3,332	5,703	−2,132	−129	−111	1
1985	4,581	5,576	−1,113	151	−34	1
1986	2,129	4,219	−1,646	−262	−184	2
1987	543	3,598	−2,297	−571	−187	—
Brazil						
1970	−111	1,700	−1,556	−363	109	−1
1975	−5,049	3,989	−6,235	−3,289	505	−19
1981	−1,499	8,072	−245	−10,842	1,354	162
1983	4,577	8,084	2,816	−7,977	1,677	−23
1985	11,265	8,567	5,791	−4,901	1,822	−14
1986	6,825	5,546	2,903	−3,467	1,670	173
1987	9,648	7,629	4,498	−4,446	1,770	190
Mexico						
1970	−1,256	294	−1,594	−40	84	—
1975	−3,579	96	−3,934	102	157	—
1981	−3,543	−1,598	−16,439	14,012	486	−4
1983	13,574	−438	−2,752	15,974	792	−2
1985	9,197	−209	−5,092	14,049	455	−6
1986	4,323	1,255	−3,053	5,716	480	−75
1987	7,771	755	−1,544	8,038	592	−70
Total Latin America						
1970	−464	4,963	−9,020	1,657	1,938	−2
1975	−8,723	8,664	−23,943	4,060	2,475	21
1981	−7,744	15,080	−49,570	19,872	6,632	242
1983[b]	28,937	17,141	−15,926	21,985	5,783	−46
1985[b]	34,541	19,372	−13,649	22,593	6,282	−57
1986[c]	15,675	18,236	−17,061	9,661	4,732	107
South Korea						
1970	−1,148	−507	−446	−127	−67	−1
1975	−2,190	−1,097	452	−1,283	−273	11
1981	−4,798	−3,875	7,865	−7,603	−1,254	69
1983	−1,797	−2,947	8,867	−6,419	−1,184	−64
1985	−853	−2,763	10,067	−6,442	−1,451	−264
1986	3,131	−2,668	12,025	−4,424	−1,724	−78
1987	6,247	−3,490	17,448	−5,273	−2,380	−58

TABLE 12.7 (*cont.*)

Source: Joint ECLAC/UNIDO Industry and Technology Division based on United Nations, Commodity Trade Statistics, Statistical Papers: various years.

a See table 12.3 for the definition of these sectors.

b Panama and Dominican Republic not included.

c Panama, Dominican Republic, and Guatemala not included.

instance, the bulk of these resources flowed into the oil sector, while lesser amounts were channeled toward the manufacturing sector and toward increasing imports of consumer goods. Consumer goods imports also rose in Argentina. However, in both Brazil and South Korea, funds acquired via external credit were directed toward the manufacturing sector. Thus, despite superficial similarities in the *levels* of external borrowing undertaken by the Latin American NICs and South Korea, the varied *uses* of these resources by each country may have noteworthy implications for their long-term development patterns and their respective capacities for industrial growth.

Capital Flight

There are indications that capital flight at times has reached considerable levels in Argentina and Mexico but has been virtually nonexistent in Brazil and South Korea. While diverse aspects of economic policy (e.g., exchange controls and interest rates) may contribute to the presence or absence of capital flight, variations in the relationship between the state and the entrepreneurial sector also play a crucial role.

Despite obvious differences in the historical backgrounds of Brazil and South Korea, the public and private sectors in both countries enjoy a strategic relationship in which entrepreneurial activity is directed toward fulfillment of carefully defined national objectives. The entrepreneurial elites of Argentina and Mexico, however, have traditionally taken a rather jaundiced view toward such notions of "national responsibility." The case of Mexico appears especially problematic. There extensive capital flight attributable to the systemic erosion of confidence between the public and private sectors has been exacerbated by Mexico's geographical proximity to the United States. While the severity of this issue warrants further discussion, a more complete analysis lies beyond the scope of this paper (see Stallings, chap. 3, this volume).

Patterns of Entrepreneurial Leadership

A comparison of patterns of entrepreneurial leadership reveals four basic differences between South Korea and the Latin American NICs. First, somewhat like Japan, South Korea benefits from close linkages between the state and an influential group of national conglomerates. Although most major firms are highly diversified, public-private sector connections appear most important for the South Korean manufacturing sector. In South Korea, the ten major conglomerates generate nearly 25 percent of the national GDP, while the leading forty-six concerns account for 43 percent of the GDP. The private national conglomerates of Latin America contribute a significantly lower share of the GDP in the countries of that region, and their linkages with Latin American state agencies are not comparable to those enjoyed by South Korean firms.

Second, according to one account: "The financial system in the Republic of Korea at the beginning of the 1980s was largely the product of government initiatives. Except for the local banks and branches of foreign banks, financial institutions were either government-created, government-owned, or government-controlled by virtue of majority shareholding" (Asian Development Bank, 1984). Public development banks in Latin America, although relatively important, coexist with a stronger private financial sector than one finds in South Korea. It is these private institutions in Latin America that play the major role in short-term financial mediation.

Two additional differences warrant mention. The subsidiaries of TNCs appear central in shaping Latin American development, concentrating heavily on internal markets. TNCs exert a far less significant overall impact on the process of development in South Korea (see Stallings, chap. 3, this volume).

Fourth and finally, the NICs differ in terms of the participation of public enterprises in investment. Given the strong influence of the oil sector over the composite pattern of development, public enterprises like Petróleos Mexicanos (Pemex) may be most important in Mexico. However, such firms exhibit greater involvement in industrial activity in South Korea than in either Brazil or Argentina.

In sum, one can identify several regional differences in patterns of entrepreneurial leadership (see tables 12.8 and 12.9). In South Korea, efforts at self-sustaining economic growth are spearheaded by the interventionist planning of state agencies, in close consultation with a relatively small number of potent national conglomerates. The influence of TNC subsidiaries over this process of industrial leadership remains circumscribed within a few strongly export-oriented sectors.

However, Latin American NICs lack such "organic" institutional articulation. Instead, the distribution of industrial functions in Latin America allows TNCs to play leadership roles in many of the most dynamic sectors of the economy. While public enterprises assume responsibility for infrastructure in Latin America, private national industries are often confined

TABLE 12.8
Relative Importance of Different Types of Enterprise

	Argentina	Brazil	Mexico	South Korea
Direct foreign investment: stock (late 1970s) (US$ millions)	$5,489 (1983)	$13,000	$3,868	$737
Participation of TNCs in total value of production (manufacturing industries)	31% (1972)	44% (1977)	39% (1970)	11% (1975)
Participation of TNCs in manufactured exports	30 + % (1969)	43% (1969)	34% (1974)	27% (1978)
Public enterprises: share of total fixed investment	20% (1978–1980)	23% (1980)	29% (1978)	25% (1974–1977)
Contribution to GNP by national private conglomerates (1978): 10 largest 46 largest	 NA NA	 NA NA	 NA NA	 23% 43%

Sources: UNCTC (1983b); Sachs (1985); Kim (1985); CEPAL (1986).
Note: NA = Not Available.

TABLE 12.9
Percentage Share of State, Private National, and Foreign Enterprises: Total Sales, 1983

	Argentina			Brazil			Mexico		
	State Firms	Private National Firms	TNCs	State Firms	Private National Firms	TNCs	State Firms	Private National Firms	TNCs
Ten Largest Enterprises	45.1	7.1	47.8	59.3	11.2	29.5	83.7	14.2	2.1
Fifty Largest Enterprises	37.1	24.5	38.4	47.4	20.8	31.8	65.9	24.5	9.6

Sources: UNCTC (1983b); CEPAL (1986).

to less dynamic and less sophisticated sectors and to the production of services, including intermediate financial activities.

A SYNTHETIC COMPARISON OF DEVELOPMENT PATTERNS

For a more parsimonious comparison of the major Latin American countries and South Korea, we have focused on four aspects of their respective development experiences. These dimensions are identical to those used in the earlier comparison of Japanese and American development patterns: (1) the consumption pattern; (2) the degree of distributive equity; (3) the pattern of economic growth; and (4) the level of international competitiveness (see table 12.10). What can we conclude from this assessment of the Latin American and South Korean development patterns?

First, figure 12.2 indicates that the South Korean graph has characteristics similar to those of Japan: high dynamism, relatively equal income distribution, high competitiveness, and austere consumption. In contrast, the Argentinian graph markedly resembles that of the United States: lower levels of growth, competitiveness, *and* equity, combined with "exuberant" national consumption. Brazil and Mexico, like Argentina, exhibit higher levels of consumption than their East Asian counterpart. In addition, while Brazil and Mexico share with Argentina the experience of substantial distributive inequality, their growth rates are significantly higher than that of their southern neighbor. Nevertheless, despite its relatively equal distribution of income, South Korea's rate of growth dwarfs those of the Latin American NICs. Further, South Korea leads all Latin American nations in international competitiveness; only Brazil approaches the South Korean performance in this regard.

The identification and discussion of these patterns of development leads to an important conclusion: The experience of the United States has provided a "model" for Latin American elites, which has been "translated" and assimilated in the different countries of the region. Despite their considerable diversity, all major Latin American countries exhibit high levels of consumption (as measured by automobile density) relative to South Korea, along with a concomitant orientation toward production for the domestic market. Indeed, the Brazilian economy is characterized by a lower level of openness than that of the United States. Intraregional variations in dynamism and distributive equity may be attributable to (1) the differing sizes of the respective domestic markets, and (2) the different degrees of "social articulation," as shaped by distinctive sociohistorical processes.

It is interesting to note that, during the late 1970s, economic planners in both Brazil and Mexico sought to reformulate their industrial strategies in light of the lessons of the Japanese development experience. The

TABLE 12.10
Economic and Social Indicators of the NICs

	GNP Per Capita, Average Annual Growth Rate, 1960–1979[a]	Equity in Income Distribution: 40 percent Lowest Incomes/ 10 percent Highest Incomes	Automobiles per 1000 Inhabitants, 1980	Engineering Products: Exports/Imports, 1979–1980
Argentina	2.5	0.40 (1970)	109	0.35
Brazil	6.3[b]	0.14 (1972)	68	0.58
Mexico	2.8	0.24 (1977)	56	0.10
South Korea	7.2	0.61 (1976)	6	0.71

Sources: World Bank (1985); CEPAL (1984); UNCTC (1983b); United Nations (1980).
[a] Estimated by adjustment of an exponential function, using the least-squares method.
[b] 1965–1979.

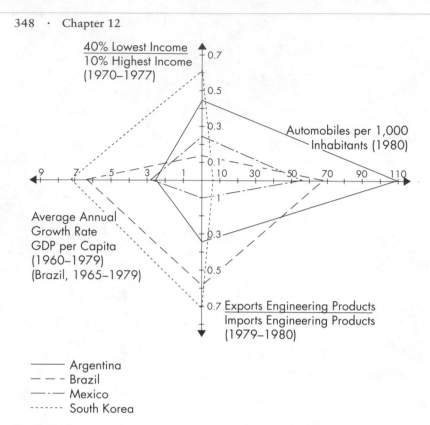

FIGURE 12.2
Strategic Profiles: Argentina, Brazil, South Korea, and Mexico.

(*Source*: Table 12.10.)

fruits of these efforts appear in the Second National Development Plan in Brazil and the Industrial Development Plan in Mexico. While policymakers in both countries intended to "complete" the Japanese production structure, they were unable to reproduce two elements crucial to the Japanese experience: (1) the condition of general socioeconomic equity, and (2) the historically conditioned leadership of Japanese entrepreneurs.

Finally, an analysis of the 1980–1985 period indicates that the area within the Latin American graphs has actually been reduced in most cases along the axes of dynamism, equity, and competitiveness. The relative improvement of Brazilian competitiveness in recent years constitutes the lone noteworthy exception to these trends.

Conclusion

Certainly Latin American nations vary considerably in a number of respects: level of dynamism, degree of socioeconomic articulation, availability of natural resources, size of domestic markets, organization and relative importance of the agricultural sector, and the legacy of the industrialization process. Despite such intraregional diversity, however, this paper has identified a single pattern of development common to the Latin American NICS. Four features are particularly important: (1) a consistent pattern of "exuberant" consumption; (2) industrial sectors oriented primarily toward the domestic market; (3) the insertion of national economies into the international system via trade in natural resources; and (4) the dubious leadership role played by national industry.

It is crucial to grasp one salient point: These four common features are *interrelated* and *mutually reinforcing*. Thus, one cannot understand the existence and reproduction of what has been termed here "showcase modernity" and the systematic orientation toward the domestic market without simultaneously considering the persistent weakness of the national entrepreneurial sector, and vice versa. On the other hand, the convergence of these three conditions helps to account for the fact that, even after several decades of industrialization, the international insertion of Latin American economies is based primarily upon natural resource exports.

Any attempt to formulate new industrialization strategies must therefore assume the interdependence of these factors and approach them as a totality. For instance, the implementation of policies that concentrate exclusively upon the need to open domestic markets could inadvertently intensify the effects of showcase modernity, weakening further the already frail domestic entrepreneurial sector and accentuating the importance of natural resources in Latin America's external economic relations.

On the other hand, efforts to strengthen the national entrepreneurial sector might focus on transferring the property of established enterprises to other economic actors, either through privatization or statization. However, such a strategy would likely sustain a pattern of national consumption that appears incompatible with economic growth. Given the negative net capital flows common in the region during the present period, this strategy could have unforeseen but critically important debilitating consequences.

In short, the experiences of Latin American countries—and others as well—suggest that successful development strategies must simultaneously address issues related to both (1) domestic social and economic articulation and (2) the mode of national insertion into the international economic order. Arguments that a more solid international insertion results from the partial exclusion of social groups and regions merely perpetuate an illusion. The latent social tensions that result from such strategies generate social and political instability and may therefore jeopardize the achievement of investment and growth.

However, concentration on internal articulation and distributive issues to the exclusion of broader concerns regarding international economic insertion may prove equally deleterious. This policy orientation can also foster political conflict due to the rising material expectations of the populace. Moreover, the improvement of living conditions requires a level of material resources available only through increased productivity. Such economic growth results from the incorporation of technical progress, which is itself stimulated via a solid insertion into the world economy.

The industrialization pattern that characterizes the contemporary Latin American NICs reflects the weakness of the "endogenous nucleus of technological dynamism" (ENTD) (see Fajnzylber, 1986). To modify the pattern of "showcase modernity" prevailing in Latin America requires the reinforcement and articulation of this ENTD, as well as the subsystems of goods and services of which it is comprised (Fajnzylber, 1983).

As noted above, the variegated expressions of the pattern of "showcase modernity" currently existing throughout the region result from the combination of *common* features—extensive consumption, production for domestic markets, international insertion via natural resources, and weak national entrepreneurial sector—with *distinctive* national social and industrial characteristics. Thus, any successful innovation in development policy must consider both these shared features and an array of distinctive national characteristics.

The Latin American NICs face the common challenge of increasing the area enclosed within their respective graphs (figure 12.2). However, each can best accomplish this by focusing on those areas that pose especially pressing problems. For instance, Argentina might well concentrate on competitiveness and dynamism, while Brazil could focus with benefit on equity-related issues. Mexican policymakers confront serious weaknesses in the areas of equity, competitiveness, and dynamism. In each of the regional NICs, however, an era of more austere consumption patterns appears essential.[7]

This analysis has demonstrated that East Asian countries have achieved higher levels of both economic growth and distributive equity than their Latin American counterparts. Recognition of the disparate performances of East Asian and Latin American NICs has fostered spirited discussion within the latter countries. Debates over development policies in Latin America have been "ideologized" in a way that parallels the recent "reindustrialization" debates in the United States noted earlier.

However, the interrelated character of those sets of structural features comprising regional development patterns makes clear the futility of any

---

[7] One should acknowledge an apparent inconsistency between these recommendations and recent trends: During the first half of the 1980s, the sole industrial sector exhibiting significant dynamism in the recuperation of the major Latin American economies was precisely that of automobile production.

effort to "reproduce" the East Asian experience in Latin America. While economic growth and equity are important goals in many developing countries, the Latin American NICs seek to accomplish these socioeconomic objectives within an institutional framework of political democracy. The importance of achieving consistency between economic objectives and resurgent democratic politics in Latin America can scarcely be overestimated.

Therefore, the purpose of this analysis of prevailing development patterns has *not* been to encourage the uncritical emulation of East Asian strategies by Latin American countries. Instead, the foregoing cross-regional comparison has sought to promote reflection on development realities in Latin America. The distinctive character of accumulated social needs and economic potentialities (i.e., the ENTD) in the major Latin American countries indicates the importance of formulating a regionally specific development model.

REFERENCES

Asian Development Bank. 1984. *Asian Development Review* 2, no. 2.

Badaracco, Joseph L., and David Yoffie. 1983. "Industrial Policy: It Cannot Happen Here." *Harvard Business Review* 61, pp. 96–105.

Bell, Daniel. 1979. "Communications Technology—For Better or for Worse." *Harvard Business Review* 57, pp. 20–45.

Birch, David L. 1981. "Who Creates Jobs?" *Public Interest* 65, pp. 3–14.

Blinder, Alvin S., Irving Kristol, and Wilbur J. Cohen. 1980. "The Level and Distribution of Economic Well-Being." In *The American Economy in Transition*, edited by Martin Feldstein. Chicago: University of Chicago Press.

CEPAL (Comisión Económica para América Latina). 1986. "Las Empresas Transnacionales en Argentina." *Estudios & Informes de CEPAL*, no. 56.

———. 1984. *Recent Problems of Latin American Industry: Reactivation and Long-Term Policies*. Santiago: CEPAL.

Fajnzylber, Fernando. 1986. "Democratization, Endogenous Modernization, and Integration: Strategic Choices for Latin America and Economic Relations with the United States." In *The United States and Latin America in the 1980s: Contending Perspectives on a Decade of Crisis*, edited by Kevin J. Middlebrook and Carlos Rico. Pittsburgh: University of Pittsburgh Press.

———. 1983. *La Industrialización Trunca de América Latina*. Mexico City: Nueva Imagen.

Feldstein, Martin, ed. 1980. *The American Economy in Transition*. Chicago: University of Chicago Press.

Graciarena, Jorge. 1976. "Poder y estilos de desarrollo: una perspectiva heterodoxa." *ECLAC Review*, first semester, pp. 173–93.

Hirschman, Albert. 1987. "The Political Economy of Latin American Development: Seven Exercises in Retrospection." *Latin American Research Review* 22, pp. 7–36.

Hirschman, Albert. 1973. "The Changing Tolerance for Income Inequalities in the Course of Economic Development." *Quarterly Journal of Economics* 87, no. 4, pp. 544–65.

Kim, Kwan S. 1985. "Industrial Policy and Industrialization in South Korea, 1961–1982." Working paper no. 39 (January). Kellogg Institute, University of Notre Dame.

OECD (Organization for Economic Cooperation and Development). 1986. *Productivity in Industry*. Paris: OECD.

Pinto, Anibal. 1976. "Notas sobre los estilos de desarrollo en América Latina." *ECLAC Review*, first semester, pp. 97–128.

President's Commission on Industrial Competitiveness. 1985. *Global Competition: The New Reality*. Vols. 1 and 2. Washington, D.C.: GPO.

Reich, Robert B. 1983. *The Next American Frontier: A Provocative Program for Economic Renewal*. New York: Penguin Books.

Sachs, Jeffrey. 1985. "External Debts and Microeconomic Performance in Latin America and East Asia." *Brookings Papers on Economic Activity*, no. 2. Washington, D.C.: Brookings Institution.

Schejtman, Alejandro. 1985. "Sistemas alimentarios y opciones de estrategia." *Pensamiento Iberoamericano*, no. 8, July–December.

Scherer, Frederic, ed. 1970. *Industrial Market Structure and Economic Performance*. Chicago: Rand McNally.

Scott, Bruce R. 1984. "National Strategy for Stronger U.S. Competitiveness." *Harvard Business Review* 62, pp. 77–91.

Sunkel, Osvaldo. 1981. *La Dimensión ambiental en los estilos de desarrollo de América Latina*. Santiago: CEPAL/PNUMA/ONU.

Thurow, Lester C. 1986. "Comment on *The Positive Sum Strategy: Harnessing Technology for Economic Growth*, edited by Ralph Landau and Nathan Rosenberg." *Scientific American* 225, no. 3, pp. 24–31.

UNCTC (United Nations Centre on Transnational Corporations). 1983a. *Transnational Corporations in the Automobile Industry*. New York: United Nations.

———. 1983b. *Transnational Corporations in World Development*. New York: United Nations.

United Nations. 1980. *Yearbook of National Accounts Statistics*, vol. 2 (International Tables). New York: United Nations

U.S. Department of Commerce. 1986. *U.S. Industrial Outlook, 1986*. Washington, D.C.: GPO.

U.S. Government. 1984. *Economic Report to the President, 1984*. Washington, D.C.: GPO.

World Bank. 1989. *World Development Report 1989*. New York: Oxford University Press.

———. 1986. *World Development Report 1986*. New York: Oxford University Press.

———. 1985. *World Development Report 1985*. New York: Oxford University Press.

CHAPTER 13

Reflections on Culture and Social Change

Ronald Dore

THESE "REFLECTIONS" began at a conference at which the papers in this volume were presented. It was supposed to be the usual final-session attempt to summarize the state of play, highlight the important insights, and send everybody home with a glow of satisfaction and achievement. Even then it wandered seriously from that task. Now, however, that the task has been so competently performed by Gary Gereffi in his introduction (chap. 1, this volume), I feel rather better entitled than I was then to add a few ideas by way of highly selective commentary on the issues discussed.

I begin with a rather tedious conceptual issue by noting that in a conference about "Development Strategies," very little was actually said about "strategies" as they were implicitly defined—as the mixture of forecasts and intentions and assumptions about probable causal sequences held by policy makers when they take economic decisions. It was not actually a concern of most of the contributors to the conference—Robert Wade (chap. 9, this volume) being a notable exception—to seek to establish by historical evidence the intentions of those who took policy decisions at particular points in time. Which is not to say that there was not a great deal of speculation on the matter. The chapters by Frederic Deyo, Robert Kaufman, and Tun-jen Cheng (this volume), for example, are predominantly concerned with charting the interest group pressures which it is *assumed* helped shape economic decisions. During the conference discussions, one heard remarks such as: "Was it that the automobile companies decided to come to Brazil? Or did the Brazilian government decide it needed to have an automobile industry? I *suspect* it was the former."

There would be value in research which sought to substitute hard historical evidence for these assumptions and suspicions—evidence from contemporary government plans and documents, and from oral history where government archives are not available. Since so much of the policy debate revolves around the question of what governments *can* do, hence what governments in the past have, or have not, "succeeded" in doing, it is as well to establish what, in the past, governments have thought they were trying to do.

If one did that, one would be in a position to answer the not uninteresting question: Do the economic decision makers in Latin America and East Asia over recent decades actually turn out to have been consciously following "strategies"? Or is what one might call the *War and Peace* version of events more appropriate—officials fumbling and stumbling from one decision to the next, reacting as pragmatically to the pressures and opportunities of the moment as Tolstoy's generals were? Gustav Ranis declared his hunch at one stage of the discussions that the latter was the more accurate view. He pointed out that the succession of pragmatic choices that constituted the New Deal was only called "the New Deal" afterward. Doubtless true, but once the New Deal name was affixed to the bundle of policies adopted in those years, it then became a discrete and graspable "strategy." It became available for thinking as a *gestalt*—a set of rationalized policy principles and instruments set in a general theoretical understanding about what policies should lead to what results. In exactly the same way, discussions in the development economics literature and academic conferences crystallize, post hoc, from the experiences of developing countries over recent decades, strategy bundles like those labeled import-substituting industrialization (ISI) and export-oriented industrialization (EOI) (however misleadingly!). It is unlikely that any of the planning offices of the countries we have been talking about would *today* be devoid of people who think and talk in these terms. But was it so fifteen or twenty years ago when the decisions whose consequences these chapters discuss were being taken? The world now moves faster than in the days of Keynes. His "practical men of affairs" in developing countries are not "victims of some long defunct economic theorist"; their influence comes (often with high leverage via places like the World Bank) from much more recent theorist generalizers distilling their patterns and their lessons (or seeking reinforcement for their prejudices) from the much more recent past.

This progressive process of making new concepts "available for thinking" does not only apply to whole strategies, of course. The distinction between durable and nondurable consumer goods which plays such a large part in the analyses of these chapters is not all that old in economics, for instance. The concept of industries in which one has (or can acquire) high, and industries in which one has low, dynamic comparative advantage is still looked on somewhat askance. A number of the categories in which East Asians do their thinking about sectors and their appropriate groupings for policy purposes (some of them adopted in these chapters) were invented in Japan and then spread, via the shared ideographic writing system, to Korea and Taiwan: "heavy and chemical," "high value-added branches of production," "information-intensive industries," etc.

PATTERNS

Categories, concepts, and whole-package strategies derive, then, from analysis of patterns of the past, and it is the substantive nature of the patterns, rather than strategies, which is the dominant subject matter of these chapters. The categories and strategy frames in which policy makers did their thinking and which thereby played some part in producing these patterns may be a matter of importance for the allocation of praises and blame, for attributing "success" or "failure." But for determining the categories in which policy makers will do their thinking tomorrow, they are not as important as the categories in which analysts like those represented in this book do their post hoc analysis of *patterns*.

What guides the analyst's search for patterns, the inevitably arbitrary decision to categorize this way rather than that—to include exchange rates, say, in the specification of a pattern and not the proportion of gross national product (GNP) spent on education or on research and development? In the first place, I suppose, what makes a pattern meaningful is its relevance to *valued* objectives. Much discussion of development is highly ideological. There are sharp divisions between those who believe that good can only come, and only good will come, from the unfettering of markets, and those who favor more structuralist explanations of how economies work, and more interventionist recipes for making them work better. Even if one can tell where most of the writers in this volume would end up if they had to topple one side of that fence or the other, the chapters are pleasantly free from passionate partisanship in this regard. There is a lot of common ground. But that is not to say that values are not important just because they are shared. For example, faster growth is universally assumed to be better than slower growth. A low Gini coefficient is universally referred to in these chapters as a better or "more favorable" distribution of income than a high one. (And this even by writers who would doubtless want to argue that equality should be subordinated to distributive justice and incentives if a rapid approach to equality in their own society began to threaten their own incomes.)

So what are these shared, assumed objectives? Fajnzylber (chap. 12, this volume) lists eight dimensions of evaluation of country performance. They can perhaps, without rising to too high a level of generality, be collapsed into three: (1) dynamic growth with a rising position in the international per-capita-income-and-technological-sophistication league; (2)

relative equality of income distribution and social cohesion; and (3) national integrity and independence. Those are pretty much shared values within the development studies community—the community of meaningful-pattern-seekers. The divisions come in the weighting: the neoclassical right puts more emphasis on the first than on the second two, and within the first on income rather than technological sophistication measures; the left, roughly vice versa.

The weighting one assigns to these objectives is likely to affect the shape of the pattern one draws out of the economic record, out of the time-series trend lines found in the statistical yearbooks. It determines what one thinks it important to include. Whether or not the division between locally and externally owned industrial capital is important and a necessary element in the specification of a "pattern" or strategy package—or the importance attached to the distribution of income, or the distribution of wealth, or the deviation of actual and shadow interest rates, or the sectoral targeting of subsidies and credit allocations—depends in part on the breadth of their ramifications (the extent to which they affect other variables); but in part, also, on which policy objectives are valued and the directness of the relation of the variable in question to those objectives.

And therein, also, of course, lies the claim of such discussions to "usefulness"—usefulness to the people who actually have to make policies in developing countries. The abstract, bloodless planner envisaged in the early planning literature may have given way to the more or less corrupt civil servant, too preoccupied with immediate issues to think much about the long-term future, vulnerable to the arbitrary whims of political masters, buffeted this way and that by the crosswinds of interest group influence. But one should not go too far in the other direction. The people who make policy in developing countries, in addition to wanting to please their tyrannical minister, or to solve their immediate balance-of-payments crisis, or to get away from the office early enough for a game of tennis, or to make a million dollars, are *also* often keen to see their country grow richer and more respected in the world. And insofar as the values they hold—and the objectives derived from those values—coincide with those we also take as a starting point, then the patterns and prescriptions we derive from them can have a claim to "usefulness."

The prescriptions can only come from understanding the causal sequences within the patterns, and it is of course here, in the why, rather than in the what, dimension, that the papers of this volume offer a variety of speculative explanations. Let us note in passing that, as any free will/determinism controversy usually concludes, it is a good thing that the explanations have to remain in the realm of speculation. If it were possible, to use Ranis's terminology (chap. 8, this volume), to "endogenize" the explanation for differences between South Korea and Taiwan on the one hand and Brazil and Mexico, or Mexico and Columbia, on the other—to explain them solely in terms of given initial conditions like resource endowment or size—then there would be no role for policy choice, and no possibility of "usefulness" for the analyst.

THE EXPLICANDUM

What then is the difference in patterns (as between East Asian and Latin American countries) which needs to be explained? (And which it is important to explain precisely because on all three of the dimensions into which we collapsed Fajnzylber's list—the growth dynamic, equality and cohesion, and national independence—East Asia seems to have done better than Latin America in recent years.) One thing that becomes clear from these chapters is that the answer is not a sharp opposition between an ISI pattern and an EOI pattern.

The common denominator of contrasting patterns which seems to emerge from these chapters might be painted, with the broadest brush, rather as follows. Both East Asian and Latin American countries start by substituting domestic production for imports of nondurable consumer goods, financing the process by exports of primary products or by foreign borrowing, and using a variety of infant-industry protectionist measures to aid the process. East Asian countries try to phase out the protection, though, so that the new industries get world-competitive and can start to export in order to earn the foreign exchange for further phases of ISI—in intermediates and capital goods as well as consumer durables. Latin American countries, however, are likely to continue the protection too long. Consequently, they fail to reach world-competitive levels, therefore achieving less in the way of growth in manufactured exports, they emphasize consumer durables rather than capital goods and intermediates in their further industrialization efforts, and they continue to finance the process by primary product exports and foreign borrowing.

COMPETING/COMPLEMENTARY EXPLANATIONS

Among the possible explanations for the difference in patterns is, of course, the possibility that they were following different strategies: South Korea and Taiwan run by graduates of the University of Chicago and the University of California at Berkeley, devotees of moralized marketism;

Latin America under the sway of the United Nations Economic Commission for Latin America (ECLA) structuralists and dependentistas who are only slowly learning the limitations of state interventions. But there seems little indication that Latin American policy makers were in fact anti-EOI in the sense of aiming for autarkic delinking and a declining export/GNP ratio—as was certainly the case with both Indian and Chinese policy elites at certain times.

But if not strategies, then perhaps models? Fajnzylber's suggestions (chap. 12, this volume) about the respective influence of the Japanese and American models—the former a model of collective effort to conquer foreign markets and move up the international pecking order of economic power, the latter a model of consumption patterns for individuals to strive for—are compelling.

Equally persuasive are Ranis's suggestions (chap. 8, this volume) that differences in country size and resource endowments must have been a powerful influence. The East Asian pattern requires tough action by a strong state—squeezing new industries into competitiveness quickly by the withdrawal of protection, insisting on growing savings to replace foreign borrowing, etc. The Latin American pattern is more of a drifter's pattern, and countries with a substantial cushion of natural resources can more easily afford to drift.

But that difference between drifter states and purposeful states must surely have to be explained in terms other than simply the ability to get by through drifting. There does seem to be a difference in what one might call the "will to develop"—the salience of the achieving of sustained growth among the policy objectives of the people who were in a position to take policy decisions. It may be true of Taiwan and South Korea too that most bureaucrats and politicians are predominantly concerned with immediate trouble-shooting—but not *quite* as true as in Latin America. They may be just as preoccupied with solving an immediate foreign exchange crisis; but in choosing among alternative methods of dealing with that problem, the effects of those alternatives on the long-run prospects for growth and for national independence, and possibly also for internal cohesion, would, I suggest, be more likely to be taken into consideration in the East Asian states. That is what I mean by a difference in the "will to develop."

Why should there be a difference in this regard between countries in the two regions? One suggested reason is that both South Korea and Taiwan had a sense of needing to prove themselves against immediately threatening quondam-compatriot states. And it is worth remembering that, in the 1950s and early 1960s in particular, North Korea had a strong growth record. It was a worthy opponent for a then stumbling South Korean regime. Taiwan's opposite number, the People's Republic of China, also seemed to hold some promise of rapid development in the same period.

But the factors conditioning the "will to develop" are probably more complex than that. Recall the essay by Alexander Gerschenkron (1962) in which he first speculated about what he called the "advantages of backwardness"—about the specific differentiating characteristics of late developers. These advantages were primarily two. First, the late developer could learn from the mistakes of the pioneers; it could *start* with institutional arrangements of which the pioneers only discovered the virtue long after they had institutionalized less suitable arrangements. Second, there was the *sense* of backwardness, shared by the intellectuals and political leaders of the late-developing country, which provided a charter for state action to mobilize resources and to take initiatives and risks. There are a number of reasons why this sense of being behind and the urgency of the desire to catch up might have been stronger among the leaders and intellectuals of Asian countries than in Latin America.

To begin with, cultural differences surely were important. What gives intellectuals in a country a sense of their nation's backwardness vis-à-vis foreign countries is often their own personal experiences in international settings. People carry into such occasions—particularly those in which they are primarily known by their national label—"our Ruritanian delegate" rather than "Mr. Hodge"—something of the status ranking that their nation holds in the international pecking order. Non-European nations, in a world that for two centuries has been dominated by European or at least Eurocentric powers, are further down the pecking order than any rating by economic strength or performance could justify.

I recall a telling story in a Japanese magazine about the Japanese prime minister, Takeo Miki, at one of the economic summits at Rambouillet in the late 1970s. Rambouillet apparently induces dinner table conversation of a classical kind. Valéry Giscard d'Estaing talked of some particular endeavor of the summit nations as being like the task of Sisyphus. Five of the other six present knew all about Sisyphus rolling his stone everlastingly up the hill, but not Miki. So there had to be a pause for a long explanation of who the unfortunate was and what he was doing with the stone and why it was important and well known. This made the prime minister, it is recorded, feel so much an outsider that he decided he would have to get a book on classical mythology before he went to the next summit. It is a trivial story, but it does illustrate the way in which the sense of outsiderness can translate into perceptions of one's position in the international pecking order. And given the nature of the "international community," it is likely to do so more poignantly for people from East Asia than for men and women from Latin America who share the same Mediterranean-rooted culture as the dominant powers—and frequently, and with justice, consider themselves to be more sophisticated and authentic exponents of it than some of their more crass counterparts from neighboring northern countries.

It is a related element of this same contrast that Latin American industrialization started much earlier. It started, albeit in more restricted enclaves of those societies, in much the same way as industrial growth in the pioneer industrial countries—that is to say, as a result of the self-interested entrepreneurial initiatives of individual people, rather than as a result of the actions of governments. And it had, within those enclaves, reached world levels. Latin America, in the 1950s, had heart surgeons who were as good as heart surgeons anywhere else; it had poets winning Nobel Prizes for work which fell squarely within European traditions. In that sense, quite apart from personal sophistication and aplomb in international settings, Latin Americans had less cause to feel a sense of backwardness about the standing of their nations, either.

The enclave nature of Latin America's keeping up with the leading powers was also important. There was a much more distinct differentiation between the Europeanized enclaves of the towns and the countryside than was ever found within the Asian countries—even in the Southern cone, and *a fortiori* in the northern, less homogeneous areas of Central America or Mexico with their racially mixed populations. Felix (1986) has recently traced one of the economic consequences of this division, combined with what used to be called "cultural dependency." The consuming upper classes of Japan, South Korea, and China created a flourishing artisan sector to furnish their indigenous forms of conspicuous and luxury consumption, which only later and secondarily came to be supplemented by imports. When industrial growth began to create and enrich a new bourgeoisie, it retained much of those older life-styles. Hence, the multiplier effects (and income-equalizing effects) in expanding the artisan, cottage-industry sector were considerable. Upper-class life-styles in Latin America, by contrast, had always been much more import-dependent, and, with the progress of industrialization, became more so. Hence, a lower multiplier effect, greater un- and under-employment, greater inequality.

To return to the theme of the "sense of backwardness" and the drive to catch up, that division was also an important conditioning factor in the development of a sense of nationhood, which is, after all, a precondition for any sense that "one's nation" is backward. For example, I suspect that a good many Japanese doctors, or even economists, would feel a lot more at ease sitting down for an evening's drinking with a Japanese farmer than with an American doctor, or economist. By contrast, a Mexican doctor, I suspect, would feel more comfortable sitting down with the American doctor than he would with an "indio" peasant—and be quite happy to swap stories with his American friend about the funny and incomprehensible ways of peasants, rather than feeling obliged to defend his countryman against the American's disparagement. In other words, the national bond is weak enough to be easily overcome by the occupational bond.

These factors count, not only because they affect the extent to which economic development will be a salient concern of policy makers, but also because they affect the likelihood that the policy of the government will be accepted as legitimate—that it will be believed to be in the *national* interest, and not some conspiracy to benefit a sectional interest group. Where there really is a sense of the national interest, there is more likely to be outrage at corruption and hence more likelihood of keeping the incidence of corruption down. And that surely must be counted as on the whole a good thing, even if an austere absence of corruption does sometimes frighten foreign investors away—as the Singapore bureaucracy is sometimes said to drive foreign businessmen into the arms of the more easygoing Malaysians.

The sense of a shared, overriding national interest is also important for the *effectiveness* of policy. Wade's chapter (this volume) suggests the conditions under which bureaucratic initiatives can be an effective means of catalyzing hesitant private-sector decisions—when the bureaucracy is generally admired, if it is recognized as having more information than business firms, etc. One might add: and if a shared national consciousness gives bureaucrat and businessman a shared perception of national problems—if it is common ground between them that the shortage of foreign exchange, say, is a real problem for both of them and all their compatriots too. In discussing, as Kaufman and Cheng (chaps. 5 and 6, respectively, this volume) have done, the much greater strength of pressure group demands on Latin American than on East Asian governments, the prescription is usually drawn: seek, therefore, the insulation of state from society. But the *degree* to which such insulation is required depends on the extent to which those who can exert pressures on the state apparatus share the objectives and perceptions of the bureaucrats.

Many of the chapters in this book have charted the differences in this insulation dimension—in the extent and intensity of interest group demands on government. They point to a number of clearly important factors: the size and social/cultural diversity of the country, the traditional religious bases for social organization, the cohesion of the military forces in their exercise of martial law, traditions of populist politics, the influence of welfare state ideologies, etc. There is another possible factor worth mentioning: the relative social prestige attaching to the bureaucrat on the one hand and the politician on the other. There is a striking difference in this regard between, say, Britain and the United States on the one hand, and Japan on the other. Japan became a meritocracy long before it became a democracy. For two or three generations, elite bureaucrats (whose elitism was guaranteed by the rigorous process of educational selection they had undergone) graduated, when they had accumulated enough seniority with merit, to the level of statesmen with only the briefest of interludes of playing—halfheartedly—the role of wheeling, dealing, brokering and persuading politician. The Anglo-Saxon countries became democracies—made politicians out of their leaders and leaders out of their politicians—long before they began to adopt meritocratic methods of selecting their public servants.

Taiwan and South Korea, marrying the Confucian traditions of the scholar-official (which they shared with Japan) to the modern recruitment and training methods acquired in the Japanese colonial period, also started as meritocratic authoritarian bureaucracies (at least if one counts post-Rhee as the start in the case of South Korea) and are only gradually becoming democracies. As in France, bureaucrats who owe their legitimacy to their youthful educational achievements have a head start over politicians in claiming to arbitrate between conflicting interests in society in ways which are consonant with the national interest (although competition in France from politicians has been a good deal stronger for a good deal longer). Indeed, bureaucrats also have a head start over the military men who breeze in and claim to take over after each periodic coup.

CULTURE AND ECONOMIC PERFORMANCE

It is these elements of culture that are at once the hardest to pin down and the most important to grasp if one wants convincing explanations of national differences in economic performance. Thanks to Protestantism and the capitalist spirit, there once was a flourishing industry in tracing the various growth potentials of Protestantism and Catholicism and Islam and Hinduism. All too often it was seen as a matter of finding the logical consonance between the doctrines of those faiths as they might be summarized in a textbook of comparative religion and certain kinds of economic behavior. But the connection between Confucianism and the patterns of East Asian development is not like that. It is much more a matter of cultural characteristics: attitudes to authority, the balance between dutifulness and hedonism in personal life-plans, the social cohesion of face-to-face groups, and levels of interpersonal trust. These are as loosely connected with the *expounded* doctrines of professional Confucianists as individualism is with Christianity.

There is, in fact, very little that is explicitly about culture in these chapters. In the conference discussions, mention of cultural factors was often hesitant and quasi-apologetic. This is partly, perhaps, a matter of the diffidence of the "soft" social scientist toward colleagues in "harder" disciplines. A "savings propensity" can be derived from time-series or cross-sectional budget data, whereas an imputation of "ascetic frugality" has to be put together from anecdotes.

But it is more than softness and hardness, too. The dominant neoclassical paradigm of the economist is about human society. It rests on the assumption that in all respects relevant to the issues discussed in this book, human beings are alike everywhere. They may contingently have different endowments of physical or human capital, but in motivational structures, human nature anywhere is much the same. Hence, given a similarity of initial conditions as measured by the economic indicators, all one needs is the correct instruments and policies (i.e., the free-market framework) and, bingo: the desired response is assured. It is hard to suppose that anybody believes exactly that, but a lot of economic writing is only intelligible on such assumptions.

A second reason for reluctance to talk about culture may be the fear of appearing racist. Talk of Confucian culture may all too easily be seen to be code talk for Mongolian genes. Genes indeed may have something to do with the matter, but whether one believes it inadmissible and racist to entertain that possibility or not has nothing to do with the possible effects of national cultures on economic performance. One should not throw away with the bath water of racism all the healthy baby hypotheses about the importance for economic growth of the "need for achievement," "empathy," "trust in people," "future-orientation," etc., which were so earnestly discussed in the modernization conferences of the 1960s. "Modernization" may still be an unfashionable concept, if not quite the dirty word it was in the early 1970s, but the importance of the issues that were addressed in its name has not diminished.

Let me try to make explicit some of the values and personality characteristics which seem to be "desirable" in the sense that their presence in a majority, or a large proportion, of a population would seem to be conducive to good national economic performance (as measured in the terms suggested earlier). The importance of many of them is implicitly assumed in a number of the chapters, but note that not all desirable characteristics need to be universal. Not everyone has to be a risk-taking entrepreneur capable of inspired leadership. Dutiful followership is also required—and probably in rather larger quantities.

Some cultural characteristics show up clearly enough in the figures. Underlying the tendency, charted in Stallings (chap. 3, this volume), for the Latin American countries to increase, and for the East Asian countries to decrease, their foreign indebtedness over time is a difference in the level and movement of domestic, including household, savings. The capacity to defer gratification—not just to prefer two pots of jam next week to one pot today, but the propensity, also, to calculate the possibility of actually getting two pots of jam next week, rather than acting on immediate impulse—must be relevant to the explanation. Differences between the two regions in consumption patterns and income elasticities of demand respectively for food and for consumer durables which Felix (1986) has recently dissected—differences which have a strong bearing on these economies' marginal propensity to import—would also seem to be rooted in differences in values and, Felix suggests, historical differences in upperclass living styles.

Other differences which one would expect to be no less important are not easily deducible from any available time-series. An example is the sense of a duty to keep promises—of importance for the secure reliability of contract, a precondition, also, for creating the kind of trust which encourages the taking of risks. No economy can run efficiently if more than a tiny minority of contracts need the courts for their enforcement. That "sense of dutifulness" is also related to the work ethic and to honesty, which have to do with corruption in government. Whatever one thinks about the ability of civil servants to pick winners, it cannot be more efficient for their credit allocations to go to their friends rather than to the potential winners they publicly declare themselves to have picked. Whether 95 percent of the subsidies are allocated by objective criteria to firms in the targeted industries, or only 50 percent, is bound to make a difference.

TECHNOLOGY

There is one other cultural characteristic that I do not recall coming across in the earlier modernization literature, and that is what might be called the inability to tolerate black boxes without wanting to take them apart—the sort of drive for intellectual mastery that makes a man or woman uncomfortable to have to use machines whose workings they do not in principle understand—and even more uncomfortable if the only people who do understand and can repair the machine are foreigners.

Most economic discussions of the growth of supply-side capacity in the newly industrializing countries (NICs) revolve around measures of capital accumulation on the one hand, and school and college enrollment figures as proxies for human capital accumulation on the other. Both have serious defects and measures of what really counts. Let us take the second first.

Technology transfer is basically a matter of learning, and enrollments as a proxy measure of human capital accumulation are a poor measure of the efficiency of the learning process. The really important part of learning for industrial development is the learning that takes place on the job. It takes place best in societies where university graduation is seen as marking the beginning of a process of learning, not—to sighs of self-satisfaction all around—its end. A recent survey of Japanese technologists included the question: "How long was it after you got out of the university before you realized that what you learned there didn't have much relevance?" The average of the answers was one-and-a-half years. Perhaps the more significant thing is that nobody challenged the premises of the question.

Technology transfer is not a simple all-or-nothing process. When a new plant is bought, and the embodied technological knowledge with it, it is one thing to learn to run the plant efficiently in normal operation. It is a significantly different thing to be able fully to repair and maintain the plant with one's own indigenous resources. It is yet another thing to understand enough about the plant, and about the scientific principles which underlie its design, to be able to reproduce it, and another thing again to be able to reproduce it with significant modifications derived from the experience of running it. All that learning takes place faster in societies with a higher density of people who suffer from the "intolerance of black boxes" syndrome. My impression from descriptive literature and businessman talk—perhaps there are survey data but I do not know of them—is that that density is rather higher among the products of East Asian universities than among the products of the more status-preoccupied higher education systems of Latin America—or of Europe, for that matter.

Finally, a word about technology and the other major measure of growth of supply-side capacity—capital accumulation. Investment figures need to be broken down carefully before they can begin—and then only can begin—to take account of those changes in levels of technological sophistication which have in fact so preoccupied policy makers in the Asian NICs. This pattern is exemplified by frequent discussions of the need to move to higher value-added branches of production, reinforced in Singapore, for example, by pushing wages up in order to accelerate the process. This concern is partly a matter of retaining export market shares in the face of competition from countries with even greater low-wage cost advantages. But partly it is also a matter of national pride; in an increasingly technology-conscious world, how close a country can claim to be to the high-tech frontiers comes to be an ever-stronger element in determining its "international standing." (Consider the current American neurosis about being overtaken by the Japanese.)

Meaningful pattern seekers need to design new breakdowns for capital investment figures in order to capture these differences. And the same applies to the figures for exports and imports. As is shown by the ability of the Japanese to retain their American markets recently in the face of a drastic shift in exchange rates and price competitiveness, the difference between predominantly price-sensitive low-tech manufactured exports and predominantly quality-sensitive high-tech exports is of growing significance in the world economy. It is especially important to the resource-poor export economies of East Asia as they seek their survival strategies in an increasingly protectionist world.

CONCLUSION

I cannot think of any central theme to summarize by way of rounding off this ramble around the issues posed by the Latin American/East Asian contrast, unless it be something like the following. Endogenize this factor, endogenize that. Show how, given the resource conditions, given a certain set of historical circumstances, this upturn in imports, that pattern of investment—even that policy decision to liberalize or impose controls—could not have been other than they were. It is still the case that the developing world is full of people with the illusion of free will, trying to understand their country's situation and trying (as well as acting in all kinds of self-interested ways) to choose a set of policies which will, by their lights, improve it. There is a lot to be said for anything which genuinely helps them either to better conceptualize their choices, or to be more self-consciously aware of the way their own choices are constrained by their circumstances and conditioned by their backgrounds—and so to choose between those constraints and influences which they accept and endorse, and those for which they wish to discount. Insofar as books like this one do that, they have a useful role beyond their primary function of providing entertainment and stimulation to academic puzzle solvers.

References

Felix, David. 1986. "Import Substitution and Late Industrialization: Latin America and Asia Compared." Working paper no. 97. Department of Economics, Washington University, St. Louis, Mo.

Gerschenkron, Alexander. 1962. *Economic Backwardness in Historical Perspective*. Cambridge: Harvard University Press.

CHAPTER 14

Explaining Strategies and Patterns of Industrial Development

Christopher Ellison and Gary Gereffi

THE PATHS of industrialization followed by the Latin American and East Asian NICs have been shaped by a diverse array of international and domestic forces. This volume offers a number of conclusions about how the strategies and patterns of industrial development have evolved in response to initial factor endowments, historical events, external shocks, political choices, the interplay of domestic interest groups, and available economic ideas and cultural traditions in each of these societies. These interpretations not only advance our understanding of industrial processes in the cross-regional set of societies in question, but they also suggest new directions for future comparative research in the political economy of development.

The findings in this volume can be synthesized along two broad dimensions: first, the *kinds of explanations* used by the authors; and second, the *scope of comparative generalizations* that can be derived from the chapters. Our purpose here is to use these two dimensions to provide a more integrated account of what we have learned about industrial development in Latin America and East Asia.

Our first task is to order in a systematic way the explanatory variables used in this volume. The degree of rigidity decreases as one moves from the structural determinants of development outcomes at the world-system and national levels to more proximate explanatory factors at the institutional and cultural levels that reflect a greater degree of choice by social actors. We begin with global conditions, major historical events, and national factor endowments; then we move to the level of domestic political, social, and economic institutions and their networks; and finally we examine factors that are closest to the behavior of individuals, such as currently available ideologies, values, beliefs, and incentives.

This is primarily a heuristic framework for discussing the determinants of development patterns and strategies in the Latin American and East Asian NICs. The most aggregated levels of explanation act as parameters or structural "boundary conditions" that affect the choice of national "development strategies" by state elites. Development strategies are comprised of sets of industrial policies that shape a country's relationship to the global economy and that allocate resources among domestic industries and major social groups. Successful industrial policies must be responsive to the institutional and cultural contexts of specific countries, and thus development strategies are domestically rooted. Policy appropriate for one kind of economy cannot be transferred to a radically different kind of economy. National development strategies, in turn, affect a country's "development pattern," which includes: a nation's leading industries, the degree to which these industries are inwardly or outwardly oriented, and the major economic agents that implement and sustain development (see Gereffi, chap. 1, this volume).

Our second task, after outlining this explanatory framework, is to loosely organize the findings from the chapters into three sorts of generalizations: (1) patterns of development that are common to the NICs in both Latin America and East Asia; (2) development outcomes that vary between the two regions, but are basically the same for the NICs within each region; and (3) aspects of the development experience of the NICs that may be unique to one country or reflect subregional rather than interregional variation.

Our broadest hypothesis is that those factors operating at the international or country-specific "initial conditions" levels of analysis, such as global economic trends, geopolitical alliances, natural resource endowments, and domestic market size, will be most useful in accounting for broad commonalities and some cross-regional patterns of variation among the NICs. Consideration of the domestic institutional arrangements and social structures of the NICs, on the other hand, should yield a richer picture of national industrial diversity and help us to explain points of subregional variation in industrial trajectories.

Instead of presenting these generalizations in a mechanical way, we prefer to embed them in our review of the main substantive arguments that can be made within each level of explanation or that serve to bridge levels of explanation. This synthesis will help to advance our historical and comparative insights about development in these two dynamic regions.

LINKING MACRO AND MICRO LEVELS OF ANALYSIS

The comparative research undertaken in this volume has several advantages in terms of its ability to produce useful generalizations. These are studies of the "small N" variety (i.e., a few cases, rather than one or many) where the authors are intimately familiar with the countries under investigation, the cases are drawn from the same bounded set (Latin

American and East Asian NICs), and the analyses typically combine historical interpretation of significant social phenomena with a search for broader causal explanations.

Many other factors related to macrosocial comparative research confound our attempts to unravel the causal complexity of the development patterns at hand, however (see Ragin, 1987, chap. 2). First, outcomes of interest to social scientists rarely have a single cause. Second, the causal arguments related to large-scale change usually are *combinatorial* and/or *conjunctural* in nature. In other words, it is the intersection of various conditions in time and space that produces a given outcome. Several different combinations of circumstances might produce the same emergent phenomenon, so there may be no necessary or sufficient conditions for an outcome of interest. Third, a particular cause may have opposite effects depending on the context. Finally, the limited number and variety of our cases impose a necessary indeterminacy to our analysis, since all the relevant variables can neither be measured nor controlled as easily as in a simple laboratory experiment.

Faced with this challenge, we have opted for a multilevel analytical framework that combines several kinds of explanations: (1) those that cite features of a larger unit in which our cases are embedded (e.g., the world-economy); (2) those that cite general features of our cases (e.g., natural resource endowments, the role of the state, national industrial structure); and (3) those that cite unique qualities of our cases (e.g., Confucian or Hispanic cultures, or the ethnic conflict between the Mainlanders and the native Taiwanese in Taiwan) (see Ragin, 1989). The four levels of explanation in our framework are: the world-system level, the national level, the institutional level, and the organizational level. These levels are *nested* in the sense that each outer (or more macro) level conditions the ones that follow it, analogous to a set of Chinese boxes. The framework is *hierarchical* in that the primary direction of causality is from international structures to a variety of conditions at the national level; to institutions and organizations at the subnational level; and finally to ideologies, values, and so on at the cultural level which most directly motivates the behavior of individuals. All of these levels are subject to some degree of choice and change over time, however, and there often is reverse causation (although less pronounced and temporally lagged) from the lower levels to the upper ones. (For similar broad-based efforts at explaining state strategies and development patterns, see Haggard, 1989; Kim, 1989; and Shapiro and Taylor, 1989.)

The most encompassing level of explanation in our "nested hierarchy" is the world-system. Following Wallerstein (1979) and others, we distinguish two main components of the world-system: the world-economy and the interstate system. The impact of the *world-economy* on national development outcomes can be seen most clearly by focusing on four kinds of transnational economic linkages (TNELs): foreign aid, foreign trade, direct foreign investment, and foreign loans. These TNELs are the key external economic resources used to finance national development. The availability of TNELs can facilitate the pursuit of particular development strategies, while the absence of these resources limits the choice of national policymakers. In addition, the use of TNELs to link nations to the world-economy can strengthen as well as weaken domestic institutions in a variety of ways (see Gereffi and Wyman, 1989).

The *interstate system* affects national development at both the global and regional levels of analysis. A key dimension of the interstate system is the degree of hegemony that prevails in a given time period. With regard to the Latin American and East Asian NICs, one of the most important shifts is the rise of the United States to hegemonic prominence in the two decades following World War II, and then the emergence of contending political and economic powers that challenge American hegemony. The response of the United States to communist nations in the Cold War period was a critical factor shaping the policies of the United States toward the East Asian NICs in the 1950s, while the relatively recent rise of Japan and West Germany as economic powers, and the reintegration of China into the international system, have altered the options of the NICs in the past two decades.

At the national level, certain conditions are relatively immutable or *static*, such as country size, resource endowments, and geographical location. Economists have long argued that foreign trade is much more important for small economies than for large ones. The Latin American NICs, with their abundant natural resources and large domestic markets, had some structural advantages that made secondary ISI feasible. The East Asian NICs, on the other hand, had few natural resources and relatively small markets, which limited their options and pushed them in the direction of EOI. In addition, the geographical proximity of nations to external markets, ocean ports, or military rivals has a strong impact on viable development options. Other factors at the national level are more *dynamic*, such as indigenous social structure (e.g., class structure and demography), political regimes (e.g., authoritarian or democratic), and the prevailing economic system (e.g., capitalism or socialism). Although these initial conditions do not fully determine policy choices and development outcomes, they represent significant opportunities and constraints that shape a country's linkage with the international economy.

A variety of political, economic, and social *institutions* have been analyzed in this volume. Of particular importance is the state, which has been dealt with in two ways: first, as an institution that generates and implements development strategies and specific economic policies that help to steer the national economy; and second, as a complex organization with various ministries, public officials, technocrats, and state enterprises falling under its jurisdiction. The issue of state autonomy refers to how the social bases of the state as an organization shape or constrain its actions and policy outcomes.

There are other economic and social *organizations*, in addition to government agencies, that are important determinants of development patterns in the NICs. Various chapters in this volume have dealt with the impact of local private firms, transnational corporations, and state enterprises on outcomes ranging from national export performance to the ability of the state to implement industrial policy. Similarly, the presence or absence of labor unions and other popular sector organizations has shaped the implementation of development strategies in Latin America and East Asia. Relevant social organizations include the family, community organizations, and class-based associations.

Finally, our explanatory framework includes a set of historical, cultural, and social network dimensions that cuts across the world-system, national, institutional, and organization levels. The development paths of the Latin American and East Asian NICs have been affected by a wide range of historical events such as economic depressions, wars and revolutions, trade and investment cycles, oil shocks, and debt crises. Each of these events calls for major adjustments by the NICs. The effectiveness of the responses by specific countries varies, however, and can only be understood by moving to the national and subnational levels of analysis.

The sociocultural factors are particularly important because they include the most proximate determinants of individual behavior, such as *ideas*, which are usually taken to include ideology, but also refer to the kinds of economic models employed by policymakers; *incentives*, which shape the individual's calculations of the costs and benefits of acting in a certain way; cultural *values*; and a variety of *social networks* based on kinship, ethic, and religious ties. These networks shape economic behavior (e.g., subcontracting relationships or export networks) as well as political outcomes (e.g., the social coalitions that form to support or oppose certain development strategies). Culture operates at several different levels of analysis. There are cultural patterns at the level of national traits (see Fajnzylber and Dore, chaps. 12 and 13, this volume); the legacy of historical events influences the behavior of political and economic elites (see Kaufman, Cheng, and Ranis, chaps. 5, 6, and 8, this volume); and culture is also a factor at the popular level (Deyo, chap. 7, this volume).

The remainder of this chapter uses this multilevel framework to synthesize the major conclusions of the various contributors to this volume. We show how world-system factors and country-specific conditions constrain but do not fully determine the options of national decision makers

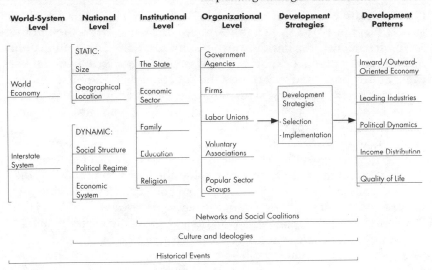

World-System Level	National Level	Institutional Level	Organizational Level	Development Strategies	Development Patterns

FIGURE 14.1
Macro-Micro Links: A Nested Hierarchy.

in the Latin American and East Asian NICs. We focus on the transitions or break points between development strategies, where it is important to distinguish between two different processes: the reasons why certain phases of industrialization come to an end and the factors that determine the choice of a subsequent strategy. Finally, we highlight the ways in which domestic institutions, social coalitions, networks, and culture condition the evolving implementation of development strategies once they have been selected.

WORLD-SYSTEM DYNAMICS

The world-system level of analysis is the most encompassing perspective in the social sciences, since it includes both a long historical view as well as attention to the interplay between the *world-economy* and the *interstate system* (see Wallerstein, 1979; Cumings, 1989; Arrighi, 1990). The various ways in which the external environment has shaped paths of industrial development in Latin America and East Asia remains a subject of intense debate. Several of the contributions to this volume shed new light on the complexities of this issue.

The impact of world-system dynamics on the paths of industrialization in the NICs can be summarized as follows. The initial impetus for ISI in both regions was a result of "situational imperatives" caused by profound change in the world-system, although the nature and timing of these imperatives were different in Latin America and East Asia (see Haggard, 1989, pp. 131–33). In Latin America, the Great Depression of the 1930s precipitated the push toward industrialization. The continuation of the primary product export model was no longer a viable option because of low prices and lack of demand for commodity exports, and because the contraction of international trade made it difficult to rely on the industrialized countries for a continued supply of imported consumer goods (Kaufman, chap. 5, this volume).

Factors in the external environment also sparked the impulse toward industrial development in East Asia. Autonomous national industrialization began during the 1950s in response to the social and economic dislocation caused by decolonization. Throughout the 1930s, both South Korea and Taiwan had been part of the regional "Greater East Asian Co-Prosperity Sphere," supplying raw materials and rudimentary manufactures to their Japanese colonizers. However, the Allied victory in World War II disrupted regional trading patterns and ended South Korean and Taiwanese access to guaranteed Japanese markets.

The subsequent divergence in industrial trajectories between the two sets of NICs at the conclusion of the "easy" phase of import substitution again reflects the impact of world-system forces, which presented very different kinds of opportunities and constraints for the two regions. In particular, the respective positions of Latin America and East Asia in the emerging postwar geopolitical order conditioned the access of regional NICs to various types of external resources, most notably U.S. aid and private foreign investment.

Throughout the 1950s and 1960s, East Asia benefited from a special relationship with the United States. This relationship was predicated on the geopolitical assumptions of U.S. policymakers, who saw Japan, South Korea, and Taiwan as important arenas of potential Cold War confrontation (Cumings, 1984). It is widely acknowledged that the South Korean and Taiwanese economies could not have survived in the 1950s without enormous amounts of American assistance. Political divisions in both countries and continuing confrontation with the communists in North Korea and Japan provided a permanent excuse for maintaining the basic framework of a political security state in the 1940s and 1950s. In the 1960s, both states adopted a neomercantile ideology of economic development with anticommunism and rapidly expanded their intervention in both the economy and society in order to actively promote EOI (Kim, 1989, pp. 70–79). Thus, one crucial effect of U.S. aid to East Asia was the strengthening of the states in South Korea and Taiwan relative to business, labor, farmers, and other social classes.

Despite the geopolitical importance of South Korea and Taiwan to the United States as bulwarks against Asian communism, American aid of this magnitude could not continue indefinitely. When U.S. aid officials announced in the late 1950s that this foreign assistance was to be curtailed, it forced both countries to address the question of where they would obtain needed foreign exchange once the aid flows ceased. The U.S. government took advantage of the vulnerability of these countries and lobbied hard to make continued aid contingent on a two-pronged shift in development orientation in South Korea and Taiwan: (1) a greater role for exports, thus supplanting the ISI approach that prevailed in the 1950s and (2) more openness to direct foreign investment. American policymakers argued that these steps would enable the East Asian NICs to take advantage of opportunities created by an expanding world economy, including access to profitable U.S. markets and relatively cheap transfers of technology (Stallings, chap. 3, this volume).

To be sure, U.S. pressure did not yield immediate results; both South Korea and Taiwan flirted with the idea of secondary ISI before making the transition to primary EOI (Cheng, chap. 6, this volume). Nevertheless, the issues of regional geopolitics and the hegemonic role of the United States in the world-economy and interstate system during the 1950s and 1960s clearly established the broad parameters within which industrial policy in East Asia could be fashioned.

The dynamics of the world-economy and the interstate system also conditioned paths of industrialization in Latin America, although the circumstances and outcomes were strikingly different. Faced with the exhaustion of the "easy" phase of ISI during the 1950s, leaders of the major Latin American nations had at least three clear options: (1) to abandon efforts at domestic industrialization, and to refocus national energies on boosting primary product exports; (2) to formulate an export-oriented industrial strategy; or (3) to intensify their programs of import substitution (Kaufman, chap. 5, this volume). In the Latin American cases, the external economic and political environment presented a set of opportunities and constraints that encouraged policymakers to opt for secondary ISI.

First, in contrast to the East Asian situation, U.S. policymakers considered capitalist hegemony in the Americas to be relatively secure. The Alliance for Progress programs of the early 1960s channeled security and development assistance primarily to smaller Latin American countries that appeared vulnerable to agrarian insurgency. Because the big Latin American nations did not appear threatened by a viable communist force, the lavish amounts of U.S. aid provided to the East Asian NICs were not forthcoming. In the late 1930s and during World War II, however, U.S. security concerns related to the global conflict gave Mexico and Brazil increased freedom of maneuver (e.g., in 1938 Mexico became the first developing country to nationalize its oil industry, expropriating the property held by British and American investors).

Second, although Latin American countries had hosted foreign investment in primary products and extractive industries for some time, American multinational corporations increasingly sought investment opportunities in the manufacturing sectors of Latin America during the 1950s. Countries such as Brazil, Mexico, and Argentina, with relatively large internal markets for consumer nondurables, were especially attractive to these firms.

Third, the Eisenhower Administration encouraged such foreign investment in the region, calling on Latin American leaders to ensure a profitable investment climate for U.S. corporations. These appeals received a sympathetic ear from prodevelopment officials in both Brazil and Mexico during the 1950s (Gereffi and Evans, 1981).

In sum, the chapters in this volume suggest three conclusions regarding the impact of the global economy and the interstate system on development strategies in the NICs. First, world-system factors are primarily important in forcing economic policymakers to consider major strategic changes (Haggard, 1989, p. 132). By foreclosing certain development options, world-system factors can make strategic shifts all but inevitable (a "situational imperative"). While global economic and political processes may narrow the parameters of policy choice, it is nevertheless domestic institutions and coalitions that determine the content of new development strategies.

Second, our analysis makes it clear that the nature of world-system ties experienced by the NICs have differed qualitatively. In contrast to South Korea and Taiwan, whose integration to the world-system in the 1950s and early 1960s was essentially *political* in character, the major Latin American countries have been linked more closely with the global *economy* (Kim, 1989, p. 72). Third, these fundamental regional divergences in the mode of world-system integration have contributed to important differences in the autonomy and capacity of domestic institutions. While U.S. aid *strengthened* East Asian states relative to civil society, direct foreign investment *weakened* the governments of the Latin American NICs. As Latin American nations pressed forward with intensified ISI strategies, the combined political clout of groups with vested interests in the continuation of ISI—including foreign investors, their local entrepreneurial allies, and urban labor unions—undermined the capacity of states to encourage competitive manufactured exports, and in fact precluded any fundamental shifts in industrial policy prior to the mid-1960s.

RESOURCE ENDOWMENTS AND COUNTRY SIZE

A standard account by economists of why the industrial paths of the Latin American and East Asian NICs diverged after primary ISI would give considerable importance to country-specific differences in initial conditions, such as natural resource endowments, population density, and country size. With few natural resources, an abundance of labor, and relatively small internal markets, it could be argued that the East Asian countries had little choice in the 1960s but to pursue EOI.

The Latin American countries, in contrast, were thought to have large enough potential markets, coupled with their diverse array of primary export commodities (minerals, petroleum, and agricultural goods), to make secondary ISI feasible. The persistence of ISI in Latin America also has been attributed to the tendency of resource-rich economies to postpone politically difficult choices regarding industrial development. Thus, the Latin American NICs were able to grow respectably through the 1960s, in part due to the export revenues and tax proceeds of primary product exports, despite a host of economic conditions that diminished industrial competitiveness: overvalued exchange rates, protected domestic markets, relatively high wages in the nonagricultural sector, low real interest rates, and inflationary pressures resulting from monetary expansion (Ranis, chap. 8, this volume).

To be sure, factors such as natural resource endowments, labor resources, and size of the internal market significantly influence a country's industrial prospects. Econometric analyses carried out by Chenery et al. (1986) show that big nations (i.e., with populations above 20 million) follow a relatively uniform pattern of industrial change: they typically enter into ISI earlier and have a higher manufacturing share of GDP than do small countries at the same per capita income level; they move further into secondary ISI activities; and their import and export shares of GDP are likely to be less than 10 percent, while a small country's shares may be more than 50 percent. Small economies, on the other hand, tend to be open and give more importance to specialized, niche-oriented industrial strategies rather than relying on rapid demand growth in their domestic markets.

However, these arguments should not be carried too far. As Balassa (1981, pp. 2–3) has observed, the East Asian NICs are not really small in market terms compared to many other developing countries. While Brazil and Mexico possess much larger populations, their highly unequal pattern of income distribution, low wages, and slow growth rates in recent years have effectively reduced the size of the domestic markets to levels closer to that of their smaller East Asian counterparts than population figures alone would suggest. More generally, the correlation between a country's size and its economic policies is far from perfect. Small, open economies as well as large, inward-oriented countries can run the gamut from *dirigiste* to market-oriented policies (Bradford, chap. 2, this volume).

The experiences of the East Asian and Latin American NICs force us to rethink conventional economic wisdom not only about country size, but also about the connection between natural resource endowments and industrial development. A country's comparative advantage (or presumed lack thereof) in natural resources should be thought of in dynamic rather than static terms. The East Asian nations have done remarkably well in creating a dynamic competitive advantage for themselves in the production of intermediate goods, such as steel and petrochemicals, despite lacking indigenous supplies of iron ore and oil. This shift toward heavy and chemical industries in the 1970s was criticized at the time for being both energy- and import-intensive, but it laid the groundwork for a far more diversified range of manufactured exports by the East Asian NICs in the 1980s (Gereffi, 1989b).

Paradoxically, resource wealth may generate as many problems as resource scarcity. Resource-rich countries often suffer from what has been called the "Dutch disease" (see Alt, 1987). The general diagnosis, which is applicable to several of the Latin American cases (Ranis, chap. 8, this volume), is that natural resource wealth increases the level of domestic consumption, favors imports over manufactured exports, benefits services more than manufacturing, and leads to rampant inflation and decreased industrial competitiveness. But the evidence from small Scandinavian countries, among others, belies the notion that resource wealth is an insuperable barrier to competitive industrial trade. Countries like Finland and Sweden have used their comparative advantages in forestry, mining, and cold-water ocean resources to become world leaders in technologically intensive backward- and forward-linkage industries such as logging and paper machinery, hardrock drilling and crushing equipment, icebreakers, paper, and paperboard. The discovery of North Sea oil fueled Norway's high growth rate and enhanced the success of its industrial exports. For the Latin American NICs to make a similar transition from natural resource wealth to technological progress will require substantial investments in the human capital needed for research and new product development, along with appropriate institutions to foster these efforts. Achieving higher levels of domestically induced technological progress is one of the keys to growth with equity in the NICs (Fajnzylber, chap. 12, this volume).

Transitions in Development Strategies

World-system dynamics and country-specific factors like resource endowments and domestic market size present both opportunities and constraints for national development. The world-system and national levels of analysis, however, are more important in identifying paths of industrialization that *cannot* be pursued than they are in determining the direction of subsequent industrial shifts in the NICs. Said differently, these outer structural boundary conditions help us understand why certain phases of development must come to an end, but they do not explain the choice of the new strategies that will replace those that are no longer viable. A more detailed examination of development strategies requires us to descend to the institutional and cultural levels of analysis.

The transitions between development strategies thus raises three distinct questions: (1) Why does a given phase of industrialization come to an end? (2) What determines the choice of a development strategy from the array of available options? (3) How are new development strategies implemented and sustained? Different levels of analysis are appropriate for each of these questions. World-system constraints (political and economic shocks) are especially important in understanding why given strategies come to an end. Country-specific differences in initial conditions, opportunities at the level of the world-system, the role of the state and influential social actors, and prevailing economic and political ideologies are critical factors in determining the choice of new strategies. Finally, the institutional and cultural levels of analysis are of utmost significance in understanding how development strategies are implemented and sustained.

Our notion of "development strategies" needs to be clarified prior to discussing their relevance to industrial transitions in the NICs (see Gereffi, chap. 1, this volume). By this term we do not necessarily mean comprehensive economic blueprints or grand designs of industrial development. Governments in developing societies do formulate and publicize such blueprints (e.g., five-year plans), and in certain cases these help to shape the development process. Often, however, these documents are crafted for the consumption of international organizations and multilateral lending institutions that are potential sources of external funding for industrial development.

As in most capitalist societies, governmental decision-making in the NICs tends to be incremental and pragmatic rather than strategic, responding to immediate crises and short-term dilemmas rather than to long-range plans and comprehensive schemes for change. For this reason, the notion of development strategy often is more meaningful "the second time around." That is, policymakers may arrive at more or less accurate post-hoc interpretations of previous trial-and-error experience, and then attempt to distill general principles and concrete lessons on the basis of this reconstructed logic (Dore, chap. 13, this volume). This incremental decision-making cum post hoc development strategy perspective is supported by chapters in this volume that analyze four key industrial transitions in the Latin American and East Asian NICs: (1) the transition to primary ISI in all the NICs; (2) the subsequent transition to secondary ISI in Latin America and primary EOI in East Asia; (3) the transition to diversified EOI in Latin America and secondary ISI (heavy and chemical industrialization) in East Asia; and (4) the transition in the 1980s to development strategies that show significant elements of convergence in the two regions.

Transition to Primary ISI

Industrial "strategies" as such did not emerge in the NICs of Latin America and East Asia until the late 1950s. The initial phase of industrialization in both regions resulted not from premeditated policy designs, but from world-system shifts that made the continuation of the primary product export model of economic growth virtually impossible. Thus, the overriding concern of government officials in Latin America in the Depression era of the 1930s was not to promote ISI but rather to stave off balance-of-payments crises, to maintain public employment, and to achieve similar short-term objectives. Similarly, the main objective of East Asian policymakers during the 1950s and early 1960s was not to promote EOI but to acquire the foreign exchange needed to purchase imports.

Nevertheless, these early responses to situational imperatives swiftly gave way to more coherent and enduring sets of initiatives aimed explicitly at furthering the process of industrial development. In Latin America in the 1950s, the "easy" ISI of the preceding two decades had provided the basis for widespread efforts at state-led development. Civilian and military elites within the state became the most important advocates of ISI, well ahead of the emerging class of industrialists themselves (Kaufman, chap. 5, this volume). Efforts to deepen ISI were further rationalized and legitimated by postwar economic doctrine from the UN Economic Commission on Latin America (Hirschman, 1961).

Transition to Secondary ISI (Latin America) and Primary EOI (East Asia)

After the mid-1950s, the overriding goal of state industrial policy in the Latin American NICs was to redress balance of payments problems, and thereby ensure economic growth by broadening the range of local production to include consumer durable, intermediate, and capital goods (Baer, 1972). To this end, albeit with some vacillation, political regimes in both countries courted foreign investment in manufacturing (see Gereffi and Evans, 1981). In both Brazil and Mexico, imports of machinery and equipment were subsidized in order to encourage manufacturing investment. These incentives were combined with a high level of protectionism—tariff walls and stringent controls on manufactured imports—that served the interests of local elites and multinational corporations producing for domestic markets. In this environment, local manufacturing increased, imports as a proportion of total consumption fell, foreign investment rose, and manufacturing industries in both Mexico and Brazil became increasingly foreign-controlled. The large foreign manufacturers became prominent in the industries that were to be the new sources of dynamism in the Latin American NICs: automobiles, electrical appliances, chemicals, pharmaceuticals, and heavy machinery (Newfarmer and Mueller, 1975; Evans and Gereffi, 1982).

In the East Asian NICs, the transition from situational imperatives to strategies was similarly gradual and uneven. Faced with the impending exhaustion of primary ISI in the late 1950s and early 1960s, the governments of both South Korea and Taiwan first sought unsuccessfully to deepen ISI (Cheng, chap. 6, this volume). Further, the subsequent dramatic success of manufactured exports was largely unanticipated, particularly in the case of South Korea (see Hong, 1979). South Korean economic development planners in the early 1960s focused almost exclusively on expanded exports of primary products, and they clearly lacked an understanding of the sectors in which South Korea enjoyed an unexpected comparative advantage in the international system. In the Taiwanese case, on the other hand, government planning documents from the early 1960s clearly identified a number of specific industrial sectors worthy of state involvement and promotion (Wade, chap. 9, this volume). Thus, at least in the case of Taiwan, the notion of development strategies as careful premeditated designs finds a measure of support.

However, as textiles and other industries began to perform well on the world market, officials in both Taiwan (1958–1960) and South Korea (1963–1965) transformed early "export-adequate" projections into systematic "export-led" strategies. Although the specific styles of EOI in the two NICs differed substantially, early EOI initiatives included several common features: reductions in import controls, currency adjustments, and the provision of various incentives to export industries (Wade, 1989, pp. 75–77). Two main points emerge in both cases: (1) in a range of industrial sectors from the late 1950s to the 1970s, coherent sets of state initiatives have aimed at stimulating efficient production and competitive exports; and (2) the mode of government leadership in promoting industrial growth differs between Taiwan and South Korea: Taiwan's government relied more on public enterprises or public research and service organizations, while the South Korean government pushed and prodded its very large private firms (Cheng and Wade, chaps. 6 and 9, this volume).

With regard to the role of the state in East Asia, Cheng and Wade cast doubt on the government "followership" arguments advanced by some neoclassical economists, but important questions remain concerning the *degree* of leadership. We need to distinguish, for instance, between policies that indicate the outright leadership of the state in the growth of a given industrial sector, and those policies that merely induce reticent private firms to commit a few resources ("tipping the balance"). Wade (1989, p. 78) refers to this as "big" leadership versus "small" leadership. This raises an important issue for future research: the question of state leadership in industrial development cannot be settled without considerably greater insight into the intentions and motives of both state planners and corporate investors.

Transition to Diversified EOI (Latin America) and HCI (East Asia)

By the early 1970s, both sets of regional NICs confronted difficulties that grew out of the inherent constraints of secondary ISI and primary EOI, respectively (Gereffi, 1989c, pp. 598–602). Mexico and Brazil found their chronic balance-of-payments deficits growing larger in the late 1960s, and inflation was getting worse in both countries. At the start of the 1970s, Taiwan and South Korea were facing a three-dimensional challenge: from *below*, by emerging NICs who were competing in many of the same low-wage manufacturing export industries that the East Asian NICs successfully exploited during the previous decade; from *above*, creeping protectionism in the major markets for their industrial exports (the United States and the nations of Western Europe); and from *within*, the shrinking labor pool and hence rising wage levels, especially in Taiwan. South Korea also faced growing political unrest.

These new situational imperatives fostered a relative convergence of industrial strategies, as each of the NICs tried to resolve the problems of secondary ISI and primary EOI by incorporating elements of the other approach (Gereffi, chap. 1, this volume). The Latin American NICs adopted the strategy of diversified export promotion, but with continued ISI deepening. In contrast to the commodity export model, the key feature of this approach was its emphasis on a diversification of exports, especially manufactures, rather than the quantitative expansion of a single commodity or a small number of commodities. Secondary ISI efforts continued in this phase, especially in the intermediate and capital goods sectors (see Villarreal, chap. 11, this volume).

The East Asian NICs, on the other hand, sought to develop heavy industries—especially steel, petrochemicals, and heavy machinery—motivated in part by defense considerations (Cheng, chap. 6, this volume). During the 1973–1979 period, both South Korea and Taiwan launched "heavy and chemical industrialization" (HCI) programs with two main objectives: (1) to develop national production capability in these sectors; and (2) to lay the groundwork for more diversified exports in the future. Moreover, in both South Korea and Taiwan these moves toward HCI resulted from careful prior planning by the state. The South Korean move toward HCI was charted in the early 1970s, while Taiwanese aspirations first became evident in the planning documents of the 1960s (Wade, chap. 9, this volume). Commonalities in the language used by East Asian economic planners suggests that this round of HCI, particularly in the South Korean case, was modeled closely on the earlier Japanese experience (Dore, chap. 13, this volume).

Elements of Convergence in the 1980s

In the 1980s additional forces furthered the convergence of industrial paths among the NICs. The oil price shock of 1979–1980, rising international interest rates, and growing protectionism in the advanced industrial countries combined to push all four of the Latin American and East Asian NICs to adopt similar adjustments in their development strategies. These trends—particularly in the Latin American cases—were amplified by pressures from the International Monetary Fund and the World Bank, which made continued lending contingent on adoption of an extensive package of neoliberal policy reforms, or "structural adjustments."

The resulting policy shifts in each of the NICs may be described as efforts to promote stabilization, privatization, and internationalization (Gereffi and Wyman, 1989). *Stabilization* measures sought to reduce inflation in the NICs by using the conventional policy tools of fiscal restraint and monetary control, together with restrictions on wage increases. *Privatization* meant a turn in all four countries toward a more market-oriented style of economic management. This involved a move away from discretionary, sector-specific intervention and toward indirect, nondiscretionary supports (such as incentives for research and development, and manpower training), deregulating foreign exchange controls, liberalizing imports, limiting the role of state-owned enterprises, and lessening government influence over banks and credit. *Internationalization* refers to measures taken in all four NICs to open up their domestic markets by removing restrictions on direct foreign investment, especially in the service sector (including banking, insurance, hotels, and retail stores).

These common themes notwithstanding, the paths of industrialization among the NICs also have shown considerable national distinctiveness during the 1970s and 1980s. Even broadly similar policies can yield divergent outcomes, as the recent experiences of Mexico and Brazil suggest. Throughout Latin America, exchange rate liberalization meant sharp currency devaluations. The results of Mexico's adjustment stem from its geographical proximity to the United States: labor-intensive manufactured exports from the *maquiladora* industries located along the border skyrocketed, and inflows of direct foreign investment also climbed in the mid-1980s. In contrast to Mexico, Brazil enjoyed expanded exports of consumer durables (e.g., automobiles), steel, capital goods, and armaments. This subregional variation reflects Brazil's more concerted and successful effort at sustained secondary ISI during the late 1970s (Hirschman, 1987, pp. 19–22; Villarreal, chap. 16, this volume).

SELECTING AND IMPLEMENTING DEVELOPMENT STRATEGIES: THE ROLE OF INSTITUTIONS AND SOCIAL COALITIONS

While processes operating at the global level, such as world economic expansion or geopolitical restructuring, have promoted strategic shifts in each of the NICs, the chapters in this volume indicate that domestic institutions and interest groups have played important roles in the selection and implementation of new strategies. National governments, particularly authoritarian states such as those in East Asia and Latin America, are responsible for both formulating industrial strategies and putting them into practice. Major firms often have been involved in policy implementation in the NICs, but their growing political clout in East Asia may signal an expanding future role in strategic planning as well. On the other hand, most elements of civil society, particularly the popular sector groups, have minimal access to policy-making channels. Social coalitions can influence, however, the ways in which strategies are put into practice.

States

Development strategies are formulated and implemented primarily by national governments. Although various social groups ranging from domestic entrepreneurs to popular sectors may articulate policy preferences, state structures differ in their permeability and receptivity to social pressures in the crucial area of industrial decision-making. States in the Latin American and East Asian NICs share a number of common features: they tend to be strong, centralized, authoritarian, and deeply involved in the national economies. There are important differences in the autonomy of these states, however, and in their styles of economic intervention, which have contributed to regional and subregional divergences in paths of industrialization.

First of all, the authoritarian regimes in Latin America and East Asia differ sharply in their historical and structural origins. Exclusionary regimes in Latin America's Southern Cone emerged in the context of strategic crises in the 1960s (see Collier, 1979). These political crises resulted from periods of populist rule during which organized labor had been a crucial pillar of state support. Different circumstances prevailed in Mexico, however. Because the patterns of compromise among the Mexican elite differed historically from those in Brazil, the Brazilian-style political incorporation of organized labor in populist coalitions did not occur

(Collier, 1982). The pervasive political dominance by the PRI has until recently stifled the emergence of alternative groups.

In contrast to the antipopulist Latin American authoritarians, the regimes of East Asia inherited large, centralized state bureaucracies from their Japanese colonizers and were assisted in consolidating their power over elements of civil society by U.S. activity during the 1950s. Thus, whereas Southern Cone authoritarians engaged in the brutal repression of previously mobilized popular sector organizations to solidify secondary ISI strategies (O'Donnell, 1973), the East Asian regimes did not confront a significant activated popular sector. Thus, they were exclusionary from the outset.

There are also substantial regional differences in the broader societal role of the military (Gereffi and Wyman, 1989). In Latin America, the nature of the threat to which armed forces are responding typically has been internal insurgency. In South Korea and Taiwan, on the other hand, there has been concern over the possibility of external invasion (forced "reunification") from neighboring communist countries. Thus, even though the military penetrates more deeply into civil society in East Asia than in Latin America, the sociopolitical role of the military may hold greater legitimacy in South Korea and Taiwan than in the Latin American NICs because of the prevalent view that economic development and social mobilization are critical for national survival (Dore, chap. 13, this volume).

As we noted earlier, the rapid industrialization of the NICs has rejuvenated ideologically charged debates over the economic role of the state (Wade, chap. 9, this volume). Influential interpreters have argued that the rapid industrial development of the East Asian NICs has resulted primarily from the implementation of neoliberal economic reforms in the early 1960s ("getting the prices right"), and from the subsequent withdrawal of the state from the economies of those nations (e.g., Balassa, 1981). However, the chapters in this volume emphatically reject this minimalist interpretation of the state's role in South Korea and Taiwan. The typology of development strategies developed by Bradford (chap. 2, this volume) makes it clear that state economic intervention is compatible with a wide range of policy orientations, including EOI. States clearly have played strong interventionist roles in *each* of the main Latin American and East Asian NICs discussed in this volume.

However, the character of government development initiatives has varied significantly across and even within regions. Of the two East Asian NICs, South Korea has pursued a far more *centralized* approach to both primary and secondary EOI (see Jones and Sakong, 1980, chap. 4; Cheng, chap. 6, this volume). In addition to sectoral policies based on import controls, domestic content requirements, entry restrictions, and sharp limitations on foreign investment, the South Korean state has pressured the leading firms directly (Wade, chap. 9, this volume). Because of the relatively high debt-equity ratios of major South Korean firms (*chaebols*), and the ability of the state to curtail generous allocations of concessional credit and foreign exchange (Wade, 1988), these pressures have generally succeeded.

In contrast, Taiwan's relatively *decentralized* approach to industrial leadership depended on fiscal incentives, more general promotion of light industry, and ample but carefully regulated flows of foreign investment (Cheng, chap. 6, this volume). Efforts to hasten the development of sectors requiring large-scale, capital-intensive production have generally involved state-owned enterprises (SOEs), which have been more prominent in the industrial policies of Taiwan than in those of South Korea. Wade (chap. 9, this volume) suggests that, given the much smaller average size of leading firms in Taiwan, SOEs have generally been the functional equivalent of the South Korean *chaebols* in the implementation of industrial policy. Recent attempts by the Taiwanese government to stimulate the growth of high-technology sectors, however, have centered on state-sponsored research and development institutes (Schive, chap. 10, this volume).

The state has also played an important economic role in the Latin American NICs. State-owned enterprises are more prominent in Latin America than in East Asia, and they are particularly concentrated in key input industries (e.g., steel and petrochemicals), natural resource sectors (e.g., oil and minerals), and infrastructure and services (e.g., transportation and communications). State-run firms have been more prevalent in Brazil than in Mexico (Newfarmer and Mueller, 1975). In addition to their direct involvement in production, government bureaucracies occasionally have mounted concerted campaigns to stimulate the interest of local and/or foreign investors in specific industrial sectors, as in the case of the Brazilian computer industry (Evans, 1986), although such activity is exceptional. On the whole, the governments of Brazil and Mexico have demonstrated little capacity or inclination to formulate comprehensive sector-specific industrial policies of the type found in the East Asian NICs. Further, the governments of Brazil and Mexico have shown less interest than their counterparts in East Asia in human capital investments, such as educational expansion. Finally, governments in both Latin American NICs have also struggled to shape the role and impact of foreign capital through various tactics that are discussed below.

Firms

The chapters in this volume indicate that the structure of leading industries in the NICs differs across and/or within regions along four basic dimensions: (1) ownership, (2) sectoral emphasis, (3) size, and (4) relative concentration. These basic patterns of industrial structure confront governments with distinctive sets of opportunities and constraints in the formulation and implementation of national industrial strategies (Hamilton et al., 1987; Gereffi, chap. 4, this volume).

First, the size of the *chaebols* and their centrality in the South Korean economy make them crucially important in the implementation of the government's economic policies. This was especially true during the heyday of HCI in the 1970s, when the government's "big push" approach—which focused on the production of capital goods, intermediate inputs, and consumer durables—was predicated on an unprecedented concentration of capital in the *chaebols*. The patriarchal command structure of these major South Korean conglomerates, their reliance on the state for credit and other resources vital for doing business, and the absence of secondary groups to attenuate the links between the state and local economic groups resulted in a co-opted big business class with little option but to serve its own best interests by accommodating government policy objectives. By the 1980s, however, the undisputed dominance of the state over the *chaebols* had weakened significantly, indicating that in the future the *chaebols* are likely to have more power in the formulation as well as the implementation of major policy choices (Kim, 1988).

In contrast, the plethora of small and medium-sized family firms that prevails in Taiwan permits no smooth implementation of national industrial strategies. Instead of the formal system of command that characterizes the *chaebols*, Taiwanese firms are operated via flexible management policies centered in informal interpersonal networks (Hamilton and Kao, 1987; Redding, 1988). For a variety of reasons related to extended family relations and the patterns of personal life-course transitions in Taiwan (see Wong, 1988), family firms tend to splinter and proliferate rather than grow by enlarging the size of the original firm. Furthermore, ethnic tensions between the Mainlander-dominated political elite in the Kuomintang (KMT) and the Taiwanese-based economic elite have generally led the party to discourage the growth of larger firms. On the few occasions when the KMT leadership has encouraged consolidation in order to facilitate economies of scale in production (as in the automobile industry), its efforts have fizzled (Wade, chap. 9, this volume).

This distinctive industrial structure in Taiwan makes the implementation of any industrial strategy problematic. The relatively large number of Taiwanese firms enmeshed in complex family webs reduces the likelihood of unified business support for state policies, and the relatively small size of these firms hinders efforts to compete with their mammoth South Korean counterparts. Further, in contrast to the *chaebols*, the smaller Taiwanese manufacturers lack access to giant trading companies to distribute their products in lucrative Western markets. The Taiwanese state has adapted to the difficulties presented by its industrial structure in several ways: (1) by formulating a "gradualist" rather than a "big push" approach to HCI (Cheng, chap. 6, this volume) and other large-scale projects; (2) by according state enterprises and research agencies a more prominent role than in South Korea (Schive, chap. 10, this volume); and (3) by pursuing short-term subcontracting relationships with large foreign buyers (Gereffi, 1989b; Gereffi and Korzeniewicz, 1990).

In the Latin American NICs, the prominence of foreign investors establishes a very different context for the implementation of state industrial strategy. The dominance of MNCs in capital goods and consumer durables industries has significantly reduced the importance of domestic capital in these sectors. Consequently, the advancement of secondary ISI strategies has been based largely on bargaining between state officials and MNC representatives over how best to reconcile global corporate objectives with national development goals.

Over time, both Brazil and Mexico have enjoyed some success in harnessing MNCs to assist national industrial strategies, Brazil by implementing both local content and export requirements, and Mexico by forcing MNCs into joint ventures with local entrepreneurs. Nevertheless, MNCs have rarely accommodated even the cautious demands of Latin American host governments with alacrity. The current era of international debt and economic liberalization may well lessen the bargaining power of states over foreign investors during the strategic drive for competitive manufactured exports.

Social Coalitions

Any development strategy draws support from its beneficiaries and evokes opposition from those elements that are adversely affected. For instance, while the traditional primary product export model in Latin America received consistent backing from powerful agrarian and mining elites, it also drew fire from an urban-centered coalition of nascent manufacturing interests and labor. The patterns of coalescence, disintegration, and restructuring among these broad alliances of social forces can exert a profound influence on the design and implementation of industrial strategies. Along with domestic institutional arrangements, these shifting social coalitions are an important source of regional and subregional variation in paths of industrialization among the NICs.

The different social coalitions that grew out of state efforts at financing early ISI help to explain subsequent regional divergences in industrial strategy. In the Latin American NICs, the decision to subsidize ISI via resource wealth fostered a particularly durable supporting social coalition, including urban industrialists, organized labor, middle- and lower-income consumers, and the civil servants who parceled out the specific benefits of ISI (Kaufman, chap. 5, this volume). Although nonelite groups rarely have played a direct role in the *formulation* of industrial strategy in any of the NICs, "distributive coalitions" built around popular sectors have influenced the *implementation* of development policies, especially during the populist phase of early ISI in Latin America (Deyo, chap. 7, this volume).

After the mid-1950s, the initial ISI coalition was restructured and secondary ISI was backed by a "triple alliance" of foreign investors, local manufacturers, and the state, along with skilled workers and upper-income consumers who can afford to purchase locally produced consumer durables like automobiles and major electrical appliances (see Evans, 1979). At every turn, the strength of these ISI coalitions reduced the willingness and capacity of states to withdraw benefits from major vested interest groups, despite the costs in terms of international competitiveness.

As indicated above, ISI financing was carried out quite differently in East Asia: the unique geopolitical position of South Korea and Taiwan during the 1950s brought lavish quantities of concessionary foreign aid. Aid flows had two important consequences for the coalitional bases of future industrialization efforts in these regional NICs. First, because political elites enjoyed discretionary authority over the allocation of these critical resources, U.S. aid led to a pronounced strengthening of state authority in these countries (Stallings, chap. 3, this volume). Second, in both South Korea and Taiwan, the U.S. assisted local regimes in the preemptive demobilization of those groups in civil society that could have formed a "distributive" social coalition, particularly peasantry, labor, and intellectuals (Deyo, 1987; Cheng, chap. 6, this volume). The combination of sweeping land reforms pressed by U.S. aid officials and early political repression of the political left paved the way for the politically smooth transition to EOI, which occurred during the late 1950s and early 1960s.

Further, the distinctive relationships between state and business forged in South Korea and Taiwan during this period have contributed to subsequent divergences in the formulation and implementation of primary and secondary EOI in each country. In Taiwan, early ethnopolitical tensions between KMT cadres and indigenous entrepreneurs have persisted, albeit in muted form. Sensitive to the potential political threat posed by the consolidation of large, Korean-style business groups, the KMT generally has looked with favor on the continued proliferation of small- and medium-sized family firms, despite the difficulties in implementing industrial policy.

In contrast, in the early 1960s the Park regime quickly yoked South Korean big business to state development objectives by threatening to prosecute uncooperative businessmen for their collaboration with the Japanese during the colonial era and for their subsequent political corruption under Syngman Rhee during the 1950s (Cheng, chap. 6, this volume). Major South Korean conglomerates and their subcontracting partners have profited handsomely from their subordinate status and until recently have lacked both the power and the motivation to challenge state industrial strategy.

While social coalitions can provide crucial support for industrial strategies, the outcomes of these strategies can also undermine or outstrip their coalitional foundations. Two recent developments in the East Asian NICs offer important examples of this unfolding process. First, the growing middle class and expanding sectors of students and intellectuals—all products of earlier economic successes—are increasingly unwilling to accept the curtailment of political and civil liberties in return for industrial growth (Cheng, chap. 6, this volume). This dissent is especially evident in South Korea, where the political situation has been complicated by a variety of factors: growing income inequality, occasionally erratic economic performance, social polarization over the reunification issue, and signs of nascent autonomy of big business vis-à-vis the state.

Second, the expansion of heavy industries (e.g., steel, petrochemicals, consumer durables) may provide new opportunities for labor mobilization in the East Asian NICs (Deyo, chap. 7, this volume). The earlier generation of light manufacturing industries (e.g., textiles, electronics) employed primarily young unmarried women, who were short-term workers often housed in temporary, sex-segregated dormitories. In contrast, the mostly male employees of heavy industrial plants tend to reside in stable, urban working-class communities. These neighborhoods may well develop authentic class cultures, informal social networks, and popular institutions. Further, the organization of work in heavy industries may facilitate more efficient communication among dissident workers.

However, these labor trends may have less impact in Taiwan than in South Korea for several reasons. First, these heavy industries are less prominent in Taiwan because of the "gradualist" (as opposed to the South Korean "big push") approach to HCI adopted by the state (Cheng, chap. 6, this volume). Second, the spatial arrangement of manufacturing industries is very different in Taiwan. The dispersal of small and medium-sized firms around the island permits many workers to rely on family agricultural incomes to supplement industrial wages; it may also maintain the primacy of conservative provincial values and impede the formation of durable working-class communities. Third, the family scale and paternalistic ethos of most enterprises in Taiwan tend to reinforce the loyalty of workers to the firms. Finally, the early decision of the KMT to make employers virtually the sole guarantors of social security in old age provides an economic rationale for labor quiescence and stable employment (Deyo, chap. 7, this volume; 1984).

In sum, recent trends demonstrate the dynamic and interactive relationship that exists between social coalitions, state strategies, and paths of industrialization in the NICs. Each configuration of social, political, and economic forces carries the seeds of its own evolution, and the "success" of development strategies may well undermine the social coalitions that originally supported them. Periodic strategic shifts have been virtually assured by alterations in world-system processes and by the inherent limitations of state industrial policies. However, the specific character of strategic change has been shaped in large measure by the opportunities and constraints presented by domestic institutions and social coalitions.

Networks

The study of industrialization may be enriched by viewing the totality of global social structure as a set of interlocking networks at multiple levels (Tilly, 1984), which may or may not be coterminous with formal political boundaries (see Berkowitz and Wellman, 1988, for a general introduction). The selection and implementation of development strategies in the NICs has been influenced by the structure of various types of exchange networks within and among domestic and international institutions. Building on the contributions to this volume and other recent research, our discussion highlights several areas where such network variations among the NICs appear especially important: subcontracting and marketing links, the circulation of policy-relevant knowledge, technology transfer, interpersonal contacts between private and public sectors, and working-class mobilization.

By *networks* we refer to sets of members (nodes) that are linked by one or more specific types of relations between them. While most uses of network analysis in development research have involved mapping trade, aid, and lending patterns among nation-states (Snyder and Kick, 1979; Nemeth and Smith, 1985), the nodes can just as easily be industrial firms or individuals, such as policymakers or workers. The ties are defined by the flow of resources (e.g., material goods, information) from one member to another. These *ties* may vary in terms of strength (the quantity of resources characterizing a relation), duration (the length of time a tie has existed), and symmetry (the extent to which exchanges are reciprocal). When the *networks* themselves are compared, they can differ according to their range (the number of members), density (the extent of interconnectedness via direct ties among members), boundedness (the proportion of all ties that stay within network boundaries), and homogeneity (the extent to which members have similar attributes), among other characteristics (Hall and Wellman, 1985, pp. 25–28).

The production and marketing of any commodity in the global manufacturing system is the result of diverse sets of exchange relationships: acquisition of raw materials and other inputs from suppliers, procurement of capital to finance business operations and expansion, subcontracting the design and production of the final commodity or its components with specialty firms, and the marketing and delivery of the product to consumers (Gereffi and Korzeniewicz, 1990). In addition to these exchanges of merchandise and capital, producers and distributors may participate in trade organizations or other networks to gain information about production techniques, market conditions, and other issues. Such networks may be sector- or even product-specific (Korzeniewicz, forthcoming). Variations in the structural properties of these networks—for instance, their boundedness and ethnic homogeneity—may affect the reliability of supplies, production, and distribution within a particular industry, and may also increase or diminish the ability of producers to respond flexibly to changing environmental conditions (see Piore and Sabel, 1984; Lazerson, 1988).

Several of the contributions to this volume suggest that variations in the structure of the subcontracting and marketing networks of South Korean and Taiwanese firms help to account for divergent styles of EOI in the East Asian NICs (Gereffi, chap. 4, this volume). In brief, the numerous small and medium-sized enterprises in Taiwan partake of networks that link them backward to suppliers and forward to consumers (Hamilton and Biggart, 1988, pp. 83–85). These business arrangements—like the day-to-day operations of the enterprises themselves—are embedded in a complex web of extended family relationships (see Greenhalgh, 1988; Wong, 1988). Thus, personalistic ties based on mutual trust and reciprocity help to reduce the otherwise high levels of uncertainty and facilitate flexibility in entrepreneurial decision-making. In contrast, the South Korean *chaebols* enter into subcontracting relations with much smaller firms or acquire such firms as part of their vertical integration process. Although more information is needed on this issue, it appears that informal networks are far less important in South Korea than in Taiwan, as state regulation and price-setting in the former country govern many subcontracting relationships.

In addition to their internal subcontracting networks, firms in the East Asian NICs also differ in their marketing arrangements. With state guidance, the products of South Korean businesses are marketed abroad by large trading companies. However, the much smaller firms in Taiwan often subcontract directly with Western distributors and retailers (e.g., K-Mart) who ultimately dispose of the products (Gereffi and Korzeniewicz,

1990). The marketing patterns in both East Asian cases differ from the predominant pattern in the Latin American NICs, which involves transfers of material and capital among the branches and subsidiaries of multinational corporations (Gereffi, 1989b).

Several writers have suggested that the rise and expansion of formal international organizations concerned with economic development may contribute to the growth of a "world political culture" among planners and policymakers (e.g., Thomas and Lauderdale, 1988). Integral to this emerging system of common values is the gradual rise of shared assumptions about (1) the appropriateness of state involvement in certain types of prodevelopment initiatives and (2) the value of common institutional forms and programs for pursuing national goals in the areas of economic growth and social welfare.

But how does "policy-relevant knowledge" circulate within and among agencies and nations (Haggard, 1989, pp. 139–40)? While it seems clear that the East Asian NICs—particularly South Korea—drew on the earlier Japanese experience with HCI in formulating their plans (Dore, chap. 13, this volume), the precise formal and/or informal mechanisms through which policymakers in the NICs and elsewhere gather such information remain unclear. Interpersonal networks centered in development-related international organizations (e.g., UNIDO) and regional groups (e.g., ECLAC) may have played a major role in stimulating discussion and informational exchanges via conferences, publications, missions, and other means (Hirschman, 1961).

Bilateral contacts are important as well. Educational and training programs established by the United States during the 1950s are thought to be responsible for common ideologies of management in South Korean business and state bureaucracies (Hamilton and Biggart, 1988, p. 82). Two additional types of transnational influence on planning knowledge and ideology deserve consideration: (1) informal economic planning missions and (2) more direct pressures from multilateral institutions, such as the International Monetary Fund, on nations to pursue predetermined packages of policy reforms (see Villarreal, chap. 11, this volume).

While these interpersonal networks may provide a crucial source of intellectual capital for national policymakers, networks also shape the capacities of domestic institutions and social coalitions to implement industrial strategies. Three brief examples suffice to clarify this point. First, technology transfer in high-tech industries such as electronics and computers is one area where interpersonal networks may play a major role, since East Asian and Latin American employees in Western companies often return to work for public or private firms and research agencies based in their home countries.

Second, recent research has explored the role of informal networks among business and political elites in Latin America and East Asia. Studies of the Japanese state bureaucracy have identified cohort and informal personal networks centered in educational institutions. In addition, "revolving door" links between public and private sector positions, formalized via the *amakudari* system, are important in facilitating a bureaucratic sense of purpose and consensus on policy issues, as well as agreements frequently made in informal settings between state officials and business leaders on matters of industrial policy (see Johnson, 1982, chap. 2). Extensive informal networks also exist among the South Korean business elite, stemming from family ties, intermarriage, educational loyalties, and regional and cultural affinities (Suh, 1989).

Third, divergent development strategies have fostered variations in the structure of working-class communities in the NICs. The residential neighborhoods and shop-floor arrangements associated with heavy industries in Latin America, and more recently in South Korea, give rise to denser and more durable interpersonal networks among their permanent, predominantly male workforce. These networks serve as channels for information and social support, providing valuable resources for labor militancy (Deyo, 1989; and Deyo, chap. 7, this volume).

While our brief discussion is in no way exhaustive, it does suggest that studying the structure and determinants of production, distribution, and information networks offers a promising approach to emerging patterns and trends of industrial development in the NICs and elsewhere. The idea of network ties offers a useful investigative tool, but it is not a theory per se. By linking the concepts and methods of network analysis with more established perspectives, future research can profitably address a wide range of issues related to contemporary industrialization.

CULTURE

The rapid growth of the East Asian NICs has refocused attention on the role of culture in national development, although this topic is only indirectly addressed in the volume. In this section, we juxtapose two divergent perceptions of "culture" in the social science literature on development. We then discuss several ways in which cultural patterns have contributed to cross-regional and intraregional differences in paths of development. Examples drawn from this volume and other recent research suggest the need to rethink the connections between culture and economy.

In conventional wisdom, the term "culture" connotes a relatively static, "deep structure" of abstract common values that shape individual behavior and social organization in a variety of contexts. For instance, one line of analysis prominent during the 1950s and 1960s focused on the role of individual attitudes and national "modal personalities" in developing societies (see Inkeles, 1983, for a review).

Drawing on the seminal work of Weber, many social scientists center their discussions of culture and development on religious values. A number of writers argue that Confucianism confers certain advantages over other traditions in the quest for economic development. First, Confucian values stress the importance of sobriety, education, achievement, and reciprocal social obligations. Second, the Confucian emphasis on hierarchy encourages harmony, cooperation, and loyalty within organizations (Kahn, 1979, p. 122). These characteristics are thought to have facilitated the national consensus around high-speed economic growth that was evident in Japan and the East Asian NICs in the 1950s and 1960s. This culturally derived capacity for cooperation led political elites, industrial leaders, workers, and other citizens to agree on the primacy of economic objectives for the society as a whole and on the means to achieve those objectives (see Johnson, 1983, pp. 6–10).

In Latin America, a divergent set of cultural norms based upon an "Ibero-Catholic" or Hispanic heritage has been identified as impeding the economic advancement of the region. According to the modernization theorists of the 1960s, this Latin American tradition is characterized by an elite culture of luxury, disdain for labor and commerce, a general affinity for ascriptive criteria in the distribution of social benefits, and other values typically found in feudal societies (see Valenzuela and Valenzuela, 1978, for a review of this perspective). Lawrence Harrison, the author of a recent book entitled *Underdevelopment Is a State of Mind*, has voiced one of the most virulent indictments against the Hispanic tradition: "In the case of Latin America, we see a cultural pattern, derivative of traditional Hispanic culture, that is anti-democratic, anti-social, anti-progress, anti-entrepreneurial, and at least among the elite, anti-work" (cited in Fishlow, 1989, p. 118).

Sweeping arguments about the impact of culture on development in East Asia and Latin America run into various problems. First, as some proponents of culturalist arguments acknowledge (e.g., Berger, 1986), regions are not culturally homogeneous; this is particularly true of East Asia. In Taiwan and South Korea, for example, Taoism and Buddhism also have important followings along with Confucianism. Further, there is a significant Christian entrepreneurial minority in some countries of the region, like South Korea (see Jones and Sakong, 1980). Even where Confucianism is predominant, there tends to be a gap between the ideal and the reality—that is, between what is believed and what is practiced (Pye, 1985).

More importantly, in terms of the timing of high-speed growth, both the Confucian and Ibero-Catholic traditions have existed for centuries. In both regions, but especially in East Asia, dynamic shifts in economic per-

formance have occurred primarily in recent decades. Although some recent treatments of Confucianism are more sophisticated, these developments pose difficulties for vulgar culturalist arguments (Leung, 1989).

Further, the same Confucian beliefs that are now thought to facilitate
rapid industrialization in East Asia were criticized by several generations
of Western scholars for inhibiting economic development (see Hamilton
and Kao, 1987). In addition, many of the stereotyped views of "Confucian" values may be empirically inaccurate. For instance, East Asian industrial relations have not always been (and are not now) harmonious
(Gordon, 1985; Form and Bae, 1988), and Chinese employees do not
identify closely with their work organizations (Silin, 1976).

Instead of a template or predetermined program that mechanically
shapes individual behavior, Ong (1987, p. 2) views culture as "historically situated and emergent, shifting and incomplete meanings and practices generated in the webs of agency and power." Further, the situational
characterization of culture recognizes that culture is mediated through
institutions. Thus, while culture highlights core societal values, there is
no direct relationship between values and behavior independent of institutional or organizational context.

The contributions to this volume offer several examples of the potential
utility of this historically contingent perspective on culture. In addition to
the hotly debated issue of a "Confucian ethic," several other cultural
themes are associated with cross-regional variations in paths of development. First, observers call attention to striking cross-regional differences
in attitudes toward the state apparatus and its personnel (Dore, chap. 13,
this volume). The early development of meritocratic educational systems
in East Asia, in contrast to the more status-oriented systems of Latin
America, partly accounts for the greater prestige and popular legitimacy
of bureaucrats in East Asia, particularly relative to electoral politicians.

Second, there is evidence of a cultural demonstration effect in international production, consumption, and development policy. In some instances, the substance and language of East Asian industrial policies
seems to have been taken almost directly from Japanese documents
(Dore, chap. 13, this volume). Further, the reemergence of Japan as a
regional power after World War II may have encouraged the East Asian
NICs to imitate Japan's relatively austere personal consumption patterns,
while the "showcase modernity" of the Latin American NICs is more in
accord with the kind of consumer-oriented lifestyle characteristic of the
United States (Fajnzylber, chap. 12, this volume).

Third, the relative ethnic homogeneity of East Asian societies like
South Korea and Japan plays a major role, along with the situational imperatives of resource scarcity, small size, and military threats in height-
ening nationalistic sentiments, which are conducive to a single-minded
emphasis on economic growth. In this regard the East Asian NICs contrast

strikingly with their Latin American counterparts, which tend to be far more culturally diverse (Dore, chap. 13, this volume).

While culture underlies cross-regional contrasts in several important ways, culture also may help to account for intraregional differences in paths of industrial development. For instance, while some discussions have focused on the relative ethnic homogeneity of the East Asian NICs, the degree of homogeneity varies within the region. Such variations may have important social and political consequences. In contrast to the high level of ethnic homogeneity in South Korea, political and economic power in Taiwan are distributed along an ethnic fault line: The Mainlander political elites of the Kuomintang (KMT) remain suspicious of any efforts by native business leaders to develop nonparty bases of power (Cheng, chap. 6, this volume). Accordingly, the KMT has encouraged the proliferation of small and medium-sized firms rather than Korean-style conglomerates.

However, these ethnopolitical cleavages are not the only cultural factors contributing to intraregional divergences in industrial structure. Gereffi (chap. 4, this volume) also underscores the importance of family structure and ideology on the size and behavior of industrial concerns in South Korea and Taiwan (see Hamilton, Orrù, and Biggart, 1987). In brief, interfirm relations in South Korean conglomerates are organized on the principle of *corporate patriarchy*; these concerns are controlled by a single authoritarian individual and operated via hirelings. This principle of economic organization facilitates close working relationships between state and private sector. In contrast to the formal system of command that prevails in South Korea, Taiwanese firms are characterized by a more decentralized form of management based on *patrilineal ties*, or personal (primarily extended kin) relationships based on reciprocal trust and loyalty. These cultural differences in family structures, managerial ideology, and industrial organization provide both opportunities and constraints for political elites seeking to guide the industrialization process.

As these examples indicate, to evaluate cultural arguments seriously one needs to turn to history and also to look at the evolution of special institutional arrangements. The impact of cultural variables is perhaps most important in outlining an acceptable range of solutions to development problems, rather than in determining specific outcomes. One of the "lessons" of East Asian development may be that the institutional bases underlying the region's growth are effective precisely because they have responded flexibly to the traditional forces in each society.

CONCLUSIONS

The patterns and strategies of industrial development in the Latin American and East Asian NICs defy easy description, let alone explanation. This volume has sought to bring together the expertise of development specialists in two very different regions of the world in order to move beyond Latin American and East Asian paradigms and search for explanations of development processes and outcomes that have global significance.

The common stereotype that Latin American and East Asian NICs can be characterized by their pursuit of inward-oriented and outward-oriented paths of industrialization respectively is profoundly misleading. What has been essential to the economic dynamism of the NICs in each region is the interplay and synergy between the ISI and EOI approaches (see Gereffi, 1989b). To merely argue for the uniform application of one set of orthodox economic policies to promote the economic recovery of Latin America or other developing nations would be to draw the wrong lesson from East Asia. Comparative analysis helps us explain *why* particular strategies perform well or poorly, or *why* certain development patterns emerge, in particular contexts. Our task is to try to identify effective styles of integration into the international political economy that are compatible with domestic institutions and circumstances.

World-system dynamics and country-specific "initial conditions" pose structural constraints to national development, but they are not binding on all countries in the same way. The oil shocks of the 1970s were a constraint to most of the Latin American and East Asian NICs, but they were at least a temporary boon to Mexico. The debt crisis became a serious problem for Mexico and Brazil, and a moderate one for South Korea, but Taiwan has achieved massive balance-of-payments surpluses. The East Asian NICs had a far greater degree of success in taking advantage of the expansion in international trade in the 1960s and 1970s than the Latin American NICs did, while the latter countries have encountered many more difficulties in harnessing multinational corporations to national development objectives. Linkages to the world-economy thus can have positive as well as negative consequences for national development, depending on how and when they are established and whether they are congruent with key elements in the domestic environment.

Natural resource endowments and country size frequently have been thought of as fairly rigid boundary conditions that shape the success of inward-oriented or outward-oriented development schemes. In fact, the experience of the NICs shows us that there is considerable room for maneuver and choice in this area as well. There are several ways to get around natural resource constraints. South Korea and Taiwan imported many of the raw materials needed to establish their heavy and chemical industries (such as steel and petrochemicals) in the 1970s in order to create a substantial domestic output of intermediate goods and machines used extensively in downstream industries. Brazil tried to cope with its shortage of oil by substituting rather than importing this needed raw material through a massive gasohol program that used processed sugar that

Brazil produced in great quantities. Some structural constraints ultimately do bind, but there are multiple examples of creativity and flexibility in dealing with structural boundary conditions in the NICs.

The role of the state has emerged as a key factor in the Latin American and East Asian NICs in terms of the state's capacity to select and implement successful development strategies. What cannot be overlooked is the fact that all of the East Asian NICs, as well as Japan, have been extremely adept at establishing a dominant national commitment to economic growth as a primary requirement for national security in the context of an uncertain and potentially hostile international environment. Economic nationalism in the Latin American NICs has been more narrowly based, with foreign economic (rather than political) domination frequently being their chief concern.

One of the most neglected and vexing areas of analysis in the comparative development field has been culture. We have advocated a more historically and institutionally grounded notion of culture that can help us explain a variety of phenomena: for example, the different varieties of nationalism in the NICs, the reasons that the East Asian nations have such a strong disposition to high savings rates compared to the Latin American NICs, and the factors that explain why Taiwan is more averse to inflation than South Korea. Cultural variables, in this broader view, are important in legitimizing an acceptable range of viable solutions to national development problems.

The chapters in this volume represent the state of the art in the field of comparative development studies, and they should inform research on industrialization in the East Asian and Latin American NICs for some time to come. Valid generalizations depend on utilizing a multilayered explanatory framework that permits us to understand both the context-dependent nature of successful development strategies as well as the general constraints and opportunities that shape broad patterns of development outcomes in different regional settings. The choice and sequences of national development strategies cannot be understood if world-system dynamics and country-specific "initial conditions" are ignored; similarly, the impact of these strategies on broader patterns of industrial development are mediated by institutional and cultural factors within societies. Only an interactive framework that integrates all these levels of explanation is adequate to the task of analyzing contemporary development experiences in diverse regional settings.

REFERENCES

Alt, James E. 1987. "Crude Politics: Oil and the Political Economy of Unemployment in Britain and Norway, 1970–1985." *British Journal of Political Science*, no. 17, pp. 149–99.

Arrighi, Giovanni. 1990. "The Developmentalist Illusion: A Reconceptualization of the Semiperiphery." In *Semiperipheral States in the World-Economy*, edited by William Martin. Westport, Conn.: Greenwood Press.

Arrighi, Giovanni, and Jessica Drangel. 1986. "The Stratification of the World-Economy: An Exploration of the Semiperipheral Zone." *Review*, no. 10, pp. 9–74.

Baer, Werner. 1972. "Import Substitution in Latin America: Experiences and Interpretations." *Latin American Research Review* 7, no. 1, pp. 95–122.

Balassa, Bela. 1981. *The Newly Industrializing Countries in the World Economy*. New York: Pergamon Press.

Berger, Peter L. 1986. *The Capitalist Revolution*. New York: Basic Books.

Berkowitz, S. D., and Barry Wellman, eds. 1988. *Social Structure: A Network Approach*. New York: Cambridge University Press.

Chenery, Hollis, Sherman Robinson, and Moshe Syrquin. 1986. *Industrialization and Growth*. New York: Oxford University Press.

Collier, David, ed. 1979. *The New Authoritarianism in Latin America*. Princeton: Princeton University Press.

Collier, Ruth Berins. 1982. "Popular Sector Incorporation and Political Supremacy: Regime Evolution in Brazil and Mexico." In *Brazil and Mexico: Patterns in Late Development*, edited by Sylvia Ann Hewlett and Richard S. Weinert. Philadelphia, Pa.: Institute for the Study of Human Issues.

Cumings, Bruce. 1989. "The Abortive Abertura: South Korea in the Light of Latin American Experience." *New Left Review*, no. 173, pp. 5–32.

———. 1984. "The Origins and Development of the Northeast Asian Political Economy: Industrial Sectors, Product Cycles, and Political Consequences." *International Organization* 38, no. 1, pp. 1–40.

Deyo, Frederic C. 1989. "Economic Sheltering and Working Class Formation in the East Asian NICs." Paper presented at the annual meetings of the American Sociological Association, August 9–13, San Francisco.

———. 1984. "Export Manufacturing and Labor: The Asian Case." In *Labor in the Capitalist World-Economy*, edited by Charles Bergquist. Beverly Hills, Calif.: Sage.

———, ed. 1987. *The Political Economy of the New Asian Industrialism*. Ithaca, N.Y.: Cornell University Press.

Evans, Peter B. 1986. "State, Capital, and the Transformation of Dependence: The Brazilian Computer Case." *World Development*, no. 14, pp. 791–808.

———. 1979. *Dependent Development: The Alliance of Multinationals, State, and Local Capital in Brazil*. Princeton: Princeton University Press.

Evans, Peter, and Gary Gereffi. 1982. "Foreign Investment and Dependent Development: Comparing Brazil and Mexico." In *Brazil and Mexico: Patterns in Late Development*, edited by Sylvia Ann Hewlett and Richard S. Weinert. Philadelphia, Pa.: Institute for the Study of Human Issues.

Fishlow, Albert. 1989. "Latin American Failure against the Backdrop of Asian Success." *Annals* of the American Academy of Political and Social Science, no. 505, pp. 117–28.

Form, William, and Kyu Han Bae. 1988. "Convergence Theory and the Korean Connection." *Social Forces*, no. 66, pp. 618–44.

Gereffi, Gary. 1989a. "Rethinking Development Theory: Insights from East Asia and Latin America." *Sociological Forum* 4, no. 4, pp. 505–33.

———. 1989b. "Development Strategies and the Global Factory." *Annals* of the American Academy of Political and Social Science, no. 505, pp. 92–104.

———. 1989c. "Industrial Restructuring and National Development Strategies: A Comparison of Taiwan, South Korea, Brazil and Mexico." In *Taiwan: A Newly Industrialized State*, edited by Hsin-Huang Michael Hsiao, Wei-Yuan Cheng, and Hou-Sheng Chan. Taipei: Department of Sociology, National Taiwan University.

Gereffi, Gary, and Peter Evans. 1981. "Transnational Corporations, Dependent Development, and State Policy in the Semiperiphery: A Comparison of Brazil and Mexico." *Latin American Research Review* 16, no. 3, pp. 31–64.

Gereffi, Gary, and Miguel Korzeniewicz. 1990. "Commodity Chains and Footwear Exports in the Semiperiphery." In *Semiperipheral States in the World-Economy*, edited by William Martin. Westport, Conn.: Greenwood Press.

Gereffi, Gary, and Donald Wyman. 1989. "Determinants of Development Strategies in Latin America and East Asia." In *Pacific Dynamics: The International Politics of Industrial Change*, edited by Stephan Haggard and Chung-in Moon. Boulder Colo.: Westview Press.

Gold, Thomas B. 1986. *State and Society in the Taiwan Miracle*. Armonk, N.Y.: M. E. Sharpe.

Gordon, Andrew. 1985. *The Evolution of Labor Relations in Japan, 1853–1955*. Cambridge: Harvard University Press.

Greenhalgh, Susan. 1988. "Families and Networks in Taiwan's Economic Development." In *Contending Approaches to the Political Economy of Taiwan*, edited by Edwin A. Winckler and Susan Greenhalgh. Armonk, N.Y.: M. E. Sharpe.

Haggard, Stephan. 1989. "The East Asian NICs in Comparative Perspective." *Annals* of the American Academy of Political and Social Science, no. 505, pp. 129–41.

Hall, Alan, and Barry Wellman. 1985. "Social Networks and Social Support." In *Social Support and Health*, edited by Sheldon Cohen and S. Leonard Syme. New York: Academic Press.

Hamilton, Gary G., and Nicole Woolsey Biggart. 1988. "Market, Culture, and Authority: A Comparative Analysis of Management and Organization in the Far East." *American Journal of Sociology* 94, Supplement on Organizations and Institutions, pp. 52–94.

Hamilton, Gary G., and Cheng-shu Kao. 1987. "Max Weber and the Analysis of East Asian Industrialization." *International Sociology*, no. 2, pp. 289–300.

Hamilton, Gary G., Marco Orrù, and Nicole Woolsey Biggart. 1987. "Enterprise Groups in East Asia: An Organizational Analysis." *Financial Economic Review* (Tokyo), no. 161, pp. 78–106.

Harris, Nigel. 1987. *The End of the Third World: Newly Industrializing Countries and the Decline of an Ideology*. New York: Viking Penguin.

Hirschman, Albert O. 1987. "The Political Economy of Latin American Development: Seven Exercises in Retrospection." *Latin American Research Review* 22, no. 3, pp. 7–36.

———. 1961. "Ideologies of Economic Development in Latin America." In his *Latin American Issues: Essays and Comments*. New York: The Twentieth Century Fund.

Hong, Wontack. 1979. *Trade, Distortions, and Employment Growth in Korea*. Seoul: Korea Development Institute.

Inkeles, Alex. 1983. *Exploring Individual Modernity*. New York: Columbia University Press.

Johnson, Chalmers. 1983. "The 'Internationalization' of the Japanese Economy." *California Management Review* 25, no. 3, pp. 5–26.

———. 1982. *MITI and the Japanese Miracle*. Stanford, Calif.: Stanford University Press.

Jones, Leroy, and Il Sakong. 1980. *Government, Business, and Entrepreneurship in Economic Development: The Korean Case*. Cambridge: Harvard University Press.

Kahn, Herman. 1979. *World Economic Development: 1979 and Beyond*. Boulder, Colo.: Westview Press.

Kim, Eun Mee. 1988. "From Dominance to Symbiosis: State and *Chaebol* in Korea." *Pacific Focus* 3, no. 2, pp. 105–21.

Kim, Suk Joon. 1989. "The Political Economy of Export-Led Industrialization in Korea and Taiwan: A Statist Approach." *Asian Perspective* 13, no. 2, pp. 69–88.

Korzeniewicz, Miguel. Forthcoming. "The Social Foundations of International Competitiveness: Footwear Exports in Argentina and Brazil." Ph.D. diss., Duke University.

Lazerson, Mark H. 1988. "Organizational Growth of Small Firms: An Outcome of Markets and Hierarchies?" *American Sociological Review* 53, no. 3, pp. 330–42.

Leung, Hon-chu. 1989. "Beyond Confucianism: Reformulating the Problem of 'Culture' in East Asian Development." Unpublished paper, Duke University.

Nemeth, Roger J., and David A. Smith. 1985. "International Trade and World-System Structure: A Multiple Network Approach." *Review*, no. 8, pp. 517–60.

Newfarmer, Richard S., and Willard Mueller. 1975. *Multinational Corporations in Brazil and Mexico: Structural Sources of Economic and Non-Economic Power*. Report to the Subcommittee on Multinational Corporations, Committee on Foreign Relations, U.S. Senate. Washington, D.C.: GPO.

O'Donnell, Guillermo. 1973. *Modernization and Bureaucratic-Authoritarianism: Studies in South American Politics*. Berkeley: Institute for International Studies, University of California.

Ong, Aihwa. 1987. *Spirits of Resistance and Capitalist Discipline*. Albany: State University of New York Press.

Piore, Michael J., and Charles F. Sabel. 1984. *The Second Industrial Divide*. New York: Basic Books.

Pye, Lucian. 1985. *Asian Power and Politics*. Cambridge: Harvard University Press.

Ragin, Charles C. 1989. "New Directions in Comparative Research." In *Cross-National Research in Sociology*, edited by Melvin L. Kohn. Newbury Park, Calif: Sage.

———. 1987. *The Comparative Method*. Berkeley: University of Califonria Press.

Redding, S. G. 1988. "The Role of the Entrepreneur in the New Asian Capitalism." In *In Search of an East Asian Development Model*, edited by Peter L. Berger and Hsin-Huang Michael Hsiao. New Brunswick, N.J.: Transaction.

Shapiro, Helen, and Lance Taylor. 1989. "The State and Industrial Strategy." Paper prepared for the UNU/WIDER Project on Medium-Term Adjustment. Cambridge, Mass.

Silin, Robert. 1976. *Leadership and Values: The Organization of Large-Scale Taiwanese Enterprises*. Cambridge: Harvard University Press.

Snyder, David L., and Edward L. Kick. 1979. "Structural Position in the World-System and Economic Growth, 1955–1970: A Multiple Network Analysis of Transnational Interactions." *American Journal of Sociology*, no. 84, pp. 1096–1126.

Suh, Jae Jean. 1989. "The Social and Political Networks of the Korean Capitalist Class." *Asian Perspective* 13, no. 2, pp. 111–39.

Thomas, George M., and Pat Lauderdale. 1988. "State Authority and National Welfare Programs in the World-System Context." *Sociological Forum*, no. 3, pp. 383–99.

Tilly, Charles. 1984. *Big Structures, Large Processes, Huge Comparisons*. New York: Russell Sage Foundation.

Valenzuela, J. Samuel, and Arturo Valenzuela. 1978. "Modernization and Dependency: Alternative Perspectives in the Study of Latin American Underdevelopment." *Comparative Politics*, no. 10, pp. 535–57.

Wade, Robert. 1989. "What Can Economics Learn from East Asian Success?" *Annals* of the American Academy of Political and Social Science, no. 505, pp. 68–79.

———. 1988. "The Role of Government in Overcoming Market Failure: Taiwan, the Republic of Korea, and Japan." In *Achieving Industrialization in East Asia*, edited by Helen Hughes. New York: Cambridge University Press.

Wallerstein, Immanuel. 1979. *The Capitalist World-Economy*. Cambridge: Cambridge University Press.

Wong, Siu-lun. 1988. "The Applicability of Asian Family Values to Other Sociocultural Settings." In *In Search of an East Asian Development Model*, edited by Peter L. Berger and Hsin-Huang Michael Hsiao. New Brunswick, N.J.: Transaction.

Contributors

Colin I. Bradford, Jr., is associate professor at the School of Management at Yale University, New Haven, Connecticut, and currently is a member of the Senior Staff of Strategic Planning at the World Bank, Washington, D.C.

Tun-jen Cheng is assistant professor in the Graduate School of International Relations and Pacific Studies, University of California, San Diego.

Frederic C. Deyo is associate professor of sociology at the State University of New York, College at Brockport.

Ronald Dore is director of the Japan-Europe Industrial Research Center, London, England, and adjunct professor at the Department of Political Science, Massachusetts Institute of Technology, Cambridge, Massachusetts.

Christopher Ellison is a Ph.D. candidate in the Department of Sociology, Duke University, Durham, North Carolina.

Fernando Fajnzylber is chief of the joint Industry and Technology Division of the United Nations Economic Commission for Latin America and the Caribbean and the United Nations Industrial Development Organization, Santiago, Chile.

Gary Gereffi is associate professor of sociology at Duke University, Durham, North Carolina.

Robert R. Kaufman is professor of political science at Rutgers University, New Brunswick, New Jersey.

Gustav Ranis is the Frank Altschul Professor of International Economics, Yale University, New Haven, Connecticut.

Chi Schive is dean of the Graduate School of Industrial Economics, National Central University, Chung-li, Taiwan.

Barbara Stallings is professor of political science and associate dean of the Graduate School at the University of Wisconsin, Madison.

René Villarreal is professor of economics at El Colegio de México, Mexico City, and general manager of Productores y Importadores de Papel, S.A., Mexico.

Robert Wade is currently visiting professor of public and international affairs at the Woodrow Wilson School, Princeton University, Princeton, New Jersey, on leave from the Institute of Development Studies at the University of Sussex, England.

The late **Donald Wyman** was associate dean of the Graduate School of International Relations and Pacific Studies, University of California, San Diego.

Index